MEDIEVAL INDIA 3

MEDIEVAL INDIA 3
Researches in the History of India

Edited by
B. L. BHADANI

CENTRE OF ADVANCED STUDY
Department of History
Aligarh Muslim University

MANOHAR
2012

First published, 2012

ISBN 978-81-7304-942-2

Published by

Ajay Kumar Jain *for*
Manohar Publishers & Distributors
4753/23 Ansari Road, Daryaganj
New Delhi 110 002

Typeset at

Digigrafics
New Delhi 110 049

Printed at

Salasar Imaging Systems
Delhi 110 035

Contents

Preface 7

1. The Role of Women in Rajput Polity During the Early Medieval Period
   Rashmi Upadhyaya 9
2. Intellectual Fervour During the Reign of Sultan Firuz Shah Tughlaq
   Aneesa Iqbal Sabir 29
3. Composite Culture: Portrayal in Architecture
   Ravindra Kumar 47
4. Agricultural Technology Depicted in Mughal Paintings
   Ahsan Jan Qaisar 77
5. The Impact of Sufi Traditions on Kabir
   Shahabuddin Iraqi 101
6. Sheikh Farid Bukhari's Relations with Some Contemporary *Ulama*
   Mohammad Umar 115
7. Akbar's Fort at Allahabad
   Ali Athar 131
8. Mughal Portraiture: An Underlying Relationship with the Renaissance Humanism in Art
   S.P. Verma 139
9. *Shajra-i-Suhraward*: A Sixteenth-Century *Tazkira* of the Suhrawardi Sufi Saints
   Iqtidar Husain Siddiqui 169
10. Shaikh Ahmad Sirhindi and the Organization of the Naqshbandi *Silsilah* in India
    Iqbal Sabir 177
11. The Position of Hindus in the Mughal *Suba* of Malwa
    Syed Bashir Hasan 197

12. Iranis and Commerce: A Case Study of Shaista Khan in Gujarat and Bengal
Mohammad Afzal Khan 227

13. Banjaron ki Baori at Sikar (Rajasthan): A Study of Medieval Hydraulic Technology
M.K. Pundhir 235

14. A Walk into Oblivion of Pargana Amarsar: The Environmental Dimension
Sumbul Halim Khan 245

15. Ecology, Social Stratification and Agrarian Production in Medieval Rajasthan
Mayank Kumar 257

REVIEWS

1. Hamid Qalandar, *Khair-ul-Majalis*
Iqtidar Husain Siddiqui 275

2. Mulla Qāti'i Harvi, *Tazkira-i-Majma'al-Shu'ra-i Jahangir Shahi*
Iqtidar Husain Siddique 279

3. Razi uddin Aquil, *Sufism: Culture and Politics, Afghan and Islam in Medieval North India*
Iqbal Sabir 289

4. Iqtidar Husain Siddiqui, *Delhi Sultanate: Urbanization and Social Change*
Parwez Nazir 301

List of Contributors 307

Preface

The Department of History started its publication of a quarterly journal *Medieval India Quarterly* in 1950 under the academic leadership of our stalwart Professor Mohammad Habib to accelerate researches in Medieval Indian History. In this series, however, only five volumes came out and unfortunately for some reasons, it was stopped in 1963.

The work of publication was revived under the able guidance of Professor Shaikh Abdur Rashid, Professor S. Nurul Hasan (the founder of our Centre of Advanced Study in History), Professor K.A. Nizami and Professor Irfan Habib with the new title *Medieval India: A Miscellany* in 1969. However, this series also came to an end in 1975. The publication was again started by Professor Irfan Habib now giving it a new title of *Medieval India* and the its first volume *Medieval India 1* edited by him was published in 1992. Its chequered publication was revived by Professor Shahabuddin Iraqi when *Medieval India 2* came out in 2008 being edited by him. This effort has been continued by me and the present volume *Medieval India 3* has now been published carrying on the legacy of our former stalwarts.

The present volume, *Medieval India 3* contains fifteen research papers on various themes of Medieval India. All these papers are based on the rigorous scientific research. Besides these, four reviews are incorporated in this volume on the books recently published by well-known scholars. The quality and standard of the papers are to be judged by the readers. The Centre acknowledges the cooperation of the colleagues and other scholars for their valuable contribution.

The Centre expresses its gratitude to Manohar Publishers & Distributors, New Delhi for undertaking the publication of this volume expediously. The colleagues and staff equally deserve my sincere appreciation for their kind cooperation and help. My young colleague Dr. Syed Bashir Hasan deserves special mention for his keen academic interest and all necessary cooperation that was involved in its publication at different stages before its final sending to the publisher and later on in setting it in line of the observations made by the editor of the publisher.

B.L. BHADANI

CHAPTER 1

The Role of Women in Rajput Polity During the Early Medieval Period

RASHMI UPADHYAYA

The inequality of women as against their male counterpart and their assertion to acquire power and independence in relation to the latter in different periods, of history, enforced the study of the history of women in modern times and, to some extent, to the study of the 'women question', which was persistently linked to understand the position of women as an index of civilization in the nineteenth-century Britain. In India the position of women had undergone a rapid transformation in the nineteenth century. The consciousness and participation of women in social change is not only to be credited for this subsequent transformation, which often undermined the traditional expectations and definitions. But the role of family or household is admittedly significant in determining the position of women, as the scene of action for women's advancement in a class or locality is the household and not community. The skills, capabilities and capacities of women in every sphere have been generally recognized by the household. However, in some cases the intra-household behaviour of women could also be related to their status and position. The role of women outside the bounds of her house did, however, exist. The royal families of India, unlike the families of modern Europe were not merely the economic units of society but also the power centres, the role of which certainly influenced the character and status of women in the socio-political life. These household incongruities of women are not beyond Altekar's paradigm with regard to the position of women in Hindu civilization.[1]

The study of the change in the position of women in the Indian society, is intimately bound up to the different historical periods. The elevated status of women in the Vedic age underwent a gradual decline. Such a decline has been referred as detrimental to significant historical changes in different periods.

The history of women as defined in prescriptive Brahmanical works, has already been reviewed by scholars.[2] Since the role of women in the composition, compilation, preservation and transmission of such texts may not be construed at any level, there is a need to explore the data which has not been composed with the awareness of an inherent bias regarding the inferior status of women, i.e. the epigraphs and contemporary texts on polity, which reflect the prevalent socio-political system and the women's place therein.

The literature and epigraphic sources of early medieval period are worthy of investigation in order to make a constructive analysis of the position of women in the royal households, which obviously constituted an important locus through which their role in the socio-political, economic and cultural life of the contemporary age is structured.

The present paper is aimed at reconstructing the position of women during the feudal era, which is significantly marked by the fratricidal struggles and heroic conquests of the Rajput rulers with the Arabs and the Turks. Owing to the ubiquitous distribution of different clans and the elements of variations within them, the position of women appears to have a sort of vivacity and variability from one dynastic order to the next. Women appear as performing various roles—as the queen mother, the chief queen, the daughter of the king (*rajputri*), the wife of the feudatories, administrators, courtiers, etc.

The queen mother, in general, occupied a place of high honour in the royal household as she had to involve herself in very many substantial activities of the state, probably as representative of the royal household or as the king's counterpart. The significant position of the queen mother can be gleaned from many of the Gahadawala land grants. The Kamauli grant of Madanapala and Govindachandra (VS 1162/AD 1105) refers to the grant of a village by *maharajaputra* Govindachandra issued with the permission of the *purohita*, the *mahattaka*, the *pratihara* and the queen mother Ralhadevi.[3] As it is not clearly referred whether the consent of the queen mother was required as merely a formality of providing respect and not as a significant member of the administrative body like the *purohita*, the *mahattaka* and the *pratihara*, her inclusion in the body politic and administrative regalia may not be regarded as negligible.

The land grants of the queen mothers are often found to have been recorded by their sons (*rajputras*). For instance, the Pali grant (VS 1189/AD 1132) in which the queen mother Ralhana Devi refers to her having donated 10 *nalukas* of land in a particular village to *thakkur* Jayapalasarman was recorded by her son *rajputra* Govindachandra.[4] In the Benares grant (VS 1181/AD 1124) Govindachandra is referred to have recorded the grant of a village in Yavallapattala to one Bhupatisarman, made by the same queen mother (*mahamatr*).[5] She is also provided with the specific credit to have performed the five great sacrifices (*pancha lagna mahadana*) in the same grant.[6] The influence of the queen mother Ralhadevi was nevertheless immeasurable as can be seen from the Kamauli grant; wherein *parambhattaraka maharajadhiraja paramesvara* Govindachandra is mentioned to have granted the villages in *Navagrama pattala* of Avimuktakshetra of Benares to one Dixit Jagusarmana in VS 1197 and 1198 respectively, in order to attain spiritual benefit after her death in next life.[7]

The queen mother was provided with land allotments for her personal expenditure.[8] That they retained proprietary right over such holdings may be deduced from a particular mention in an inscription regarding the land grant of Queen Analadevi, mother of Kelhanadeva (*matr-rajni*), measuring one plough out of her own *rajkiyabhoga* [9] to *tirthankara* Mahavira. It is, however, notable that the grant was made not in individual capacity but with the permission of the king.[10]

Further, the authority of the queen mother to make donations of land and money under the Kalachuris reflects their influential and effective role in contemporary politics. The Bheraghat stone inscription (VS 907/AD 1155) records the gift of two villages as endowment to the temple of Shiva under the name of Vaidyanath by the dowager Queen Alhanadevi, the mother of Narasimha.[11] She appears to have assigned at one place the income from the village of Namaundi in the Jaulipattala, probably without the permission of the king, which may be inferred by the absence of any reference to such permission taken for the transaction.[12] Similarly, in the Kumbhi plate, mother of Vijaisimha, is attributed to have granted the village of Choralayi in the Sambala pattala to a brahmin named Silhasarma.[13]

Literary sources throw valuable light on the position of the queen mother in different dynasties. Jayanaka, in his *Prithvirajavijaya*, attributes the entire credit for the early victories and judicious administration of the great Chauhan leader Prithviraja III, to the authority of his mother, Karpura Devi, who was made the regent for her minor son by the ministers, in the absence of any heir.[14] The prosperity of the Chahamana kingdom during her regency and her successful administration of affairs of the kingdom in spite of her hostile neighbours on almost every side, has been eloquently accounted in *Prithvirajavijaya*.[15] The same text also refers that she was ably assisted by minister Kadambavasa in the administrative affairs.[16] Similarly, Mynalladevi, the mother of the Chalukya king Sidhharaja Jayasimha, managed the affairs of the kingdom in place of her minor son, in cooperation with her ministers and councillors. She remained an able advisor to the king even after his assumption of full responsibilities of the government, and acted as a motivating and inspiring force behind many of his campaigns.[17]Another noble Chalukya lady, Naiki Devi, is referred to have fought and defeated the army of the Turko-Afghans, probably in the capacity of regent for her minor son Mularaja II.[18] Karma Devi, a Chalukya princess and queen of Rai Samarsi of Chittor, after the death of her husband took the reigns of administration in her hands and maintained the kingdom in the capacity of regent while her son Karan was still a minor.[19]

The honourable position of the queen mother resulted in the possession of tremendous political influence and power by her. Her will was never overlooked even in the most significant decisions, such as release of prisoners or making peace treaties. *Kathakosa* narrates the role of Queen Madanrekha, wife of the king of Avanti, who acted as negotiator while a battle was ensuing between her two sons. The peace was finally, restored between the two brothers at her initiation.[20] The Ratanpur Stone inscription (KE 866) refers that Somesvara after being defeated was imprisoned along with his ministers and wives, by Jajalladeva, but was released quickly at the behest of his mother.[21] Sometimes, the abolition of important taxes was also made at her instance. *Prabandhacintamani* refers that the Chalukya king Siddharaja Jaisingh while on a pilgrimage to Somnath along with his mother Mayanalla, abolished the tax imposed on the Saiva mendicants at Bahuloda at her behest, which yielded seventy-two lakh (probably *drammas*) to the royal treasury annually.[22]

The respectable position of the queen mother is also reflected in the writings of contemporary political thinkers and jurists.[23] Medhatithi, while commenting on Manu, regards the honour of the mother as the highest duty of a son and advices him to always do what is agreeable to her. Obedience to her is regarded by Manu as the best form of austerity.[24] Again, a son is advised by him not to perform even meritorious acts without her prior permission.[25] Kshemendra refers to a mother's position as superior to that of even the guru.[26] Laxmidhara while quoting Baudhayana and Gautama, recommends a son to abandon his father if he adopts immoral practices but never his mother, even if she is excommunicated.[27] Chandesvara and Sukra, however, provide the dictum of equal respect to both mother and father.[28] Rajshekhara in his *Balramayana* regards a mother as surpassing a thousand fathers in point of the respect and honour that should be paid to her.[29]

The evidences of literary accounts are complemented by the epigraphs, wherein the mothers of the Rajput kings have got specific mention. The practice of mentioning the mother's name seems to have been customary among the Kalachuris. The Khaira Plate of the Kalachuri king Yasahkarna refers to his mother Avalla Devi.[30] Similarly, in the Bheraghat Stone inscription of Narasimha[31] and the Kumbhi plates of Vijaisimha, the mothers of the respective rulers find mention. In some instances the kings before introducing themselves give references to their mothers.[32] The profound respect and regard paid to Gosaladevi by Vijaisimha is reflected in the Kumbhi Plate, which describes her as 'one whose glance is a veritable shower of nectar, whose company is an excellent treasure and whose speech is wish fulfilling jewel'.[33]

Kings are found to have made gifts of villages or lands as charitable endowments for the enhancement of spiritual merit and glorification of his mother.[34] Such grants were usually made by the king on the death anniversary of his mother. Thus, the Chandellla king Devavarman, on the occasion of the death anniversary of his mother, Queen Bhuvanadevi, granted a village to a Brahman named Abhimanyu.[35] The Kadi grant of VS 1299/AD 1242 refers that the Chalukya king Tribhuvanpala, the successor of Bhima, granted two villages in Dandahi pathaka to feed *karpatikas* (mendicants) at the almshouse built by *rana* Lunapas for the spiritual benefit of his mother *rajni* Sallakshanadevi.[36]

The powerful and influential feudatories also provided grants as pious donations in order to gain spiritual merit for their mothers. The Nadlai inscription of Maharaja Rayapala (VS 1200), a feudatory of the Chalukyas, records that Rauta Rajdeva, on the occasion of *rathyatra*, organized for the sake of his mother, made a religious benefaction consisting of one *vimsopaka* coin from the *pailas* accruing to him and two *palikas* from the *palas* of oil due to him from every *ghanaka* or oilmill.[37] The Kot Solankiya inscription of Vanavira (VS 1394) refers to the grant by one *rauta* Mularaja and his wife Jakhaladevi consisting of a *vadi* or orchard for the spiritual merit of his parents in the presence of two other *rautas*.[38]

Besides the queen mothers, the epigraphic records account of the high respect bestowed on the queen by the reigning king. The queens were accorded a highly respectable place in the royal house and administration. It is known that the Rashtrakuta ruler, Dhruva ruled over a considerable part of northern India in the eighth century in the joint authority of his queen Silla Mahadevi. She held such a high place in administration that sometimes orders were given to the provincial governor and other officials not by the King Dhruva but by Silla Mahadevi, who is found to be entitled as *paramesvari* and *param bhattarika*.[39]

The queens also are referred as doing works of public utility and making land grants to religious centres. The chief queen had a position of authority, having her own distinct paraphernalia. Under the Gahadawalas, the chief queen (*pattamahadevi*) was endowed with all royal prerogatives (*samastarajaprakriyopeta*) and was empowered to make grants to the brahmins with the consent of the king.[40] The gifts made by the queens had to be announced by the reigning king. Thus, the grant of the village of Gatiara to *thakkura* Kulhe made by *pattamahadevi* Gosaladevi with the consent of the King Govindachandra was announced by the latter.[41] The practice of granting land by the queen was also prevalent under the Chedis. The Karitalai inscription of Somesvara, minister of Laxmanaraja, records that his queen *mahadevi* Rahada granted the village of Chakrahadi to the temple of Vishnu, which was built by Somesvara and at which an inscription was evidently found.[42] The Paramara queens also made land grants to religious centres. It is known from the Ajhari inscription of VS 1240/AD 1183 that in the victorious reign of King Dharavarsha of Chandravati, the wife of King Prhaladana granted a certain piece of land to Arhata Jogadeva.[43] An inscription of the Paramara Yasodhavala also records a grant of the village Ajari by Saubhagyadevi, queen of Yasodhaval Paramara of Abu (AD 1145-63).[44] It is further noted from the Jhalodi inscription of VS 1255/AD 1198 that Sringardevi, Dharavarsha's queen granted in her own right a few orchards to the temple of Santinatha.[45] The Bombay Grant of Paramara king Naravarmana refers to the religious endowment consisting of some pieces of land to a brahmin by the king's wife Mahadevi in VS 1154/ AD 1097-8.[46]

It is notable that all the grants by the queens were made for spiritual purpose and none were made to any state official. Probably such religious endowments were made by them with the consent of the king not in any official capacity but as consorts participating with him in religious activities, following the Sastric injunctions, according to which religious acts should be performed by husband and wife together and the accomplishment of the invisible purposes of a man depends on his wife.[47]

Some of the queens had their own *bhandagaras* or treasuries consisting possibly of the marriage gifts, bath and toilet money from the father or husband or income from property settled at the time of marriage by the husband and other similar personal gifts and funds.[48] Some had the right to appoint and promote particular administrative officials for their assistance and carrying out the administrative affairs. One such case of unique importance in the Gahadawala records is the appointment of Jambuki as the foremost of all *pattalikas* by Kumaradevi, the queen of Govindachandra.[49] The political status of the queens under the Gahadawalas is also clearly signified by the particular mention of *rajan*, *rajni*, *yuvaraja* followed by the list of royal officials, who were informed about the grants.[50] However, it is not clear whether it refers to the royal queen or to the family of feudatory chiefs, who generally assumed the title *rajan* during the feudal times. It is clear that these queens, who were significantly informed about the grant together with other officials, were intimately connected with the political system of that time. This tradition of informing about the grants was also practised by the Kalachuris. Their land grants included the queens in the customary list of the officials and persons, who were informed about each and every detail of the proposed endowment of land.[51]

The queens are often mentioned in possession of villages and *bhuktis* as fiefs possibly as the allotments to them by the kings for their maintenance.[52] It is evident that Sanderaka, the westernmost outpost of the Chahamanas, was included in the *bhukti* of Queen Jhalanadevi and was governed by her through a deputy.[53] Some of them were also empowered to issue coins. Somalladevi, Ajayaraja's queen is known to have issued a considerable number of silver and copper coins.[54] *Prithvirajavijaya* makes a vague reference to the issue of new coins daily by her.[55] Under the Kalachuris, sometimes the inscriptions were also executed at the behest of the queens. The Vadner plate of Buddharaja (KE 360) refers that this record was written at the behest of Queen Anantamahayi.[56] Under the Chahamanas, the important edicts were often promulgated by the queen.[57] The rightful position of the queen in the execution and promulgation of inscriptions is indicated by the particular mention of the genealogy of their paternal families with glorification of their fathers and forefathers.[58]

The queens possibly also had certain control over the activities of the *rajputras* and other officials. The Larlai stone inscription of Kelhanadeva VS 1233/AD 1176 refers to the grant made by *rajputra* Lakhanapala and *rajputra* Abhayapala, who were the proprietors (*bhoktr*) of Sinawana, conjointly with Queen Mahibaladevi during the reign of Kelhanadeva at Nadula in the presence of the village *panchkula,* for celebrating the festival of god Santinath. The grant consisted of barley corn measuring one *haraka* from an *arghatta* (water lifting machine) belonging to a village of Bhadiyaduva.[59] An interesting fact revealed from this inscription is that the two *rajaputras* mentioned therein were not the sons of the king but that of his younger brother Kirtipala. Mahibaladevi is not referred as their mother but simply as the queen, i.e. the wife of King Kelhanadeva. The making of a grant in conjunction with *rajputras* thus reveals that the queen either might have had a certain share in the proprietorship of the two *rajputras* or was probably keeping her hold over their activities as the representative of the king.

The inscriptions assigned to the queens refer them for their indulgence in pious and benevolent activities like the construction of temples, tanks, reservoirs, wells, etc. Svetalladevi, Vallabharaja Kalachuri's queen is found in the Ratanpur Stone inscription of Prithvideva II of KE 910 to have caused the construction of a tank of her own accord.[60] The queen of Bhima Chalukya (AD 1023-65) named Udayamati caused the construction of a new reservoir in Pattana which was better than even the Sahasralinga lake excavated by Siddharaja. The same queen is also credited with the digging of a well at Anahillapataka, which is now known by the name of *rani ki vav*.[61] Mayanalladevi, the wife of Karna I and daughter of the Kadamba king of Karnataka Jayakesin, who acted as regent for her minor son Siddharaja, caused the excavation of Mansar Lake near

Viramgam and another known as Malav at Dhavallaka or Dholka in Ahmedabad.[62] The Ajaigarh record of VS 1317 was issued to record the construction of a well with perennial water, a hall for the supply of its water and a tank at Nandipura by Kalyandevi, the chief queen of Viravarmana.[63]

The queens actively participated in the temple building activities and laid foundations of many of them. The Pratihara queen Jayamati built a temple of Paramesvara at Buchkala Rajya ghangakam in AD 815 and Queen Chitralekha, wife of Mahipala constructed the temple of Vishnu at Bayana in AD 955.[64] Nohala, the chief queen of Yuvarajadeva I, the Kalachuri king (tenth century) built a lofty temple of Shiva under the name of Nohalesvara and endowed it with the gift of several villages.[65] Somaladevi, the second queen of Bhima II and daughter of Lavanaprasada erected the Somalesvara temple sometimes before AD 1239.[66] Jayatalladevi, queen of Tejasimha Guhila constructed a temple of Parsvanath in Chittor in VS 1335/AD 1278. Alhanadevi laid the foundation of the temple of Shiva under the name of Vaidyanath at Bheraghat with a *matha*, a hall of study and gardens attached to it. For the maintenance of this establishment the queen assigned two villages in the land adjoining the hill.[67] Kumaradevi, the queen of Gahadawala Govindachandra, is referred to have restored an image of *dharmachakra jina* and erected a *vihara* for the Buddhist monks.[68] Kamaladevi, the crowned queen of Pratapsimha Chahamana is referred to have renovated the temple of Vaesvara Shiva together with a *linga* inside it.[69] It is also referred that for the daily offerings to the God, a gift was made of a field and two *pailas* on every maund of each commodity from the customs house.[70] Some of the temples were constructed, repaired and renovated by the wives of the feudatories. Dayika, the queen of Vachharaja, possibly a feudatory of Vigraharaja Chauhan, repaired the temple of Sankaradevin in AD 1055.[71] The Udaipur inscription of the Guhila king Aparajita (VS 718/AD 661) records the renovation of the building of the temple of Vishnu by Yasomati, the wife of Varahsimha, mentioned as the chief leader (*praneta*) of the king.[72] Lahini, the sister of Purnapala of Abu and widow of King Vigraharaja of Vasantagarh is credited to have repaired the temple of Sun God and to have founded a tank at Vatpura in AD 1042 during the reign of Bhoja Paramara (*c.* AD 1000-55).[73]

It is a notable fact that the records regarding the constructional works by the queens do not refer directly to the permission of the king for such activities. It thus indicates indirectly to their significant position in the contemporary political structure and independence in economic matters.

Glorification of the queens is often found in epigraphic records. The Chandella queens got high praise in the inscriptions as consorts of the kings. In the Khajuraho inscription of VS 1059 of Dhanga, his queen Pappadevi is stated to have hailed from a reputed family and as equal to Sachi, wife of Indra.[74] The Ajaigarh rock inscription of VS 1317 refers to Kalyandevi, the chief queen of Virvarmana, as an object of reverence for the kshatriyas.[75] Hiradevi, the mother of Hamira and wife of Jaitrasimha Chauhan, is also praised for her qualities by Nyayachandra Suri, the author of *Hamiramahakavya*.[76] The Chahamana queens often acquired divine affinity as the kings sometimes ordered to name the deities on the names of their queens in order to glorify them.[77] Some of the queens under the Chahamanas are even referred as the rulers of some sacred lands or territories. Asaraja's queen Delhanadevi, the mother of Alhana, is described in the Ojha grant 2 as the ruler of the sacred Saraswat land.[78] The position of the queens under the Kalachuris was also supreme. Nohala, the chief queen of Yuvarajadeva I, the Kalachuri king, influenced the religious policy of her husband king by introducing her own religion and inviting ascetics from her home country.[79] Likewise, Queen Roopsundari of Anhilawada, the wife of the king of Panchasur named Jayashekhar, had her own spiritual preceptor.[80]

The important feudatories ruling as the kings defied their queens by carving out the images together with the deities in the forts or palaces.[81] Some also made offerings and granted lands for the spiritual welfare of their wives. According to an inscription a certain Narapati during the reign of *maharajakula* Samantasimha of the Chahamana of Jalor, granted a *bazaar* building or warehouse for storing goods to be exported for the spiritual welfare of his wife Nayakadevi.[82]

Besides making grants of land for the attainment of spiritual merit,[83] the wives of the feudatories and officials also played important roles in the political affairs.[84] They looked after the administration of estates probably in the capacity of governors or in charges and managed the staff of officials and ministers under them. The Bhor State Museum plates dated Saka 1001/AD 1079 refers to the ministers of Sridevi and Mahaladevi, queens of a feudatory of the Chalukya king.[85] Sometimes the lands or villages were provided by the powerful feudatories to their queens for their maintenance. The Bali Stone inscription of Asvaka (vs 1200), a feudatory of *maharajadhiraja* Jaisinghdev of Chalukya dynasty shows that the village of Valahi was in the enjoyment of Queen Tihunaka as her *grasa*.[86] They were also empowered to pass general orders of some significance in the estates enjoyed by them. The Ratanpur Stone inscription of the reign of Kumarapala, records the publication of an order of Girijadevi, the *maharajni* of Purnapakshadeva, successor of *maharaja* Rayapala (Nadol Chahamana) prohibiting slaughter of animals on some specified dates.[87] The strictness of the order may be guessed from the mention in the same record that in case of violation of the order, the violator will be punished with a certain amount of fine. Not only this but even the potters were prohibited to burn their pots on the day of the holy *amavasya* (new moon day) to prevent the non-killing of living beings on that day.[88] Sometimes the queens of the feudatories are mentioned to hold a title in order to identify them with the office or post of their husbands. Thus the wife of some chief and the mother of Jagapala, an official of the Kalachuri king Prithvideva II, Udaya, is found referred as *thakkurajni* in an inscription.[89]

The queens of the Rajput dynasties of the age are known to have attended court meetings and participated in deliberations. *Manasollasa* of Somesvara gives a graphic account of the royal ladies, who came to attend the assembly hall in *palquins* fitted with curtains and accompanied by staff bearers.[90] The Arab traveller, Abu Zaid also records the presence of royal women in court meetings without any veil on their faces.[91]

The references are not scanty where the Rajput ladies put up stiff resistance to the enemy forces fighting in good spirit.[92] That women during their childhood used to receive a good amount of military training is confirmed from *Tilakamanjari*, which refers to the girls of royal blood learning *Dhanurveda* (knowledge in the use of bow).[93] The wives and female relatives of the kings usually accompanied the king in the military campaigns. *Kavyamimamsa* of Rajshekhara refers to the sport of ladies present in the advancing army of the king.[94] *Kamasutra* of Vatsyayana states that women also served in the state and accompanied the king in their *darbars*, campaigns, pleasure trips, etc.[95] They rode horses in arms and some of them are reported to have been captured in war.[96] The presence of ladies in the army is referred as one of the causes of the weakness of the fighting force by Kamandaka, who regards it as an uncustomary practice.[97] The Rashtrakuta rulers had also followed such practice in the military system. The Gwalior inscription refers to Bhoja having subdued demons (*asuras*) with the help of women which might have included the royal ladies also.[98] The Bilhari Stone inscription of the Kalachuri King Yuvarajadeva II indirectly refers to the presence of women in the military camp.[99] It is also known that Amoghavarsha was born while his father's camp was pitched at the foothills of the Vindhyas during his campaign in central India.[100] Akkadevi, the elder sister of the western Chalukya king Jayasimha III, is referred in the Belur inscription as a *bhairavi* in battle and in destroying the hostile kings while governing the district of Kisukad.[101] The Rajput women also find mention in the Persian inscriptions. For instance, Persian inscription of H 680 *rabi* II 25 referring to the military conquests of Ghiyasuddin's reign, makes mention of Rajput Jajala with his wife Rajasri Ratnadevi. His son Hariraja's two younger brothers are mentioned with their sister Virada Ranadevi.[102]

The involvement of some of the queens and queen mothers in court intrigues and treacheries may not be overlooked. They played an important role in turning out the court politics by participating in matters of succession and war. The rival queens vied with one another for securing the nomination of their own sons as heir.[103] Cases are not unknown when they sided with the enemy against their own husbands in order to satisfy their greed for wealth. *Prabandha-cintamani* refers how Suhava, wife of Jayachandra Gahadawala, invited the Turks with the desire to kill her husband being repellent at the latter's resentment to bestow the office of crown prince on her son.[104] Thus, the author of *Samaraichhakaha* in one story also refers to Queen Nayanawali, the wife of Surendradatta, who attempted to murder her husband in order to avoid living a monastic life with him, which he had decided to adopt.[105] *Niti-vakyamrita* and *Yashastilaka* refer to a number of traditions with slight variations, which, illustrate stories of assassinations of kings by women in their own ingenious ways.[106] It was indeed against the foul character of the royal ladies that the contemporary writers asked and advised their masters to guard themselves while maintaining relations with women.[107]

Sometimes the royal ladies also acted as a cause of war or strife between two dynasties. The war between the Chalukya king Kumarapala and the Chahamana king Arnoraja was caused according to a story in *Prabandhakosa*, by the sister of Kumarapala, who while feeling offended by her husband Arnoraja went to Pattana and reported the matter to Kumarapala, who at the initiation of his sister determined to engage in a battle against the former.[108] The story is somewhat differently mentioned in *Kumarapalaprabodha*.[109] Similiarly, the ill treatment of Anandbai, sister of Prithviraja by her husband Rai Jagmal, the king of Sirohi, is known as the cause of attack by the former on the latter.[110] The cases are not missing when the queens roused the spirit of their husbands acting as encouraging and exciting force during wars.[111] Instances are also there when peace was concluded on the advice or initiation of the queens.[112]

In some cases the wives of the officials or feudatories proved as true loyalists and patriots. *Kanhadade Prabandha* refers to how the wife of Sejawal, probably the keeper of the fort of Jalor struck her husband on being informed of his treacherous game against his master by revealing the secret pathway leading to the fort, to the Turks. After striking her husband she conveyed the whole matter to *rawal* Kanhadade.[113]

Apart from the respect paid to the women by the families of their husbands girls were also accorded an independent status even after marriages in the household of their parents. The Belur inscription of the time of Jayasimha III refers that his elder sister Akkadevi governed the district known as Kisukad in Saka 944 in the memory of her brother Tribhuvanamalla Vikramaditya and to have made a grant of Perur *agrahara* to feed and clothe 500 students with the providence of free quarters.[114] She ruled Banavasi in conjunction with her husband, the Kadamba chieftain Mayurvarmana. Daughters were often utilized as political weapons while given in marriage to the enemy in order to make peace. Kanchanadevi, the daughter of Siddharaja, was given in marriage by her father to Arnoraja as a result of the struggle with the latter.[115] Association of the girls with their paternal families and their independent status in the family of husbands is revealed from the manner in which the queens have given the genealogies of their paternal families without intending to suggest the inferiority of their husband's families in the least.[116] Girls often took active part in the matters of administration and were given their share out of the assignment of the revenue.[117] They also had their own council of management with the right to appoint minor officials.[118] Like the queens, some of them also showed interest in the construction of temples. Rudaladevi, the daughter of Chahmana king Samarsimha, built a temple of Shiva at Jalor.[119] Another daughter of Samarsimha, who is mentioned in the inscription as queen (*rajni*), (probably of Bhima Chalukya) built the temple of Bhimesvara and Lilesvaradeva at Lilapur.[120] Padmavati, the daughter of Jagaddeva

Parmara is known from Jainad (Jainath) inscriptions to have founded a temple of Nimvaditya in an *agrahara*.[121]

After examining the above evidences one feels contented to accept the fact that women had significant involvement in the contemporary feudal organization of the state, i.e. in the procedure of granting land, acting as regents, appointing some minor officials, enjoying certain royal prerogatives for their personal maintenance, issuing coinages, attending court sessions and even fighting as soldiers in battles at times. The lack of assumption of any official designation by these queens, however, suggests that such roles might have been played by them in the capacity of an important member of the royal household as well as the companion of the king in all matters, including state politics.

NOTES

1. A.S. Altekar, *The Position of Women in Hindu Civilization*, Benares, Motilal Banarsidass, 1956.
2. P.V. Kane, *History of Dharmasastra*, Poona, Bhandarkar Oriental Research Institute, vols. I, II, III, IV; J. Jolly, *Hindu Law and Custom*, Calcutta, Greater India Society Publication, 1928.
3. *Epigraphia Indica*, New Delhi, Archaeological Survey of India, vol. II, 1894, pp. 358-81 (hereafter cited as *EI*).
4. Pali Grant of Govindachandra and his mother Ralhanadevi (VS 1189/ AD 1132), *EI*, vol. V, 1898-99, p. 114. Ralhanadevi and Ralhadevi are the names of one and the same queen (see *EI*, vol. V, p. 114 , also see ibid., vol. IV, 1896-7, p. 113).
5. *Journal of Asiatic Society of Bengal*, vol. LVI, pt. I, pp. 113-18, cf. Roma Niyogi, *The History of the Gahadawala Dynasty*, Calcutta, Oriental Press, 1959, pp. 249-50.
6. Ibid.
7. *EI*, vol. IV, pp. 113-14.
8. Macchlishahr copper-plate inscription of Harischandra of Kanauj (VS 1253) refers to a piece of land possibly belonging to *maharajni* Ghosaladevi in the previous years (*EI*, vol. X, 1909-10, pp. 93-100).
9. The term is translated by D.R. Bhandarkar as the king's personal property. U.N. Ghoshal regards it as periodical supplies of fruits, firewood, flowers, etc., which villages had to furnish to the king (for details see Dashrath Sharma, *Early Chauhan Dynasties*, Delhi, S. Chand and Company, 1966, p. 210). Whatever had been the meaning of the term, the *Rajkiyabhoga* as it is mentioned in the inscription appears an assignment to the queen mother made by the king for her own maintenance.

10. Sanderav Stone Inscription of Kalhandeva of VS 1221, *EI*, vol. XI, 1911-12, p. 47.
11. *EI*, vol. II, p. 13, vv.29-30.
12. Bheraghat Inscription of Alhanadevi, KE 907, *EI*, vol. II, p. 13, v. 29.
13. *Corpus Inscription Indicarum, Inscriptions of the Kalachuri Chedi Era*, ed. V.V. Mirashi, vol. IV, pt. II, Appendix 4, p. 649, v. 27 (hereafter cited as *CII*).
14. G.N. Sharma, *Rajasthan Through the Ages*, vol. II, Bikaner, Rajasthan State Archives, 1990, p. 221.
15. *Prithvirajavijaya*, chapter IX, cf. Dashrath Sharma, *Early Chauhan Dynasties*, op. cit., pp. 72, 199.
16. Ibid., p. 72. The author of *Hammirmahakavya* refers that Somesvara lived a retired life after providing the kingdom to Prithviraja (*Hammirmahakavya*, ed. Nilkanth Janardan Kirtane, Education Society Press, Byculla, 1879, pp. 15-16) Karpuradevi then took over the charge as regent for her son (ibid.).
17. *Prabandhakosa*, Shantiniketan, Singhi Jain Granthmala (hereafter SJG), no. 6, pp. 90-1.
18. *Prabandhacintamani*, Bombay, SJG, no. 1, 1933, p. 154.
19. *Great Women of India*, ed. Swami Madhavananda and R.C. Mazumdar, Calcutta, Sri Gauranga Press Limited, 1st edn., 1953, pp. 320-1. James Tod, *Annals and Antiquities of Rajasthan*, vol. I, Delhi, Low Price Publications, 1993, p. 303.
20. *Kathakosa*, tr. C.H. Tawney, New Delhi, Oriental Book Reprint Corporation, 1975, pp. 25-6.
21. *CII*, vol. IV. pt. II, no. 77 (Text), p. 413, v. 22.
22. *Prabandhacintamani*, SJG, p. 58.
23. B.P. Mazumdar, *Socio-Economic History of Northern India (*AD *1030-1194)*, Calcutta, K.L. Mukhopadhyay, p. 136.
24. R.M. Das, *Women in Manu and his Seven Commentators*, Bodhgaya, Kanchan Publications, 1961, p. 242.
25. Ibid.
26. B.P. Mazumdar, op. cit., p. 135.
27. Ibid., pp. 135-6.
28. Ibid., p. 136, *Sukranitisara*, Hindi tr. with text by Pt. Mihir Chandra, Bombay, Sri Venkateshwar Steam Press, chapter 3, p. 84.
29. Ibid.
30. *CII*, vol. IV, pt. I, no. 56, text, pp. 293-4, vv. 13-14.
31. *EI*, vol. II, pp. 7-17, *CII*, no. 60, vv. 21-2.
32. *CII*. vol. IV, pt. I, no. 60, v. 24, text, p. 316, *EI*, vol. II, p. 12, v. 24.
33. *CII*, vol. IV, pt. II, Appendix 4, p. 649, v. 26.
34. *Vastupala Tejapalaprabandha* in *Puratanaprabandha Sangraha*, ed. Jinavijayamuni, Calcutta, SJG, no. 2, 1936, p. 57.

35. *Indian Antiquary*, Delhi, Indological Book Reprint Corporation, vol. XVI (hereafter cited as *IA*),1887, pp. 205-7, v. 8.
36. *IA*, vol. VI, 1877, pp. 208-10, cf. H.C. Ray, *Dynastic History of Northern India*, New Delhi, Munshiram Manoharlal, 1973, vol. II, pp. 1034-5.
37. *EI*, vol. XI, pp. 41-2. *Pala* is the abbreviated form of *palika*. *Paila* signifies a unit of measuring weight. *Vimsopaka* was probably a coin which is equal to the 1/20 of the rupee prevalent in that period (ibid.).
38. Ibid., pp. 62-3.
39. Jayashri Mishra, *Social and Economic Conditions under the Imperial Rashtrakutas* (AD *750-973*), New Delhi, Commonwealth Publications, 1992, p. 57. Also see A.S. Altekar, *The Position of Women*, p. 189.
40. The *Pattamahadevi Maharajni* Nayanakeli Devi endowed with all royal prerogatives made the donation of the village of Dharavali to *Purohita* Jagusarmana with the consent of the king. The purpose of the grant was sacred. (Kamauli Plate of Govindachandra and his queen Nayankelidevi, *EI*, vol. IV, pp.107-9). The Bahuvara grant or Messrs Terry and Company Grant (VS 1164) refers that *Maharajni* Prithvisrika granted Bahuvara village in Bhailavata *pattala* to *Purohita* Devavarmana and others with the consent of the king. (H.C. Ray, op. cit., vol. I, p. 512). The king's name is not mentioned with reference to the queen but the editor took the donor as the queen of Madanapala (ibid.).
41. Bangavan Plate of Govindachandra and his queen Gosaladevi, VS 1208/AD 1150 (*EI*, vol. V, pp. 116-18).
42. *EI*, vol. II, p. 177, v. 32.
43. Pratipal Bhatia, *The Parmaras (c. 800-1305* AD), Delhi, Munshiram Manoharlal, 1970, p. 173, fn. 4.
44. *IA*, vol. LVI, 1927, p. 12.
45. Bhatia, op. cit., p. 173, fn. 4 (viii).
46. Ray, op. cit., vol. II, p. 882.
47. Das, op. cit., pp. 161, 171-5.
48. Thus Hathia-dah Pillar Inscription (VS 1207/AD 1151) records the excavation of a tank by several *thakkuras* of whom the chief is Belhana *thakkura as bhandagarika* of queen Ghosaladevi, the chief queen of Govindachandra (A. Cunningham, *Archaeological Survey of India Report*, vol. I, Delhi, 1972, pp. 95-6). Under the Kalachuris the head of the treasury department was known as *mahabhandagarika* or *bhandagarika* (R.K. Sharma, *Kalachuris and Their Times*, Delhi, Sandeep Prakashan, 1989, p. 13). According to Roma Niyogi, who made a study of the Gahadawala inscriptions, this was an important personage comparable to the treasurer or Collector General (*samaharta*) of *Arthashastra*, though the literal meaning of the term is to be regarded as officer-in-charge of the royal store. She suggested that besides the state *bhandagarikas* there were some in-charge of the personal *bhandaras* of the important members of the ruling family including the queens (see Niyogi, op. cit., p. 152).

49. Sarnath Inscription of Kumaradevi (Undated), *EI*, vol. IX, 1907-08, p. 325, v. 22.
50. Copper plate Grant of Chandradeva and Madanapala (VS 1154), *IA*, vol. XIII, p. 13, also see Copper Plate Grants of Madanapala and Govindachandra VS 1166, ibid., p. 18, Benares College Copper Plate Grant of Jayachandra of (VS 1232), ibid., p. 131. The tradition of informing about the land-grants to the queens was possibly started by the Senas, who are described to have brought about a significant change in the formula of royal land grants so as to include the queens in the list of the king's informants (Mazumdar, op. cit., p. 140).
51. The Kahla Plate of Sodhadeva Kalacuri refers to a *maharajni* and *maharajaputra* in the same context (Niyogi, op. cit., p. 147, fn. 2.).
52. The Tantoti Image Inscription (VS 1251/AD 1194) refers that the village of Tamtuthi (modern Tamtoti) was in the fief of Pratapadevi, the queen of Hariraja (Ray, op. cit., vol. II, p. 1093).
53. Sanderav Stone Inscription of Kelhanadeva, VS 1236, *EI*, vol. XI, pp. 51-2.
54. The copper coins issued by her bear the figure of horsemen on the obverse and the queen's name on the reverse, while the silver coins which are comparatively rarer, popularly known as '*gadhaiya ka paisa*' bear on the obverse the legend Sri Somaladevi and on the reverse a degraded representation of a king's head. (Dashrath Sharma, *Early Chauhan Dynasties*, op. cit., p. 41, also see, Ray, op. cit., vol. II, pp. 1071-2).
55. Dashrath Sharma, *Early Chauhan Dynasties*, op. cit., p. 41, fn. 58.
56. *CII*, vol. IV, no. 69, l. 1.
57. Kiradu Stone Inscription of Alhanadeva (VS 1209), *EI*, vol. XI, pp. 44-6.
58. The Ajaigarh Stone Inscription (VS 1317) of the chief queen of Virvarmana, Kalyanadevi refers to the genealogy of the dynasty to which the queen originally belonged (A. Cunningham, *Archaeological Survey Report*, vol. XXI, 1883-84, p. 51). The Bilhari Stone Inscription of the Kalachuri king Yuvarajadeva II describes the genealogy of Nohala, the chief queen of Yuvarajadeva I, who belonged to the Chalukya lineage (*CII*, vol. IV, no. 45, pt. I, pp. 211-12, vv. 30-7). The Bheraghat Stone Inscription of Narasimha of KE 907 refers to the entire pedigree of Alhanadevi, the wife of Gayakarna Kalachuri and the daughter of Vijaisimha Guhila (*CII*, vol. IV, pt. I, no. 60, p. 316, vv. 17-22).
59. *EI*, vol. XI, pp. 49-50.
60. *CII*, vol. IV, pt. II, no. 95, p. 499, vv. 29-30.
61. *Prabandhacintamani*, tr. C.H. Tawney, Delhi, Indian Book Gallery, 1982, p. 78.
62. *Great Woman of India*, p. 363, also see, A.K. Forbes, *Rasmala*, Delhi, Heritage Publishers, p. 1973, p. 83.

63. *EI*, vol. I, pp. 328, vv. 18-20.
64. Harihar Singh, 'Women's Patronage to Temple Architecure', in Kumkum Roy (ed.), *Women in Early Indian Societies*, New Delhi, Manohar, 1999, p. 292 (hereafter cited as Women's Patronage). Also see B.N. Puri, *The History of the Gurjara-Pratiharas*, Bombay, J.V. Patel Pubs., 1957, p. 156.
65. Bilhari Stone Inscription of Yuvarajadeva II, *CII*, pt. I, no. 45, p. 212, vv. 40-5.
66. Women's Patronage, op. cit., p. 294.
67. *EI*, vol. II, pp. 12-13.
68. Sarnath Inscription of Kumaradevi (undated), *EI*, vol. IX, p. 325, vv. 20-2.
69. Sanchor Stone Inscription of Pratapsimha, *EI*, vol. XI, pp. 65-7.
70. Ibid., p. 67.
71. Dashrath Sharma, *Early Chauhan Dynasties*, op. cit., p. 37.
72. *EI*, vol. IV, pp. 29-32, vv. 6-8.
73. Vasantagarh Inscription of Purnapala of VS 1099, *EI*, vol. IX, pp. 12-15.
74. *EI*, vol. I, p. 144, vv. 40-2.
75. Ibid., p. 328, vv. 14-20.
76. *Hammirmahakavya*, op. cit., text, p. 36.
77. Ojha Grant, no. 3, vv. 20-2, cf. Dashrath Sharma, *Early Chauhan Dynasties*, op. cit., p. 133.
78. Ibid., p. 131.
79. *CII*, vol. IV, no. 45, l. 18.
80. *Rasmala*, p. 29.
81. Image Inscription of Ajaigarh Fort, VS 1345/AD 1288, cf. P. Prasad, *Sanskrit Inscriptions of Delhi Sultanate*, New Delhi, Oxford University Press, 1990, pp. 142-3.
82. Jalor Stone Inscription of Samantasimhadeva, VS 1353, *EI*, vol. XI, pp. 61-2. The ancestors of Narapati, the grandfather and great grandfather are styled as *thakkuras.*
83. See supra, op. cit., pp. 8-9.
84. The Kanker Copper Plate Inscription of Pamparaja VS 965/AD 1213 refers to the grant of a village with a fixed revenue to the village priest by the feudatory of the Gurjara-Pratihara in the presence of his queen Laxmidevi, the prince and eight government officials including the minister as witness. *EI*, vol. IX, p. 168.
85. *EI*, vol. XXII, pp. 188, 190.
86. *Rajni sri Tihunaka grasa bhujyamanavalahigramasya* (*EI*, vol. XI, p. 33).
87. Ratanpur Stone Inscription, Ray, op. cit., vol. II, p. 980.
88. Ibid.

89. Rajim Stone Inscription, *IA*, vol. XVII, 1888, p. 137. Kielhorn regards her as the mother of Jagapala.
90. *Manasollasa* (or *Abhilasitarthacintamani*) of Somesvara, Baroda, Gaekwad Oriental Series, vol. II, no. 84, p. 100, vv. 63-6, *Adhyaya* 11, *vimsati* 3.
91. H.M. Elliot and J. Dowson, *The History of India as Told by its Own Historians*, Delhi, Low Price Publications, 2001, p. 11.
92. *Prabandhcintamani*, SJG, p. 97. James Tod, op. cit., vol. I, pp. 303-4, see supra, p. 4.
93. *Tilakamanjari*, Bombay, Nirnayasagar Press, 1938, p. 156.
94. R.K. Sharma, op. cit., p. 117.
95. K.A. Nizami (ed.), *Politics and Society during the Early Medieval India*, vol. I, New Delhi, Peoples' Publishing House, 1974, p. 219.
96. Ibid.
97. Kamanadaka, *Nitisara*, XIV, 69, XVIII, 45 cf. A.S. Altekar, *The Rashtrakutas and Their Times*, Poona, Oriental Book Agency, 1934, p. 255 (hereafter cited as *The Rashtrakutas*).
98. *EI*, vol. XVIII, 1925-6, pp. 109, 114, v.22.
99. *CII*, vol. IV, pt. I, ins. no. 45, v. 21, p. 210.
100. Altekar, *The Rashtrakutas*, op. cit., p. 254.
101. Belur Inscription of Saka 944, *IA*, vol. XVIII, 1889, pp. 273-4.
102. V.S. Bendrey, *A Study of Muslim Inscriptions: With Special Reference to the Inscriptions Published in Epigraphia Indo Moslamica(1907-1938)*, Delhi, Anmol Publications, 1985, p. 18.
103. *Agni Purana* warns the king against trusting a wife who has got a son (Eng. tr. M.N. Datt Shastri, vol. II, Varanasi, Chaukhamba Sanskrit Series, chapter 224, p. 42).
104. *Prabandhacintamani*, tr. Tawney, p. 185.
105. *Samaraicchakaha* of Haribhadra, ed. H. Jacobi, IV *Bhava*, Calcutta, Bibliothica Indica, no. 169, 1926 cf. K.K. Handiqui, *Yashastilaka and Indian Culture*, Jinaraja Jain Granthmala, no. 2, Sholapur, 1968, p. 44.
106. Somadeva Suri, *Yashatilakam*, Bk. IV, ed. Kashinath Sharma, Bombay, Nirnayasagar Press, 1903, pp. 152-3, *Nitivakyamrita*, see chaper on *Rajraksha*, Manikchandra D. Jain Granthmala, no. 22, Bombay, 1922, cf. K.K. Handiqui, *Yashastilalaka and Indian Culture*, pp. 104-5.
107. The treacherous character of women had been seriously tackled by the author of *Nitivakyamrita* providing lessons in detail to adopt precautionary measures while associating with women and not to eat anything coming from the ladies apartment (*Nitivakyamrita*, chapter 24 (24.32). Also see chapter on *rajraksha*.) The mind of women is referred as extremely fickle and superficial by the author of *Nitivakyamrita* (ibid.). Kalhana in his *Rajatarangini* also refers the same opinion

regarding the fickleness of women (tr. M.A. Stein, Delhi, Motilal Banarsidass, 1979, vol. I, p. 335, VII, p. 857).

108. *Prabandhakosa*, SJG, pp. 50-1.
109. *Kumarapala Charitra Sangraha*, ed. Muni Jina Vijaya, Bombay, SJG, no. 41, 1956, cf., S.P. Narang, *Dvasraya Kavya: A Literary and Cultural Study*, New Delhi, 1972, p. 112.
110. *Virvinod*, vol. I, Delhi, B.R. Publishing Corporation, 1986, p. 350.
111. While Parmala, the Chandella king, finally decided for war against the Chahamana king Prithviraja, his queen Malanadevi 'upbraided his uncommonly spirit and bid him head his troops and go forth to the fight' (James Tod, op. cit., vol. II, p. 728).
112. Tod accounts that when Prithviraja Chauhan of Delhi abducted the daughter of the prince of Sameta 'some of the wounded, who had covered his retreat were assailed and put to death by the Chandella king Parmala and to avenge that Prithviraja invaded the territory of the Chandella king and defeated some of the Chandella troops at Sirswa'. After this initial victory of Prithviraja 'the Chandella king called a council and by the advice of his queen Malanadevi demanded a truce of his adversary on the plea of the absence of his chieftains Alha and Udala' (James Tod, op. cit., vol. II, pp. 715-16). It is further accounted by Tod that Parmal summoned a grand council constituting all his chiefs, the mother of Banaphar chiefs and Malanadevi, the chief queen of Parmala, who took active part in the final deliberations of this council and after a long course of discussion and deliberation, Malanadevi keeping in view the fierceness of the Chauhans advised to make peace by paying tribute in order to save Mahoba (ibid., p. 722).
113. Padmanabha, *Kanhadade Prabandha*, tr. V.S. Bhatnagar, New Delhi, Aditya Prakashan, 1991, pp. 90-1.
114. Belur Inscription of the Time of Jayasimha III, Saka 944, *IA*, vol. XVIII, 1889, pp. 273-4.
115. Dashrath Sharma, *Rajasthan Through the Ages*, vol. I, Bikaner, Rajasthan State Archives, 1966, p. 265.
116. Ibid.
117. A.K. Forbes, *Rasmala*, Bk. I, p. 28.
118. Ibid.
119. Sundha Hill Inscription, v. 41, cf. G.C. Chaudhari, op. cit., p. 161.
120. Kadi Grant (VS 1263/AD 1206), cf. Ray, op. cit., vol. II, p. 1007.
121. Ibid., p. 878.

CHAPTER 2

Intellectual Fervour During the Reign of Sultan Firuz Shah Tughlaq

ANEESA IQBAL SABIR

In the history of the Delhi Sultanate, the age of Firuz Shah Tughlaq (AH 752-90/AD 1351-88) was the most prolific as far as the writing of historical and religious literature is concerned. If on the one hand it saw the production of Ziauddin Barani's *Tarikh-i-Firuzshahi*,[1] Afif's *Tarikh-i-Firuzshahi*,[2] Firuz Shah's *Futuhat-i-Firuzshahi*[3] and the *Sirat-i-Firuzshahi*,[4] and on the other hand, works like *Al-Fatawa-al-Tatarkhaniah*,[5] *Fawaid-i-Firuzshahi*,[6] *Fiqh-i-Firuzshahi*[7] and *Fatawa i-Jahandari*[8] (appeared during this period, on the principles and procedures of maintaining records there appeared the *Dastur-ul-Albab-fi-Ilm-ul-Hisab* while in *Insha-i-Mahru*, many documents of the period were put together). The reign of Firuz Shah Tughlaq is important in the history of the Delhi Sultanate for not only its political role but also cultural achievements.

It was after the death of Muhammad Tughlaq that the nobles and the *ulama* selected Firoz, the nephew of Ghiyas-ud-din Tughlaq, to the throne of Delhi. The reign of this Sultan is remembered in the history of India for peace and public welfare. The first thing he did was to release those prisoners whom Muhammad Tughlaq had thrown into prison. He gave compensations to the survivors of those who had been murdered on the instructions of his predecessor.

Sultan Firuz Shah Tughlaq (AD 1351-88) was deeply interested in the promotion of Islamic education and learning. N.N. Law writes 'In the long list of preceding Mohammedan emperors there was none who tried so much for the diffusion of education among his subjects.'[9]

Nothing is known about the early education of Firuz but the wide interest he took in *fiqh* (law) religion, theology, astronomy, medicine and natural sciences as revealed in the *Sirat-i-Firuzshahi*[10] and his composition and dictation of *Futuhat-i-Firuzshahi*, it can be safely deduced that he was well educated and Ghiyas-ud-din Tughlaq must have made good arrangements for his education just as that of Muhammad Tughlaq. He was only twelve when Ghiyas-ud-din died and after that Muhammad bin Tughlaq always kept Firuz in his company and explained to him all important state affairs. Ibn Batuta[11] opines that Malik Firuz was the closest chamberlain to the Sultan who used to dine with him which was a rare privilege. Thus he was thoroughly trained in the art of administration.

Firuz Shah Tughlaq's intellectual level and learning may have been less as compared to Muhammad Tughlaq, but he possessed a variety of literary interests. He was enthroned in Sindh by a group of religious men including Shaikh Nasir-ud-din Chiragh. During the course of his journey from Sindh to Delhi he visited shrines and *khanqahs* of saints and gave stipends and endowments to *khanqahs* which had suffered during the previous reign.[12] His political administration was of an entirely different nature. He abhorred from making any bold experiments like Muhammad bin Tughlaq. He entrusted the routine administrative responsibilities to his *wazir* and directed his attention and energies to projects of public welfare and undertook several programmes of educational development.[13]

Contemporary Persian sources unanimously acclaim the greatness of Firuz Shah Tughlaq. He has been described as 'the most gentle, modest, gracious, benevolent, grateful, faithful, and firm believer in the tenets of Islam after Muhammad bin Sam'.[14]

Firuz Shah Tughlaq was of a deeply religious bent of mind. He regularly performed the obligatory prayers in a congregation, recited the Koran daily, was deeply interested in Islamic jurisprudence, banned the use of silver and gold vessels in the court, and regulated the visit of women to tombs and festivals and use of silken clothes, etc. But there was another side to his character without which the picture will be incomplete. That he was very fond of wine, had deep interest in astronomy, believed in omens, auguries, amulets and charms and loved music. Azra Alavi rightly observes: 'Firuz Shah projects an image of his religious personality in the pages of *Futuhat* which is correct so far as it goes, but is not complete.'[15]

The Sultan (AD 1351-88) was a highly accomplished and versatile man of literary and artistic tastes. In his devotion to learning, literature, and architecture he surpassed all other Sultans of Delhi. Himself a fairly educated monarch, he devoted his energies to the spread of Islamic learning and literature. The establishment of many *madrasas* and the lavish grant of subsistence allowances and stipends to the learned greatly enhanced his reputation as a patron of learning. Not only did he build *madrasas* he also renovated and repaired the old buildings, mosques and *madrasas*, which he has mentioned in his *Futuhat-i-Firuzshahi*, where he writes,

One of the favours of God, bestowed on the humble servant (was that) he was enabled to construct works of public utility, I erected numerous mosques, *madrasas* (colleges) and *khanqahs* so that the *alims* and *mashaikh* (devotees and pious men), might devote themselves to the worship of the true God and help with prayer the founder of charitable institutions.[16]

It is interesting to learn from the Sultan himself some particulars about the provisions made for building operations:

Provisions for the future repairs and rebuilding of these *madrasas* and tombs was made from their old endowments, which were to remain attached to their respective institutions. And where no income had been settled before, I assigned villages whose revenues are always to be used in meeting the needs of visitors and for providing, carpets, light and other requirements of the places concerned.

Again, thus I contributed the grants of villages, lands and old endowments attached to madrasahs, tombs and graves of the victorious Sultans of the past and the great *mashaikh* for meeting the needs of visitors and providing necessary materials required for the holy places. In addition if there was no endowment or other provision at any place, an assignment was made for it so that the noble work might continue for ever and travellers and learned and holy men might rest there and remembered them and me in their prayers.[17]

He further informs:

Portions of the *madrasa* of Sultan Iltutmish with whom God may be pleased had fallen down. These were likewise, rebuilt and furnished with sandalwood doors. . . . In the mausoleum of Sultan Ruknuddin, a son of Sultan Shamsuddin, which is situated in Malikpur, the enclosure was repaired, a dome was built and a '*khanqah* constructed'.[18] Also, Sultan Alauddin Khalji's mausoleum was repaired and furnished with sandalwood doors. Walls of the water reservoir and the western walls of the mosque which is within the *madrasa* and ground floor were also repaired.[19]

According to the testimony of Nizamuddin Bakhshi and Ferishta,[20] the Sultan established no less than thirty *madrasas*, appointed learned teachers there and provided them a handsome salary. However, Abdul Baqi Nahawandi has recorded in his *Maasir-i-Rahimi*, that he opened as many as fifty *madrasas.*[21] Although the number of *madrasas* differs in different accounts there were definitely several of them existing in a flourishing state.

The *madrasas* of Firuz Tughlaq's period became popular because of the high standard of education and excellent teaching arrangements there. The Firuzi Madrasah and the Madrasah-i-Shahzada Buzurg[22] were well known throughout the country.

Perhaps the only detailed account of a *madrasa* founded by any Sultan of Delhi is that of Firuzi Madrasah of Delhi, on the southern bank of the Hauz-i-Khas,[23] Firuz Shah built this magnificent *madrasa*[24] in AD 1352.[25] 'Its magnificence,' writes Barani, 'architectural proportions and pleasant air make it so unique among the great buildings of the world that it would be justifiable if it claimed superiority over the Khwarnaq built by Simar or the palace of Kisra.'[26]

The Firuzi Madrasah was a double-storeyed building with arched *dalans* and projecting windows overlooking the tank.[27] As soon as one entered the doorway one found oneself in a blooming garden adorned with pathways and passages.[28] This two-storeyed structure was in itself a fine example in the art of building. It stood on strong pillars and there were many domes made over it. The location of this *madrasa* was excellent and it was built on a large, extensive campus. There were spacious courtyards in between the different buildings of the *madrasa*, which had wide galleries and corridors. The scenic beauty, gardens laden with beautiful colourful flowers added explicit charm to this *madrasa*.

Barani describes the beauty of this *madrasa* in the following words:

از بناهای مبارک خداوند عالم مدرسه فیروز شاهیست که بس بوالعجب عمارتی بر سر حوض علائی بنا شده است وعمارت مدرسه مذکور از رفعت گنبدها وشیرینی عمارتها وموازین صحنها ولطافت نشست جاشهائے ومحلهای مروج وصفهای دلآویز گوی لطافت از عمارتهای که در عالم معروف است ربوده است.... از شیرینی عمارت وموازین عمارت وهوای دل کشای ازان بناها نادره است[29]

What greatly God gifted is the Madrasah-i-Firuz Shahi that wonderful buildings are situated near the Alai Tank. The buildings of the *madrasa*, because of the glory of their domes, sweetness of their construction, open courtyards, comfortable seats, beautiful palaces and attractive lines of students, have left behind the buildings of other places in the world. In attraction and comparison, and also from the point of view of air, these monuments are rare.

Another beautiful description of this *madrasa* in poetic form has been done by the famous poet Mutahhar of Kara[30] who praises the Firuzi Madrasah in these words:

صحن او روح فزا ساحت او جاں
خاک او مشک فشان نکهت او عنبر بار
سبزه وسنبل وریحان وگل ولاله درو
رسته وآراسته چندانک کند با تو کار

Its courtyard, both external and internal are because of their construction very comfortable,
Its dust is scented with musk, its air is ambergrised,
There are greenery, spikenard, sweet basil, rose and popy flower in side it,
All its ways are beautifully decorated

The Firuzi Madrasah covered a capacious area besides several lecture halls, it had within its campus, commodious hostels for both teachers and the taught, guest houses for casual visitors, a huge mosque, rooms for *imams* and *mu'ezzins* and *hujrahs* (small rooms) for those who wished to spend their time in meditation.[31] Comfortable and pleasant looking carpets of Shiraz, Yemen and Damascus were spread in every corner of the *madrasa*.[32]

In the words of Mutahhar:

وزبساط یمن مفرش شیراز ودمشق
همه آراسته بیرون ودرونش چو نگار

Its carpets have been brought from Yeman, Shiraz and Damascus,
Both its outside and inside are beautifully decorated

Other than its beauty, magnificence and excellence in building, the *madrasa* was famous for its cultured and experienced teachers who were experts in their subjects. Amongst the most famous was Maulana Jalal-ud-din Rumi (not the famous philosopher and author of the *Mathnawi* Jalal-ud-din Rumi (AD 1273). Barani has used the title (استادمتفنن), i.e. teachers of arts and crafts, for him.[33] But it is clearly evident from the following verses of Mutahhar that Jalal-ud-din Rumi was the principal of this *madrasa*:

صدر آن محفل وسر دفتر آن استادی
کہ زسرتا بقدم صورت عقل ست و وقار
گفتم این عالمِ آفاق جلال الدین است
کہ رومی آن کزنسبتش رے کند و روم فخار[34]

The head of the gathering and the incharge of its office is a teacher;
Who, from top to bottom, is the face of intellect and honour?.
I said this world-fame teacher is Jalal-ud-din Rumi,
Of whose genealogy the cities of Ray and Rum, take pride.

Mutahhar has called him a great master of Koran, *hadith* and *fiqh* and has acknowledged of himself benefiting from the teachings of Jalal-ud-din Rumi.

راوی ہفت قراءت سند چارده علم
شارح پنج سنن مفتی مذہب چار
پس شنیدم زگفتارش انواع علوم
اخذ کردیم ز تفسیر واصول واخبار[35]

He knows seven dialects of *qirat* and he is an authority in fourteen sciences,
He is interpreter of the five collection of *hadith* and the *mufti* of all four schools of jurisprudence.
In short, I heard from him about different sciences,
I derived lot from his *tafsir*, *usul* and *hadith*.

Sir Syed Ahmad Khan and other modern writers[36] have named Syed Yusuf Bin Jamal Haseeni as the most famous and renowned teacher of the Firuzi Madrasah and have even said that he was buried in the courtyard of this *madrasa*. Others have mentioned him as the principal teacher of the *madrasa* which was built close to Hauz Alai but was some other *madrasa* and not the Firuzi Madrasah.[37] The syllabus of the *Madrasah-i-Firuz Shahi* included both traditional (*manqulat*) and rational (*ma'qulat*) sciences.

In it the following subjects were taught:

- *Fiqh* (Jurisprudence)
- *Qir'at* (method of recitation of the Koran)
- *Usul-i-Kalam* (Principles of scholasticism)
- *Usul-i-Fiqh* (Principles of jurisprudence)
- *Tafsir* (Exegesis)
- *Ahadis* (Traditions of the Prophet)
- *Ma'ani-o-Bayan* (Rhetoric)
- *Nahv-o-Sarf* (Syntax)
- *Ilm-i-Nazar* (Science of observation)
- *Ilm-i-Riyaazi* (Mathematics)
- *Tabi'i* (Physical sciences)
- *Illahi* (Theology)
- *Ilm-i-Tibb* (Medicine)
- *Tahrir-o-Khatt* (Calligraphy).[38]

Barani particularly refers to the teachings of *tafsir* (Koranic exegesis), *hadith* (Traditions of the Prophet) and *fiqh* (Muslim jurisprudence).[39] As Firuz Shah was deeply interested in astronomy history and medicine, there is a possibility that these subjects were taught in this *madarasa*.

Moreover, the reign of Sultan Firuz Shah Tughlaq was generally famous for the domination of the sciences of *fiqh*, but as regards the interest of the rational sciences and the instruction in these sciences and its compositions were also actively carried out. In some of the *madrasas* of this period, logic, philosophy and scholasticism were included in the course, the evidence of which is available. During this time Jalal-ud-din Rumi, Jalal-ud-din Kirmani, Azuddin Khalid Khani, Abdul Aziz Dehlavi, etc., and several other scholars were present who had a deep knowledge and understanding of subjects such as philosophy *hikmat*, and physical sciences. Jalal-ud-din Rumi was the pupil of Shaikh Qutbuddin Razi, the interpreter of *Shamsiyah*. Teaching was his special profession. The last mentioned two *ulama* had translated some Sanskrit works of astronomy into Persian. It is the best proof of their deep knowledge in this field.[40] Moreover there was no shortage of scholars of medicine. The appearance of many hospitals during this period testifies to the keen interest of the Sultan in this field.[41]

No information on the uniform of the students is available, but the teachers of this institution wore the Syrian *jubbah* and the Egyptian *dastar*.[42]

Contemporary sources bring out the fact that other than teaching and learning, the process of holding debates and seminars was also present in the Firuzi Madrasah and the students were given opportunity to debate on a particular topic of significance. Khaliq Nizami[43] has narrated that the Muslim method of middle ages laid great emphasis on seminars and mutual discussions amongst the students. The purpose was to make use of their intelligence and improve their standard as intellectuals. The Firuzi Madrasah did not neglect this, very important method of imparting knowledge. To prove this, Nizami has used this particular verse of Mutahhar:

هم چنان یک دگر از طالب علمان هر سوی بر فلک برده صدا غلغل بحث و تکرار[44]

In this way the pupils were conducting discussions and debates in every corner and their voices echoed in the heavens.

Liberal grant were provided by the state to finance this *madrasa* and meet all the expenses of the teachers and the students. Royal arrangements were made for the boarding and lodging of students. According to Mutahhar, the following dishes were served at mealtimes: 'Pheasants, partridges, herons, fish, roasted fowl and fattened kids, fried loaves, sweets, of different kinds and other things, were heaped everywhere in large quantities.' Pomegranate syrup, prepared with the mixture of sorrel, was served as a drink. Betelnuts were brought in gold and silver dishes after the meal.[45]

Barani writes about the religious atmosphere prevailing at the *madrasa*:

واز انکه مدرسه فیروز شاهی معدن خیرات وحسنات است و دراو عبادت لازمه وهم عبادت متعدیه موی شود
وفرایض خمسه بجماعت مسنون می گذارند وصوفیان نماز چاشت واشراق وفی زوال واوابین وتهجد ادا می کنند
ولیلا ونهارا ذکر میگویند وبدعا وثنای بادشاه مشغول می باشند... وهر روز حافظان در ختمهای قرآن مشغول می باشند
ومسافران آواز تکبیر بآسمان می رسانند

Because this *madrasa* is a monument of good works and public benefaction, prayers obligatory and supererogatory are constantly being offered within its precincts. The five compulsory prayers are offered in congregation according to Sunnah. The Sufis offer the *chasht* Prayer (offered between sunrise and meridian), *ishraq* (prayer offered soon after sunrise), *fayaz-zawal* (prayer offered immediately after sunset) and *tahajjud* (prayer offered in the latter part of the night), praise God night and day and send benediction on and sing and praise the Sultan constantly. People who know the Koran by heart recite the full text every day; the travellers raise their voices to the heavens when they cry Allah-o-Akbar.[46]

Barani writes that the beauty of the Firuzi Madrasah was *par excellence* and the satisfaction and peace that one experiences after entering this *madrasa* could not be availed or felt in any other place which he expresses in the following words:

واگر چه دار الملک دهلی بادشاهان گذشته طاب ثراهم عمارتها بسیار کرده اند مالهائے بے اندازه دران خرچ شده

ومواطن دیوان و پریان گشته ام شیرینی، روحی وراحتی که مدرسه فیروزشاهی دارد هیچ بنائے نیست وبدین زیبائی

عمارتی مشاهده نشده است [47]

Although the former rulers have built a number of attractive monuments in Delhi and spent heavy amount in their beautification and decoration, yet the prettiness, pleasure and comfort which are in the Madrasah-i-Firuz Shahi are not seen elsewhere.

The Firuzi Madrasah was a great centre of Muslim learning in the East, and people gathered there from different parts of the country, simply to see it:

از پئے نظاره دیدار او شرق وغرب

کاروان در کاروان وقافله در قافله

With a view to have a look at it (people from) the east and the west (come) in caravan after caravan.[48]

The second *madrasa* of the Firozian period was built at Siri which also has been praised by Barani who records that Maulana Syed Najm-ul-Millat Waddin Samarqandi, a great scholar of the time was the principal of this *madrasa*.[49]

Another very famous seat of learning in Delhi was the Madrasah-i-Shahzada Buzurg.[50] It was named after the eldest son of Firuz Shah, Fath Khan, who died in AD 1374. A footprint of the Prophet was placed on the grave.[51] The area therefore came to be known as *Qadam Sharif*.[52] With in the enclosure the Sultan built a charity house (*langar khana*), a *madrasa* and a mosque consisting of three chambers, covered with domes with a courtyard attached to it surrounded by walls.[53]

The doorway of this *madrasa* was engraved with the following lines:

> The guide of those who have lost (their way) Muhammad
> The Preacher of Preacher Muhammad
> Glorious is the *madrasah*, the pulpit and the house
> In the midst of which is read the praise of Muhammad
> For the broken hearts he is (Healing) balm
> For the afflicted in the heart Muhammad is a comfort, etc.[54]

The aforementioned discussion on the educational centres of Islamic higher learning shows that these centres were found all over the Sultanate and imparted education in different branches of learning at a higher level.

Amongst the scholars of the Firuzi period was the compiler of the famous Arabic dictionary *Qamus*, Maulana Majduddin Firuzabadi, who came to India during this period. Three other people worth mentioning of the Firuz Shahi period were Maulana Ahmad Thaneshwari, Maulana Khwajaji, who was the teacher of Qazi Shihabuddin Daulatabadi, and Qazi Abdul Muqtadir Dehlawi. The most famous amongst the Sufis (*mashaikh*) was Makhdum Nasiruddin Chiragh of Delhi.[55] Sultan Muhammad bin Tughlaq had disrespected him but Firuz Shah paid him great honour. It was the *shaikh* who, after the death of Muhammad bin Tughlaq persuaded Firuz Shah, who was intending to leave for Hajj and other pilgrimages, to become the Sultan of Delhi. Firoz, on becoming the Sultan, sought his advice on several occasions. Shaikh Sadruddin Multani was another famous *shaikh* (Sufi) of that time whom the Sultan had granted the title of *Shaikh-ul-Islam*.

It appears that poetry and the composition of verses was not very popular in Firuz's reign as compared to others. However, some famous poets of the time find mention—one of them is Masud Bak, who is said to be a relative of Firuz Shah. His *diwan*, the collection of his verses and poems, has been published from Hyderabad Deccan. His real name was Sher Khan. Perhaps Masud Bak was his title. For a long time he lead the life of an aristocrat. Later he was attracted to the *darweshi* (the mystical life) and joined the discipline, becoming a *murid* (disciple) of Shaikh Ruknuddin bin Shaikh Shihabuddin. He wrote several works on Sufism (*Tasawwuf*), for instance *Tamhidat* and *Mirat-ul-Arifin*. Shaikh Abdul Haqq Muhaddith Dehlavi writes about him:

در سلسلۂ چشتیہ ہیچ کس این چنین اسرار حقیقت را فاش نگفتہ، و مستی نہ کردہ کہ او کردہ

In the Chishti order nobody disclosed the secrets of reality and got intoxicated with the love of God as he did.[56]

The other poet was Hamid Qalandar who compiled the *Khair-ul-Majalis*,[57] the *Malfuzat* of Hazrat Chiragh-i-Delhi. Amir Khusrau's son Amir Ahmad was also a poet of pleasing nature but we do not come across any *diwan* of his.[58] In the same period, Shihabi, who was a physician, composed a *mathnawi* entitled *Tibb-i-Shihabi*. But the best poet of that time was Mutahhar, who belonged to Kara (near Allahabad). He praised Firuz immensely and was an eulogist of Firuz Shah and his time. A noble known as Malik-ul-Sharq, Malik Ain-ul-Mulk, whose *Insha-i-Mahru*[59] is famous, was also one of the celebrated personalities whom he praised. Badayuni writes that the *diwan* of Mutahhar consisted of fifteen to sixteen thousand verses.[60] But it was not easily available even in the time of Shaikh Abdul Haq Muhaddith. Fortunately, a copy of this *diwan* has been discovered by Wahid Mirza. The latter and Maulvi Muhammad Shafi, Principal, Oriental College, Lahore wrote invaluable articles in the *Oriental College Magazine* and revived the name of the poet.[61]

Besides composition of verses and poetry, *fiqh* (jurisprudence) also was highly developed in those days. We are informed of several famous works of *fiqh* of the Firuzi period. Among the old works of Indian *fiqh* the *Fiqh-i-Firuzshahi* (also known as *Fatawa-i-Firuzshahi*[62] is very famous. Moreover, *Khan-i-Azam* Tatar Khan, who was a noble of Firuz and died a few years after AD 1357, got edited monumental works of religious science. One of them is the exegesis (*tafsir*), of the Koran and the other is concerned with *fiqh* which contains thousands of problems of *fiqh*, differences amongst jurists and their *fatawas* about every problem. A copy of this work in nine volumes and translated during the ninth century, is preserved in the *Kutub-Khana-i-Asafiyah*, the Asafiya Library, Hyderabad. The work is entitled *Al-Fatawa-al-Tatarkhaniah*. Its compiler is Maulana Alam bin Alauddin Hanafi. People of that age were so interested in *fiqh* that a *murid*; of Shaikh Nasiruddin Chiragh wrote a long *mathnawi* concerning the subject of *fiqh* under the title *Tarfat-ul-Fuqaha*. It contains more than thirty thousand verses.[63]

According to the author of *Sirat-i-Firuzshahi*, Firuz had listened from beginning to end most books on jurisprudence. The *Fatawa-*

i-Firuzshahi was prepared at his instance. The *Fawa'id-i-Firuzshahi*[64] of Maulana Sharaf Ibn Muhammad al-'Atai was another book on *fiqh* dedicated to Firuz Shah, considered in the broad perspective of trends in Muslim religious scholarship, the age of Firuz Shah was pre-eminent for the production of *fiqh* literature. Firuz Shah was responsible for encouraging this trend.[65]

During Firuz Shah's reign there was considerable development in the field of medicine also. The *Sirat-i-Firuzshahi*[66] gives a list of diseases and medicines indicating the Sultan's interest in the subject. The science of surgery was also developed. New instruments of operation were also invented. There was an instrument which was used to find out the position of a child in the womb of the mother.[67] He also established a hospital (*Dar-ul-Shifa*) where the general public were treated. In fact, Firuz adopted a modern approach by putting mentally ill patients in the hospital for treatment.[68] There was immense progress in the fields of astronomy and mechanical sciences as well.

The Sultan's keen personal interest gave further fillip to *tibb* (medicine). During his time it was included in the syllabus of the government colleges. He used to write prescriptions like Muhammad bin Tughlaq and prepared under his personal supervision, a comprehensive treatise on medicine entitled *Tibb-i-Firuzshahi*,[69] dealing with various diseases and their treatment. He was also interested in veterinary science and discussed the diseases and treatment of animals in a brochure entitled *Shikar Nama-i-Firuzshahi*.[70]

During his period we find evidence that the hospitals (which were called *Darul Shafa*, *Bimaristan* or *Sahatkhana*) other than providing treatment and remedy for various ailments also functioned in the capacity of centres for providing training and knowledge in the field of medicine.[71] In *Afif's Tarikh-i-Firuzshahi* there is mention of only one hospital but in the *Tarikh-i-Ferishta* the number of hospitals established by Firuz Shah Tughlaq is five[72] and in the *Tabaqat-i-Akbari* it is four.[73] Thus the hospitals other than being health service centres also played the role of a mode through which medical training and education were imparted.

Firuz Shah Tughlaq under his personal supervision established an excellent astrolabe and erected it on a minaret (tower) along with a sundial, which functioned as a storehouse too for the study, observation and conducting experiments in the field of astronomy. Here for the scholars of astronomy were provided facilities for observation and research.[74] Both the astrolabe and the sundial were also important aids in sea navigation, and by the thirteenth-century Chinese magnetic compasses (floating needles) were in use in ships in the Indian seas.[75] Firuz also established a unique mobile astrolabe.[76] Sultan's deep interest and abiding love for astronomy is also evident by his getting a Sanskrit work on astronomy translated into Persian which became famous as *Dalail-i-Firuzshahi*.[77] Thus we can infer that observatories were established by the Sultans so that research and experiment could be conducted in the field of astronomy, which led to enormous progress in this field. His passion for astronomy reached such an extent that even hunting of different animals was undertaken according to astronomical calculations.[78]

Firuz Tughlaq deposited a large number of books on astronomy and astrolabes in the royal library (*Kitab-khana-i-khas*) and desired that these be made available to all those who wished to make use of them.[79]

For the teaching and training of various arts and talents other than the private centres or household firms or home industries which provided domestic training, there were also workshops or centres of industrial training under the supervision of the administration called *karkhanas*. These *karkhanas* were specially established for manufacturing commodities for the use in the royal household and those of the nobles and officers. Hence under the supervision of expert artisans, craftsman, handicraft workers, training was imparted by expert artisans through the system of apprenticeship where the trading classes maintained their own schools for the instruction of their children or other people from which all took advantage. This system of providing training in various skills and industry was prevalent in the villages and towns of the Sultanate and was free from complex formalities.[80] In fact, the *karkhanas* of the royal household were factories to manufacture articles needed at the court.

Detailed evidence is available of the establishment of *karkhanas* and centres of industrial training during the period of Firuz Shah Tughlaq. There was a special department for technical training and teaching of different arts and skills for slaves (*diwan-i-bandagan*) during his period. Here it is clear that other than religious teaching and training, the Sultan was deeply interested in providing industrial training and technical knowledge to his slaves. In these *karkhanas*, under the supervision of skilled artisans and expert craftsmen, training in different arts, crafts, skills was provided to the royal slaves. In this way according to Afif approximately 12,000 slaves became efficient artists and artisans.[81]

The development in the mechanical science can be gauged from the list of mechanical devices listed by Afif: [82]

1. *Tas ghariyal*, a gong, meant to regulate the time of prayers. It was prepared by Firuz Shah in cooperation with astronomers and was placed on the *darbar* hall of Firozabad.
2. Large sized revolving *cauldrons*, for cooking ten fat sheeps.
3. *Claundron stands*, with ten legs to carry the 'revolving cauldrons'.
4. *White dome*, with a special portico (*fariza*), a part of royal camp.
5. *Azhdar Peel*, fixed on the backs of elephants.
6. Huge drums tied to the backs of elephants during hunting expeditions.
7. Two astrolabes (*usturlabs*) indicating direction.

CONCLUSION

Firuz Shah Tughlaq's reign is popular for its vibrant cultural tradition. His versatile personality and keen interest in the promotion of art and learning glorified and enhanced the cultural achievements of the Tughlaq dynasty. During his reign numerous intellectuals, scholars and poets flourished, who greatly enriched the field of knowledge by their erudite contribution. Not only did these scholars write on literature but also on religion, law, medicine and astronomy—books were written testifying the comprehensive progress made in all fields of learning during Firuz's reign.

NOTES

1. Ed. Sir Syed, *Bibliotheca Indica*, Calcutta, Asiatic Society of Bengal, 1862.
2. Ed. Maulvi Vilayat Husain, ibid., 1889-91.
3. Ed. Abdur Rashid, Dept. of History, Aligarh, 1954.
4. MS Bankipur Library (Catalogue VII, 547).
5. By Alim bin Ala-al-Hanafi, MSS Asiatic Society of Bengal (ASB) (405), Bankipore (19/14-16, No. 1715-19), Asfiyah (II, 1052), Rampur (III/240, No. 2454) and British Museum (1139), five volumes have been edited by Qazi Sajjad Husain, i.e. *Al-Fatawa-al-Tatarkhaniah* (ed. Qazi Sajjad Husain), Dairat-al-Ma'arif-al-Usmani, Hyderabad, 1984-9.

6. By Sharaf Muhmmad al-'Atai, MS Azad Library, AMU, Aligarh 297.3/27 (Subhanallah Collection).
7. By Maulana Sadr-ud-din Ya'qub Muzaffar Kirmani and others, MSS Maulana Azad Library, Aligarh, No. 260 (Punjab University).
8. Ziauddin Barani, *Fatawa-i-Jahandari*, ed. Afsar Salim Khan, Lahore. Idarah-i-Tahqiqat-i-Pakistan, 1972, English tr. *The Political Theory of the Delhi Sultanate*, by Mohammad Habib and Afsar Salim Khan, Delhi, 1957.
9. N.N. Law, *Promotion of Learning in India During the Mohammedan Rule*, Delhi, Idarah-i-Adabiyat-i-Delhi, 1963, p. 56.
10. For details see Anonymous, *Sirat-i-Firuz Shahi*, Fascimile edition of the manuscript, Patna, Khudabaksh Oriental Library, 1999, pp. 297-356.
11. Ibn Battuta, *The Rehla of Ibn Battuta*, English translation and commentary, Agha Mahdi Husain, Baroda, Oriental Institute of Baroda, 1976, pp. 58, 64.
12. Ziauddin Barani, *Tarikh-i-Firuz Shahi*, ed. Sir Syed Ahmad Khan, Aligarh, Sir Syed Academy, AMU, 2005, pp. 538, 539.
13. *Sirat-i-Firuzshahi*, op. cit., p. 142.
14. *Tarikh-i-Firuzshahi* (Barani), op. cit., p. 548.
15. Firoz Shah Tughlaq, *Futuhat-i-Firuzshahi*, ed. Azra Alavi, Delhi, Idarah-i-Adabiyat-i-Delhi, 1996, p. 8.
16. Firuz Shah Tughlaq, *Futuhat-i-Firuzshahi*, ed. Abdur Rashid, Aligarh, Department of History, 1954, p. 11.
17. Ibid., p. 15.
18. Ibid., p. 13.
19. Ibid., p. 14.
20. According to Nizamuddin Ahmad and Ferishta, Firuz Shah built 30 *madrasas*, Nizamuddin Ahmad, *Tabaqat-i-Akbari*, Lucknow, Newal Kishore, 1875, p. 121; Muhammad Qasim Ferishta, *Tarikh-i-Ferishta*, vol. I, Lucknow, Newal Kishore, 1864-5, p. 151.
21. According to Abdul Baqi Nahawandi, he erected 50 *madrasas*, *Ma'asir-i-Rahimi*, 1st edn., M. Hidayat Husain, Calcutta, Asiatic Society of Bengal, 1924, p. 30. There is no denying the fact that Firuz Shah erected a large number of *madrasas*, but it is very difficult to give the exact number on the basis of the accounts of later authorities.
22. *Sirat-i-Firuzshahi*, op. cit., p. 208.
23. An extensive tank covering an area over 70 acres of land, constructed by 'Ala-ud-din Khalji in 1296. It was later repaired and cleaned up by Firuz Shah. See Carr Stephen, *The Archaeological and Monumental Remains of Delhi*, Allahabad, Kitab Mahal, 1967, p. 83.
24. Yahya bin Ahmad Bin Abdullah Sirhindi, *Tarikh-i-Mubarakshahi*, tr. K.K. Basu, Karachi, Karimsons, 1977, p. 127. The remains of the *madrasa* possess a historical or Quranic epigraph and the only inscriptional decorations one comes across in it are the plastered discs inscribed with one or the other of the following phrases: Hasbi Allah, Sultan Allah, ul

Mulk Allah, see *Memoirs of the Archaeological Survey of India*, no. 47, p. 77. A record of all the Koranic and non-historical epigraphs on the protected monuments in the Delhi Province, by Maulvi Muhammad Ashraf Husain, Calcutta, Government of India, 1936, p. 77.

25. *Tarikh-i-Firuzshahi*, however, is silent about the date of establishment of this *madrasa*. K.A. Nizami mentions AD 1352 in his *Studies in Medieval Indian History and Culture*, Allahabad, Kitab Mahal, 1966, p. 73, but Sir Syed in his *Asar-us-Sanadid*, has given the date as AD 1354. Sir Syed Khan, *Asar-us-Sanadid*, 1st edn., Khaliq Anjum, Delhi, Urdu Academy, Delhi, 1990, p. 329.
26. K.A. Nizami, *Studies in Medieval Indian History and Culture*, Allahabad, Kitab Mahal, 1966, p. 73; R.C. Jauhri, *Firuz Tughlaq* (*AD 1357-88*), Agra, Shivalal Agrawal & Company, 1968, p. 158.
27. Hasan Zafar, *Monuments of Delhi: Lasting Splendour of the Great Mughals and Others*, III (Mehrauli Zail), New Delhi, Aryan Books International, 1920 (rpt. 1997), pp. 179-80; Azra Alavi, op. cit., p. 14.
28. Diwan-i-Mutahhar, *Oriental College Magazine*, May 1935, p. 136.
29. *Tarikh-i-Firuzshahi*, op. cit., pp. 562-3.
30. Diwan-i-Mutahhar, op. cit., p. 136.
31. *Tarikh-i-Firuzshah* (Barani), op. cit., pp. 563-5.
32. Diwan-i-Mutahhar, op. cit., p. 137.
33. *Tarikh-i-Firuzshahi* (Barani), p. 564.
34. Diwan-i-Mutahhar, op. cit., p. 137.
35. Ibid., p. 137.
36. Syed Abdul Hayy, *Hindustan Islami Ahd Mein*, Lucknow, Majlis-i-Tahqiqat wa-Nashriyat-i-Islam, 1973, p. 159.
37. Shaikh Abdul Haqq Muhaddith Dehlavi, *Akhbar-ul-Akhyar*, Delhi, Matba-i-Mujtabai, 1332 AH, p. 150.
38. *Sirat-i-Firuzshahi*, op. cit., p. 142, *Tarikh-i-Firuzshahi* (Barani), op. cit., p. 564.
39. *Tarikh-i-Firuzshahi* (Barani), op. cit., p. 564.
40. Abdu'l Hayy Al Hasani b. Fakhru'd-Din, *Nuzhat-u'l-Khawatir*, vol. 2, Hyderabad Osmania Oriental Publications Bureau, 1966, pp. 15, 22, *Tabaqat-i-Akbari*, vol. I, op. cit., p. 234.
41. Firuz Shah Tughlaq, *Futuhat-i-Firuzshahi*, Aligarh, Department of History, 1954, pp. 15-16; *Tabaqat-i-Akbari*, vol. 1, op. cit., p. 121.
42. Diwan-i-Mutahhar, p. 137.
43. K.A. Nizami, *Studies in Medieval Indian History and Culture*, p. 77.
44. Diwan-i-Mutahhar, p. 137.
45. Ibid., p. 138.
46. *Tarikh-i-Firuzshahi* (Barani), op. cit., pp. 563-4.
47. Ibid., p. 565.
48. Ibid., p. 564; K.A. Nizami, *Studies in Medieval Indian History and Culture*, op. cit., p. 56.

49. Ibid., p. 565.
50. *Sirat-i-Firuzshahi*, op. cit., p. 208.
51. Zafar Hasan, *Monuments of Delhi Lasting Splendour of he Great Mughals and Others*, vol. II, New Delhi, Aryan Books International, 1919 (rpt. 1997), p. 241. It is related that Firuz Shah secured it as a gift from the Prophet by sending his spiritual guide Makhdum Jahanian Jahan Gasht to him. The Sultan received this relic with great reverence and expressed his desire that after his death it should be placed over his grave. But when his favourite son Fath Khan died before him in AD 1374 it was placed on his grave.
52. E. Thomas, *The Chronicles of Pathan Kings of Delhi*, New Delhi, Munshiram Manoharlal (Oriental Publishers), 1967, pp. 297-8.
53. Zafar Hasan, II, op. cit., pp. 242-4; Carr Stephen, pp. 147-78.
54. Carr Stephen, op. cit., p. 147.
55. M. Ikram Shaikh, *Aab-i-Kauthar*, Delhi, Taj Company, 1987, p. 430; R.C. Jauhri, op. cit., p. 158.
56. *Akhbar-ul-Akhyar*, op. cit., p. 169
57. The *Khair-ul-Majalis* is record of one hundred mystic gatherings of Shaikh Nasir-ud-din *Chiragh-i-Delhi*. For details see Hamid Qalandar, *Khair-ul-Majalis*, ed. K.A. Nizami, Aligarh, Dept. of History, 1959. Not only is it a source of information of the lives of several Indo-Muslim saints but also supplies information on the political and economic conditions of the time.
58. Abdul Qadir Badayuni, *Muntakhab-ut-Tawarikh*, ed. M. Kabiruddin Ahmad Ali, Calcutta Asiatic Society of Bengal, 1868, pp. 255-6.
59. The *Insha-i-Mahru* is collection of 134 documents drafted by Ain-ul-Mulk, some for himself, some on behalf of the government and some for others. For details see Ain-ul-Mulk Mahru, *Insha-i-Mahru*, ed. S.A. Rashid, Aligarh, AMU, 1954.
60. *Muntakhab-ut-Tawarikh*, I, op. cit., p. 257.
61. Muhammad Shafi, Mutahhar Kada, *Oriental College Magazine*, Lahore, May 1935.
62. The work is a revision and enlargement of the original draft of Sayyed Yaqub Muzaffar Kuhrami. This is a comprehensive work on Islamic law compiled to give guidance to the *qazis* and *muftis* in particular and to the Muslims in general, Zafarul Islam, *Fatawa Literature of the Sultanate Period*, New Delhi, Kanishka Publishers, 2005, pp. 21-2.
63. M. Ikram Shaikh, op. cit., p. 433.
64. The manuscript of the work are preserved in the Maulana Azad Library, AMU (Subhanallah Collection No. 293.2/27, Jawahar Collection, No. 687). Asiatic Society of Bengal, Calcutta (Catalogue, pp. 517-18, No. 1069) and Khudabakhsh Oriental Public Library (Catalogue, vol. XIV/1225).

65. K.A. Nizami, *Salatin-i-Dehli Kay Mazhabi Rujhanat*, Delhi, Nadwat-ul-Musannifin, 1981, pp. 396-8.
66. For details see *Sirat-i-Firuzshahi*, op. cit., pp. 93-7, 236-41, 320-55.
67. Ibid., pp. 320-1.
68. Ibid., pp. 336, 338, that physicians were employed in the hospital (*shifakhana*) and medicines were distributed is clearly stated in the detailed accounts of the hospital in ibid., pp. 235-42; *Tarikh-i-Firuzshahi* (Afif), op. cit., pp. 357-9.
69. *Sirat-i-Firuzshahi*, op. cit., p. 53.
70. Nizami, *Royalty in Medieval India*, op. cit., p. 132.
71. *Tarikh-i-Firuzshahi* (Afif), op. cit., pp. 355-9; *Sirat-i-Firuzshahi*, op. cit., pp. 235-6; *Futuhat-i- Firuzshahi*, op. cit., pp. 15-16; Abdul Majid Salik, *Muslim Saqafat Hindustan mein*, Lahore, Idarah-Saqafat-i-Islamia, n.d., p. 294.
72. *Tarikh-i-Ferishta*, vol. 1, op. cit., p. 151.
73. Nizamuddin Ahmad, *Tabaqat-i-Akbari*, Lucknow, Newal Kishore, 1875, p. 121.
74. Anonymous, *Sirat-i-Firuzshahi*, Facsimile edition of the manuscript, Patna, Khudabaksh Oriental Library, 1999, pp. 300-5.
75. The evidence has been exhaustively studied in an Urdu work, Sayyid Sulaiman Nadvi, *Arbon Ki Jahazrani*, Azamgarh, Darul Musannifin, 1935, pp. 148-52; also Joseph Needham, *Science and Civilization in China*, IV(1), Cambridge, Cambridge University Press, 1962, pp. 247-8.
76. *Tarikh-i-Firuzshahi* (Afif), op. cit., p. 370, Iqtidar Husain Siddiqui 'Science and Scientific Instruments in the Sultanate of Delhi', *Hamdard Islamicus*, 17/3, Autumn 1994, pp. 11-12.
77. *Sirat-i-Firuzshahi*, op. cit., p. 301; *Muntakhab-ut-Tawarikh*, vol. 1, op. cit., p. 249; Nizami, *Salatin Dehli Ke Mazhabi Rujhanat*, op. cit., p. 399.
78. *Sirat-i-Firuzshahi*, op. cit., pp. 95-6.
79. Ibid., p. 320.
80. Krishnalal Ray, *Education in Medieval India*, Delhi, B.R. Publishing Corporation, 1984, pp. 53-5.
81. *Tarikh-i-Firuzshahi* (Afif), op. cit., p. 270; for details, see J.M. Banerjee, *History of Firuz Shah Tughlaq*, Delhi, Oriental Publishers, pp. 183-4.
82. *Tarikh-i-Firuzshahi* (Afif), op. cit., pp. 255, 369-70; Jauhri, op. cit., p. 179.

CHAPTER 3

Composite Culture: Portrayal in Architecture

RAVINDRA KUMAR

Every country needs to make an assessment of its past periodically and take an account of its historical, political and other resources under changing circumstances to compose a view of itself. Medieval Indian history has traditionally had two competing visions suggesting alternative ways of defining India. One is that of a unique civilizational identity embedded in an institutional framework that got sustenance from some basic values and sensibilities innate to this land. The other is of an Indian civilization that has been open to the influences of others, its content being synthetic in orientation committed to the values of tolerance, self-restraint and universality. The notion of a composite culture revolves around this pluralist vision of India as the conviction is that this synthetic orientation transcends the barriers of space and time and manifests itself in the area of culture-syntheses occurring in arts, literature, architecture, technology, social life, etc. For a country like India cultural history becomes a very broad and eclectic field, in terms both of subject matter and diverse historiographical perspectives. A historian's enquiries often encounter a tension between the need to build-up holistic syntheses and the need for close reading. Rather than take a 'Cox & Kings Tour' of composite culture in medieval India this essay engages in the act of critical close reading in ways a composite architectural form evolved as a consequence of an interface between the architectural practices of ancient India and the 'new' devices and methods that percolated here from about the end of the twelfth century-beginning of the thirteenth century onwards.

Use of arch as the main structural form spanning voids and spaces, and round dome as the main device to provide covering/roofing over walled spaces is generally considered the hallmark of medieval

Indian architecture. 'Introduction' and large-scale use of lime mortar as a cementing material for joining individual structural elements used in raising arches and domes has been an associate feature. It is generally believed that since the application of lime mortar suited the rough and porous surfaces of bricks and smaller surface areas allowed the cementing properties of mortar to act more efficiently, the constructions in brick began to match constructions in stone at least numerically, if not in size, in the urban landscape of medieval India. It is contended that this 'new' architectural device—arches made of bricks (or of such other material) held in place by lime-mortar—was an 'advance' over earlier methods and had even made masonry construction an 'affordable' proposition. One would therefore believe that the 'new' form would have supplanted the earlier column-and-beam structures or substituted them heavily. Instead, the two allied and gave rise to a composite style generally identified as the Indo-Islamic architecture. That this style contains two different structural forms, is often cited as an attribute, though it should also be admitted that sometimes this combination is treated as bordering on the grotesque and having incongruous structural elements.

A close reading of this composite architecture is the focus of this essay. It requires detailed examination of the design and structural behaviour of the forms and devices that were used in the buildings and other structures. 'New' forms and the structural actions that come into play as they are actually used in the buildings, their inherent potentialities, the ways in which they facilitated construction, the manner in which they allied with the structural form/s practised in the earlier period and the overriding considerations, if any, of the available building material, and the considerations of the 'economy' of time consumed in completing the construction are some of those areas that fall in the ambit of close reading. The actual subsequent exploitation of this composite architectural form in built structures based on the 'wide range of choice' made available to the builders is an area of ancillary interest. It may please be noted that in most built structures the elemental structural forms (e.g. arch, column-and-beam, etc.) have grown as essential parts of a larger building and have very rarely developed in isolation. The structural actions are therefore more complex sometimes than the simple understanding about them presented here.

It is interesting to note that structural forms generally imbibe influences from the past and are rarely conceived in a manner so as to suggest insulation from the past. Since the technical resources for an understanding of the structural actions of built forms were more limited in the past than they are today, structural actions of the earlier forms would be rendered intelligible to the architects through experience than through abstract principles of design. The process of development of these forms and the constraints surrounding this development was largely contingent on the successes and failures of structures using these forms over a period of time. The present-day understanding of the structural action/s should therefore be viewed with care in arriving at any qualitative judgement about their technical suitability at specific periods of time in history.

The principal structural form in use in India at the time of the Turkish invasion was the 'column-and-beam' in which logs of timber or beams of stone were supported horizontally by two vertical columns. The space so spanned formed part of a roof or an entrance in a wall. In making a roof, in fact, a number of horizontal elements were set at short distance apart and the in-between space was covered with slate, reed or such other material. The columns were also carved out of timber or stone or were also made of bricks. The beam and column have been the simplest of all elemental forms but their primary structural actions—internal tensions and compressions—are perhaps the most complex ones to be subjected to an analysis.

It is an axiom to say that the basic requirement in architectural compositions is that the structure remains standing and does not collapse under conditions which are at some deviation from the 'normal'. While local deformations may occasionally take place, the main objective in choosing the structural form is that the deformations are kept within acceptable limits and they do not in general jeopardize the stability of the structure. For this overall stability there are some basic imperatives: 'active loads' should be balanced against resistances, the foundations should be able to bear the loads passed on by the structure, and sufficient margins of strength and stiffness should be available in the structural elements used for construction.

Let us understand these imperatives and associated features a little more closely. In a structure there are several types of load that become operative once the structure is completed. The gravitational self-weight of the structural elements and the load of other material used in the construction is foremost. In addition there are external pressures exerted by the users and by the environment on the structure. The user pressure is accounted for the people and the articles and material kept or carried through the structure. The pressure of wind, heat or the impact of coldness, and natural calamities as earthquake and lightning, etc., constitute the environmental action on the structure. The self-weight of the structural elements is called the 'dead load'; it does not change under normal circumstances and is determined by the nature of the building material. The external pressure is called the 'live load'; the magnitude of this load is not fixed and is determined by the regularity and frequency of use of the structure as also by the manner of its construction. In addition we have the 'reactive loads' which become operative at the points where the structure is supported and where it terminates. Generally the reactive load offsets the force exerted by the dead and live loads, and depends on the manner in which the structure is terminated either at the plinth level or at or below the foundation. The points of junction of different structural elements too show reactive loads.

The forces or loads discussed here, namely the dead and live loads—collectively called the 'active loads'—and the reactive loads, have a normal tendency/proclivity to generate displacement which is in the direction in which the loads work. As a result, a miniscule movement or displacement occurs; this gives rise to a resistance in the structure that attempts to defy the displacement. The structure remains intact under the forces so generated due largely to the fact that they are balanced by each other. The strength or stability of a structure is its ability to attain balance without too much displacement or deformity. It is also important to understand that these loads generally act quite slowly. This permits the development of a resistance that keeps pace with the force of displacement, and the stability of the structure does not get endangered. Yet there may be situations in which the changes in the loads are swift, causing resistance to not grow at the same pace, and thus bring deformities in the structure. Earthquakes, emanating vibrations of great amplitude, are illustrative instances of such actions.

It is thus clear that in choosing a configuration for a structure and in selecting the manner of its construction, most of the subsequent forces operative on the structure are in a way pre-decided. While it is not possible to accurately predict the subsequent behaviour of a structure under the impact of loads likely to be borne by the structure, it is still possible to take care of some general structural requirements at the time of making the choices as above. These requirements are in addition to the selection made with respect to the structural form/s and the building material/s. In the first place is the requirement to organize the assembly of structural elements and their joints in such a manner that the structure becomes a stable order and not an assemblage of loosely joined and disarrayed elements. Next is the requirement of having structural elements and their joints of such characteristics as to provide the requisite strength. It is true that in complex structures, i.e. those having multiple components, it is not easy to discern these requirements and meet them for individual elements. It is more practical to account for the balance of forces at work in the structure at various points or to achieve, what in the technical term is called, a static equilibrium of the forces at work in the structure.

Now, to get back to the column-and-beam constructions, it is generally understood that beams do not exert any appreciable horizontal force and the sizeable actions are only along the vertical lines. In fact, the dead load of the beam gets distributed over its length quite unlike several other structural forms, such as arches and catenaries, where the dead load gets resolved into two resultants and operates at the points at which the arches and catenaries are supported. In general terms it can be said that the beams supported on vertical pillars or columns work as an 'arch' and a 'catenary' simultaneously. Thus the two structural forms where loading actions operate conversely become combined in the beam; the resultant has a propensity to neutralize these converse loading actions (Fig. 3.1).

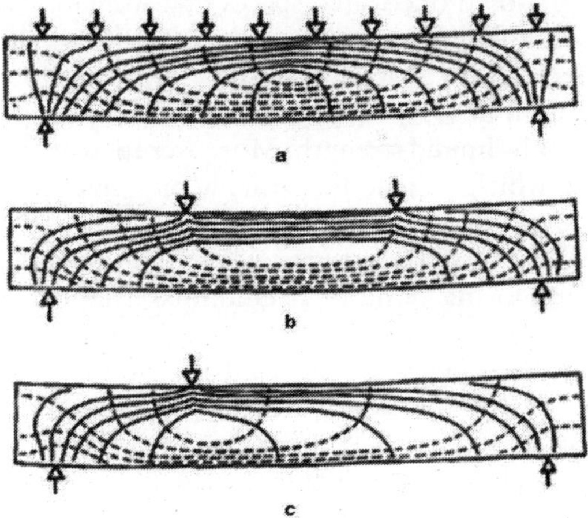

Fig. 3.1: Loading Actions

However, it is not easy to even approximate the axes or lines through which these actions or forces operate. We only know that normally the two forms remain in a state of equilibrium and it is only under the impact of any changed load on the beam that a readjustment in the two forms takes place. The beam gives way when this readjustment crosses a threshold point and fails. Either the 'arch' or the 'catenary' gets disrupted and the collapse of the beam does occur.

The column-and-beam architecture was practised in India from a very early time and this long experience had taught architects and builders many practical lessons. The structures were built in all the three principal materials, viz., timber, stone, and brick and generally it was a combination of all in which one predominated and the other materials used for other specific purposes. Extremely valuable documentation of early Indian architecture has been done by Coomaraswamy and relief panels from early *stupas* cited by him that testify this feature. The strength of this architecture lay in its simple methods of construction and the abundance of building materials. It is true that stone has not been a 'friendly' medium for easy visual embellishment of the surface. Yet the Indian artisan had mastered the sculptural techniques to an immaculate perfection. The surface in these stone buildings as also in other structural media was adorned with iconic figures of marvellous beauty. There were hardly any areas that were left undressed. The column-and-beam architecture was massive and composed of covered spaces that were long and narrow and where the columns were closely spaced. This architecture, however, suffered from at least one major structural shortcoming. The stone (or even timber) beam used for the purposes of spanning the spaces had only limited strength. Moreover there was a maximum size (length) in which it could be naturally procured. As a result the span that could be covered by the stone beam remained constrained by the 'limited' size of the beam. Attempts to increase the span further necessitated employing additional columnar support. Not many ingenious expedients were available to override this deficiency. The situation could be somewhat redeemed by the use of corbel with stepped soffits as another device to span openings or cover roofs (Fig. 3.2).

A characteristic feature of this form is that all the structural blocks (usually of stone or bricks) remain embedded horizontally on one another. As they rise to bridge the opening or to roof the enclosure

Fig. 3.2: Corbel

they project slightly beyond those of the course below. Thus the gap to be spanned is narrowed progressively and eventually at the centre either the two sides meet or they approach near enough to be finally spanned by a single block.

The temple had come to typify the architectural form using column-and-beam device. Temple structures had sprung up in many variants in different parts of India since the time of the Gupta rulers.[1] Beginning with flat-roofed simple structures having a pillared pavilion in front of the door-frame, the temple structures of the later periods came to signify one of the most elaborate and embellished constructions in India. Many experiments with their plans and designs and equally expansive extensions in front of the architrave housing the deity resulted in the emergence of large rectangular stone (and occasionally brick) buildings that were also visual delights. On the basis of their style, Indian temples have been classified into three categories—*Nagara*, *Dravida* and *Vesara*. It is not our purpose here to delve deep into the architecture of temples. The intention is to stress the fact that quite diversified attributes of the temples were achieved with the use of the column-and-beam device. High pyramidal superstructures marked by the *shikhar* and profusely decorated outer surface having iconic representations from all hues of social and religious life became the distinguishing features of temple architecture.[2] Thus when Turks came to India they encountered temples as the principal architectural form and column-and-beam as the main structural form practised by the builders here.

The advent of the medieval period in India also marks the beginning of a new expression in architecture. New structural forms are introduced and the new forms—arch and vault/dome—are employed in architectural construction in many innovative ways. Arch and vault/dome are such versatile structural forms that they present numerous exciting possibilities to the architects. It will therefore be worth our while to seek to comprehend their structural characteristics and the actual mechanics of their usage, to truly appreciate their application in medieval Indian architecture mostly in conjunction with column-and-beam to give birth to the composite architecture.

The arch is usually a curved form and is normally made of wedge-shaped component blocks (in stone, brick or even concrete) fixed together firmly either by neatly dressing the adjoining surfaces of component blocks for a tight joint or with the help of a cementing material (Fig. 3.3).

The curved form endows the arch with very special structural characteristics. Geometrically, arch is an unstable form prone to cracking or collapsing at one or more points along its curvature. The same curved form, nevertheless, attains stability and acquires remarkable load-bearing properties if its component blocks (voussoirs, to be technically accurate) are rigidly joined so as to form a continuous masonry. It is important for an arch to retain its curved shape to be able to retain all the remarkable properties that are generally associated with arches. It is equally important for this curved formation to support itself at the two end points of the curve on firm bases. Once these essential conditions are met arch achieves an equilibrium in which the dead load gets resolved into two parts each exerting a thrust at the point of support. This thrust operates through the line of tangent drawn along the curve on both sides. Since the end points

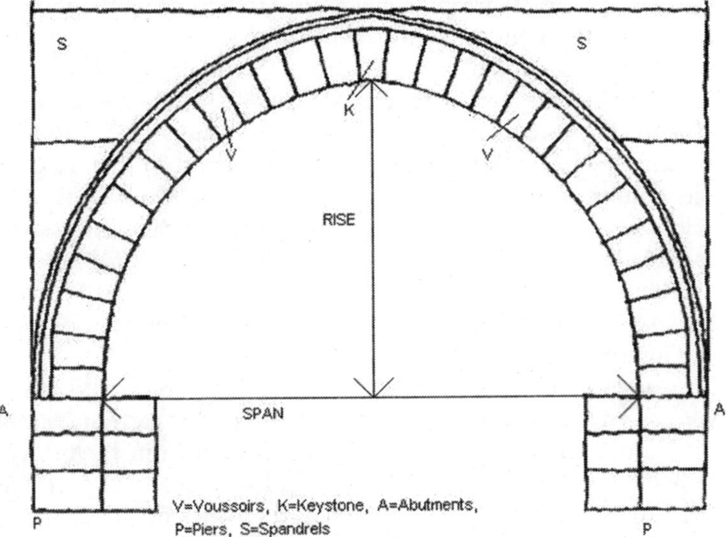

Fig. 3.3: Arch and its Parts

are firmly rooted on the supports, the thrust gets resolved at this point into two components, the vertical downward thrust and the horizontal outward thrust (Fig. 3.4).

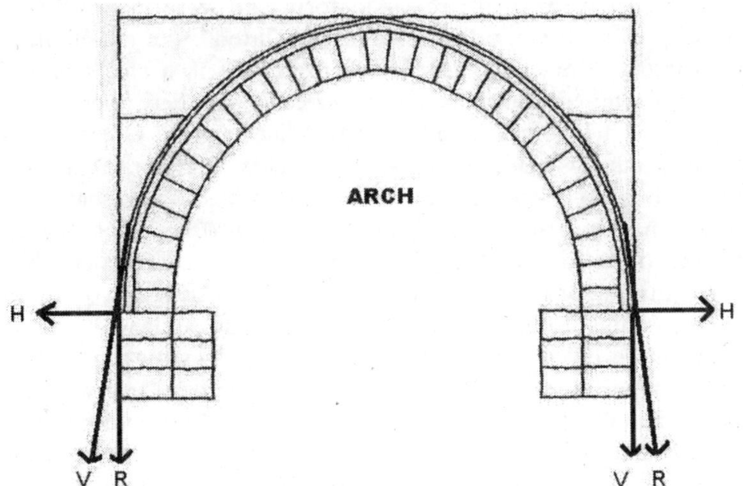

Fig. 3.4: Dead Load Thrust

The vertical thrusts are generally transmitted through the supports to the foundations and only horizontal thrusts try to destabilize the arch. The net effect of all these forces is that the destabilizing action is generated by only a part of the total dead load while the remaining dead load is absorbed by the foundations. If the arch is burdened with active loads, by the same principle only a part of it and not the whole would try to destabilize the arch. The practical aspects of this principle were of great value to the architects. It may have resolved their difficulty in not being able to increase the dead load beyond a certain limit, as was the case in column-and-beam structures. Moreover larger spans could now be covered by arches without the necessity of any intermediate support.

The architectural use of the arch was first attempted by the Egyptians. Mud-brick arches dating back to a period early in the third millennium BC have been reported from Reqaqnah in Egypt. They were perhaps of the window arch type and were made of only a few bricks.[3] Arch was, however, not preferred by ancient Egyptians as a structural form and the reasons for this were perhaps similar to the arch not finding a favour with the architects in ancient India. It was much later that adoption of arches began in the larger structures. In seventh century BC we find brick archways of fairly wide span surviving in Thebes in middle Egypt. The use of stone in making arches began in Greece and Italy and later in Rome around the fourth century BC. These arches were semi-circular in form and were made of stone voussoirs of such workmanship that they fitted quite closely in the semi-circular profile. In these arches there was no use of mortar. It seems the semi-circular shape was preferred so that these finely worked voussoirs would remain intact even without mortar.[4] Great advance in using arch was made by the Romans. They refined the technique and introduced some very useful modifications in the shape. The design and construction of Roman arches also have a bearing, if indirect, on making arches in India during the medieval period.

The making of Roman arches involved the construction of support walls/columns up to the point from where the arch would spring up. At this level a false-work was raised having the same semi-circular shape as was desired for the arches. This was perhaps a cumbersome process and needed the support of carpenters who would create the false-work (centring) in wood. It is of interest that a semi-circular profile could be easily attained in wood and not in other materials. The next stage in construction was to accurately fix the voussoirs in place from both ends. The craft of chiselling stone voussoirs was perfected by the Romans to such an extent that the two adjacent voussoirs joined together without leaving any crevice in between. This type of tight-fit was an absolute necessity for the principle of load transfer on the supports to come in operation. As the crown was reached the keystone was tightly fitted in the available space. The keystone was a critical element that was to keep the semi-circular profile in place and was to bring the tangential thrusts of the two halves of the semi-circle to become operational at the points of support or the springing of the arch. Once this stage of construction was done the false-work or centring was removed, leaving the arch standing in place. The structural characteristics of Roman arches that emerge from this detail are of interest: the semi-circular arches were not capable of accommodating even the slightest movements of its supports, otherwise they would collapse; the curvature of the soffits had to be truly semi-circular, that is, no horizontal profile at any point was admissible otherwise the voussoirs would slip on each other causing them to fall; the Romans used joggled voussoirs as an expedient to minimize the likelihood of slipping and also found it useful in situations where false-work was not very firm and required an additional contrivance to keep the voussoirs in place at the time of construction.

A few more innovations made by the Romans are also noteworthy. From about the middle of the first century AD, brick-faced concrete arches came into use. An interesting feature of these concrete arches was that they were penetrated by full bricks at regular distance. Perhaps the attempt was to create voussoir-like sections as component blocks of the arch. In technical terms, though, the concrete would have behaved in much the same fashion as the concrete structures of today would—as a complete monolithic curved formation. Towards the later part of the Roman Empire along with semi-circular profile of the arches segmental profile was also introduced (Fig. 3.5).

It seems that in this process only slight departures from the semi-circle were initially done. These departures were more a consequence of errors of construction than any deliberate attempt to experiment with a new profile. Subsequently, arches with markedly segmental profiles were used in their structures, though, in an irregular manner.

The departures from the simple semi-circular profile have been of seminal value in the development of the arch as a structural form.

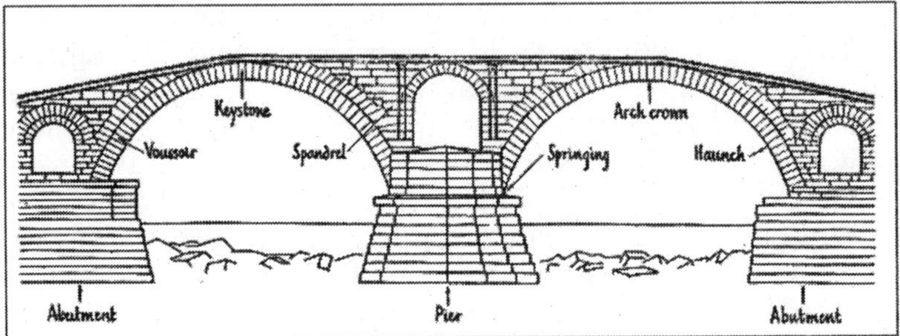

Fig. 3.5: Segmental Arch

The departures, as we have noted above, came about initially from the slight structural errors during the construction stage. But once the benefits of these 'errors' became evident, the departures became deliberate. Lessons were perhaps drawn from the observation that profiles at deviance from semi-circle were also quite strong. It would have been hard to anticipate the actual behaviour of the 'departed' profiles but practical observations and strength and longevity would have assured the architects about their utility. The most significant new profile was the pointed arch. It offered advantages in construction that were impossible to ignore. These were: easy setting out of the arch; possibility of using lighter centering than was required for a semi-circular or segmental arch; and the propensity to adjust its profile marginally to offset minor settlements due to a poor foundation. The pointed arches appeared first in the Islamic world in Jordan in the eighth century AD and soon became one of the main features of Islamic architecture of the region.[5] The popularity of pointed arches speaks for the advantages they offered in construction. The regions of its early spread were wide deserts and jagged rocky uplands that were barren of forest or vegetation. The architects were therefore deprived of the advantage of creating a centering made of timber unlike the Roman practice. Under these circumstances pointed arches were the most suitable proposition since they did not require an all-timber centering in their construction. In fact, material other than timber which could be locally procured was used in the centring. This material was brick and a combination of timber with brick or sometimes bricks alone were used in making the centring. A bottom layer of light centring was constructed first and then a thin layer of bricks was placed on top of it. If needed, another concentric layer of brickwork was also added over it and the arch was raised over these layers of bricks. Often these two layers of brickwork acted as permanent shuttering for the arch (Fig. 3.6).

Since a pointed arch would impose lesser load on the centring and a smaller horizontal thrust at the support than a semi-circular profile, the method described thus worked quite efficiently. The horizontal thrust in the pointed profile was minimized because the rise in pointed arches was greater than the span. The line of thrust at the support would therefore resolve into horizontal and vertical thrusts such that the vertical thrust increased and the horizontal thrust got reduced in the same proportion. This arch was therefore found better equipped than the semi-circular arch in dealing with conditions where stable foundations were difficult to obtain and/or timber was not easily available for raising the false-work.

It would appear, at first sight, from this account that for the architects it was a rational choice to opt for the pointed arch. The architect's freedom to choose its form when a structure is to be constructed, however, is a complex process in which many inter-connected factors come into play. In addition to the basic structural requirements of the building and the availability of the material, architects had to contend with the application of particular techniques of construction within the available mechanical aids and human skills. It has often been found that architects have developed ingenious methods to cope with such situations and suitable adjustments in the structural form/s have been made to overcome constraints at least partially if not completely. The introduction of the arch—the pointed arch in medieval India—presents a somewhat similar situation. The

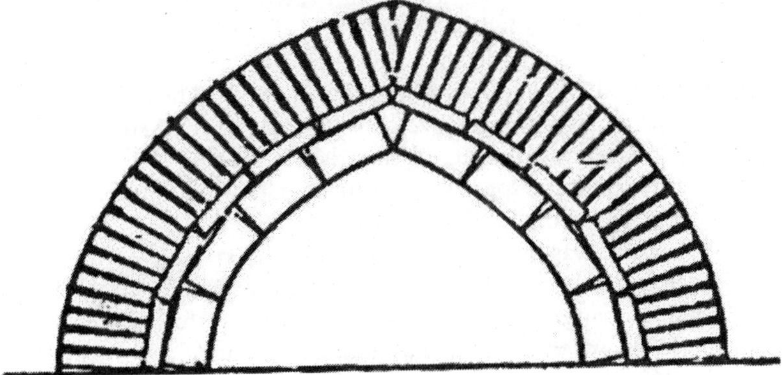

Fig. 3.6: Brickwork Layers

architects employed by the new rulers—the early Turkish Sultans—were given the task of assembling a built form that would in shape be a pointed arch. The assurance gained in their homeland about the strength of the pointed arch was now to be translated into practice in 'alien' conditions. The architects had also to tackle with the problem of securing adequate stability and strength to the arch at intermediate stages of construction. The availability of building material and its fabrication into desired shape, and the methods of joining them together were also issues seeking a resolution. The first buildings were raised under such conditions.

The first structure raised by the new rulers was the mosque in the Qutb area at Delhi popularly known as the Quwwatul Islam Mosque, which was completed in AD 1195. It was built on the ruins of a temple by integrating its plinth within the plinth of the mosque. The material for the mosque was not fabricated afresh but the material (stone) used in twenty-seven other temples of the area and demolished by Qutbuddin was largely reorganized to serve the purpose.[6] It is logical that at such an early stage of their rule the Sultans were ill-equipped to use an architectural method very different from the one already practised in India. The mosque—its prayer hall and the colonnade—was built by using the column-and-beam device. Pillars—sculpted ones—from the demolished temples were reused as columns and beams and were put in place with the help of brackets to complete the colonnade. The craftsmanship of the mason in assembling the mosque from the spoils collected from temples is remarkable. Obviously, the principal consideration was architectural exigency as aesthetics had perforce to take a backseat. The columns, brackets, and lintels were reused without being reworked in any significant manner and the mosque was completed (Fig. 3.7).

The covered colonnade all around the central courtyard was also provided with shallow domes at periodic intervals. These were corbel domes built by laying successive courses of horizontal stones where each upper layer was projected slightly inward. As the top of the dome was reached the space was gradually narrowed. Finally a round stone at the top completed the form.

The mosque was begun in AD 1191-92 and completed by 1195. It was a completely column-and-beam structure with no arches. The first notable change in the structural form was effected four years later, in 1199, when a screen was added in front of the prayer hall. It was in this screen that arches were introduced though they were

Fig. 3.7: Reused Material

of the 'false' order—not having stones arranged in the form of true voussoirs. A detailed analysis of this early arch form is of great significance in gaining an insight into the processes and methods at work in the emergence of composite architecture. We have noted that the process of construction during the early phase of Sultanate architecture operated within certain constraints—having to work with skills and aids not of the desired competence and the availability of only a particular type of building material, the spoils of temples chiefly. It is evident that these 'false' arches (corbels) were chosen so that the requirement of raising any temporary support during the different pre-completion stages of construction would be minimized and as described earlier the two halves of the arch would be raised as stable halves independent of each other (Fig. 3.8).

It is logical to assume that in this kind of over-sailing elements architects would have learnt that it was always necessary to keep the length of the projections in the upper course small, but under no circumstances to exceed half of its length. Similarly, the total weight of the stone elements, or for that matter the other masonry used in making each half of the 'arch', was also to be distributed such that the weight behind the projection would be more—much more—than

Fig. 3.8: False Arches

the weight of the projection itself. Such an arch was therefore generally stable for moderate spans. When the span was to be increased it was necessary to use sufficiently long stone blocks and it was equally necessary to anchor them properly to the mass of the support wall on either side.

The shape of the 'false' arches built in the screen was a pointed ogee having a slight curve at the crown. It is evident that in raising these arches centering was not needed. But it is equally true that due to technical limitations the scope of widening the span was also limited. The screen built by Qutbuddin was subject to two extensions subsequently, one by Iltutmish and the other by Alauddin Khalji. Both the extensions today retain only the jambs or walls on which the (false) arches were raised, but the arches do not survive. Since the two extensions were also bigger in proportion, it is most likely that the arches failed either the test of horizontal friction or of the anchor. Noteworthy is the fact that the arches of smaller span in these extensions have survived and only the central wider arches have perished.[7] Sufficient confidence to build structures having true arches was not gathered soon and the practice of using corbel and column-and-beam device was continued for a little over a century since the construction of the Quwwatul Islam mosque. During this period no major changes were introduced in the methods of construction except perhaps a few experiments made with the shape of the arches. We note that the ogee form employed in the screen by Qutbuddin was altered when the first extension was carried out by Iltutmish. The ogee cusp was replaced with a simple pointed arch formation which, as noted by Percy Brown, was 'not very dissimilar from the pointed arch of Decorated Gothic style appearing about the same time in England'.[8] In fact, this form was closer to the four-centred arch of the Lodi and Mughal periods; we can see this form in the central arch of the screen added by Iltutmish to *Arhai-Din-Ka-Jhompra* mosque originally built by Qutbuddin at Ajmer (begun in AD 1200). A new form that makes an appearance in the Ajmer structure is the trefoil pointed arch, used in the two side arches on each flank. The two end arches of the seven-arched screen are again of the four-centered type.

After more than a hundred years of experimentation with corbel and column-and-beam methods, and the use of 'false' arches, the next logical stage was the construction of the true arch which appeared for the first time in Alai Darwaza (Fig. 3.9), an entrance gateway

Fig. 3.9: True Arches

built by Alauddin Khalji at the Qutb complex in AD 1311. Like Iltutmish, another extension of the Quwwatul Islam mosque was planned by Alauddin. The scheme was to double the size of the complex. Thus the structure originally built by Qutbuddin, and subsequently extended by Iltutmish, was meant to be expanded to more than four times its size. In the new layout, four gateways were planned such that each was an elaborate complex on its own. Today only the southern gateway survives and is popularly known as Alai Darwaza. Perhaps this was the only one to have been completed as indicated from the site and ruins of the proposed extension of the mosque under Alauddin. The gateway has four arched openings, one in each wall. The three, in the east, west and south walls, are pointed ogee arches while the fourth one, in the northern wall, is a semi-circular arch. As stated above, the true arch (having structural elements arranged as voussoirs) appears in a medieval building in India for the first time in Alai Darwaza.[9] Significantly, the semi-circular arch too makes a brief appearance here as it is not found used in other contemporary buildings and also vanishes almost completely from the buildings of the succeeding period (Fig. 3.10).[10]

Fig. 3.10: Semi-Circular Arch

All the arches in Alai Darwaza have been built of freshly fabricated stone unlike the usual earlier practice of reuse of temple stones (Fresh stones were, in any case, cut and dressed for the screen built by Qutbuddin and later extended by Iltutmish). The three pointed arches have been built of stone slabs measuring approximately 2.75 m in length. Interestingly these arches have been constructed of full length stone slabs; the practice of making several concentric rings of arches of smaller width has not been employed here. As a matter of fact the pointed arches in Alai Darwaza are built with such long voussoirs that they in effect constitute a vaulted passageway. It seems plausible that at such an early stage of constructing the arch the architects were not confident about their methods; hence the use of long voussoirs instead of smaller elements and the method of making several layers of concentric rings of arches. The span of these pointed arches is only a little more than 3 m each. This is not a very wide span and understandably so at this (probably the) first use of the true arch having voussoirs. There is no direct evidence available to give us information about the different stages of construction of these arches. We may, however, safely assume that they were built with the aid of centering—the fine finish of their joints and the thin, uniform thickness of the cementing material providing the testimony.

The northern entrance arch, as noted above, is a semi-circular arch. But its manner of construction indicates a certain indecisiveness on the part of the architect. It seems, an attempt has been made to use the semi-circular form in the same material as was fabricated for the pointed arches. The keystone is not as pronounced as it should normally have been in a semi-circular arch. The voussoirs have been arranged such that they appear as a combination of 'horizontal' and 'curved' soffits. The arch stands intact because the depth of its voussoirs is sufficient to resist the 'slip' resulting from such construction. It is evident that some experimentation with the form of arches was definitely on at the time of building the Alai Darwaza. The favour shown to the pointed arch in other contemporary buildings and in the subsequent period too did not mean that attempts, even though sundry, were not made to use the other forms, particularly the semi-circular form. It may be interesting for us to know that the confidence gained with the use of the pointed arch was soon translated into its application in more utilitarian structures such as in building bridges across rivulets and streams of not very long spans. A three-arched bridge stands extant across a seasonal stream in front of Siri, Alauddin's new capital at Delhi. Another larger bridge of eleven arches was built to provide passage across river Gambhir below Chittaurgarh Fort. One of the arches of this bridge is a semi-circular arch while all the remaining ones are pointed arches of the same type as built in Alai Darwaza (Fig. 3.11 & 3.12).

Fig. 3.11: Pointed Arches

Fig. 3.12: Pointed Arches

We note that the column-and-beam method was not forsaken altogether in favour of the constructions using arch as a dominant form; the extension proposed by Alauddin in the Quwwatul Islam mosque complex was undertaken by employing the column-and-beam device as is evident from a small surviving portion located in its south-east corner.

The wider application of arch, made possible from the successful experiment of the Khalji period, also brought into focus the question of achieving an overall stability of the building in addition to the durability and load-bearing properties of individual structural elements. It was important to ensure that individual structural elements in a completed building were not so arranged that the collapse of one would jeopardize the entire structure. It is noteworthy that the column-and-beam buildings were more stable in this respect because the structural elements acted almost completely in tension. Destabilizing forces of moderate intensity generated small displacements in these elements. As against this, the arches were the type of structural forms that acted in compression. Even small displacements in such cases had the tendency to inflict larger instabilities. We have already noted why semi-circular arches were replaced with pointed arches in regions where destabilizing forces could not be regulated with precision. Therefore, if the arches in a complete structure were so arranged as to be interlinked with each other structurally (such as in a long arcade), it was an added risk that the collapse of one arch was likely to result in the collapse of the entire building. It was then important to either structurally 'de-link' arches or to introduce an additional element in the arch having a different pattern of loading action from that of the arch. Sometimes the addition of a beam to the arch was thought to be an adequate device to address this issue. Tughlaq period buildings, where large-scale use of arches was practised and a new material—the rubble—was employed in major building projects, show the adoption of some new and interesting features. Foremost is the use of a pointed arch having a profile much closer to the profile of a four-centred arch. This was a significant change as it allowed two major advantages to the architects: the first was to give a leeway in extending the span of the arches without, in the same proportion, raising the height of the arches; and the second was to give an additional strength to the arch since it now worked as composed of four instead of two parts. We can even call this form a more 'squat' arch than the pointed arch used hitherto (Fig. 3.13).

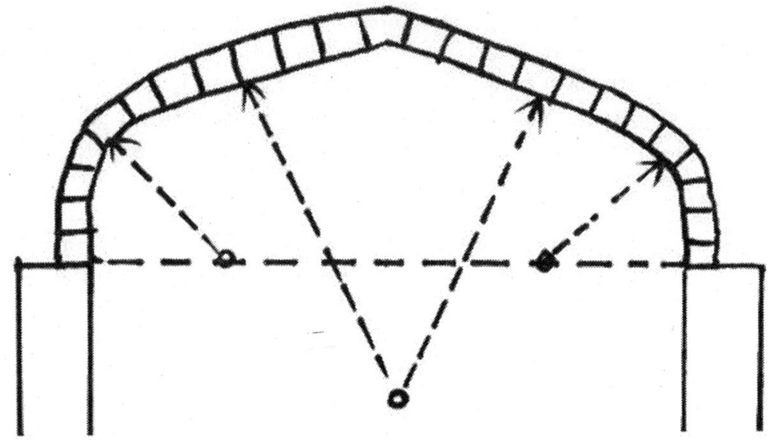

Fig. 3.13: Four-Centred Arch

The other notable feature, also accepted as the brand-Tughlaq attribute, is the use of an 'extra' beam or lintel invariably in association with the arch (Fig. 3.14).

Fig. 3.14: Extra Beam in Arch

The beam/lintel always appears at the base of the arch that is spread across the span of the arch at the springing point or at a point a little lower than that. The addition of a beam in this manner has been mostly considered as 'technically irrational', not having any structural merit and as a mere ornamentation or a continuance of an old habit. We have already noted that structures using several arches needed a composition in which the failure of one arch was not likely to endanger the other arches and thereby the entire structure. The introduction of beam/lintel as different structural form was perhaps an expedient to guard against an interlinked structural dependence of multiple arches in a single structure. The large-scale use of rubble would have reinforced the arch-beam arrangement. In fairness to the medieval architects, though, it must be said that it took them quite some time to realize that in practice no standing structure behaved as closely interlinked as to suffer a collapse due to the failure of one or more of its structural elements.

Before we move ahead, it is necessary to comprehend the meaning and significance of the change in building material from ashlars to stone rubble on a large scale under the Tughlaqs. The readily quarried sandstone, mostly with rough and random surfaces, required a slightly different treatment. The architects were sure about the durability of this material—strength of stone as a structural element is time tested. Perhaps what they doubted was the strength of the structure built in rubble and the load bearing capacity of the forms created in rubble. The 'contrivance' employed in arch-making—combining the arch with an additional beam—was seemingly to provide added strength to rubble arches. The other structural device used conspicuously in buildings in Tughlaq's time was the sloping effect in walls, columns, etc., by unusually widening the base and reducing this width gradually upwards. A detailed comment made by Percy Brown, specifically for the structures of Firuz Tughlaq's period, holds equally good for the entire Tughlaq period:

> The materials and method of construction employed by the Firuzian builders naturally reacted on the character of the architectural style. With masonry of this loosely knit order, additional strength and stability was assured by building certain portions thicker at the base than at the top, an expedient which gives the illusion of greater power, although no such angle of batter is really structurally necessary. This effect of slope is emphasized in many of the examples by the attachment of tapering turreted buttresses at the quoins, and by projecting conical bastion-like towers crowned with low domes from the four corners of the building.

Evidently, the strength of the structure made of rubble was uppermost in the minds of architects while resorting to the extra wide bases of walls and tapering them upwards.

A subject we have not broached so far but which can no longer be deferred relates to the medium in which the rubble was set, in other words the cementing material used in joining the rubble for raising the structure. It is quite clear that the requirement of cementing material or mortar in construction work based on rubble was much more than in ashlars. Simultaneously the construction method used in raising the arch was also dependent on a good quality cementing material that would hold the voussoirs in place and would allow the loading actions in curved shape to operate tangentially, as illustrated earlier. Therefore the development of the arch as a structural form and its application in different situations in structures demanded the ready availability of a strong cementing mortar. This cementing material was *lime mortar*; the recognition of its adhesive properties and its early use in masonry construction is generally attributed to the Romans. It is said that the cementing action of lime was discovered 'accidentally' when it was employed in the form of rubble fillings between the two faces of walls made of dressed stone and inside a square or rectangular dressed stone pier. The device was used to economize on construction in making walls and piers of extra thickness. With the passage of time, it was discovered, the casing walls had given way but the rubble fillings remained intact and exhibited appreciable strength. It seems the Romans soon found out the wonderful cementing properties of pozzolana and also the more satisfactory manner of its application than a mortar using lime as the basic ingredient.

It is significant that references to the use of lime mortar, independently of its discovery by the Romans, have also come from India, and they date back to the second century BC. Citing *Archaeological Survey of India Report (Annual Reports), 1913-14* (p. 205), Percy Brown writes:

> Lime mortar appears to have been known at this time although but only two instances of it have come to light, one in the foundations of a temple at Besnagar (Bhopal, Madhya Pradesh) of the second century BC, and the other at Budh Gaya, where it was sparingly employed. The character of the brickwork excavated at Besnagar is very remarkable for so early a date, as the beds of the bricks were grooved to hold the lime mortar, which on being analysed was found to be of a kind far in advance of the Phoenician and

Greek varieties, and approaching more closely to that used by the Romans.[11]

This information finds support in a study conducted by R.V. Karanth, K. Krishnan and K.T.M. Hegde of M.S. University, Baroda. This team of scholars collected samples of ancient Indian lime plaster from the excavation site of a seventh century AD baked brick structure of a temple located at Karavan in Gujarat and subjected the samples to a comprehensive chemical and petrographic analysis. The conclusion reads: The study

> shows that the ancient mason was skilled enough to select and treat the raw materials to produce good quality plaster. He sieved the sand to eliminate larger particles that would project when plaster was applied to the wall. He possessed the necessary understanding and technology to construct a lime kiln for calcining kankar modules to obtain quicklime and for handling the strong exothermic hydrolysis reaction. Sand and slaked lime were mixed in a desirable proportion of 3:1 to obtain a durable plaster. He selected the upper finer part of the slaked lime to apply as a surface finish. This was burnished to render the plaster smooth.[12]

The use of lime mortar as a cementing material in the Islamic world had gained added importance in view of the fact that the pointed arch had been adopted as a preferred form and this needed the stone or brick voussoirs to be cemented firmly to hold the pointed form in shape. As noted earlier, in the case of semi-circular arches (especially of the Romans) there was no such cementing requirement if the keystone was accurately fitted. There is some ambiguity about the precise nature of the main ingredient used in the mortar in the Islamic world. George Michell notes:

> Although it is not always easy to distinguish whether 'gypsum' or 'lime' is meant in the records, gypsum was the more easily prepared, and was a common bonding agent for mortar in the Ancient World, continuing to be used in much of the Islamic World throughout the medieval period. There is some evidence, however, that mortar manufactured from lime wherever available, was preferred for the foundations and the corners of buildings. Gypsum mortar was then used for pointing the joints of face stonework or brickwork, in which case the mortar of the inner faces and cores of walls was seldom more than a local clay grout, occasionally mixed with chaff or straw.[13]

Use of lime mortar and/or gypsum mortar in medieval India has not been documented in detail. One study that discusses the making of mortar relates to Mughal India.[14] It is, however, not very unreasonable to assume that most of the inferences drawn there, if not all, would also hold for the Sultanate period.

The use of both lime- and gypsum-mortar in medieval India was widespread. Several kinds of lime were in use and the use of special types of mortar for specific parts of the building was also a common practice. Lime was obtained from three principal sources—limestone, gravel, and marine shells. The preparation of mortar had gradually developed into a specialized craft. In the Mughal period the mortar was improved for its adhesive properties by mixing 'a number of gelatinous, glutinous, resinous and non-resinous cementing agents'.[15] Much in the Roman manner of adding ingredients such as crushed under-fired brick, tile, or potsherds, in medieval India too lime mortar was mixed with 'pounded' bricks.[16] There is also mention of the preparation and application of mortar for special purposes—for constructions that required prevention from water-leakage, e.g. indigo-vats, and for plastering on the walls of the structures. It is important to note that the effective use of lime mortar was possible only on 'small' and porous surfaces. If the joints were wide, the adhesive property of the mortar was not likely to generate adequate compressive strength that was so vital a factor for holding structural forms such as an arch or a dome intact. Therefore bricks as building material, were found to be of greater utility in making arches and domes which used lime mortar as the main cementing agent.

Now, returning to the developments in the arch we discover that the experimental four-centred arch of the Tughlaqs finally blossomed into a proper four-centred arch under Akbar. The curvature changed such that the arch could now be divided into four segments each having a different centre of gravity. In architectural terms the great advantage derived from such a shape was that the architect could henceforth increase the span and yet would have to give only marginal increase in the height that is, the rise of the arch. It not only provided technical advantages but also introduced a certain elegance in compositions employing this arch. In red sandstone, Akbar's favourite building material, this arch assumed a distinctly recognizable character. The only other change in arch-making came when marble was introduced as a building material on a wide scale in the seventeenth century. The curves of the arch were modified from the continuous line profile to a multi-foliated profile. Generally there were nine cusps in each arch, four in each half and one at the crown (Fig. 3.15).

Fig. 3.15: Multi-Foliated Arch

Cusps were, however, increased in situations where the span of the arches were fairly big. The introduction of foliates was decorative in essence without altering the structural characteristics of the arch.

Thus, by the close of the sixteenth century most of the distinctive features of composite 'Indo-Islamic' architecture had come in place. It was in fact a combination of two different structural forms—column-and-beam and arch—that was judiciously used for particular structural purposes. Arch was used principally in gateways and buildings needed for congregations of people for various purposes (e.g. *barahdari*, *diwan-i aam*, etc.). Column-and-beam method was used for roofing, in colonnades and in entrances to chambers and also in other buildings. The objective clearly was to economize on construction, that is, to achieve greater output from the efforts put in composing the complete structures. The stability and the load-bearing capacity of the two forms had also been grasped. The parts of building where greater stresses were likely to occur were provided with arches; in those parts where load arranged for near vertical transference to the foundations, columns and beams were used in association with brackets and capitals, constituting a discernible element of construction technology. Clearly, there was no necessary conflict between the two; in fact they complemented each other. This gave a cultural depth to the composite architecture and gave it a wider context in which the users always took a fluid and porous view of their forms and crossed their boundaries without inhibition. Lastly, we must not mistakenly believe that this composite form homogenized the identity of medieval Indian architecture and hovered over various local and regional traditions like a spectre. The fact is local/regional traditions flourished alongside this composite form and produced interesting modifications as demanded by locally available material and compatible devices. We need to undertake detailed investigation of these traditions to uncover their actual worth.

NOTES

1. 'It is among the hilly wooded tracts of Madhya Pradesh, on the southern fringes of the Gupta Empire, that the majority of the earliest surviving free standing shrines are to be found. They are mostly from late in the Gupta period.' [J.C. Harle, *The Art and Architecture of the Indian Subcontinent*, Middlesex, Penguin Books, 1986, p. 111].
2. For a comprehensive and extremely valuable study of the temple architecture see Stella Kramrisch, *The Hindu Temple*, 2 vols. (pages in continuity), Delhi, Motilal Banarsidass, 2002 (first published by the University of Calcutta, and reprinted at Delhi in 1976 by the above publisher).
3. See Rowland J. Mainstone, *Developments in Structural Form*, Architectural Press, Oxford, 2nd edn., 1998, p. 98. He cites J. Garstang, *Tombs of the Third Egyptian Dynasty at Reqaqnah and Bet Khallaf: Report of Excavations at Reqaqnah 1901-2*, Constable, 1904 as the source for this information.
4. See Rowland J. Mainstone, *Developments in Structural Form*, p. 101.
5. Used in the palace of Mshatta, dated AD 744. See George Michell (ed.), *Architecture of the Islamic World, its History and Social Meaning*, London, Thames and Hudson, 1978, p. 136.
6. An inscription placed on the inner lintel of the eastern gateway of the mosque gives this information. See J.A. Page, *An Historical Memoir on the Qutb: Delhi*, Memoirs of the Archaeological Survey of India, No. 22. Published originally in 1926 by the Archaeological Survey of India, New Delhi, rpt. 1998, Appendix II (a), p. 29 where the text and the English translation of the inscription has been given.
7. It may be noted that 'false' arches were built in several structures at Delhi and in other regions controlled by the Sultans of Delhi, e.g. *Arhai Din Ka Jhompra* at Ajmer (built by Qutbuddin Aibak and later some additions made by Iltutmish), Iltutmish's and Alauddin's extensions of the 'screen' at Quwwatul Islam mosque at Delhi, Sultan Ghari's tomb (Iltutmish's eldest son, Nasiruddin Mahmud, who died in AD 1229 at Lakhnauti,

Bengal), Iltutmish's tomb at Delhi, Jami Mosque at Budaun (built by Iltutmish in AD 1223), and Ukha Masjid at Bayana (built during the reign of Iltutmish).

8. Percy Brown, *Indian Architecture* (*Islamic Period*), Bombay, D.B. Taraporevala Sons & Co., 5th edn, 1968, p. 13 (originally published in 1956).
9. There is some dispute about the use of the true arch in Balban's tomb, which is a structure dated earlier than the Alai Darwaza. Syed Ahmad Khan (in *Asar-us Sanadid*), is of the view that Balban's tomb contained a true arch which, however, did not survive. J. Burton Page, though, finds this assertion unacceptable ('Indo-Islamic Architecture: A Commentary on Some False Assumptions', in Dalu Jones, ed., *Art and Archaeology Research Papers*, no. 6, December 1974, pp. 14-21). Since the 'arch' did not survive even at the time Syed Ahmad Khan wrote his book, the story of its existence was perhaps pieced together from the fragmentary survivals of the rubble at the site and from local traditions. Page finds even the identification of the structure as Balban's tomb implausible.
10. The only other instance, in my knowledge, of the use of semi-circular arches is in the Ahom period (sixteenth century AD) temple in Sibsagar, Assam.
11. See Percy Brown, *Indian Architecture* (*Buddhist and Hindu Periods*), Bombay, D.B. Taraporevala Sons & Co., 6th rpt., 1971, p. 45.
12. R.V. Karanth, K. Krishnan and K.T.M. Hegde, 'Petrography of Ancient Indian Lime Plaster', *Journal of Archaeological Science*, 1986, London, Academic Press, pp. 543-51. The cited text is on p. 550.
13. See George Michell, *Architecture of the Islamic World*, op. cit., pp. 134-5.
14. Ahsan Jan Qaisar, *Building Construction in Mughal India: The Evidence from Painting*, New Delhi, Oxford University Press, 1988. The information on lime mortar is largely drawn from this study.
15. Ibid., p. 20.
16. Ibid.

CHAPTER 4

Agricultural Technology Depicted in Mughal Paintings

AHSAN JAN QAISAR

Most historians of medieval India have been interested in the political, administrative and economic aspects of the period, while some have exhibited a fondness for religious and cultural history, albeit in a limited manner. Of late, new sectors of study have been explored: for example, the development of technology during the medieval period.

The history of technology has emerged as a distinct discipline in India since the last two decades. Long ago, P.K. Gode's contribution to this area of study was so enormous that today we look upon him as the 'godfather' of this discipline.[1] After Gode (d. 1961), efforts of other scholars of medieval India in this respect have fructified in diverse directions.[2] Several aspects have been explored or are in the process of being examined, viz., the technology of shipbuilding, textiles, building construction, metallurgy, etc.

It must be underscored, however, that mere *verbal* description of the production-process or technique is not enough; in fact, technology cannot be properly studied without the aid of *visual projection*. This statement is fully strengthened by the tomes of *Science and Civilization in China* produced by Joseph Needham and his associates. Precisely, in this respect scholars of the history of technology in India find themselves inconvenienced. To date we have not come across any Persian treatise with sketches and drawings pertaining to medieval India on specific production technology *per se*. The same is true of sources in non-Persian Indian languages. Exceptions are there, but illustrations even in such cases are available only *en passant* in works of a *general* nature, such as *Sirat-i Ferozeshahi* or *A'in-i Akbari*. Sculptural or other non-verbal evidences including artefacts—albeit sporadic—are of a different category. Thus, in the absence of illustrated treatises on production-technology concerning our period, we turn to paintings, especially of the Mughal school, which have generously yielded evidence on material culture in general and on technology in particular, to the extent that we have now been enabled to establish paintings as an important historical source for our purpose.

In this article, I have attempted to present briefly the result of my study of Mughal paintings after collecting evidence therefrom bearing on agricultural technology.[3] Supplementary evidence has been taken from literary sources, whenever needed, for elaboration and verification. It is necessary to point out here that the pictorial material referred to in this paper relates to the territorial expanse north of the Vindhyas. This, by and large, is the unique feature of the Mughal school.

PLOUGHS AND PLOUGHING

Depictions of ploughs in Mughal paintings are not numerous, but they do show its traditional form. We have selected four paintings for this purpose—all executed during the second half of the sixteenth century under the patronage of Akbar.

Not a single composition displays a hoe or hoeing, which is not surprising since the use of ploughs in the time-scale can *definitely* be traced back to the advent of the Aryans into India, or perhaps a little earlier.[4] The Iron Age, identified with the 'Aryan' settlement in the Gangetic plain, contributed to the development of the plough in the sense that while initially the entire frame was of timber, the coulter now was of iron.[5] This iron piece in the plough immensely helped in the tillage of comparatively harder soil. For soft soil, it could have been dispensed with, the more so as the price of iron was high. For example, John Fryer records in the 1670s about the 'combies' (*kumbies*) in south India that 'their coulters [are] unarmed mostly, Iron being scarce, but they have hard wood which will turn their light ground'.[6] At any rate, it is not easy to detect the iron piece very clearly in paintings.

In one composition, the part of the plough where the share or coulter should be expected, is not visible as it has gone underground (Fig. 4.1).[7] In another painting the case is similar.[8] Nor is it visible in the *Tarikh-i Alfi's* composition (bottom left) (Fig. 4.2).[9] The plough in the *Khamsa* illustration is on such a tiny scale that even its blow-up would not have disclosed the iron piece.[10] One non-Mughal painting, however, exhibits the iron coulter prominently.[11]

Fig. 4.1: Ploughing (*Anwar-i Suhaili*, Bharat Kala Bhavan, Varanasi, f. 61, detail)

This can be explained by the fact that this composition occurs in a Persian glossary which seeks to highlight it under the entry *zinjir* (=share, coulter). On the other hand, the ploughs in Mughal paintings

Fig. 4.2: Ploughing (British Museum, Dep. Oriental Antiquities, 1934-1-13-01, *Tarikh-i Alfi,* detail)

happened to be there just incidentally and, therefore, the artist does not seem to have been interested in projecting the iron piece clearly. At any rate, the existence of the share and coulter, though very important, was taken for granted by the artists.

Regional variations in the size and weight of ploughs in a sprawling country like India must be expected—from a light plough that could be carried by the tiller on his shoulders, to the heavy one meant for harder soil.[12] But we have not discovered in any composition such light ploughs being carried upon the shoulders. And yet, our paintings leave the impression of light ploughs only.

Tillage was performed by harnessing a pair of oxen to the plough with three basic things: a long wooden beam or shaft attached to the plough was fastened to the middle of the yoke placed over the depression between the neck and the hump of the animals; and two ropes, one for each ox, the one end of which passed through the nostrils of the oxen while the other end was held in the hands of the tiller. The Europeans did not normally use the yoke because of the anatomical differences of their bullocks, having no sufficient hump. Their common practice was to tie the animal's horns with ropes attached to the plough; sometimes ropes were tied to the animal's neck-harness or its tail.[13] Oxen were driven by the Indian tiller with a stick or a small whip in his one hand to goad the animals while he held the ropes in his other to guide them. Cows do not appear to have been put to ploughing, nor have any rituals been depicted on the eve of tillage. Unlike in Europe, neither horse nor bullock-drawn wheeled plough nor mould-board were ever used in India.[14] Our plough responded to what William Terry, an English traveller to India (*c.* 1612) called 'foot-plough'.[15] As for the method of ploughing, the *Khamsa* painting gives a clear hint that tillage was routinely done in a circular manner.[16] In Europe, due to strip farming, only longitudinal cultivation was possible before the enclosures. Cross-cultivation was practised in India but it is difficult to interpret it in the paintings. In Europe it was out of the question since the holdings were mostly narrow and longitudinal in shape.

The next process was to break the clods or lumps of earth and level the ground. This was done with the help of wooden boards called *patela* in some parts of the Hindi-speaking belt. Only two paintings display this device. In one of these, the board is large and rectangular in shape upon which a man stands controlling the oxen in a manner similar to ploughing (Fig. 4.2).[17] The yoke is there but harnessing is different from ploughing: two ropes are fastened to the centre of the yoke, the other ends being attached to the levelling board. This device eliminates the wooden beam or shaft used in the plough. The other composition shows a squarish board upon which the operator stands.[18] But it differs from the above in some details: the man supports himself by holding the long and curved stem of a broad plank which is attached (or nailed?) to the levelling board. The harnessing, too, is dissimilar: instead of the wooden shaft we discover two ropes tied to the outer ends of the yoke whose other ends are lashed with the stem to the broad plank. But the ropes which should have worked as 'reins' are missing. Literary sources do not furnish information on these two types of levelling boards.

SOWING

It is held that, in the global context, four ways of sowing seeds were known: broadcasting, seed drill, sowing in a row, and dibbling.

Mughal paintings depict the first method only in connection with gardening. So far I have been able to collect only two such compositions. The *Baburnama* illustration shows three persons working in a garden one of whom is scattering seeds which he takes out from the improvised cloth-bag slung over his shoulder (Fig. 4.3).[19] This can be compared with what a woman is doing in similar fashion in a European illustrated manuscript.[20] Another Mughal garden scene displays a man holding a large, flat and shallow dish-like container in one hand and throwing seeds on the ground with the other.[21] It is a rather sophisticated way of broadcasting.

As for the seed drill, this is not the proper place to discuss its antiquity in India back to the Vedic Age, as has been suggested first by Jules Bloch.[22] At this stage, we can only say that we do not agree with Bloch's interpretation of some Vedic verses bearing on this issue. In any case, that the seed drill was known in medieval India cannot be denied. The only positive evidence for its use comes from Duarte Barbosa, who came to India during the early sixteenth century. He reports about a place near Bhatkal along the western coast that '[. . .] they plough the land as we do with oxen and buffaloes yoked in pairs, and the ploughshare has a hollow in it wherein the rice is carried

Fig. 4.3: Seed broadcasting (British Museum, Oriental 3714, *Baburnama,* f. 173b, detail)

when the land is flooded, and as the share ploughs the rice goes on setting down under water and earth. On dry land they sow by hand.'[23] Other information comes from Halcott and Buchanan, pertaining to south India during the eighteenth and early nineteenth century.[24] Undoubtedly, seed-drills were used in India and China, centuries before Europe did so.[25] But, unfortunately, Indian ploughs as discussed above do not exhibit this devise which was much better than broadcasting. For that matter, there is no specific term for this technique or even for broadcasting in our contemporary Persian or non-Persian Indian literary sources. However, dibbling had been taken note of in regard to cotton cultivation.[26] In essence, the practice of sowing in a row by hand or dibbling may be considered as 'controlled broadcasting'.

IRRIGATION

Mughal paintings reveal only those irrigational devices which were oriented toward drawing water from wells. Water supply to the fields from canals or tanks has not been represented. These wells were more often than not masonry ones with raised walls and enclosures or platforms, the latter being octagonal or squarish. Both bricks and stones were used to construct wells. These wells were usually set inside with terracotta rings which are clearly visible in some compositions. These are known as 'ring-wells' among archaeologists, and they have been found in many excavations of ancient sites in India. They are called 'draw-wells' if the rings are found sunk deep down to the water-table; in case of shallow depths, they are taken to have been used as barns, refusepits or soakpits.[27] Our paintings do not display *kachcha* wells, that is, those without bricks, stones or terracotta rings. Such wells could not have been durable or strong enough for extensive water-lifting purposes.[28]

Our paintings display five devices or techniques to raise water from wells. Drawing upon R.J. Forbes, we can put them into two broad categories: (a) intermittent or discontinuous water supply devices; and (b) a continuous supply system.[29] Four methods belong to the first and only one to the second category. Again, depending upon the nature of the operative source, the five techniques could be divided into two types, that is, human power (by hand) and animal power. In this case, only two respond to the first and the rest to the second. Since water had to be raised from wells, all the devices except one, shared two things amongst them: rope and bucket or bags, the latter varying in size commensurate to the 'power' used.

Type A. The most simple technique was to draw water with rope and bucket by hand without any mechanical aid.[30] Obviously, then, the bucket was small in size and, thus, this operation would not have adequately served to water large fields. In fact, none of our paintings clearly shows the use of this method for irrigation; instead, water was drawn for domestic purposes. But we cannot deny the use of rope-bucket technique for irrigating small fields for crops, most probably vegetables, that did not require much water.

Type B. The second method was the employment of pulleys combined with the ropebucket contraption which was, once again, activated manually (Fig. 4.4). Undoubtedly, the pulleys needed lesser amount of human energy and, therefore, comparatively larger bags or buckets could have been used. Some of these have been depicted in a rural setting with the adjacent field being ploughed.[31] This suggests very strongly the irrigation function of this method. However, one composition shows a lady drawing water from a small, unsophisticated ring-well located by the side of her house.[32] In this instance, water was being drawn for domestic use and, perhaps, it might also have been used for watering a 'backyard' vegetable field. Often we come across this device being operated by women to carry water back home in pitchers.[33]

Type C. An improved variety of the rope-bucket-pulley contraption was the employment of a pair of oxen to replace man-power. At this stage it has become a very specialized method for drawing water intended *specifically* for irrigation. We have not seen any composition where this animal-powered device has been shown for any other purpose. In some areas of north India it is still in operation known as *charasa*. The latter is a huge leather bag enabling one to raise an immense quantity of water from the well in one single haul-up. It is unfortunate that the bag is not visible in our paintings.[34] But the very fact that a pair of bullocks were harnessed to draw water should convey the impression of its large output. Babur, the founder of the Mughal Empire (1526), gives a fair observation of its main mechanism:

> In Agra, Chandwar, Biana and those parts, again, people water with a bucket; this is a laborious and filthy way. At the well-edge they set up a fork of wood, having a roller [read pulley] adjusted between the forks, tie a rope to a large bucket, put the rope over the roller, and tie its other end to the bullock.

Fig. 4.4: Pulley (*Anwar-i Suhaili*, Bharat Kạla Bhawan, Varanasi, f. 61, detail)

One person must drive the bullock, another empty the bucket. Every time the bullock turns after having drawn the bucket out of the well, that rope lies on the bullock-track, in pollution of urine and dung, before it descends again into the well [. . .].[35]

But this is not enough. James Forbes in his *Oriental Memoirs* (1770s) adds more information:

> The wells at Surat are large, and deep, enclosed with strong masonry; a walk of an easy descent is formed from the surface, ten or twelve feet wide, its length corresponding with the depth of the well: on the surface, opposite to each other, are stone pillars, supporting an horizontal beam, from which is suspended a large leather bucket, running by a strong rope over a pulley; to the other end of the rope is fastened a yoke of oxen which, as they descend the sloping walk, elevate the bucket containing the water; this is emptied into a reservoir, and from thence conducted by the gardener into small streams, to every tree and shrub in the garden. Many of the wells and walks are sufficiently large to admit two or three pair of oxen drawing water at a time; and some of them are erected for the public use by charitable individuals, at the expense of many thousand pounds.[36]

Surprisingly, Babur's account is not illustrated in any copy of the *Baburnama* at all. Out of three paintings, the only, comparatively clear, depiction is from the *Khamsa* of Nizami which reveals this contraption outside the walls of a mansion (Fig. 4.5).[37] The two men are very much there, one standing over the 'well-edge' emptying the bucket and the other sitting on the ropes tied to the yoke. This man drives and guides the animals. This is a new information which Babur and James Forbes withhold, or perhaps they did not take notice of it. The bullock track was like a ramp (not mentioned by Babur) which R.J. Forbes has chosen to call 'draught-plane'.[38] This sloping path is clearly exhibited in the *Khamsa* composition. Moreover, its length is quite impressive, giving an idea of the depth of the well. Incidentally, it also confirms the statement of James Forbes, that is, the length of the path corresponded with the depth of the well. Babur speaks of pulleys put up between wooden forks, but James Forbes mentions stone pillars with a horizontal beam, most probably of wood, which supported the pulley thereby excluding the use of a fork. Babur must have seen small *charasa* devices for small-scale irrigations; alternatively he has confused the fork-pulley of our type B with the pillar-beam-pulley type C. The *Khamsa* painting supports James Forbes on this point: obviously, the wooden fork could not have borne the weight of the huge quantity of water raised from the well in the large bucket.

That the water of the well could not have been used for drinking, cleaning utensils or for washing clothes is substantiated by what Babur says about the ropes being polluted with urine and dung 'before it

Fig. 4.5: *Khamsa* (*Khamsa* of Nizami, BM Or. 12208, f. 45a)

descends again into the well'. Of all the five methods of irrigation under study, this was not a multi-purpose one: it was solely devised for irrigation, a fact which has not been realized till now.

Type D. The fourth technique was what R.J. Forbes considered to be semi-mechanical as it worked on the first class lever principle.[39] A long rope is lashed to the fork of an upright beam or trunk of a tree (especially meant for this purpose) to put it in a swinging position. The bucket is fastened to a rope whose other end was tied to the one end of the swinging pole hovering over the well. The pole's other end carries a 'counterweight', a little heavier than the bucket when filled with water. Thus, the fulcrum forms at the centre of the pole, with weight and counterweight (effort) at its two ends. In one painting, the latter has been shown as a big lump of mud, a little tapering, bound with some material, most probably reed or some such thing (Fig. 4.6):[40] Stones or any heavy material could have been used, as it is done even today. This contraption requires only a little effort on the part of the person operating it: he has only to give a light upward thrust when the bucket is drawn up full of water; the counterweight at the other end of the pole does the rest of the work. Slightly more effort, however, should have to be mustered by the operator when he forces the empty bucket downwards. This device is known as *shaduf* in Egypt. It is called *tula* (balance) in Sanskrit, but in Bihar and Bengal it is known as *dhenkli* or *lat/latha*.[41] It was a multi-purpose mechanism, but our two paintings place them in the vicinity of a garden.[42] In one Sanskrit source, the *tula* has been

Fig. 4.6: *Shaduf/tula/dhenkli* [R. Ettinghausen, *Paintings of Sultans and Emperors of Delhi* (New Delhi, 1961), Pl. 5, detail]

glossed as the 'water-lifting devise used by gardeners'.[43] But, even today, variants of this technique could be seen in Bihar and Bengal. Set up in rural areas in open field for irrigation, not gardens alone. It is strange that Babur did not take notice of this device.

Type E. The fifth and the last water-lifting method illustrated in our paintings is what is called the 'Persian wheel'. None of the four mechanisms described above required wheels as their basic component. This waterwheel or *saqiya* could well claim to be called *jal yantra* (water machine) because of the employment of the gear system. The other four devices were simple contraptions; only one (type C) being semi-mechanical; none of these were 'machines'. With gears, we enter upon a very advanced stage in the technological sense: it has been surpassed only now by electric tube wells.

Much controversy has cropped up about the origins of *saqiya*, that is, whether it existed in India prior to the advent of the Muslims, or whether it was a foreign importation through the latter's agency.[44] This controversy should never have started if we would have looked at this mechanism in its evolutionary context as well as the development of its components separately.

Its earliest form was one wheel with pitchers or pots of clay attached around the rim of the wheel (Fig. 4.7). This form itself forced it to be set up over shallow water on open surfaces—stream, reservoir or even rivers where water would level up to its banks. Thus, its use over wells was absolutely out of the question. This device called noria—a corruption of the Arabic *na'urah*—was worked by manpower only.[45] The second stage was to exploit it over wells. This was done by releasing the pots lashed around the rim of the wheel and, in its

Fig. 4.7: A model of the *noria* (Deutsches Museum, Munchen)

place, a chain or garland (Hindi: *mala*) of pots was provided which was long enough to reach the water level of the well (Fig. 4.8). The *mala* or chain was made of double ropes without open ends between which the pots were secured with timber strips. This contraption was so arranged that a part of it must remain in direct touch with the rim of the wheel as a result of which, when the wheel was operated by manpower, the pot-garland, too, revolved along with the wheel, enabling the pots to take water when going down and then to discharge at the moment when they came up and turned once again to go down:[46] It is important to know that there is no separate term for this contrivance in Arabic or Persian. In Sanskrit, however, it was called *ghatiyantra* (pot-'machine'), although the words *araghatta* and *arahatta* continued to be used for both the types of *noria*.

At the third stage, we find three developments to have taken place: (a) addition of two more wheels; (b) gear mechanism; and (c) the use of animal power. This is the 'Persian wheel' or *saqiya*. Babur describes this device as below:

> In Lahor, Dipalpur and those parts, people water by means of a wheel. They make two circles of ropes long enough to suit the depth of the well, fix strips of wood between them, and on these fasten pitchers. The ropes with the wood and attached pitchers are put over the well-wheel. At one end of the wheel-axle a second wheel is fixed, and close to it another on an upright axle. This last wheel the bullock turns; its teeth catch in the teeth of the second, and thus the wheel with the pitchers is turned. A trough is set where the water empties from the pitchers and from this the water is conveyed everywhere.[47]

Fig. 4.8: *Noria* with pot garland (*Archaeological Survey of India – Annual Report, 1909-10* (Calcutta 1914) Pl. XIIV, panel in Jain temple, twelfth century AD, Marwar)

Thus there were three wheels: (a) the lantern-wheel set up on an upright axle to be moved by animal power round-and-round horizontally. This wheel was provided with vertical pegs at regular intervals; (b) the pin-wheel arranged vertically with a shaft or an axle connected with; (c) the third wheel over the well that carried the pot-garland (we will call this last wheel the 'water-wheel'). The pin-wheel carried teeth or cogs to get enmeshed with the pegs of the lantern-wheel when the latter was moved by the animals. This acted as a gear system, making the pin-wheel revolve vertically which, in turn, transmitted its vertical motion through its axle to the 'water-wheel' with pot-garland over the well. Thus, in order to exploit animal power in the improved variety of *noria*, a knowledge of gears was imperative (Fig. 4.9). Essentially, the point was to convert the original horizontal motion of the lantern-wheel into a vertical one for the 'water-wheel': hence the pinwheel and the gear system.

The confusion of some modern scholars in this controversy is to identify the two stages of *noria* with *saqiya*, the latter being radically different not only in its conception but also in its components. The Sanskrit/Indian word *araghatta* or *arahatta* (common as *rahat*)

Fig. 4.9: *Saqiya*/Persian wheel
(*Khamsa* of Nizami, BM Or. 12208, f. 294b)

seems to have been originally used for noria and, later on, applied to the second stage of the *noria*, too. The first two stages were quite indigenous inventions. A blunder was committed when the same terms were used for the *saqiya* when the Muslims brought it in the early medieval period. This semantic pitfall led some modern scholars into thinking that the *saqiya* existed in India before the advent of the Muslims.[48] Usher reprimands those who fail to distinguish between the *noria* proper and the pot-garland *noria*. He says:

> The wheel was applied at an early date to the task of raising water to great heights; there are two forms, the *noria* or Egyptian wheel and the chain of pots, which is frequently, though inexcusably, confused with the *noria*.[49]

Moreover, there is no evidence of water-wheels being operated by animals in ancient India.[50] To the best of our knowledge, the gear mechanism was perhaps unknown in that period.[51]

Mughal paintings do not depict the two stages of *noria* at all, but the *saqiya* is ubiquitous. However, a sculptural evidence of the twelfth century from Rajasthan shows the *ghatiyantra*, that is, *noria* with pot-garland (Fig. 4.8).[52] Again, a Rajasthani painting of the eighteenth century, too, displays the same contraption over a tank.[53] Harbans Mukhia mentions a painting done at Lucknow in the 1770s which shows the *ghatiyantra*.[54] Thus, the improved version of *noria* had not totally gone out of use in India. But it must be stated emphatically that the Persian wheel was most widespread in certain parts of north India than other water-raising devices.

A few features of the *saqiya* depicted in the painting must be noted:

(a) Lantern and pin-wheels could be set either hanging high in the space, or put just above the ground.[55]

(b) The animal driver, in most cases, has been shown sitting on a plank whose long, narrow stem was attached to the vertical shaft of the lantern-wheel. Only one man did the job, unlike in *charasa* for which a mate was needed to bail water from the bucket. This was performed by the pots automatically due to their position at a certain point and the force of gravity.[56]

(c) It was multi-functional, that is, it was used for water-supply to large residential buildings for a variety of purposes, as well as for providing water not only to the palace-gardens but also to the fields for crops.[57]

(d) The other four contraptions supplied water intermittently when in operation. But the *saqiya* did so continuously without break as long as the animals were made to work. Sujan Rai, a seventeenth-century historian observed that more than a hundred pots were used and that the quantity of water discharged in one complete motion of the 'waterwheel' was hundreds of 'maunds'. It is not possible to compare this rough estimate with the output of the *charasa* since we do not possess any evidence for the latter.[58]

(e) The drawn-up water was first collected in a small reservoir or cistern by the side of the well, from which water flowed out to the garden of field through channels. No evidence is available in the paintings studied by me of water-supply for domestic use through pipes as reconstructed for Fatehpur-Sikri on archaeological basis.

It must be pointed out that no metal was employed in any of the water-lifting devices described above. Even the bucket was made of leather. Sujan Rai reports that three hundred and sixty timber pieces—small and large were sometimes used to fabricate the wheels.[59] Most probably, the bulk of these pieces was meant for the wheel over the well (water-wheel). One Mughal painting reveals a huge 'water-wheel' with a pot-garland, half of which is hidden.[60] Perhaps only such gigantic wheels carried more than a hundred pots as Sujan Rai wrote.

HARVESTING, THRESHING AND WINNOWING

One unique Mughal painting displays four important agricultural activities (Fig. 4.10).[61] It shows one man cutting the crop with a semi-circular sickle; another making bundles of the harvested crop; the third driving a single bullock upon a threshing-floor, and the fourth has been depicted in the act of winnowing the threshed-out material.

Two main methods for threshing, among others, were practised worldwide: first, by employing animals and second, by using flails or sticks.[62] The latter are not represented in our paintings. However, Fryer mentions both in the context of south India with the unwarranted comment that the Hindus did the job with a 'stick' and the Muslims used animals for threshing.[63] Another English traveller did not notice

Fig. 4.10: Harvesting, threshing and winnowing (*Razmnama*, Prince of Wales Museum, Bombay, Accession no. 43.35, detail)

the use of flail or stick.[64] He wrote in the 1770s that in Surat, 'the corn is trodden out by oxen, walking over the ears, as described by Homer,

> where round and round, never-varied pain,
> The trampling steers beat out th'unnumber'd grain.

'Wind power' was exploited for separating the chaff from the grain: the threshed-out matter was first put in a basket and, then, it was shaken at a set pace throwing the contents outside the basket when the lighter matter, that is, the chaff got scattered by the wind and the grain fell on the ground.[65] We can also see the winnowed grain collected in a heap nearby. These heaps were the focus of superior rights staked by various social groups, the State's share being the largest. Such millions of heaps of grain were the symbolic foundation of the Mughal empire, to which the Mughals owed their grandeur, glory, splendour and power.

The above survey of paintings, especially of the Mughal school, in pursuit of discovering depictions of the various aspects of agricultural technology has been substantially fruitful. In fact, we must recognize paintings as primary documents for the study of technology in general, keeping in view the meagre information in literary sources in this respect. My own studies related to shipbuilding, glass technology, building construction, etc., and those of others (e.g. those concerning textile technology) prove my contention. However, it does not mean that paintings alone would give us the complete picture. As I said at the outset, literary sources should also be consulted for elaboration, corroboration or for further information. Moreover, many terms related to agriculture are still used in different regions of India (for example, *patella*, *charasa*, *dhenkli*, etc.). Thus, there is a need for fieldwork, too, in so far as the local terms are concerned, for the simple reason that these terms are not always available in literary sources. Also, fieldwork would give us an opportunity to find out the continuity as well as the changes in the medieval agricultural technology.

NOTES

1. See the collection of his articles in three volumes: *Studies in Indian Cultural History* (Vishveshvanandan Vedic Research Institute, Hoshiarpur, 1961; Poona 1960; and 1969).
2. To name a few: Irfan Habib, Harbans Mukhia, M.A. Alvi, Iqtidar Alam Khan, A.J. Qaisar, Qaisar Zaman, Iqbal Ghani Khan, Ishrat Alam and others.
3. For an excellent article on agricultural technology, see Harbans Mukhia, 'Agricultural Technology in Medieval India', in A. Roy and S.K. Bagchi, eds., *Technology in Ancient and Medieval India*, Delhi, Sandeep Prakashan, 1986, pp. 107-27.
4. For archaeological evidence of the use of the plough in the Indus Culture (at Kalibangan), see *Indian Archaeology, 1968-9: A Review*, Archaeological Survey of India, New Delhi, 1971, pp. 29-30. Also, Plate XXXIV. But doubt remains whether it was drawn by men or oxen. Plough cultivation employing oxen during the Vedic Age is a well-established fact, for which see Jules Bloch, 'La Charrue vedique', *Bulletin of the School of Oriental and African Studies* 8, 1935, p. 412. See also Gyula Wojtilla, 'Some Problems of the Sanskrit Terminology of Agriculture', *Sanskrit and World Culture*, SCHR, OR 18 Berlin 1986, p. 360.

5. For this inference, see R.S. Sharma, 'Class Formation and its Material Basis in Upper Gangetic Basin (*c.* 1000-500 BC)', *The Indian Historical Review*, ICHR, New Delhi, July 1975, p. 2. For material evidence of iron share at Atranji Khera (a painted Gray Ware site identified with the 'Aryan' settlement) in Uttar Pradesh, see R.C. Gaur, *Excavations at Atranjikhera: Early Civilization of the Upper Ganga Basin*, Delhi, Motilal Banarsidass, 1983, p. 429 and Fig. 123, no. 6 on p. 430.
6. John Fryer, *A New Account of East India and Persia & C, 1672-81*, II, ed. W. Crooke, London, Hakluyt Society, 1912, p. 108.
7. Cf. *Anwar-i Suhaili*, Varanasi, Bharat Kala Bhavan, f. 61.
8. Ibid., f. 113.
9. British Museum (henceforth BM), Department of Oriental Antiquities (henceforth OA), no. 1934-1-13-01 (a scattered folio from *Tarikh-i Alfi*).
10. BM Oriental (henceforth Or.), No. 12208, f. 19a (*Khams* of Nizami).
11. See Muhammad Shadiyabadi, *Miftah-ul Fuzala'* (*c.* 1469. Manuscript illustrated *c.* 1630: Mandu School), BM Or. 3299, f. 145a, *s.v. zinjir.*
12. Cf. N.G. Mukherji, *Handbook of Indian Agriculture*, Calcutta, 1915, pp. 83, 99. For the Malabar region, see the Report of General Sir Alexander Walker (*c.* 1820), in Dharampal, *Indian Science and Technology in the Eighteenth Century*, Delhi, Impex India, 1971, p. 181.
13. See Robert Trow-Smith, *Man the Farmer*, London, Priory Press Limited, 1973, p. 15, and the figures on p. 41 (above) and p. 46.
14. For ox-drawn wheeled plough, see ibid., fig. on p. 41 (above) and p. 46. For horse-drawn plough, ibid. fig. on p. 55; also Frank E. Huggett, *The Land Question and European Society*, London, Thames and Hudson, 1975, fig. on 85. For horse-drawn wheeled plough, see ibid., fig. on p. 24.
15. Cf. William Terry's Account in W. Foster, ed., *Early Travels in India* (rpt.), Delhi, S. Chand, 1968, p. 298.
16. BM Or. 12208, f. 19a (*Khamsa* of Nizami).
17. *Tarikh-i Alfi*, BM OA, no. 1934-1-13-01.
18. See Toby Falk and Simon Digby, *Paintings from Mughal India*, London, Colnaghi, 1979, pl. 18, *c.* 1610: 'King Dara Meeting Herdsmen in a Landscape'. From the H. Kaverkian Collection.
19. *Baburnama*, BM Or. 3714, f. 173b.
20. Cf. Trow-Smith, *Man the Farmer*, 40.
21. See Michael Goedhuis, *Indian Painting*, London, 1978, p. 118, pl. 93. It is a dispersed folio of a *Baburnama* manuscript.
22. Bloch, 'La Charrue vedique'.
23. *The Book of Duarte Barbosa, 1500-17*, tr. I.H. Longworth Dames, London, Hakluyt Society (rpt.), 1967, p. 192.
24. See the Report of Captain Halcott (1795-96) on Drill Husbandry in Dharampal, *Indian Science and Technology*, pp. 209-14 (also pl. V);

Francis Buchanan, *A Journey From Madras Through the Countries of Mysore, Canara and Malabar* (rpt.), New Delhi, Asian Educational Services, 1988, p. I, pl. XI; p. III, pl. XXIV.

25. J. Needham, *Science and Civilization in China* VI, pt. 2 (rpt.), Cambridge, 1986, pp. 251-76 (on agriculture by Francesca Bray); Huggett, *Land Question*, p. 68 and note, figure on 85.
26. Irfan Habib, *The Agrarian System of Mughal India*, New Delhi, Asia Publishing House, 1963, p. 25 and n. 7 (the evidence is from *Nuskha dar fani falahat*, India Office Library, f. 306).
27. Cf. R.C. Gaur, *Excavations at Atranjikhera*, pp. 246, 249.
28. The Dutch factor at Agra during Jahangir's reign states that 'large numbers of wells have to be dug in order to irrigate the soil [. . .]', see *Jahangir's India*, tr. W.H. Moreland and P. Geyl (rpt.), Delhi, 1972, p. 48. Irfan Habib takes this statement to be a reference to the annual construction of *kachcha* wells since these 'seldom survived the Monsoons', see Irfan Habib, *Agrarian System*, p. 28, n. 23.
29. R.J. Forbes, *Studies in Ancient Technology*, II, Leiden E.J. Brill, 1955, pp. 38-9.
30. For example, see *Baburnama*, BM Or. 3714, f. 314 and 320.
31. Cf. *Anwar-i Suhaili*, Varanasi, Bharat Kala Bhavan, f. 61.
32. *Nafahat-ul Uns min Hazrat-ul Quds*, BM Or. 1362, fl. 142a.
33. See BM OA 1920-9-17-0297: 'Shah Jahan visiting a Shaikh'; T.W. Arnold and J.V.S. Wilkinson, *The Library of A Chester Beatty: Catalogue of the Indian Miniatures*, II, Bloomsbury, 1936, pl. 75 (b): 'Shahid meets Wafa at Well'; Falk and Digby, *Paintings from Mughal India*, pl. 26.
34. *Khamsa* of Nizami, BM Or. 12208, f. 45a: 'Shapur Kneeling before Shirin'. Also see BM OA 1920-9-17-013(2): 'Mary Worshipped by Angels'.
35. *Baburnama*, II, tr. Beveridge, rpt., Delhi, 1979, p. 487.
36. James Forbes, *Oriental Memoirs: A Narrative of Seventeen Years Residence in India*, I, London, 1834, p. 167. The accounts of Babur and Forbes should be compared with what Francis Buchanan wrote concerning the Bangalore territory in south India: '[. . .] the ground for sugar-cane is watered by the machine which the Mussulmans call *Puckally* and the natives *Capily*. It consists of two bags of skin raised by a cord passing over a pulley, and drawn by two oxen, or buffaloes, descending on an inclined plane. The great imperfection of this contrivance seems to be, that the cattle are forced to reascend the inclined plane backwards.' Buchanan's observation that the cattle were forced to reascend the inclined plane 'backwards', is not substantiated by Babur and Forbes. It would seem foolish to make the animals perform this feat. See Buchanan, *Journey from Madras*, I, p. 356.
37. *Baburnama*, II, tr. Beveridge, p. 487.
38. Forbes, *Studies in Ancient Technology*, p. 38.

39. Ibid.
40. See R. Ettinghausen, *Paintings of Sultans and Emperors of Delhi*, New Delhi, 1961, pl. 5: 'The Golden City of Dvarka' (from a dispersed folio of a *Razmnama* manuscript in the Freer Gallery of Art, no. 54.6).
41. A.K. Coomaraswamy, 'The Persian Wheel', *Journal of the American Oriental Society* 51, 1931, pp. 283-4.
42. Ettinghausen, *Paintings of Sultans*, pl. 5; S. Tyulayev, *Miniatures of Baburnama*, Moscow, 1960, pl. 25 (left, upper corner).
43. Coomaraswamy, 'Persian Wheel', op. cit., p. 283.
44. Irfan Habib is the first scholar to suggest that the *saqiya* or Persian wheel was a foreign importation (see his 'Technological Changes and Society: 13th and 14th Centuries', in: *Proceedings of the Indian History Congress*, Varanasi, 1969, pp. 12-15. See Harbans Mukhia, 'Agricultural Technology', n. 96; for a few names of scholars who hold opposite views on this issue. We can here add two more who mistakenly think that the Persian wheel was indigenous: Coomaraswamy, 'Persian Wheel', and R. Nath, 'Rehant versus the Persian Wheel', *Journal of the Asiatic Society of Bengal* 12 (1970), pp. 82-4.
45. See B. Laufer, 'The Noria or Persian Wheel, *Oriental Studies in Honour of Cursetji Erachji Pavry*, ed. A.V.W. Jackson, Oxford, 1933, p. 238. Laufer, too, confuses *noria* with Persian wheel.
46. Cf. the pot-garland of the *saqiya* in *Akbarnama*, Victoria and Albert Museum (hereafter V&A), pp. 86-117.
47. *Baburnama*, II, tr. Beveridge, p. 486.
48. Habib, 'Technological Changes', op. cit., pp. 12-15.
49. A.P. Usher, *A History of Mechanical Inventions*, Boston, Beacon Press, 1959, p. 129.
50. R. Nath, one of the warm advocates of Indian origin, of the Persian wheel, cites several Sanskrit sources for the use of the words *araghatta* and *ghatiyantra* (which he mistakenly identifies with *saqiya*); but none of the sources cited by him inform us that the wheel was moved by animals. Actually, one of the sources cited by him says that the wheel was rotated by foot (*padawart*). This draws the following comment by Nath: '[. . .] at times. the mechanism was not worked by bullocks but, instead, by a man, who used to ascend the latters of the wheel and this continuously helped it to rotate'. It is indeed fantastic to visualize that *saqiya* could be operated by feet. See Nath, 'Rehant versus the Persian wheel', pp. 82-3.
51. See Habib, 'Technological Changes', 12; see also Harbans Mukhia, 'Agricultural Technology', n. 96.
52. Cf. *Archaeological Survey of India—Annual Report, 1909-10*, Calcutta, 1914, pl. XLIV (panel in Jain temple, twelfth century AD, Mandor, Marwar).

53. BM OA 1959-4-11-02 (*c.* 1790, Marwar, 'A Boar Hunt by Raja Dulal Singh of Gajner').
54. Harbans Mukhia, 'Agricultural Technology', n. 96.
55. For the wheels hanging high in the space, ed. *Baburnama*, National Museum, New Delhi, f. 122; see its reproduction in M.S. Randhawa, *Paintings from the Baburnama*, New Delhi, National Museum, 1983, pl. VI; for another composition, see V&A no. D. 383-1885: 'A Prince Holding a Party in a Garden'. For two more of such depictions, see *Khamsa* of Nizami, fols. 65a and 99b. BM OR 12208. For the wheels just above the ground, cf. Arnold and Wilkinson, *Library of Chester Beatty*, pl. 49(a); *Khamsa*, f. 294b; BM OA 1921-4-11-04: 'Bullock and Ass at a Well'.
56. See *Akbarnama*, V&A 86-117 (bottom left).
57. Ibid. For watering fields, see BM OA 1920-9-17-0297: 'Shah Jahan Visiting a Shaikh', Sujan Rai, *Khulasat-ut Twarikh*, ed. Zafar Hasan, Delhi, G. and Sons, 1918, p. 79 says that the water thus drawn with *saqiya* was helpful for agriculture (*zira't*).
58. Ibid.
59. Ibid.
60. Arnold and Wilkinson, *Library of Chester Beatty*, pl. 23: 'Akbar Receiving Congratulations on the Birth of Murad'.
61. See a folio from the *Razmnama* lodged in the Prince of Wales Museum, Bombay, Accession no. 43.55. I am grateful to my colleague, Dr S.P. Verma, who kindly provided me a copy of this painting.
62. For flail in Europe, see Trow-Smith, *Man the Farmer* 38 (the lower figure). For-threshing in China, see Needham and Bray, *Science and Civilization in China* VI, pp. 345-62.
63. Fryer, *New Account*, p. 108.
64. James Forbes, *Oriental Memoirs*, p. 168.
65. The Chinese used baskets, trays, sieves and even fans for winnowing. It was also done with shovels and forks by tossing the harvest. See Needham and Bray, *Science and Civilization in China* VI, pp. 363-78.

CHAPTER 5

The Impact of Sufi Traditions on Kabir

SHAHABUDDIN IRAQI

The Bhakti movement in northern India emerged under Ramananda (1400-70) during the fifteenth century. Its spiritual leaders played a vital role in the development of regional dialects of the vernacular. But the literature produced by them appears to have been largely influenced by the Sufi traditions. In the present paper an attempt has been made to trace the impact of those traditions on Kabir (1440-1518).

Sufism was not a challenge to Islam, Quran or the Prophet but simply a reaction against the formal or external attitude of the *ulama* (Muslim theologians). The Sufis tried to replace the static theology by dynamic and progressive ideas in order to achieve a universal character. In his systematic account of Sufism in the twelfth century, Imam Ghazali (1058-1111), a great mystic philosopher, has differentiated between *ulama-i zāhir* (externalist scholars) and *ulama-i bātin* (saints or mystics) by saying that while the former proceed from knowledge to action, the latter proceed from action to knowledge.[1]

On the other hand, the Bhakti saints, particularly those of the Nirguna Bhakti,[2] appeared in northern India as a reaction against Vaishnavism or Hinduism. They not only protested against the religious orthodoxy and formalism but also challenged the incarnation theory, idol-worship and even the scriptural authority of the Vedas. The Nirguni saints and their followers developed their own scriptures in the form of compilations like the *Bijak* of Kabir, *Guru Granth* of the Sikhs and the *Panchavani* of the Dadupanthis, which were and are still followed and usually recited in their respective sectarian centres as essential part of their religious obligations. The philosophical base of such radical saints was founded on Islamic monotheism and Vedantic Advaita (i.e. later Vedic monism).

Kabir, a great Nirguna Bhakti saint, was neither a *sannyasi* (ascetic) nor a monk but a *grihastha* (householder) like the Sufis. Influenced by the Sufi concept of *tark* (renunciation), he believed in detachment, not from worldly life as such but from worldly desires and materialism. It was for this reason that though he led a family life but adopted an attitude of indifference to worldly pursuits.[3] Kabir denied to be recognized either as a Hindu or a Muslim, or identified as such with any of the religious orders.[4]

Kabir was not satisfied with the traditional system of religious knowledge and, therefore, he emphasized the need for *anubhava gyan* or direct knowledge from personal experiences, as is evident from his following verse:

पोथी पढ़ि पढ़ि जग मुआ पंडित भया न कोय।
एकै आखर पीव का पढ़ै सु पंडित होय।।

People were dead by studying books, but no body could become the learned. Those who understood the meaning of one word of God, became the learned.[5]

This reminds us of the famous statement of Imam Ghazali that true knowledge could be achieved only through personal experiences, and that theological doctrines could not be proved by speculative methods but by direct knowledge with which God floods the heart of the devotee.[6]

Kabir associated himself with a movement that conformed neither to Hinduism nor Islam, but to a universal religion. He, rather, denounced the whole system and all norms of traditional institutionalized form of religion. He laid very strict condition on his followers by saying that only those could go with him who had burnt their own religious house and cultural identity:[7]

जो घर फूंके आपना, चले हमारे संग

The *Sant Sahitya* (literature of the Bhakti saints) as a whole seems to have been influenced by the Sufis and their literature which, though indirectly, affected not only its poetic and linguistic forms and ways of expression but also even more specifically its thought contents. Tara Chand's assessment in this context is important when he says that the Indian saints were greatly under the impact of the language used by Sufis, so much so that they usually employed their language. With regard to Kabir, he remarks, the saint 'used both Sanskrit and

Persian terms' and 'employed both forms of the *Bhasa*, i.e. the Sanskritized Hindi and Persianized Urdu'.[8] It is estimated by Keay that more than two hundred words of Persian, Arabic and Turkish origin which were prevalent during those days are used in Kabir's *Bijak* alone.[9] Holding the same view, Tara Chand concludes that 'an analysis of these words shows how deeply his mind was imbued with Sufi doctrines'.[10]

Apart from the general poetic forms adopted in Bhakti literature like *sakhis*, *sabads*, *ramainis*, etc., Kabir has also used the form of Persian and Urdu *rekhtas*. It is significant that his *Das Muqami Rekhta*, which contains the inward flight of the Prophet Mohammad, is surprisingly in accordance with the Persian poetry in view of both the form and content. Besides, his *ramainis* dealing with the theory of cosmos may also be placed in the same category.

An evidence comes from the *Khazinat-ul-Asfiah* of Ghulam Sarwar, where he refers to Kabir as a 'Shaikh Kabir Julaha and a disciple of Shaikh Taqi' (himself a Julaha from Manikpur, d. 1574).[11] Another Persian work, the *Akhbar-ul Akhyar* of Shaikh Abdul Haq Muhaddis Dehalvi, remarks that though the theologians were not sure whether Kabir was to be reckoned as a Muslim or a *kafir* (infidel), his verses were read and quoted in the *sama* (audition parties) of the Sufi centres in Delhi and Agra both in the beginning of the sixteenth century.[12] This is obviously because the Sufis and Kabir both reacted against the religious orthodoxy almost in the same spirit and stressed the need of a universal religion. Like the Sufis, Kabir also addressed the people of all castes and communities without any distinction. He tried to establish a very strict monotheism exactly in accordance with the unique Islamic concept of *La ilaha-illallah* (i.e. none is there except one God to be worshipped). The Islamic impact drawn through Sufism is explicitly gleaned from the following verses of Kabir, though composed in his own style:

> There is no God but Him, The One Creator
> Kabir loudly proclaims, there is one God for the Hindu
> as for the Mohammedan
> Pure is God alone who has neither form nor limits[13]

There is a Quranic verse in Sura Luqman, 'and if all the trees on earth were pens and the ocean (were ink), with seven oceans behind it to add to its (supply), yet the words of Allah (God) would not be exhausted (in the writing): for God is Exalted in power, Full of Wisdom'.[14] The impact of this Islamic concept on Kabir is quite clear from his following verse, 'were I to make the seven oceans my ink, the trees of the forest my pens, and the earth my paper, I should not succeed in writing God's praises'.[15] Similarly, in describing the qualities of God as saviour, merciful, beautiful, happy and perfect, Kabir comes very close to the well known God's names as contained in the Quran.

There is, of course, a marked difference of approach in addressing God between the Persian poetry and that of Hindi. While in Persian God is presented as the beloved and devotee as the lover, the Bhakti saints adopted just the reverse position by calling Him the lover and themselves as the beloved. Similarly, while in Sufism the inclination of love or affectionate behaviour emanates from man towards God, the attitude of the Bhakti saints is opposed to it. They describe God as paying much attention towards the beloved or devotee who, on the contrary, appears to be rather indifferent towards the lover or God. Though Kabir also maintained this traditional approach of Bhakti poetry by calling God as 'Father', 'Husband', etc., he seems to be more inclined towards the Sufi method of describing the nature and attitude of God. If the Sufis speak of God as the 'beloved' having 'lovely gestures' and 'affectionate behaviour to the devotee', Kabir thinks of Him as the spouse, for whom the wife (devotee) abandons her home, goes out in the night full of darkness, storm and rain. Tara Chand says that Kabir like the Sufis 'frequently speaks of the wine and the cup of love, of the lover (*ashiq*, *habib*) and the beloved (*mashuq*, *mahbub*) . . . '.[16] This shows as to how much Kabir was under the impact of the Sufis in his symbolic expressions.

Though Kabir's monistic ideas were based on the Vedantic concept of *Tat Tvam Asi* (Thou art That), his mode of expression seems to be very close to that of the Sufis' *Wahdat-ul wajud* (Unity of God). This is evident from the following verses of Kabir:

> God Himself is the fire, himself the wind . . . .
> On my tongue dwells God, in my eyes dwells God,
> and in my heart dwells God[17]

Moreover, Kabir often holds the idea that the nature and essence of God is 'Light' (*nūr*), as is apparent from the following reference from his account:

> Every heart is gladdened by God's light. . . .[18]

This resounds with the Sufi concept of God as *Nūr-i Qahir*, whose essential nature consists in 'perpetual illumination'. This concept of God led Kabir to believe in God also as transcendent and beyond approach. But he also presents Him as one with whom personal interaction can be developed. 'Enjoy yourself in intercourse with the Lord.'[19]

In fact, wherever Kabir has described God as being close to the heart of the devotee, he appears to be, in spirit, under the Sufi impact. Two of his hymns are important in this context: 'Kabir having searched and searched himself, hath found God within him' and 'Search in your heart, search in your heart of hearts; there is His place and abode'.[20] It was due to this concept of God in Kabir's mind that he discarded not only idol worship and its related rituals, but also the incarnation theory. He declared that the incarnation of God did not concern him, because his 'Master is such a Lord as hath neither father nor mother'.[21]

Besides, the way of expression in describing the relationship between God, man and the universe seems to have also been derived from Sufism. He often compares the relationship between God and soul as that of 'the ocean and its waves' and thereby makes a link between God and the universe. In some of his verses, Kabir makes an attempt to reproduce the scheme of nine spheres through which creation develops in accordance with the Muslim philosophy.[22] It appears from Kabir's account of *ramainis* that there is a curious similarity between his concept of cosmology and that of the early Sufis. In fact, both Kabir and the Sufis start with one God pre-existing, who later created the idea of ideas, i.e. *Haqiqat-i haqaiq* of the Sufis and *sabda* (word) of Kabir. In this process Kabir's Brahma created an egg or the white chrysolite, i.e. *Yaqut-al baidha* of the Sufi concept, from which evolved the fourteen regions of Kabir (the seven heavens and the seven earths).[23] Besides, Kabir has adopted almost the same symbols showing the essential oneness of God and the universe, which the Muslim mystics have used. See the following verse of Kabir:

> As ice is made from water, and as ice will become water and vapour, so is the reality from that, and therefore this and that are the same.[24]

Kabir has expressed the whole process of commixture (*imtizaj*) by saying that soul and God are separated by *maya* and when it is thrown away, they are united.[25] He attaches no importance either to *avagaman* (transmigration of soul) or heaven, but to absorption into the essence of God: 'The soul is free from birth and death . . . it shall for ever be absorbed in God.'[26] This covers the famous Sufi concept of *Fana-Fit-Tauhid*, i.e. annihilation into the essence of God.

The Nirguna Bhakti meant for devotion to one God without any visible object with the spirit to apprehend Him by the inner (mystical) experiences. Kabir's Bhakti was ideal in this respect, for which he wanted to dedicate the whole of his life.[27] He believed that true devotion would itself illumine the devotees' heart with all sorts of knowledge and good actions. There should be no consideration of reward and punishment in spiritual observances or in having faith in heaven or hell.[28]

That true Bhakti cannot be achieved by formalities is described in many of his verses. In the process of spiritual perfection in Sufism, the role of a Shaikh (spiritual teacher) was always important. Kabir went further, considering the position of the *guru* no less than that of Govinda (God). This was because he substituted the human *guru* with God himself as *Satgur* and said: 'गुर गोबिन्द तो एक है, दूजा सब आकार'.[29] Besides, there are several verses in Kabir's account in which he, like the Sufis, has expressed a deep consciousness of sin within the heart and a profound sense of his unworthiness before God. But a sense of self-consciousness or self-respect is also gleaned from many of his verses. He asked the poor to maintain their self-respect by saying that 'poverty could be made bearable by self-labour and by chanting the name of Hari'.[30] He also criticized *sadhus* (saints) who stake the doors of royalty like hungry cows in a green field:[31]

राजदवारै यौं फिरै, ज्यौं हरहाइ गाइ।

Some of his verses also reflect the Sufi concept of *tawakkul* (trust in God). He emphasized the value of satisfaction and contentment with what one has got.[32]

Selfless devotion and freedom from worldly attachment were considered by the Sufis as the most important preliminary steps to be taken to prepare the self for spiritual advancement. The same spirit seems to be running in the thought of Kabir, when he speaks thus:

Lay hold on your sword, and join in the fight,
Fight, O my brother, as long as life lasts. . . .
In the field of this body a great war is going on
against passion, anger, pride and greed.
It is in the kingdom of truth, contentment and purity
that this battle is raging, and the sword that rings forth
most forcefully is the sword of God's name.[33]

Kabir asserts that pride should also be abandoned in this process: 'Kabir, what availeth it to abandon worldly love, if pride be not also abandoned . . .'.[34]

Like the Sufis, Kabir has also expressed the difficulties and pains of the traveller (*musafir*) in the way of spiritual advancement through various stages and stations (*muqam*). Tara Chand has provided in this context the following references from Kabir's account:

> The path is 'like walking on the keen edge of a sword', having 'terrible obstacles'. Again, 'the clouds gather, the evening falls, the rain pours down, the fourfold blanket becomes wetter and wetter and the burden gets heavier and heavier', and yet again, 'walking, walking the feet are aching'.[35]

As union with God was the main consideration of the Sufis, they laid much less importance to heaven or hell. Kabir also reflects the same idea by saying, 'What is hell and what is heaven, the wretched places', 'As long as you expect paradise (*vaikuntha*), so long will you delay dwelling at the feet of the Lord'.[36]

The most important factor of spiritual life is love or emotion and the Sufi *malfuz* literature is full of such references. As the Sufis considered it religious faith (*aqeeda*) and practice (*amal*), Kabir took it as *sadhan* (means) and *sadhya* (object). Tara Chand has rightly observed that 'like the Sufis Kabir too invites his fellow travellers to inebriate themselves with the wine of love and throw worldly discretion to the winds'.[37] He considered love superior to religious knowledge: 'My Guru has taught me the subject of love, now there is nothing to be read out.'[38]

For the Sufis, love is like wine which should be consumed for spiritual perfection. They also believed that intoxication or a trance caused by love is necessary for a mystic to be absorbed in the deepest meditation to God. A similar symbolic expression of love may be noticed in the following phrases of Kabir:

> My mind is intoxicated with God's elixir', or 'Drink Gods elixir, O Kabir

and

> Turning from the way of the world I have obtained this wine, a cup of which causes divine intoxication.[39]

There are many verses in which Kabir describes how one having intoxicated by the wine of love, goes out of one's senses and what sort of things can be experienced during spiritual intoxication. For instance,[40]

हरि रस पीया जानिए कबहूं न जाय खुमार।
मैं मंता घूमत फिरुं नाही तन की सार।।

Besides, the Sufis usually believed that it is with the help of love that the soul realizes its unity with the Ultimate Reality and finds his individuality merged in it. Amir Khusrau's famous verse bearing this idea is:

من تو شدم تو من شدی، من تن شدم تو جاں شدی
تاکس نگوید بعدازیں، من دیگرم تو دیگری

The same idea has been well depicted in the following verse of Kabir:

. . . (as) God and Kabir have become one,
no one can distinguish between them.[41]

The idea is further clarified in the following verse:

जब मैं था तब हरि नहीं, अब हरि हैं मैं नांहि।
सब अधिंयारा मिटि गया, जब दीपक देखा मांहि।।

There remained no more the consciousness of myself, when God was realized within self;
The whole darkness ended, when the heart was enlightened by the grace of God.[42]

At a stage in the process of spiritual perfection the devotee feels that when his soul is absorbed in the essence of God, the destiny of both also becomes identical. Kabir has expressed this stage very well in the following verse:[43]

हरि मरि हैं तो हमहूं मरि हैं।
हरि न मरैं हम काहे को मरि है।।

Imam Ghazali has emphasized the concept of three orders of existence, i.e. *malak-ul-mulk*, *malak-ul malaqut* and *malak-ul jabarut*, which was followed by later mystic philosophers. Kabir has also described the concept in the following manner:

Abandoning the actions pertaining to humanity (*nasut*), one sees the sphere of the angels (*malaqut*); then leaving even the sphere of majesty (*jabarut*) one gets the vision of divinity (*lahut*); but when these four stages are left behind then comes *hahut*, where there is neither death nor separation and where *yama* (god of death) finds no entrance.[44]

Moreover, Kabir is said to have also expressed that '*Nasut* is darkness, *malaqut* is angelic, in *jabarut* shines the Majestic Light (*nur jalal*), in *lahut* one finds the Beautiful Light (*nur jamal*) and *hahut* is the dwelling place of truth (*haq* or God)'.[45]

Thus, Kabir has observed the various orders of existence almost in the same way as described by the early Muslim mystics and philosophers. But the problem is that most of his such accounts are found in his *Ultwasian* which are most often quite obscure and meaningless.

With regard to other matters also, Kabir seems to have been greatly inspired by the Sufi views and concepts. In fact, the motivation of all of his spiritual and social views was conditioned by the two fundamental concepts of Islam or Sufism, i.e. 'unity of God' and 'unity of human being'. The liberal ideas of the Sufis suited Kabir. Westcott says that 'his condemnation of pride and commendation of humility are much more in accordance with the teachings of Sufi saints than with the practice of the Hindu Pandits'.[46] Tara Chand also says that 'the expression of Kabir's teachings was shaped by that of Sufi saints and poets'.[47]

In some of Kabir's verses there appear the echoes of the thoughts of early Persian poets and Sufis like Sheikh Sadi and Jalal-ud-din Rumi. For instance, see the following lines of Sadi and Kabir:

یاد داری کہ وقت زادن تو ہمہ خندہ بوندو تو گریاں
ہمچناں زی کہ بعد مردن تو ہمہ گریاں شوندو تو خنداں

आया था संसार में जग हंसा तू रोय।
ऐसी करनी कर चलो तुम हंसो जग रोय।।

The meaning of both is the same that when you came to the world, the people laughed but you wept. Conduct yourself in a manner that after your death people should weep but you smile. It seems that Kabir's verse is just a paraphrase of Shaikh Sadi's lines. Besides, Kabir has emphatically argued that the superiority of a man is determined not by birth but by action.[48] The concept of *Insan-i Kamil* (perfect man) as defined in Sufism seems to have also been well reflected in many of his verses. He lays even more strict conditions for a devotee to become perfect:

Every servant of God ought to be perfect like God Himself.

As a result he says, 'it so happened to me that God did what was pleasing to my mind'. Not only this, at this stage God is bent upon fulfilling his wishes: 'Kabir, once whose mind is pure as Ganga water,

God follows him, saying "Kabir! Kabir" '.[49] Such ideas remind us of Iqbal's concept of *khudi* and his verse:

خودی کو کر بلند اتنا کہ ہر تقدیر سے پہلے
خدا بندے سے خود پوچھے بتا تیری رضا کیا ہے

Elevate yourself so high that while deciding about your fate, God should take care of your wishes.

Kabir was a practical man believing in action rather than theory. He adopted a strict approach to those who preached without practising:

कथनी कथी तो क्या भया, जौ करनी न ठहराइ

What is the use of that speech which does not correspond to action.[50]

The unity of preaching and action represents a great moral force for uniting human beings. So, like the Sufis, Kabir has set ideal examples of ethical and moral values by saying:

जहं दया तहं धरम है, जहं लोभ तहं पाप।
जहं करोध तहं काल है, जहं खिमां तहं आप।।

No religious faith is fit without mercy, selfishness carries only sin; revenge leads to destruction and forgiveness to God.

सांच बरोबर तप नहीं, झूठ बरोबर पाप।
जाकै हिरदै सांच है, ताकै हिरदै आप।।

No worship is better than honesty, and no sin is equal to telling a lie; God is only with those who are honest.

ऐसी बानी बोलिए, मन का आपा खोइ।
अपना तन सीतल करै, औरों की सुख होइ।।

Speak in a soft language that appeals to others and satisfies yourself.[51]

This was the reason why Kabir, like the Sufis, was held in high esteem by Hindus and Muslims alike.

In spite of the fact that Kabir derived much from Sufi traditions, he could not follow them all. The Muslim mystic systems were too varied and well planned to be imitated fully by a saint like Kabir who was neither willing nor in a position to do so. Hence, there seems to be little weight in the assessment of Tara Chand that Kabir had experienced all the conditions which the Muslim mystics describe.[52] In spite of the fact that Kabir's love was deep, he could not follow all aspects of Sufism. For instance, it appears from a passage of *Khazinat-ul Asfia* of Ghulam Sarwar that though Kabir taught the

Sufi doctrine of *wisal* or union (with God), he was silent about its counterpart, *firaq* or separation.[53]

There is no doubt that Kabir contributed much to the development of Sufi traditions in India. J.N. Farquhar considers Kabir as one of the most popular Indian propagandists of Sufism in India.[54] It was by his time that the condemnation of polytheism, idol-worship and caste distinction became very frequent and emphatic. But an even more important aspect of his contribution is an adequate and simple fusion of Indian Vedanta and Muslim *tasawwuf* which he brought together successfully. Kabir's emergence marks a new era in the history of Indian thought. Though the Bhakti movement was already popular in northern India under Ramananda and others, Kabir gave a new impetus and orientation by introducing to it some vital elements of Sufism, such as communal harmony and universal brotherhood.

It was also the impact of particularly the Chishti saints that Kabir was suspicious of the rulers and the ruling class. He warns 'those people at whose doors *naubat* (drum) is played ten times a day, at whose gates proud elephants stand, and before whom drums and other instruments are beaten when they move out; their pride is of no use, as death is the ultimate reality'.[55] Kabir not only himself disliked political and powerful figures but also asked his followers not to be associated with them.[56] In spite of this, his influence, as observed by Tara Chand, 'continued to spread under the Mughal rule', and Akbar 'attempted to make it (Kabir's ideology) a religion approved by the State'.[57] Akbar's *Tauhid-i Ilahi* seems to have been an echo of Kabir's philosophy.

NOTES

1. Shibli Nomani, *Al Ghazali*, Delhi, Helal Press, 1914, p. 187. The sharp division between the two trends of thought represented by the *ulama* and the *mashaikh* is evident from the discussions that took place on the issue of *sama* (audition party) at a *mahzar* (convention of the learned) in the court of Ghayas-ud-din Tughlaq. K.A. Nizami, *Tarikh-i Mashaikh-i Chisht*, vol. 1, Delhi, Idara-i Adabiyat-i Dehli, 1980, p. 424. The same controversy had also appeared during the time of Iltutmish. See K.A. Nizami, *Some Aspect of Religion and Politics in India During the 13th Century*, rpt., Delhi, Idara-i Adabiyat, 1978, pp. 302-3.
2. Nirguna Bhakti means devotion to one God without any visible object, since the saints of this *marga* (path) believed that God was one, without attributes and manifested everywhere. Some of the important saints of this school were Kabir, Nanak and Dadu.

3. See *Sri Rag*, Gauri VI, Macauliffe, *The Sikh Religion*, vol. VI, rpt., Delhi, Low Price Publication, 1993, pp. 142, 145. For details about Kabir's life, see Shahabuddin Iraqi, *Bhakti Movement in Medieval India: Social and Political Perspectives*, Delhi, Manohar, 2009, pp. 144-7.
4. Kabir deliberately refers to himself in his verses as *kori* and *julaha* both (i.e. Hindu as well as Muslim weaver) and calls God both as Ram and Rahim, for the simple reason of not being identified either as Hindu or as Muslim. It is, therefore, not surprising that the complaint against Kabir to Sikandar Lodi was lodged by the religious leaders of both the communities, which reads thus: 'Those who paid heed to what Kabir said remained neither Hindu nor Muslim'. See Macauliffe, op. cit., p. 132.
5. *Kabir Granthawali*, ed. P.N. Tiwari, Prayag, Hindi Parishad, 1961, *sakhi* 33-3, p. 241; also *Kabir Granthawali*, ed. Shyam Sundardas, Varanasi, Nagari Pracharini Sabha, 1975, *sakhi* 19-4, p. 30.
6. See, D.B. MacDonald, 'The Life of Al-Ghazzali', *Journal of the American Oriental Society*, vol. XX, 1899.
7. Kabir *slok* LXXXIII, Macauliffe, op. cit., vol. VI, p. 291; also *Kabir Granthawali*, ed. P.N. Tiwari, *sakhi* 5-13, p. 160.
8. Tara Chand, *Influence of Islam on Indian Culture*, Allahabad, Indian Press, 1963, p. 159. The compound which Kabir prepared by mixing these two forms of the vernacular and the way in which he employed it, made his language unique and sometimes very difficult to understand. Keay has discussed certain features of the unique language used by Kabir by providing some examples of each. See F.E. Keay, *Kabir and his Followers*, New Delhi, Mittal Publication, 1967, pp. 64-7.
9. Ibid., p. 51.
10. Tara Chand, op. cit., p. 153.
11. Ghulam Sarwar, *Khazinat-ul-Asfiah*, cited by G.H. Westcott, *Kabir and the Kabirpanth*, Calcutta, Susil Gupta, 1953, pp. 15-16.
12. See Abdul Haq Mohaddis Dehlavi's *Akhbar-ul Akhyar* (a collection of short biographies of certain Sufis, compiled in 1590-1), ed. Muhammad Abdul Ahad, Delhi, Mujtabai Press, 1914, p. 300, Urdu tr. Subhan Mahmood, Delhi, 1990, p. 591; also Ch. Vaudeville, *Kabir*, vol. 1, New Delhi, Oxford University Press, 1974, p. 34.
13. For these references, see Kabir's *slok* CXXXIII, *Asa* XXIX, and *Bhairo* 3, Macauliffe, op. cit., vol. VI, pp. 299, 212 and 258, respectively.
14. *The Holy Qu'ran* (Text, Translation and Commentary) by A. Yusuf Ali, Islamic Foundation, U.K., 1975, chapter XXXI, *Sura Luqman*, verse 27, p. 1087.
15. Kabir's *slok* LXXXI, also *Ashtapadi* 11, Macauliffe, op. cit., vol. VI, pp. 268-9, 290.
16. Tara Chand, op. cit., p. 152.

17. For these and other such references see *Gauri* XXXIII and XI, Macauliffe, op. cit., vol. VI, pp. 157, 160, 248, 276.
18. Basant 1, ibid., p. 269.
19. It appears from a hymn of Kabir, *Gauri* IX, that though God is without attributes, one may have interaction with Him. Macauliffe, op. cit., p. 147.
20. See *Bhairo* VII, *Prabhati* II, ibid., pp. 260, 276.
21. *Gauri* LXX, ibid., p. 179.
22. Referring to the two speculations found in *Siddharta Dipika*, Tara Chand says that one denotes that everything is created from water, while the other speaks of the creation as a mechanical process. See Tara Chand, op. cit., p. 157.
23. Ibid., p. 156.
24. Ibid., p. 152.
25. For the role of *maya* as elaborated by Kabir, see *Bhairo*, XIII, Macauliffe, op. cit., vol. VI, p. 263.
26. See *Asa* 1 and *Gauri* IX, ibid., pp. 147, 196.
27. For instance, see *Gauri* VI, VII and VIII, Macauliffe, op. cit., pp. 145-7.
28. See *Gauri* X, *Bhairo* XVI, ibid., pp. 148, 265-6.
29. *Kabir Granthawali*, ed. P.N. Tiwari, *sakhi* 1-28, p. 139.
30. Hazari Prasad Dwivedi, *Sant Kabir*, Bombay, Hindi Granth Ratnakar, 2nd edn., 1947, *sakhi* 12-47, p. 52.
31. *Kabir Granthawali*, ed. P.N. Tiwari, *sakhi* 21-8, p. 213.
32. For instance, *Asa* XVI, *Kedara* VI, Macauliffe, op. cit., pp. 204, 257.
33. As cited by Tara Chand, op. cit., p. 160.
34. Macauliffe, op. cit., p. 302.
35. Tara Chand, op. cit., p. 161.
36. *Gauri* X, *Bhairo* XVI, Macauliffe, op. cit., pp. 148, 265-6.
37. Tara Chand, op. cit., p. 161.
38. Quoted by R.K. Verma, *Kabir Ka Rahasyavād*, 9th edn., Allahabad, Sahitya Bhawan, 1961, p. 35.
39. *Shri Rag* 11, *Gauri* VIII and *Kedara* III, Macauliffe, op. cit., vol. VI, pp. 143, 147, 256, respectively.
40. *Kabir Granthawali*, ed. P.N. Tiwari, *sakhi* 12-15, p. 178.
41. Macauliffe, op. cit., p. 139.
42. *Kabir Granthawali*, ed. P.N. Tiwari, *sakhi* 9, p. 166.
43. Quoted by Verma, op. cit., p. 27.
44. Kabir, *rekhta* no. 22 and *Siddharta Dipika* 15, quoted by Tara Chand, op. cit., pp. 161-2.
45. *Siddharta Dipika* 14, as cited in ibid., p. 162.
46. G.H. Wescott, *Kabir and the Kabirpanth*, 2nd edn., Calcutta, Susil Gupta, 1953, p. 29, fn. 3.

47. Tara Chand, op. cit., p. 151.
48. *Gauri* VII, Macauliffe, op. cit., vol. VI, p. 146.
49. For these references, see Kabir *sloks* CXLIX, LXXI, and LV, ibid., pp. 301, 289, 286.
50. *Kabir Granthawali*, ed. P.N. Tiwari, *sakhi* 33-4, p. 241; also *Kabir Granthawali*, ed. Shyam Sundardas, *sakhi* 18-1, p. 29.
51. For these references, see *Kabir Granthawali*, ed. P.N. Tiwari, *sakhis* 15-33, p. 190; 15-16, p. 187; and 15-75, p. 195.
52. Tara Chand, op. cit., p. 161.
53. See the passage cited by Westcott, op. cit., pp. 15-16.
54. J.N. Farquhar, *An Outline of the Religious Literature in India*, rpt. Delhi, Motilal Banarsidass, 1984, p. 284.
55. For this and other such references, see Hazari Prasad Dwivedi, *Sant Kabir*, *sakhis* 12-2, 24-20, pp. 21, 31.
56. For details of Kabir's ideas about politics and government, see Iraqi, op. cit., pp. 154-7.
57. Tara Chand, op. cit., p. 165.

CHAPTER 6

Sheikh Farid Bukhari's Relations with Some Contemporary *Ulama*

MOHAMMAD UMAR

Shaikh Farid Bukhari was one of the nobles of the court of Akbar. By the 30th regnal year of Akbar's reign he rose to the rank of 700, and after ten years was given the rank of 1500. He was also appointed *Mir Bakhshi*. Due to the incompetence of the *Divan-i-Tan*, for some time Bukhari also held charge of that department and distributed *jagirs*.[1]

During the reign of Jahangir, he rose to prominence as he rendered meritorious services to the emperor at the very outset of his rule. Though in the beginning he was in collusion with Raja Man Singh[2] and Mirza Aziz Koka[3] in the conspiracy to enthrone Prince Khusrau after Akbar, he later decided to support Jahangir.[4] He came out of the fort with his contingent, and congratulated Jahangir as emperor. Jahangir confirmed him in the post of *Mir Bakhshi* and conferred on him the title of *sahibu-s-saif wa-qalam*, and promoted him to the rank of 5000.[5]

Shaikh Farid successfully suppressed the rebellion of Prince Khusrau. In reward, the title of Murtaza Khan was conferred upon him and he was appointed governor of Gujarat[6] and subsequently sent to Punjab on the same post.[7] He died in AD 1616[8] and was mourned by Jahangir.[9] He left nothing but 1,000 *ashrafis* in cash.[10]

During his governorship of Gujarat, Shaikh Farid constructed the *sarais* and the mosques in the city of Ahmedabad and named the city as Bukhara. Besides, he built a mosque and a grand building on the grave of Shaikh Wajihuddin. He used to make great efforts to provide financial aid to the old families and no one was left out from his patronage. He got prepared a list of the Saiyads, women, old men, children, and even the pregnant women living in Gujarat and fixed for them daily allowances. For the marriage of the daughters of the poor a fixed amount was kept aside which was to be used when they grew to marriageable age. Shaikh Farid Bhakkari writes that during 1626-7, this money was utilized for the assigned purpose in Gujarat.[11]

Shaikh Farid Bhakkari says that Shaikh Farid Bukhari was adorned with inward and outward excellence. He was well known for his generosity. Anyone who approached him for any kind of help never returned disappointed. On his way to court, he used to distribute garments, sheets and shoes, money and *ashrafis* to the poor and the needy.[12]

According to Shaikh Farid Bhakkari, his generosity benefited the whole of Hindustan. The Sheikh provided financial help to the *dervishes* who lived in their *khanqahs* reposing trust in divine help. Thereafter he took care of the Sufis, the people of noble families, wealthy men, destitute and those widows whose husbands had died during their service. According to their status, their *wazifahs* (pension or stipend) were fixed. The sons of men who served him and died in harness, were adopted by him. The helpless people of noble descent, the widows whose husbands got *wazifah* for their maintenance were also taken care of. Whenever he sat in his office, these children were found around him like his sons. Whatever they asked for was provided to them.[13]

In his own *jagir*, the Shaikh had given away *madad-i-ma'ash* lands to such an extent that the income of a whole *pargana* was distributed in a way of salary. For some deserving men *madad-i-ma'ash* grants were made, to some six monthly, for others annual stipends were fixed. Whether they were present or absent, without showing the *sanads*, they were paid the amounts.[14]

In Delhi, Ahmedabad, Faridabad, Lahore and wherever else he went, the Shaikh built *bazars*, *mosques*, *sarais*, *katras*, and *khanqahs*, where travellers could stay without paying rent. The salaries of the caretakers were paid from the income of the shops built around those buildings. Wherever he built mosques, he appointed an *imam*, *mu'ezzin* and a sweeper. The income of the *bazars* was reserved for their salaries.[15]

On the authority of his father, Shah Abdur Rahim, Shah Waliullah records that Shaikh Farid had constructed a mosque in Delhi for the use of the general people. On its completion, he arranged a banquet, inviting the Sufis and the *masha'ikh* of the city.[16] He decorated the inner parts of the shrine of Shaikh Nizamuddin Auliya.[17]

Shaikh Farid Bukhari never constructed any *haveli* (house) of his own because he thought of himself as always on a journey. It is recorded that 'From the time of Akbar to the reign of Jahangir, he never entered a dwelling house (of his own). He always passed his nights in a camp.'[18]

After describing Shaikh Farid Bukhari's virtues and pious deeds, Shaikh Farid Bhakkari also records his frailties. He drank wine before meals as prescribed by his physicians; besides, he was very revengeful and cruel to the peasants.[19]

Shaikh Farid Bukhari was endowed with a sensitive heart and impressive mind. He felt great and ardent devotion and attachment to the *masha'ikh* and the pious *ulama*. Mutamad Khan remarks, 'Inward and outward life (of Shaikh Farid) was abundantly pure, chaste, and orderly. Greatness and wealth got respect and honour due to him not because he was honoured on account of his greatness and wealth.'[20]

The Shaikh used to take interest in religious matters, and it seems, in spite of his daily routine engagements, he spared time in his own way for this work. The *ulama* and the *masha'ikh* of the period, realizing his religious inclinations and sentiments, fully appreciated his financial help to them and honoured him.

The *ulama* and the *masha'ikh* had selected some religious-minded nobles to seek their cooperation in the task to eradicate prevailing unhealthy religious conditions of the Muslim community during the sixteenth century. Shaikh Farid Bukhari was one of them. Khwaja Baqi Billah (1564-1603) had received commendable support from him in propagating the teachings of the Naqshbandi *silsilah* and strengthening it in India during the last days of Akbar's reign. Sheikh Abdul Haqq appealed to his high sense of honour and religious sentiments, so that he should lend his assistance for the revival of the *sunna* and the restoration of Islamic law. In the same way Shaikh Ahmad Sirhindi sought cooperation from him for his mission relating to the reform of Muslim society. It was due to his cooperation in the task of the welfare of the people that Shaikh Farid was held in great esteem by the *ulama* and the Sufis of the period.

In his letters to Shaikh Farid, Khwaja Baqi Billah addressed him with such epithets as *qibla-gahi salamat bashund*. In an assembly of his disciples, the Khwaja said, 'The Shaikh (Farid) has many rights on us, and due to his grace and existence we have enjoyed great spiritual pleasures.'[21]

Among the nobles of Akbar's court, Khan Azam Mirza Aziz Koka, Qulij Khan,[22] Qutbuddin Mohammad Khan,[23] Shahbaz Khan[24] and others were well known in the circles of the *ulama* and *masha'ikh* for their religiosity and piety. But Shaikh Farid was conspicuous among them, for the help which he rendered to the saints of the Naqshbandi *silsilah* had a deep impact on the religious history of medieval India.

On the other hand, some of the worldly *ulama* and *masha'ikh* and the so-called rationalists like Shaikh Mubarak, Shaikh Abul Fazl, Shaikh Faizi, Haji Ibrahim Sirhindi,[25] and Mulla Sa'id[26] were mainly responsible for creating some ideological confusion which was adversely affecting the religious unity of the Muslims. In general the nobles kept themselves aloof from intellectual exercises in the sphere of religion. Hence, men like Mullah Mohammad Yazdi,[27] made great sacrifices for their protests against some of the administrative measures of Akbar which directly clashed with the religious sentiments of the Muslims. While a majority of the nobles yielded to the pressure of the court, and accepted certain newly established customs and practices, some like Shahbaz Khan Kambo, Qutbuddin Mohammad Khan and Khan Azam Mirza Aziz Koka courageously warned the king against interference in religious affairs. When this bore no fruit, they utilized their influence to counter unhealthy trends of the period that were flourishing under the patronage of Akbar, and prevented them filtering down into the lower strata of Muslim society.

In short, it is very clear from the letters of Shaikh Ahmad Sirhindi (1564-1624) and the theological works of Shaikh Abdul Haqq (1551-1642) that they made concerted efforts to counter those administrative measures of Akbar that were sapping the very foundation of the socio-religious unity of the Muslims. Both of them received help from Shaikh Farid Bukhari on their mission.

An attempt has been made in this article to examine critically whether or not there existed any kind of relationship between Shaikh Farid and Shaikh Abdul Haqq and Shaikh Ahmad Sirhindi.

SHAIKH ABDUL HAQQ AND SHAIKH FARID BUKHARI

The letters which Shaikh Abdul Haqq had written to Shaikh Farid reveal a cordial friendship based on sincerity. These letters have been preserved in the *Kitab-al-Makatib-al-Rasail.*

Every word of these letters bears significance if they are studied in the light of the then prevailing situation. These letters not only throw very interesting and useful light on the relationship but also on contemporary socio-religious tensions. If we presume that most of those letters were written during the reign of Akbar, the critical situation emerges.

In his first letter to him, Shaikh Abdul Haqq laid emphasis on three principles regarding man's attitude towards his religious faith. Ardent longing was to be developed for the realization of God; the vices and virtues of all action were to be kept in mind; and harmony was to be developed between inward and outward actions. Then he explained to him the inherent meaning of the term *talab-i-sadiq* (real desire).[28]

Shaikh Abdul Haqq reminded him that there was no time to remain idle, whatever he could do, he should do it in time, not considering it a trivial task. God had fixed rewards for each and every work.[29]

In another letter he drew the attention of Shaikh Farid to the fact that there were two arms of the *din* (faith). Respect for the command of God and magnanimity towards the creatures of God were essential. After explaining the importance of these terms, he said,

> The importance assigned to the respect for the command of God is higher, but lending support to the propagation of the commands of the faith is even higher than that. In that task he (Shaikh Farid) should exert to the best of his ability and lend full support to this cause . . . even if he finds himself surrounded by an army of the opponents. God would provide him help from others.[30]

Whatever hopes Shaikh Abdul Haqq had pinned on the nobles in the cause of strengthening of the arms of *din*, he explained them explicitly in the above passage. The sincerity of the friendship may be gauged from the letter which Shaikh Abdul Haqq wrote to Shaikh Farid inquiring about his health after an indisposition. 'Praise be to God! Due to the good fortune of the *faqirs* and *dervishes*, and the prayers of (your) sincere well-wishers, you have recovered within a short period. Your self is an asset and your blessed existence is a mystery of God.'[31]

In another letter he acknowledged his gratitude to him.[32] Sometimes Shaikh Abdul Haqq wrote to him about the needs of the people and about his own affairs.[33]

Sheikh Abdul Haqq did not believe in criticizing others openly for their lapses, but he expressed his views and objectives in subdued tones, while Shaikh Ahmad Sirhindi was straightforward in expressing his objectives and views.

The letter which Shaikh Abdul Haqq had written to Shaikh Farid after Akbar's death shows the confidence in which he was held. This letter also helps us to dispel the impression that a noble of Shaikh Farid's stature could have cordial relations with critics of his patron-king's administrative policies. In this letter Shaikh Abdul Haqq had pointed out the acts of omission of Akbar and at the same time had warned his successor (Jahangir) not to follow that path. This letter is very significant. With other contemporary sources it gives a clear indication regarding Shaikh Abdul Haqq's reactions to Akbar's interference in the religious matters of the Muslim community.[34]

However, during the reign of Shahjahan, Shaikh Abdul Haqq's contributions to the dissemination of religious education were highly appreciated,[35] and his son, Shaikh Nurul Haqq, an eminent scholar, was appointed as a *qazi* of Agra. He died in AD 1662.[36]

SHEIKH AHMAD SIRHINDI AND SHAIKH FARID

The letters of Shaikh Ahmad Sirhindi addressed to Shaikh Farid indicate their relations was intimate. Had it not been so, he would have not ventured to so frankly open his heart to him, or taken the liberty to compare him with a 'soft-bodied beloved', who felt injured even by the touch of a gentle breeze.[37] Moreover, he had deferred his pilgrimage since he could not personally consult Shaikh Farid in this regard. In his letter, Shaikh Ahmad Sirhindi informed him of the reasons for this postponement.[38]

In another letter Shaikh Ahmad communicated to Shaikh Farid that whether he was in his attendance or not, he was always busy praying for his welfare and prosperity. Shaikh Ahmad considered himself as one of the well-wishers of Shaikh Farid.[39]

Shaikh Ahmad wrote 23 letters in all to Shaikh Farid—the largest number to a noble. Most of these have been preserved in the first volume of the *Maktubat* published in 1617. Some of the letters of this volume were written during the reign of Jahangir. Since Shaikh Farid died in AD 1616, we do not find any letter in his name in the second and third volumes, published in 1619 and 1622 respectively.

Most of the letters written by Shaikh Ahmad were replies to letters he had either received directly or indirect messages conveyed through the letters that Shaikh Farid had written to some of his companions.

In his letters, Shaikh Ahmad had expressed high regard for Shaikh Farid, not only because he was one of the great nobles of the Mughal court, but also because he was a great patron of the *ulama* and *masha'ikh*. Moreover, Shaikh Farid was one of the descendants of the Prophet. On this account too, he had rendered great services to the Naqshbandi *silsilah* in India.[40] Shaikh Ahmad stressed time and again that he should play his role in the restoration of the heritage of his great ancestor, the founder of Islam, at a time when it was not receiving due attention from the ruling classes.

Certain plausible objections have been raised regarding the relations of Shaikh Farid with Shaikh Ahmad Sirhindi. The following points have been stressed. Did Shaikh Ahmad enjoy any influence over Shaikh Farid? Did Shaikh Farid ever take Shaikh Ahmad's advice? There is no proof that Shaikh Farid received those letters at all, or, at least in the form we have them now. It seems difficult to believe that such a high official of the Empire dared to entertain such letters which spoke in abusive terms of the reigning king's father? Shaikh Farid commissioned Ilahdad Faizi Sirhindi to write a history of Akbar's reign till 1601 but he did not refer to Shaikh Ahmad Sirhindi.[41] Let us consider each of these points.

The subject and nature of the letters to Shaikh Farid show that Shaikh Ahmad Sirhindi enjoyed the full confidence of the addressee and had a considerable influence over him. It is best to remember, as referred earlier, that Shaikh Farid was on intimate terms with Khwaja Baqi Billah for whom he had fixed daily allowances when he was the Governor of Lahore.[42] Later, when the Khwaja came to Delhi, Shaikh Farid continued those provisions for him and his close followers in the *khanqah*. The Khwaja's relations with Shaikh Farid were such that his critics pointed out the success which the Naqshbandi *silsilah* had achieved in India was due to Shaikh Farid's patronage.[43] It is recorded in the *malfuzat* of Khwaja Baqi Billah that 'Some block-headed and short-sighted people allege that the basis for the *Shaikhdom* of the Khwaja was his friendship with Shaikh Farid whom he addresses as *qibalah gahi salamat bashund*. On the part of a saint such a kind of flattery is unbecoming.' The Khwaja replied, 'Shaikh Farid had many rights over us and due to his blessed existence we have enjoyed great spiritual benefits. Even now we do not find any injunction of the *shar* to sever the friendship.'[44]

Shaikh Farid continued to patronize the Naqshbandi *silsilah* even after the death of Khwaja Baqi Billah. Shaikh Ahmad had written a letter to Shaikh Farid after the Khwaja's death. As a result of Shaikh Farid's close and sincere association with the Naqshbandi *silsilah* his relations with Shaikh Ahmad would have been very close as he became the head of the *silsilah* after the death of Khwaja Baqi Billah.[45]

Since the letters which Shaikh Farid had written to Shaikh Ahmad have not yet been discovered, there is no evidence to show that he had in fact written to him. It is the letters of Shaikh Ahmad Sirhindi that furnish information suggesting that Shaikh Farid did receive letters from Shaikh Ahmad Sirhindi that he acknowleged them, directly or indirectly. It seems that Shaikh Farid had invited Shaikh Ahmad to meet him, but the latter preferred to meet him after *Ramazan*.[46] Shaikh Ahmad wrote to Shaikh Farid recommending that Maulana Hamid be paid his stipend in the same way as he had received the previous year.[47] This letter is important because Shaikh Ahmad had desired that he should work for the restoration of Islamic laws in the state and pull Muslims out of their wretched condition. There is a letter in reply to the message Shaikh Farid had sent to Shaikh Ahmad through his letter to Maulana Qulich that some money was being sent for the distribution among the *ulama* and the *sufis*.[48] In another letter Shaikh Ahmad suggested to Shaikh Farid that authentic books like those of Makhdum Jahanniyan[49] be read in his assemblies.[50] After telling Shaikh Farid that he could not meet him because he had already left Delhi for a campaign, Shaikh Ahmad informed him in a letter that he was busy praying for his well-being.[51]

Many events indicate that the nobles, if they found their stand was justified, could ignore the wishes and pressure of the emperor. This aspect of the character of the Mughal nobility requires to be thoroughly investigated. Shaikh Farid gave shelter to Hakim Ali Gilani who had been charged with causing the death of Akbar due to a wrong prescription during his last illness. Jahangir and the women of the *haram* were angry and the Hakim went to the camp of Shaikh Farid to seek shelter.[52] So if Shaikh Farid could provide shelter to an alleged killer of the king, what prevented him from acknowledging letters from Shaikh Ahmad? After his accession to the throne, Jahangir had deputed Shaikh Farid to conduct some important affairs of the state, and till his death in 1616, Jahangir had never expressed any doubt about his loyalty. On Shaikh Farid's death, he expressed his grief about the loss of such a loyal servant of the state.

On the death of Akbar, as pointed out earlier, Shaikh Abdul Haqq had written to Shaikh Farid and instructed him to show the letter to Jahangir, although it contained criticism of Akbar.[53]

Shaikh Farid was not an exception, some other important nobles of the reigns of Akbar and Jahangir had been in close and intimate contact with Shaikh Ahmad Sirhindi and Shaikh Abdul Haqq, both of whom were considered severe critics of some of the administrative measures of Akbar. Both of them had written letters to Qulij Khan Andjani,[54] whose daughter was married to Daniyal, the eldest son of Akbar. Abdul Rahim Khan Khanan[55] (d. AD 1627), Aziz Koka Muhammad Khan 'Azam (d. AD 1624),[56] Sadr Jahan,[57] Fathullah Shirazi,[58] Khwaja Jahan[59] and Darab Khan were among the other important nobles.[60]

The loyalty of Abul Fazl and Shaikh Faizi to Akbar is beyond doubt, but even then both the brothers maintained contacts with Shaikh Ahmad and Shaikh Abdul Haqq, while they were staying in Fatehpur Sikri.[61] Shaikh Faizi had intense love for Shaikh Abdul Haqq as is evidenced from his letters to him.[62] When Shaikh Faizi was occupied in compiling his *Tafsir-i-Sawat al Iham,* his greatest desire was 'to send the manuscript at the earliest' to Shaikh Abdul Haqq because 'the knowledge of my friend is very deep and exhaustive'.

When he did not receive a reply for long, Shaikh Faizi wrote, 'It is long since that the gentle breeze has not come from that direction to this direction. May the hurdle disappear, and you be in the security of God.'[63]

In another letter Shaikh Faizi addressed Shaikh Abdul Haqq as *mahabbat panaha* (the refuge of love).[64] On the other hand, Shaikh Abdul Haqq took up the cudgels for his deviation from the right path and his impudent remarks about Muslims.[65] Shaikh Abdul Haqq addressed a letter to Shaikh Faizi under the caption, *tasbiyat al qadam ali al astabar tabarak suhbat al azad wa al-aghiyar.*[66] Even so, Shaikh Faizi had expressed his keen desire to meet Shaikh Abdul Haqq.[67]

In fact, two historical works were written at the instance of Shaikh Farid. Shaikh Nur al-Haqqi, son of Shaikh Abdul Haqq, after making certain additions to the history of his father, the *Tarikh-i-Haqqi,* completed his own work, *Zabdat al Tawarikh,*[68] which contains severe criticism of Akbar.[69]

The scope of Shaikh Alahdad Faizi Sirhindi's work was limited. According to the instructions of Shaikh Farid, he was to record those military campaigns of Akbar which he had personally conducted, and the military achievements of some of his nobles.[70] The author was under such strict limitations that he did not record in detail, the acts of generosity and piety of Shaikh Farid.

It is a fact that Shaikh Ahmad finds no mention in the contemporary chronicles[71] but it is very significant that the emperor not only mentions his name but also says, 'Shaikh Ahmad of Sirhind . . . had sent into every city and country one of his disciples, whom he called *khalifah*.'[72]

Dara Shukoh spoke about him with great respect. He not only defended Shaikh Ahmad against the charges[73] levelled by his opponents, but exonerated him by saying those charges were trumped up and were unfounded.[74]

The absence of Shaikh Ahmad's name in the contemporary historical literature is not of any significance. We do not find any reference to either Khwaja Moinuddin Chishti or Khwaja Qutbuddin Bakhtiyar Kaki in the contemporary historical literature. The answer will be negative.[75]

Was it possible for a man like Shaikh Ahmad Sirhindi, very conscious of his integrity and unyielding before the Mughal throne, to have written letter after letter to a person without getting any acknowledgement? Since Shaikh Ahmad had written about two dozen letters to Shaikh Farid. Apart from the evidences available in his letters, it is correct to say that Shaikh Farid did receive those letters and acknowledged them.[76]

It is also contended that the original letters might have been somewhat different from those in published form. It is suspected that some additions and deletions were made in the phraseology and contents of the letters. It is to be remembered that all the three volumes had been published between 1616 and 1622. Shaikh Farid had already died in 1616 and he was not there to object to any changes. But Aziz Koka (d. 1624) and Abdur Rahim Khan Khanan (d. 1627) could, without any inhibition contradict and disown the published letters. The originals would have been with them and, if they were afraid of the emperor, they could easily compare the originals with those that appeared in the published form.

It is also to be remembered that in 1619,[77] Jahangir had incarcerated Shaikh Ahmad but had set him free after a year. Shaikh Ahmad opted to stay with the Imperial camp.[78] During his stay in the imperial camp, the Shaikh had several private meetings with the emperor. In a letter to Khwaja Ma'sum, his son, the Shaikh described his conversations with the emperor.

> The conversations which were carried on in the assemblies of the *sultan*, praise be to God! all were very commendable. Affairs and gestures of this side are worthy for the prolongation of the conversations. Meetings are

wonderful (*'ajib-wa-gharib*). Due to the grace of God, in these conversations there is no slightest negligence or dissimulation concerning the affairs of the *din* and the cardinal principles of Islam. The same phraseology that I generally used in my private and special gatherings, with the grace of God, I have used in these meetings. If I write an account of a *majlis*, it would become a book. Especially tonight, on the 17 *Ramazan*, the conversation covered such issues as the mission of the Prophet, the instability of *aql* (intellect), faith in the *akhirat* (the invisible world), reward and punishment therein; proof of the vision of God; the cessation of the Prophethood with Prophet Muhammad; appearance of a *Mujaddid* at the end of the millennium; imitation of the practices of the *Khulfa-i-Rashidin* (Pious Caliphs); the propagation of the traditions of the Prophet; false notions regarding the transmigration of soul; covering demons, punishments and rewards to them, and other matters relating to them, were discussed in detail. The Emperor patiently listened my discourses. Similarly, matters about the *aqtab*, *abdal*, *autad* and peculiarities of so and so came under discussion. Praise be to God! He (the emperor) remained sitting unmoved, and no change was perceptible in his posture or on his face. God was a witness to these meetings.[79]

Jahangir continued to write his *Memoirs* up to 1624, but did not mention these meetings with the Shaikh. The publicity of these letters must have been disappointing to some of the favourite courtiers of the emperor, who were against Shaikh Ahmad and were responsible for his earlier imprisonment, but none among them came forward to refute the claims of the Shaikh. The third volume not only contained a letter about the emperor himself, and could be interpreted one way or the other, it also divulged the nature of his conversations with the Shaikh. Had there been any interpolation or an iota of falsehood, Jahangir could not have so easily and silently swallowed such on allegation about himself.

Hence on the basis of the evidences furnished by the letters of the Shaikh and the circumstances, the authenticity of the contents of the letters is beyond doubt. The objection regarding possible interpolations in those letters needs to be substantiated by positive evidences.

A significant fact that has generally been ignored deserves our attention. In 1623, after he set Shaikh Ahmad free, Jahangir gave him Rs. 2,000 on the occasion of the 18th anniversary of his rule,[80] which he accepted without any hesitation. The remaining amount was distributed among the needy persons and the beggars. This gesture of the emperor strengthens the view that since 1620, Shaikh Ahmad was on cordial terms with Jahangir and there is no evidence in the *Memoirs* to show that the Shaikh's relations with him were lacking in cordiality. Between 1620 and 1624, Jahangir observed complete silence about the activities of the Shaikh. This shows that he bore him no ill will.

Shaikh Ahmad was impressed by the treatment Jahangir meted out to him in 1620 on the occasion of his release. Perhaps it was during this period that he wrote a letter to the emperor drawing his attention towards his obligations to his religion. He told him that Islamic laws were to be given due consideration and that in the name of *faqr* (asceticism) and with the hope that my benedictions may be accepted, I do not find myself indifferent to offering of the prayers for the stability and prosperity of the mighty empire.[81]

In short, the letters of Shaikh Abdul Haqq and Shaikh Ahmad addressed to Shaikh Farid provide us ample evidence to show that the emperor's relations with the two principal *ulama* of the time were close and intimate. But it is not possible to determine the magnitude of the influence they had on him.

NOTES

1. Mutamad Khan, *Iqbal Nama-i-Jahangiri*, Lucknow, Nawal Kishore, AH 1286, p. 512. For biographical notices see, Abul Fazl, *Ain-i-Akbari* (Eng. tr.), vol. I, H. Blockmann, ed. S.L. Goomer, Delhi, Adesh Book Depot, 2nd edn., 1965, no. 99, pp. 454-8; Shaikh Farid Bhakkari, *Zakhirat-ul Khawanin*, ed. Saiyad Moinul Haqq, Karachi, Pakistan Historical Society, 1961, vol. I, pp. 126-48; Shah Nawaz Khan, *Ma'asirul Umara*, Eng. tr. H. Beveridge, ed. Baini Prashad, 2 vols., Patna, Janaki Prakashan, 1979, vol. I, pp. 521-7.
2. *Ma'asirul Umara*, Eng. tr., vol. II, pt. I, pp. 48-57; *Zakhirat-ul Khawanin*, I, p. 240.
3. *Ain-i-Akbari*, Eng. tr., vol. I, no. 21 pp. 343-7; *Zakhirat-ul Khawanin*, I, pp. 81-2.
4. *Ma'asirul Umara*, Eng. tr., vol. I, p. 327; *Zakhirat-ul Khawanin*, vol. I, pp. 127-8.
5. Nuruddin Muhammad Jahangir, *Tuzuk-i-Jahangiri*, Eng. tr. Alexander Rogers and H. Beveridge, Delhi, Munshiram Manoharlal, 1978, 2 vols., p. 13; *Iqbal Nama-i-Jahangiri*, p. 512.
6. *Iqbal Nama-i-Jahangiri*, p. 516; *Zakhirat-ul Khawanin*, vol. I, op. cit., pp. 136-8.
7. *Tuzuk-i-Jahangiri*, Eng. tr., vol. I, p. 178.
8. Ibid., p. 324; *Ain-i-Akbari*, Eng. tr., vol. I, op. cit., p. 456; *Zakhirat-ul Khawanin*, vol. I, p. 137.
9. Jahangir paid a tribute to Shaikh Farid Bukhari for his loyalty. 'I was much grieved in mind at this news; in truth, grief at the death of a loyal follower

is only reasonable. As he had died after spending his days in loyalty, I prayed to God her pardon for him', *Tuzuk-i-Jahangiri*, vol. I, op. cit., pp. 324-5.

10. *Zakhirat-ul-Khawanin*, vol. I, op. cit., p. 137.
11. Ibid.
12. Ibid., p. 140.
13. Ibid., p. 138.
14. Shah Waliullah, *Anfasul Arifin*, Delhi, Matba Ahmadi, 1897, pp. 182-3.
15. Shaikh Mohammad Ikram, *Rud-i-Kausar*, Lahore, Firoz and Sons, 1958, pp. 182-3.
16. *Zakhirat-ul-Khawanin*, vol. I, p. 141.
17. Ibid., vol. I, pp. 145-6; *Iqbal Nama-i-Jahangiri*, p. 512.
18. *Iqbal Nama-i-Jahangiri*, p. 512.
19. *Kalamat-i-Taiyabat*, ed. Ahmad Moradabadi, Matba Matlaul Ulum, Moradabad, 1891, p. 82.
20. *Iqbal Nama-i-Jahangiri*, p. 512.
21. *Ain-i-Akbari*, Eng. tr., vol. I, no. 28, pp. 197-231, 233.
22. Ibid., no. 42, pp. 380-2.
23. He was proverbial for his piety and his enormous wealth. His opposition to Akbar's. New Faith has been recorded on page 197 (*Ain-i-Akbari*, vol. I, Eng. tr.) 'The Emperor tried hard to convert Qutbuddin Muhammad Khan and Shahbaz Khan and several others. But they staunchly objected'. Qutbuddin Khan said, 'What would the kings of the West, as the sultan of Constantinople, say, if he heard all this. Our faith is the same, whether a man hold high or broad views'. His Majesty then asked him, if he was in India on a secret mission from Constantinople, as he showed so much opposition; or if he wished to keep a small place warm for himself, should he once go away from India, and be a respectable man there; he might go at once. Shahbaz got excited, and took a part in the conversation; and when Bir Bar—that hellish dog—made a sneering remark at our religion, Shahbaz abused him roundly, and said, 'you cursed infidel, do you talk in this manner? It would not take me long to settle you'. It got quite uncomfortable when His Majesty said to Shahbaz in particular, and to others in general, 'Would that a shoeful of excrements were thrown into your faces'. *Ain-i-Akbari* (2nd edn.), Delhi, Oriental Reprint Corporation, 1977, vol. I, pp. 197-8.
24. *Ain-i-Akbari*, Eng. tr., vol. I, no. 80, pp. 436–40.
25. *Ain-i-Akbari*, Eng. tr., vol. I, pp. 111, 180, 183, 198, 617; Badauni, *Muntakhab-ut-Tawarikh*, Eng. tr., vol. II, pp. 175-90, 191, 205, 212, 213, 214, 216, 285.
26. *Muntakhab-ut-Tawarikh*, Eng. tr., vol. II, p. 45.
27. Ibid., Eng. tr., vol. II, pp. 214, 270, 271, 284, 285, 297. He had issued a *fatwa* insisting on the duty of taking the field and rebellion against the emperor. The consequence was that Muhammad Masum Kabuli,

Muhammad Masum Khan Faran Khudi, Mir Muizul Mulk, Niyabat Khan and Arab Bahadur, etc., fought some desperate battles. Badauni, Eng. tr., vol. II, pp. 276-8.

28. *Kitabul Makatib*, p. 74.
29. Ibid., p. 76.
30. Ibid., p. 161.
31. Ibid., p. 111.
32. Ibid., p.112.
33. Ibid., p. 102.
34. See the text of the letter in K.A. Nizami, *Hayat-i-Shaikh Abdul Haqq Muhaddis Dehlavi*, Delhi, Nadvatul Musannafeen, 1964, pp. 378-85.
35. Abdul Hamid Lahori, *Badshah Nama*, ed. Maulavi Kabiruddin Ahmad and Maulavi Abdul Rahim, Calcutta, 1867, vol. I, pt. II, pp. 341-2; Muhammad Salih Kamboo, *Amal-i-Salih*, vol. III, Lahore, Majlis Taraqqi-i-Adab, 1960, pp. 377-8.
36. *Amal-i-Salih*, vol. III, p. 378. He died at the age of 90 in 1662 and was buried in the tomb of his father near the grave of Khwaja Qutbuddin Bakhtiyar Kaki. Mir Ghulam Ali Azad Bilgrami, *Masirul Kiram*, ed. Abdullah Khan, *Matba Mufeedi-Am*, Agra, 1910, pp. 201-2.
37. *Maktubat-i-Imam-i-Rabbani*, Nawal Kishore Press, Lucknow, 1877, vol. I, Letter 233. *Yar nazuk badon az bad-i-hawa me runjad; Hamchun gulbar zy asayb-i-sala me runjad.*
38. *Maktubat*, vol. I, Letter 233, p. 248.
39. Ibid., vol. I, Letter 233, pp. 247-8.
40. *Gulzar-i-Abrar* (Urdu tr.), Agra, p. 477.
41. Irfan Habib, *The Political Role of Shaikh Ahmad Sirhindi and Shah Waliullah*, Proceeding of the Twenty-third Session, IHC, Aligarh, 1960, pt. I, Calcutta, 1961, pp. 12-13.
42. *Gulzar-i-Abrar*, op. cit., p. 477.
43. *Rud-i-Kausar*, op. cit., p. 191.
44. Ibid., p. 184, *Maktubat*, I, Letter 45.
45. *Maktubat*, I, Letters 45, 54.
46. Ibid., I, Letter 51, p. 68, also see, I, pp. 61-3.
47. Ibid., *Hamid ruqqa niyaz nama Maulana az sarkar iqbal asar wazifa darad, parsal neez ummid war amda ast.*
48. Ibid., I, pp. 66-7.
49. His name was Mir Saiyid Jalaluddin Bukhari, but popular among the masses as Makhdum-i-Jahaniyan Jahangast.
50. *Maktubat*, I, pp. 71-2, Letter 193.
51. Ibid., I, pp. 247-8.
52. *Rud-i-Kausar*, pp. 177-8.
53. *Hayat Shaikh Abdul Haqq Muhaddis Dehlavi*, op. cit., pp. 378-85.
54. He was very generous, ascetic and sincere to his faith. He was found

constantly occupied in theological studies. During the days of his governorship of Lahore, he used to spend one watch of the day in a *madrasa*, reading. *Zakhirat ul Khawanin*, I, pp. 172-5. Shaikh Ahmad Sirhindi treated him as his own son. *Maktubat*, I, Letters 73 and 74.

55. He adhered to the principles of his adopted faith but he was suspected of observing *taqiyya*. His sons were strict Sunnis. *Zakhirat-ul-Khawanin*, vol. I, pp. 31-63. *Maktubat* I, Letters 23, 62, 68, 69, 70, 191, 198, 214, 232, 268; vol. II, 8, 62, 66, and 125. Shaikh Ahmad in his letter (no. 68) discusses the contents of a letter which Abdur Rahim had written to him. It is also to be borne in mind that vol. II saw the light of the day in 1619, when Jahangir was emperor.
56. 'When Akbar sent for the Mirza in the 39th year, 1001/1592-3, he became suspicious of some evil intention and went off to the Hijaz. They say that as he could in no way accept the prostration to the king (*sijda*), the shaving off the beard and the other innovations which had become established at court, but in opposition to them kept on a long beard, he perceived that going to the Presence would be disagreeable and so wrote excuses. At last the king wrote in reply, 'You are making all these delays in coming; evidently the wool of your beard weighs heavily on you'. They say that the Mirza also wrote sharp and sarcastic things about the matter of religion, such as, 'Your Majesty has put Faizi and Abul Fazl in the place of Osman and 'Ali. Well, whom have you appointed in the room of the two Shaikhs'. *Ma'asirul Umara*, Eng. tr., I, pp. 325-6. For the reasons leading to the imprisonment of Aziz Koka, *Iqbal Nama-i-Jahangiri*, pp. 516-17, *Ain-i-Akbari*, Eng. tr., vol. I, no. 21, pp. 343-6, For Shaikh Ahmad Sirhindi's letter to him, see *Maktubat*, Letters 65 and 66, pp. 82-4.
57. *Maktubat*, vol. I, Letters 194 and 195.
58. Ibid., Letters 80 and 85, pp. 102-6 and 108-9.
59. Ibid., Letters 25, 72.
60. He was the eldest son of Abdur Rahim Khan Khanan. There is a letter of Shaikh Ahmad in his name. Ibid., no. 71, Jahangir had honoured him with a *Nadiri* and the next year he was promoted to a *mansab* of 5000 *zat*. For biographical notices, see *Zakhiral-ul-Khawanin*, vol. II, pp. 277-8.
61. For details, see *Hayat Shaikh Abdul Haqq Muhaddis Dehlavi*, pp. 421-2.
62. Faizi had written twenty letters to Shaikh Abdul Haqq. See *Hayat Shaikh Abdul Haqq Muhaddis Dehlavi*, pp. 345-77. For Mirza Nizamuddin (the author of *Tabaqat-i-Akbari*) to Shaikh Abdul Haqq, ibid., pp. 3348-9. He was a Mansabdar of 5000 during the reign of Akbar.
63. *Hayat Shaikh Abdul Haqq Muhaddi's Dehlavi*, Letter I, p. 340.
64. Ibid., Letter 4, p. 352.

65. Ibid., p. 243. Badauni, *Muntakhab-ut-Tawarikh* (Eng. tr.) Idarah-i-Adabiyat-i-Delhi (rpt., 1973), vol. III, p. 413.
66. *Makatib-al Rasail*, pp. 98-9.
67. *Hayati-i-Shaikh Abdul Haqq Muhaddis Dehlavi*, Letter 10.
68. Nurul Haqq Dihlawi, *Zibdat-ul-Tawarikh* (Rotograph no. 18), Department of History, Aligarh, AMU, ff. 4b-5a.
69. For details *Zabdat-ul-Tawarikh*, Eng. tr. Elliot and Dowson, *The History of India as Told by its Own Historians*, Allahabad, Kitab Mahal, 1st edn., 1964, vol. VI, pp. 189-91.
70. Shaikh Alahdad Faizi Sirhindi, *Akbarnamah* (Rotograph no. 163), Department of History AMU, Aligarh, ff. 6ab.
71. Two contemporary *Sufi Tazkiras* give an account of Shaikh Ahmad Sirhindi, *Gulzar-i-Akbar*, written about AD 1613 (Urdu tr.), pp. 477-80, Shaikh Abdul Haqq Muhaddis Dehlavi, *Akhbarul-Akhyar*, ed. Muhammad Abdul Ahad, Delhi, Matba Mujtabai, 1232 (AH 1914), pp. 323-6.
72. *Tuzuk-i-Jahangiri*, Eng. tr., II, pp. 91-2.
73. See the charges which compelled Jahangir to imprison the Shaikh in 1619, *Tuzuk-i-Jahangiri*, Eng. tr., I, p. 92.
74. Dara Shukoh, *Safinat-ul-Auliya*, Kanpur, Matba, Newal Kishore, 1884, pp. 197-8.
75. Minhajuddin Siraj, the author of *Tabaqat-i-Nasiri*, a contemporary of Baba Farid, does not refer to the saint at all.
76. *Maktubat* I, letter 44, p. 60, *Marhamat nama girami sami dar aghari az manah sharf warud yaft, ba mutafa'a musharraf gusht. Marhamat nama girami ky az ruwi wa mumtaz farmuda budund, bamutala's mazmun an musharraf gusht, Maktubat*, I, letter 52.
77. It seems that Jahangir had read the first volume of the letters in its published form. He must have specially read those letters which were in the names of his trusted nobles, *Tuzuk-i-Jahangiri*, Eng. tr., vol. II, p. 92.
78. Shaikh Ahmad Sirhindi's imprisonment created unrest among the people. *Tuzuk-i-Jahangiri*, Eng. tr., vol. II, pp. 92-3.
79. *Tuzuk-i-Jahangiri*, Eng. tr., vol. II, pp. 272-3.
80. *Maktubat*, III, letters 43 and 47, were addressed to the emperor. In the *Khazinat-ul-Asfiyah*, there is a detailed account of Shaikh Ahmad's meetings with Jahangir. Ghulam Sarwar, *Khazinat-ul-Asfiyah*, Kanpur, Newal Kishore, 1894, vol. I, pp. 607.
81. *Tuzuk-i-Jahangiri*, Eng. tr., vol. II, p. 276. 'Among those I gave Rs. 2,000 to him'.

CHAPTER 7

Akbar's Fort at Allahabad

ALI ATHAR

The Ilahabas or Allahabad Fort was founded by Akbar to utilize it as a military base for subduing the eastern Indian territories.[1] He viewed the site from the boat and only after satisfying himself with its strategic locale, he ordered the foundation of the fort city on the 2nd Azar 991 (mid-November 1583).[2]

Allahabad was one of the forts of Akbar's rapid constructional activities, who had already constructed the forts of Jaunpur, AD 1566; Ajmer 1570; Lahore 1580; and Attock 1581. All these forts were constructed with the idea of having a military base to check recalcitrant activity and assure consolidation of the empire. Akbar was fully involved in all the architectural projects and Allahabad was no exception. Abul Fazl informs us that Akbar planned four forts:

> In each he arranged lordly residences. The beginning (of the city) was the place where the rivers joined. In the first (fort) he fixed that there were to be twelve buildings. In every one there were delightful apartments. There was a garden which was the special private chambers of the Shahanshah. In the second, there was a place for the *begums* and the princes. In the third there were to be residences for the distant relatives and for personal attendants. The fourth was for soldiers and subjects. The engineers produced masterpieces, and in a short time the first (fort) was admirably completed. Everyone had a place suitable to his rank. In a short time a great city was established.[3]

The name of the architect is mentioned as Himmat Aali.[4]

Badauni adds that when Akbar visited the site, the *amirs* laid the foundations of a great building and it 'was determined that thenceforth that place should be the capital'.[5]

Abul Fazl's idea of four model forts does not seem feasible since there are no such examples existing of Akbar's architecture. The implied aspect of his version appears that a single fort incorporating all the buildings, like the palace, the *haram*, etc., was to be constructed. Its remains stand till today, although in a dilapidated condition.

The architectural features of the Allahabad Fort imbibe both domestic and Transoxanian features, i.e. trabeate or 'post and beam' structures, which is in conformity with the tradition of Akbari architecture. The fort was originally triangular in shape[6] and surrounded by massive walls made of red sandstone. It had three gateways. One opened to the Ganges in the east, the other to the Jamuna on the south and the third, the main gateway, on the land side.[7] The main gateway has a dome on top with the interiors decorated with beautiful stone carvings and frescoes (Fig. 7.1).[8] Peter Mundy has made a similar observation regarding the gate.[9]

William Finch gives important details of the fort in his account. He states that 20,000 people were initially employed in the construction of it and when he visited Allahabad, 5,000 men were still at work.[10]

The outer walls are of an admirable height, of red sand stone, like Agra castle; within which are two other walls nothing so high. You enter thorow

Fig. 7.1: The Interior of the West Gate to the Allahabad Fort by Seeta Ram, 1814-15 (British Library)

two faire gates into a faire court, in which stands a pillar of stone. . . . Passing this court you enter a lesse; beyond that a larger, where the king sits on high at his dersane to behold elephants and other beasts to fight. . . . Right under him within a vault are many pagodas. . . . Out of this court is another richly paved where the king keeps his derbar; beyond it another, whence you enter into a moholl large, divided into sixteen several lodgings for sixteen great women, with their slaves and attendants. In the middest of all, the kings' lodgings of three storeys each contayning sixteen rooms; in all eight and forty lodgings, all wrought over head with rich pargetting and curious paintings in all kind of colours. In the midst of the lowest storie is a curious tanke. . . . In the waters side within the moholl are divers large devoncons, where the king with his women often passé their times in beholding Gemini paying his tribute to Ganges. Between them and the waters side at the foot of the wall is a pleasant garden, shaded with cypress trees and abounding with excellent fruits and flowers, having in the midst a faire banqueting house, with privie staire to take boats.[11]

Peter Mundy describes the fort as:

An excellent faire castle, compleate one to beholde of red stone. As before the Principall Gate is a semi-circle, takeinge a great Compasse, in which are five other gates, where you must passé through (I meane one of them), before you come to the greate gate. It has faire battlements, adorned with a number of Copulaes (cupolas) small and great [Fig. 7.2]. It stands just in that poynt of land which the river Ganges and river Jamina (Jamna) doe

Fig. 7.2: A view of Allahabad Fort by William Hodges, 1787 (British Library)

make att their meetinge together, soe that 2 sides there of are washed with theis two rivers. Towards the waterside, without the walls, some seaven yards from the ground, there is built in the said Castle wall a verie faire stone gallerie for the people to pass round about the part that lyes in the water [Fig. 7.3].[12]

Among the structural remains of the Allahabad Fort is the *zanana* (harem) enclosure which is based on the model of the Ajmer Fort (1570). The *Khilwatgah-i-Khas* (Fig. 7.4) imitates the imperial pavilion of Fatehpur Sikri. It is built of red sandstone with sloping balconies with beautifully carved brackets and domed canopies. This rectangular structure is supported by excellent pillaring of the outer veranda. The inner hall is replaced by a 'block on nine-fold plan'. 'The vault over the central hall is the first transformation into sandstone of the Khurasanian vault type rendered in stucco in the Imperial Haram of Fatehpur Sikri.[13]

The *Challis Satun* (forty-pillared hall) (Fig. 7.5), was a continuation of the Mughals fancy for 'iwan' structures. The *Challis Satun* was preceded by the Panch Mahal at Fatehpur Sikri. Retaining the trabeate

Fig. 7.3: A view of Allahabad Fort from 'Illustrated London News' 1857

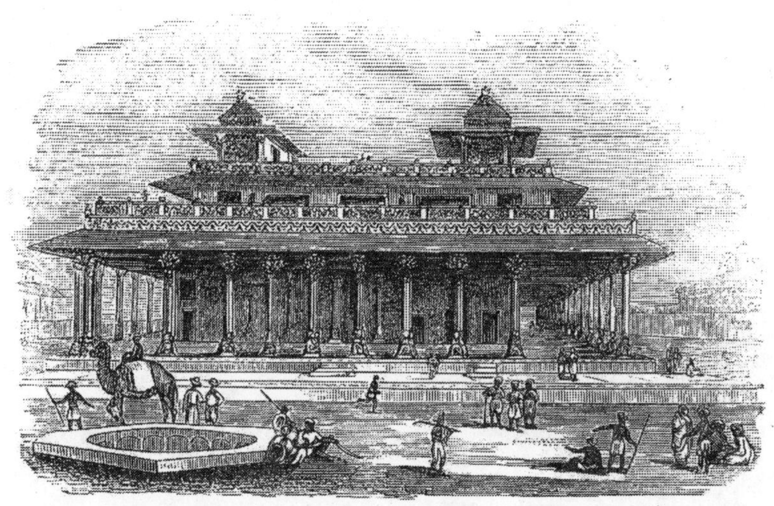

Fig. 7.4: Rani ka Mahal or *Khilwatgah-i-Khas* Mentioned as the Palace of Allahabad in an English history book, 1851. www.columbia.edu/allahabadfort.html

Fig. 7.5: 'Chaliss Satun' by Thomas Daniel, 1795 (British Library)

Fig. 7.6: View of Allahabad Fort, Robert Montgomery Martin, *The Indian Empire*, vol. 3, 1860. www.archive.org/details/indianempirehist03martuoft

stepped construction, the *Challis Satun* at Allahabad Fort was three-storeyed octagonal structure surmounted by a dome. It was constructed at the river front of the Jamuna (Fig. 7.6).[14]

Chroniclers of Akbar and Jahangir's reigns portray the fort of Allahabad as unrivalled. Finch remarks, 'it will be one of the most famous buildings of the world'.[15] An estimate of the expenditure incurred on the construction of the fort at Agra and the palace complex of Fatehpur Sikri as compared to the Allahabad Fort does show that though the Allahabad Fort was a major undertaking it did not in financial terms come anywhere near the Agra Fort, as shown below:

	Years taken to complete	Cost
Agra Fort	15-16	Rs. 35,00,000 = 14,00,00,000 dams[16]
Fatehpur Sikri	5	Rs. 16,00,000 = 6,00,00,000 dams[17]
Allahabad Fort	5	Rs. 12,00,000 = 4,80,00,000 dams[18]

Although Allahabad Fort was an important fort which was well planned and handsomely constructed, it served only as a seat for the governor of the province of Allahabad. Though initially as per Akbar's habit, his interest in its construction led to the erection of beautiful structures, his subsequent difficulties with Prince Salim, based in Allahabad, led him to lose interest in the for.

NOTES

1. Abul Fazl, *Akbar Nama*, ed. Maulvi Abdur Rahim, *Bib. Indica*, Calcutta, 1886, vol. III, pt. II, p. 415. The site was called Ilahabas, p. 88 and later Allahabad, p. 287, while referring to it as a *suba* it was again mentioned as Ilahabas, p. 327; and thence onwards Allahabad.

   Murtaza Husain Allahyar Usmani, *Hadiqat-al Aqalim*, Lucknow, Newal Kishore, 1879, contains information on Allahabad. In it is mentioned that Shah Jahan had coined the name Allahabad, p. 663.
2. Ibid., pp. 415-16. Abul Fazl also adds that since it was a place of pilgrimage for the Indian people (Hindus), Akbar thought it to be an ideal spot for the construction of a new city. *Akbar Nama*, vol. III, pt. II, p. 415.

   Abdur Qadir Badauni, *Muntakhab-ut Twarikh*, ed. W.N. Lees, *Bib. Indica*, Calcutta, 1864, Badauni writes that on 23rd of the month of *Safar* 982 Akbar laid the foundation of a great building and left the name of the city Allahabad, p. 176. On Akbar's pleasure trip to Allahabad in AH 991 (1583) the site was already a completed project, p. 334.
3. *Akbar Nama*, vol. III, pp. 415-16, Eng. tr. H. Beveridge, 1902-39, Delhi, Low Price Publication, vol. III, pp. 617-18.
4. Nizamuddin Ahmed, *Tabaqat-i-Akbari*, ed. B. De, *Bib. Indica*, Calcutta, 1931, vol. II, p. 286.
5. Badauni, op. cit., p. 335.
6. *Hadiqat-ul-Aqalim*, p. 663.
7. Ibid., p. 664.
8. *District Gazetteers of United Provinces*, Nainital, 1909, vol. 23, pp. 209-10.
9. *The Travels of Peter Mundy in Europe and Asia 1608-1667*, ed. Lt. Col. Sir R.C. Temple, vol. II, *Travels in Asia 1628-1634*, London, 1914, pp. 107-8.
10. William Foster, *Early Travels in India 1583-1619*, New Delhi, Oriental Books, rpt., 1985, p. 177.
11. Ibid., pp. 177-8.
12. *The Travels of Peter Mundy in Europe and Asia 1608-1667*, op. cit., pp. 107-8.
13. Ebba Koch, *Mughal Architecture*, Munich, Prestel-Verlag, 1991, p. 62; *District Gazetteers of the United Provinces*, vol. 23, pp. 209-10; Catherine B. Asher, *Architecture of Mughal India*, Cambridge, Cambridge University Press, 1993, p. 48; N.R. Farooqi, *Akbar's Ilahabas* in *Allahabad: Where*

the Rivers Meet, ed. Neelam Saran Gour, Mumbai, Marg, vol. 61, no. 1, September 2009, pp. 45-55.

14. The structure is preserved only in the painting of Thomas Daniel, 1795, British Library. The view from the river end is available in the painting of William Hodges, 1787. British Library and also in Robert Montgomery Martin, *The Indian Empire*, 1860 www.archive.org/details/indianempirehistory.martuoft. N.R. Farooqi wrongly ascribes it to be a surviving Mughal structure. *Akbar's Illahabas*, plate 4, p. 48.
15. Foster, op. cit., pp. 177.
16. *Tuzuk-i-Jahangiri*, ed. S. Ahmed, Aligarh, 1864, p. 2. Badauni, p. 74, has '3,00,00,000 money' (presumably *tankas*) calculated by S. Moosvi, to 6,00,00,000 *dams. The Economy of the Mughal Empire, c. 1595: A Statistical Study*, New Delhi, Oxford, 1987, p. 266, fn. 63a.
17. F. Pelsaert, *Chronicles*, Eng. tr. Brij Narain and S.R. Sharma, *A Contemporary Dutch Chronicle of Mughal India*, Calcutta, Susil Gupta India Ltd., 1957, p.18.
18. Ibid., p. 21, *Hadiqat-al-Aqalim* mentions the cost of construction of Allahabad Fort was Rs. 2 crore and some lakh, p. 663.

CHAPTER 8

Mughal Portraiture: An Underlying Relationship with the Renaissance Humanism in Art

S.P. VERMA

Portrait painting, widely practised in classical Indian art, flourished during Mughal era, blending Persian and European art traits those of India, but with a touch of originality. Mughal artists' special emphasis on the delineation of the characteristic details served as an essential basis in the formation and development of a definite style of portraiture. Babur's comment on the portraits done by Bihzad, 'Of the painters, one was Bihzad. His work was very dainty but he did not draw beardless faces well; he used greatly to lengthen the double chin (*ghab-ghab*), bearded faces he drew admirably', show the Mughal patrons conscious feeling for an exact rendering of the facial contours, or the likeness of an individual.[1] Babur's picturesque descriptions of individuals exemplify his preference for the most possible accuracy. For example, of his father Umar Shaikh Mirza, he writes in *Baburnama*:

> He was a short and stout, round-bearded and fleshy-faced person. He used to wear his tunic so very tight that to fasten the strings he had to draw his belly in and, if he let himself out after tying them, they often tore away. He had no choice in dress or food. He wound his turban in a fold (*dastar-pech*), all turbans were in four folds (*char-pech*) in those days; people wore them without twisting and let the ends hang down. In the heats and except in his Court, he generally wore the Mughal cap.[2]

His grandson Jahangir, too, gave precise description of an individual's appearance. Of his father, the emperor Akbar, he writes:

> In his august personal appearance he was of middle height, but inclining to be tall; he was of the hue of wheat; his eyes and eyebrows were black, and

his complexion rather dark than fair. He was lion-bodied, with a broad chest, and his hands and arms long. On the left side of his nose he had a fleshy mole, very agreeable in appearance; of the size of half a pea.[3]

These 'pen-pictures' suggest a definite attitude of the Mughal patrons towards life-like representations. In this context, the definition of picture (*taswir*), given by Abu'l Fazl, is relevant; Drawing the likeness of anything is called *taswir*.[4] It was Akbar himself, who in line with his genius for innovation and love of history (as witnessed by Abu'l Fazl's great historical work, the *Akbarnama*), commissioned the preparation of an album of portraits of his nobles.[5] So great was the anxiety of the Emperor for having authentic portraits that he especially sat for the painter who drew his likeness.[6]

A pictorial colophon of the MS *Khamsa* of Nizami (BM, Or. 12208, dated 1596-7, folio 325b) shows an artist Daulat executing the likeness of the scribe Abdur Rahim, seated before him.[7] In another instance, the MS *Masnavi* of Zafar Khan (RAS, dated 1662) contains a double-page illustration which shows an artist (Bishandas [?], as suggested by J.P. Losty) drawing the likenesses of the nobles present at Zafar Khan's court.[8] These pictorial evidences confirm that the Mughal artists drew the portraits of the individuals from life.

The album of portraits from Akbar's studio does not seem to have survived. Nevertheless, a good number of Mughal portraits from his time are known which fairly represent the achievements of the sixteenth-century artists.

Jahangir, too, like his father, had portraits made of his nobles, which he compiled in albums. This emerges from an anecdote narrated in the *Zakhiratu'l Khwanin*.[9] While looking at the portraits of the nobles, Jahangir had commented on 'Abdulla Khan, Saiyid Safi Khan and Rana Ramdas that they had not served well in the Deccan. As against these nobles, 'Ali Mardan Khan had performed commendably he remarked, so the Emperor ordered the latter's portrait to be included in the *Jahangirnama*.

Jahangir had portraits made not only of the nobles of the Mughal court but also of Safavid and Uzbek princes and nobles. He states:

At the time (1619) when I sent Khan 'Alam to Persia. I had sent with him a painter of the name of Bishandas, who was unequalled in his age for taking likenesses, to take the portraits of the Shah and the chief men of his State, and bring them. He had drawn the likenesses of most of them and especially had taken that of my brother the Shah exceedingly well, so that when I showed it to any of his servants, they said it was exceedingly well drawn.[10]

A few portraits of Shah 'Abbas and his courtiers, ascribed to Bishandas and lodged in various art collections, are thus the result of the artist's direct observation.[11] Jahangir was so pleased with Bishandas's achievement that he honoured him with the gift of an elephant—a status symbol in Mughal India.[12] Jahangir had similarly a number of portraits prepared of Uzbek rulers and nobles. He also took care to check the authenticity of the portrait with those who had seen the person portrayed. A Central Asian scholar Mutribi, who visited his court in 1626, informs how Jahangir strove to secure accuracy in the portraits he was collecting:

Today the Emperor showed me the pictures of Uzbek Khans. I recognized 'Abul Be there.[13]

I presented myself before the Emperor. His Majesty was holding a paper bearing a picture in his hand and was looking at the picture. Favouring me with his attention, he called me near him and said, 'See these pictures. Do you know whose portraits (*surat*) they are'? When I looked at them, I found that one was the portrait of 'Abdulla Khan Uzbek and the other of 'Abdul Momin Khan. His Majesty said, 'Are they really their likenesses (*shabih*) or do you have some comment to make? If you have some comments do speak out'. I said, 'The portrait of 'Abdulla Khan shows him as plump and his beard has been shown as straight. He was not like this. He had little flesh on his body and his beard tended to incline to one side'. His Majesty asked, 'Was the inclination of the beard to the right or to the left'? I said, 'To the left'. His Majesty summoned the painter (*musauwir*) and whatever I had said he repeated that to him. Thereafter he said, 'Have you got anything to say on the likeness of 'Abdul Momin Khan'? I said, 'The artist has shown 'Abdul Momin Khan as of dark complexion. But he was not like this. His dark complexion was inclined towards fairness and he tied his turban's sash (*ilaqa*') in front, two fists in length. It looked very well'. His Majesty said, 'Take off your turban and show us how his turban's sash looked'. I took off my turban and showed how it was made. His Majesty told the artist, 'Make your picture this way'. The next day the artist brought his pictures drawn in the way that I had indicated. This won His Majesty's approval. 'Abul Be Uzbek, known as Bahadur Khan being present, said, 'When I was a servant of 'Abdul Momin Khan, he did not wear the turban's sash (like this)'. The Emperor said, 'The *akhund* (present author) is referring to the time when he ('Abdul Momin Khan) was a prince, i.e., 15 years of age.[14]

Besides the portraits of emperors, princes (persons of royal lineage) and nobles, a large number of identified portraits of well-known Mughal courtiers, saints, scribes, artists, musicians, etc., executed during the sixteenth and seventeenth centuries, are found in volumes available in various government and private collections at museums and libraries.

The love of portraiture and pictorial records amongst the Mughals is reflected in the blend of colours and portrayal of figures. Vincent Smith observes:

> The works of the Indo-Persian draughtsmen and painters furnish a gallery of historical portraits, lifelike and perfectly authentic, which enable the historian to realize the personal appearance of all Mughal emperors and of almost every public man of note in India for more than two centuries. It may be doubted if any other country in the world possesses a better series of portraits of the men who made history.[15]

The criticism of the portraits of Shah Jahan's time by Toby Falk and Mildred Archer that 'The prime purpose was no longer accuracy of a character study, but the maintenance of the grandest possible standard for the album itself'[16] is not borne out by a careful look at the actual portraits, especially those executed by master-painters like Anup Chhatar,[17] Balchand,[18] Bichitr,[19] Chitarman,[20] Hashim,[21] Hunhar,[22] Mirar,[23] Muhammad Nadir[24] and Payag.[25] Indeed Niharranjan Ray's impression is the opposite to that of Falk and Archer:

> As in Jahangiri *durbar* scenes, so in such scenes in the paintings of the regimes of the next two emperors [Shah Jahan and Aurangzeb] as well, the emphasis was on the individualization of facial features and expression so that every single human figure became more or less identifiable.[26]

Pinder-Wilson also writes: 'Among the many portraits of the period, those rendered in line and lightly tinted have an unexpectedly intimate and personal character.'[27]

II

The Mughal school was not admittedly indigenous, since it grew out of, and reflects both conceptual and stylistic expressions of Persian art. Not to be overlooked is the subsequent impact of European Renaissance art on this school, which became so pervasive that Mughal painting has been described by a critic as a 'hybrid blend' of the East and West. It is true that with the gradual rise of the influence of Renaissance art, the growth of both Indian and Persian elements lost their dominance in Mughal style and Mughal school cannot be described adequately without a knowledge of Renaissance art. This major aspect of Mughal painting has been taken up by numerous scholars, particularly Richard Ettinghausen, Milo C. Beach, Ebba Koch and Gauvin Alexander Bailey. However, though there is little to cavil with and much to admire in their work. What has been overlooked in the technical studies is the larger role of humanism in drawing the Mughal artist (or his patron) to Renaissance art.

The term 'humanism' has been especially applied to the Renaissance movement, chiefly carried on in Italy during the late fourteenth, the fifteenth and the early sixteenth centuries, embracing the literary and cultural work of the great figures of the Renaissance. Humanism came to reflect itself in the arts of the Renaissance in various ways. Notably, it gave rise to a new theory of art and its techniques, especially in the use of *chiaroscuro,* the sense of volume, and the illusion of the three dimensions, through perspective. One may recall here Leon Battista Alberti's approach to art since it illuminates the way in which Renaissance humanism penetrated into the arts. He was himself not only a thinker but a noted artist as well:

> In his *Della pittura* (1435-36) Alberti emphasized three necessary elements in painting: the evocation of spatial and historical activity by a combination of artificial perspective and a system of proportion and scale based on the human figure; the invention of an *storia* (theme, dramatic situation, or historical episode to be depicted); and its elaboration through the use of appropriate colour, light, proportion, composition, and effective movement in such a way as to communicate a living, moving visual drama that would edify, terrify, instruct, or please the viewer. In advocating a knowledge of geometry and optics to achieve perspective (which, as will be seen, spring from a view point analogous to the humanists' new attitude toward history) in expressing the notion of a transformation of poetic into visual beauty, and in urging the goal of moving the viewer to appropriate insight, emotion, and action, his treatise embodied a historical, literary, and rhetorical—in short, a truly humanist—conception of art.[28]

Though Alberti's views were not shared universally by the painters, these became the principles by which paintings came to be judged during the sixteenth-seventeenth centuries. Besides, humanism showed great concern for the dignity of man, as a result of which a new importance was attached to human values and the qualities and achievements of man tended to be highlighted.

The Renaissance artists' notion of space viewed in linear perspective comprising seemingly three-dimensional human figures, etc., gave rise to the search for mathematical and scientifically accurate methods of creating illusions of reality on a two-dimensional plane. This specific aim combined with the moral and emotional aspect of painting which defined an artists' status, as a practitioner of an intellectual discipline. A Renaissance artist was no more just a craftsman or an imitative worker. The newly-discovered principles of a vanishing-point perspective fully emphasized an accurate representation of buildings and other objects. The presentation of a diagonal view and foreshortening of proportions involved greater sense of mathematics. The proposed system of perspective in painting thus brought together the knowledge of mathematics and art.

Under the impact of humanism where 'man happened to be the measure of all things' there naturally tended to be greater emphasis on well-formulated anatomical presentation of the human body. This gave an impetus to the collaboration of anatomists and the artist. The Renaissance artists themselves sought to acquire a minute knowledge of human anatomy. In this context the contribution of Leonardo da Vinci (1452-1519) is considerable. His anatomical drawings are of a purely scientific character. Other notable figures are that of Albrecht Durer (1471-1528) and Michelangelo Buonarroti (1475-1564), who made a profound study of anatomy. Such a realistic presentation of the human figure led nescessarily to an idealization of the human form in the same way as earlier in classical Greek art; it certainly reached its highest point in Renaissance art. Studies of the human body in the nude were designed to exhibit the actual anatomy of the human body in maximum possible details. The nude as a motif in Renaissance art, built-up an ideal of perfection of human beauty and its physical charm. Men and women received a new ideal image based on their physical form seen in the greatest detail.

Another mode of idealization was to depict the subject by presenting the figure larger than life or in isolation, dominating the whole composition. The image of man, being associated with perfection, appeared more beautiful and in idealization his figure appeared almost godlike. Nevertheless, technically all such images were extensively marked by naturalism.

The humanists' interest in man gave rise to the development of portraiture where the portraits with a landscape setting in the background presented an innovative form of landscape painting. In such examples, nature appears complementary to the human form. Under the impress of 'human', portraiture aimed at revealing unseen mysteries of the soul.[29] It is remarkable that this new principle should find an analogue in Abu'l Fazl's evaluation (1595) of the work of Khwaja Abdu's Samad '*Shirin Qalam*', recognized as one of the founders of the Mughal school:

> Though he was skilled in this [art of painting] before joining [Mughal] service, by the Emperor's keen insight he achieved a high station, *and from bringing out mere forms he came to bring out the inner meaning*. Masters who became his pupils, shone forth by learning from him.[30]

Realism was further reflected in Renaissance art by a new sense of mass and volume, and chiaroscuro, i.e. the management of light and shade.

The Italian humanism of the late fourteenth, fifteenth and early sixteenth centuries greatly inspired the Renaissance art of Europe on which the Mughal school so greatly drew. The visual realism, scientific accuracy and careful modelling of light and shade—much against the concept of overall brightness in oriental art—seen in the Mughal school, all attest to it.

An emphasis on naturalism which held a prominent place in Renaissance art, is reflected in the Mughal art, the affinity being mostly with the High Renaissance style (1500-27). What is of particular interest is that the influence of Renaissance art begins to be seen in Mughal art already by the 1570s. The most notable aspect of the miniatures of the *Tutinama* (one of the earliest illustrated manuscripts from the Mughal school, datable to 1570-5) is the lively effect achieved in the depiction of figures with emphasis placed on establishing psychological relationship between them. As a result, the figures appear highly animated. Undoubtedly, these express a naturalistic and expressive quality of art—a major feature of the developed Mughal style. An application of deep shading in the modelling of the figures and landscape shows an improvement on the strictly two-dimensional pictures of the Persian and Western India schools of painting. In the *Tutinama* MS, Beach takes note of Basawan's work, 'Hunter offers the mother-parrot to the king' (folio 36v) where the representation of the curtain and clothing of the central figure (the hunter) is heavily modelled. This technique of shading employed to create a three-dimensional effect and physical tangibility was not known to the Persian and Indian artists of the time. Beach interprets it as a straightforward adaptation of methods introduced through an access to European Renaissance painting (*c*.1350-1550).[31] Still, here only a rudimentary knowledge of humanistic painting is observable, such as the technique of shading to represent mass and volume. An advance towards a better appreciation of perspective is made in the *Hamzanama* paintings (Mughal school, *c.* 1556-80) which sometimes exhibit human figures in the background as comparatively diminutive in size compared to those in the foreground. Similarly, distant buildings shown on a diminished scale, too, emphasize depth in the painting. Two important elements in Renaissance art, modelling and perspective had thus begun to find a place in Mughal art by 1580.

Mughal painters obviously derived their knowledge of humanism and Renaissance art from European pictures, engravings, specimens of decorative art and textiles, etc. These could well have been obtained by the early 1570s. Akbar had contact with Europeans at least since 1573. Abu'l Fazl writes:

> One of the occurrences of the siege [of Surat] was that a large number of Christians came from the port of Goa and its neighbourhood to the foot of sublime throne and were rewarded by the bliss of an interview. . . . They produced many of the rarities of their country, and the appreciative Khedive received each one of them with special favour and made inquiries about the wonders of Portugal and the manners and customs of Europe.[32]

Abu'l Fazl further notices the visit of Pietro Tavares to Akbar's court at Fatehpur Sikri in 1578.[33] Badaoni, too, mentions the presence of Portuguese priests at Akbar's court during 1575-6.[34] Father Francis Julian Pereira, invited by Akbar to his court in 1578, was present at Fatehpur Sikri when the first Jesuit mission led by Rudolph Aquaviva and Monserrate from Goa arrived in February 1580.[35] Most probably Akbar had already acquired some specimens of European art much before 1580. Monserrate notices that European pictures of Christ, Mary, Moses and Muhammad were already there in the royal dining-hall when the Jesuit mission arrived.[36]

During this period, Goa itself was a thriving centre of Christian art comprising especially devotional themes. Besides the Indian artists, European artists too were active in Goa. They include the Flemish Jesuit sculptor Father Markus Mach (known as Marcos Rodriguez, died 1601) and the Portuguese Jesuit painter Manuel Godinho (active during 1580s).[37] The latter specialized in reproducing images of Virgin Mary. The Christian pictures still extant in 'Maryam Palace' at Fatehpur Sikri are the earliest evidence of an Indian artists' work in Italian Renaissance style. Some such pictures are described as representing the 'Anunciation' and the 'Fall'.[38]

The first Jesuit mission on its arrival presented a copy of Plantyn's *Royal Polyglot Bible* (printed in Antwerp between 1568 and 1573) to Akbar in 1580.[39] Its 8 volumes, sumptuously bound, and clasped with gold were illustrated with several pictures engraved by Flemish artists of the school of Quintin Matsys (1466-1530), including the work of P. Huys. These remained in the imperial library till 1595, when these were returned to the third Jesuit mission. These presumably served as one of the sources of Christian art of the Renaissance at the Mughal atelier.[40] The traces of the work of other Flemish artists, for example, Theodar Galle (1571-1633), Hieronymus Wierix, Johann Sadeler (1550-1600) and Raphael Sadeler (1555-1618) are found in paintings in the royal albums of the Mughal school.[41] Undoubtedly, the large number of the small engravings introduced from Europe during the late sixteenth and the beginning of the seventeenth century contributed much to the absorption of Renaissance Humanism by Mughal art in both technique and spirit.

Father Jerome Xavier's account confirms the presence of a Portuguese painter in the entourage of the Jesuit Fathers, to whom Prince Salim (Jahangir) turned for making a copy of the picture of the 'Virgin' brought by the Fathers.[42] Bailey has discovered two pictures preserved in the Mughal albums: 'Madonna and Child with Angels' (*c.* 1595) after an engraving by Antoon Wierix (1552-1624) after Martin de Vos (1532-1603), and 'Suzanna at her Bath Surprised by the Elders' (*c.* 1590) after Antoon Wierix, which seem to have been executed in oil on paper by an anonymous Portuguese painter.[43] In these pictures there is nothing Mughal except the broad margin painting characteristic of Jahangir's studio. In another instance, the miniature representing 'Deposition of Cross' too bears no sign of Mughal art, and it is clearly the work of a Portuguese artist. Roe also had an amateur artist named Robert Hughes, whom Jahangir desired to be presented before him with his work, in 1616.[44]

In 1618, Roe notices another European painter, Hatfield and describes him as 'a very good workeman both in Iymming and oyle'.[45] This painter was in Steel's entourage, and also had access to Jahangir. He is known to have executed the emperor's portrait from life in the same year.[46]

European pictures brought to India were in the form of illustrations in printed books, woodcuts, copper engravings, coloured pictures and prints of European specimens published by Plantin's firm at

Antwerp. Besides, European tapestries both silken and woollen 'worked with stories from the Old Testament' were also brought to the Mughal court. Quite often, the engravings were preserved in the Mughal albums in their original form.[47] Sometimes the Mughal painters also tinted the engravings and provided them with Mughal surroundings. Rogers has noticed a late sixteenth-century French engraving representing Dauphin, Francois of Valois, son of Francis I of France, on a Mughal folio (*c.* 1610-20).[48] He also takes note of an engraving 'Sea of Galilee with Gadarene Swine', tinted and pasted on a Mughal album page with margin decoration (*c.* 1650).[49] Jesuit sources tell us that for the colour reproduction of the engravings and their prints in monochrome, Mughal artists consulted Christian Fathers:

> He [Jahangir] had ordered his artists to consult the Fathers as to the colour to be given to the costumes and to adhere strictly to what we told them. The figures to be painted were selected by the King himself from his collection of prints and he decided where they were to be placed. He got his painters to make large size sketches on paper of all the prints which he wished to have painted and the Fathers then stated how the painting should be done.[50]

The display of Christian paintings on sacred subjects in the Jesuit chapels and churches, open to the public in general, must have enabled many artists to get still more familiar with the art of Europe of Renaissance period. Monserrate thus records the visit of Akbar and his sons to the Father's chapel at Fatehpur Sikri:

> When the king heard of their arrival he came alone to their house, and proceeded straight to the chapel, where (having laid aside his turban and shaken out his long hair) he prostrated himself on the ground in adoration of Christ and his Mother. He then began to talk about divine things. A week later he brought three of his sons (Salim, Murad and Daniyal) and several nobles to see the chapel. . . . The King himself accepted with the greatest delight a very beautiful picture of the Virgin, which had been brought from Rome and was presented to him by the Fathers in the name of the superior of the Province.[51]

The display of European pictures on Biblical themes held at Fatehpur Sikri in 1580,[52] was followed by one at Agra in 1602[53] and at Cambay during Jahangir's reign.[54]

A large number of European pictures and engravings were gifted to the emperor, princes and nobles by the Jesuits.[55] European portraits too were in demand, and in 1602, the Fathers at the Mughal court presented to Akbar two historical portraits, one of Albuquerque and the other of the then Portuguese Viceroy of India, Ayres de Saldagna.[56]

Jahangir, even when he was prince, showed considerable interest in Christian pictures and tried to acquire them. Xavier's letter, mentioned earlier tells us that prince Salim was very angry with those who had conducted the Fathers, because they had not brought him any picture of Our Lady from Goa; 'and speaking to another, who was about to set out those parts, he charged him to buy certain pieces which he desired to have, bidding him above all things not to forget to bring a beautiful picture of Our Lady'. Jahangir often showed off his collection of Christian pictures.[57] In 1608, Xavier notices that Jahangir's collection included the pictures of Sardanapalus, the Circumcision, God the Father, Crucifixion, and David kneeling before Nathan.[58] He had his audience and private assembly halls at Agra decorated with such pictures.[59] William Finch in his minute account of a picture representing Jahangir, his ancestors, princes and nobles, etc., seen in 1611 on the walls of the retiring rooms in the Fort at Lahore, also takes notice of the pictures of Christ and the Virgin Mary.[60] Thevenot's account of 1666, based on hearsay, corroborates Finch's observation:

> There are great many Pictures upon the walls, which represent the Action of the Great Moghuls, their Fore-fathers that arch pompously painted there and on one Gate there is a Crucifix and the picture of the Virgin on another. . . .[61]

In our times, the wall-paintings comprising Christian themes in the Fort of Lahore are confined to the vault of the Kala Burj; and these do not seem to answer to Finch's description.

Roe, in 1616, similarly observed the panels of pictures on walls including the likenesses of French kings and Christian princes in the garden-house called Chashma-i Nur near Ajmer.[62]

> . . . your pictures not all worth one penny; . . . Here are nothing esteemed but of the best sorts: good cloth and fine, and rich pictures, they coming out of Italy over land and from Ormus: soe that they laugh at us for such as wee bring.[63]

Again in 1616, he writes:

> With theis: Some cushions, cabbennetts, glasses, standishes and toyes of use for others. Pictures of all sortes, if good, in constant request, some large storie; Diana this yere gave great content.[64]

Pictures often formed part of list of items desired as gifts from Europe for Jahangir. Such a list provided by Muqarrab Khan to an Englishman also contained 'pictures on cloth'.[65] Roe too took special note of large pictures executed on cloth: 'Pictures, lardge, on cloth, the frame inpeeces; but they must be good, and for varyetye some story, with many faces, for single to the life hath beene more usual.'[66] Qaisar notices that Jahangir's desire for European pictures had become 'almost embarrassing'—in the year (1613?), out of £695 spent by the English East India Company on articles as presents in India, £255 were for pictures alone.[67] Pictures on secular subjects, in addition to Biblical themes, were also in demand. The English factors selected portraits of kings and queens and pictures of women. Besides, there were pictures representing battles and comic scenes including nude studies. Roe notices the display of the pictures of 'the King of England, the Queen, my lady Elizabeth, the Countesse of Sommersett and Salisbury, and of a citizen's wife of London; below them another of Sir Thomas Smyth, Governor of the East India Company in the Mughal Court on *Nauroz* (11 March 1616)'.[68] In the succeeding year also he saw these pictures on the wall behind the Emperor's throne.[69]

Though little is known about Shah Jahan's interest in European pictures, the surviving pictures from his atelier is clear evidence of the continuing adaptation and incorporation of European art. Nevertheless, this feature seems largely confined to the incorporation of landscape motifs and European symbols and figures.

Yet Shah Jahan while a prince had certainly some enthusiasm for European pictures. Roe writes in 1616:

> I went to the Prince and delivered the conditions demanded on my part, and withall a breefe of what I required in his *firmaen*; to all which he agreed. I gave him for a present a silver watch very small, which he took kindly; but told me the pictures I showed his father the night before; if I had given him, he would have better accepted then anything, demanding if I had no more.[70]

Shah Jahan's interest in the picture of Diana is attested by his reported purchase of a painting on this subject while he was a prince.[71] But copies of European engravings (prints) and pictures were not made on the kind of scale witnessed during Jahangir's period. This would possibly suggest that Shah Jahan's interest in European art did not last long. Aurangzeb forbade art in his court, and showed no interest in paintings, either Indian or European.

There was considerable demand for European pictures among nobles. In 1616, Roe presented to Muqarrab Khan '13 pictures of Christ and a set of 12 of the Apostle'.[72] In the same year he presented to Jamaluddin Hasan Inju a book containing 48 sheets of pictures, illustrating the entire life of Christ.[73] Mirza Beg and Asaf Khan were other nobles to whom Roe presented pictures.[74] Aziz Koka, the foster brother of Akbar, also showed interest in Christian pictures and tried to acquire the picture of Madonna del Popolo from the Jesuits.

He also expressed a desire to understand the mystery of this Lady, and offered, in the event of the Fathers being willing to part with the picture, to give them whatever price they asked for; if this was impossible, he begged them to procure him another like it, promising to defray all the expenditure incurred.[75]

Mahabat Khan[76] and Zulfikhar Khan,[77] too, had Christian pictures in their possession.

Referring to the demand for European work, Pelsaert writes in 1626:

> I will now specify various rarities which have been recommended to me by different nobles or great men, and which should be sent here by our ships, but the quantity supplied of each should be small:
>
> 2 or 3 good battle-pictures, painted by an artist with a pleasing style, for the Moslems want to see everything from close by: also one or two maps of entire world; also some decorative pictures showing comic incidents, or nude figures.[78]

III

The European pictures and engravings, available to the Mughal patrons and the painters, largely transformed their views towards painting and aesthetic attributes. The Mughal artists, under the influence of the Renaissance humanist movement in art, added a new chapter in Indian art which is neither a direct continuation of the pre-Islamic Indian traditions, nor explicitly Persian. The Mughal painting, eclectic in character, evolved with the interaction of various traditions—predominantly Indian, Persian and European. The context of naturalism, scientific perspective and *chiaroscuro*—contrasts in light and shade—in Mughal painting is the gift of humanism as practised by the European artists of Renaissance. The Mughal artists assimilated and absorbed the new methods and techniques which characterized Renaissance art which flourished during the fifteenth and sixteenth centuries in Italy and other countries of Europe. The linear art of

Persia alone did not fascinate the Mughal connoisseurs and painters. Akbar's urge for realism in art is quite clear when he sat for his painters, obviously to obtain a true and lively portraiture. Abu'l Fazl's description of the state of the Mughal painting in 1590s prescribes the criteria for judgement on painting which fall in line with the tenets of humanism: 'The minuteness in detail, the general finish, the boldness or execution, etc., now observed in pictures, are incomparable: *even inanimate objects look as if they had life.*'[79]

A portrait in the humanistic sense is defineable as a faithful portrayal of the character of an individual. An artist was now expected to work from memory by looking at the subject and not from imagination. The Mughal paintings exhibiting artists at work bear an evidence of human portrait being drawn from the life/model.[80] Thus, fine naturalistic drawings were produced with the combined effect of light and shade and perspective. These obviously differed from the archetypes of the past.

In the Italian Renaissance, anatomical presentation of the human body received utmost attention and it reached its culmination in the works of Leonardo da Vinci, Durer and Michelangelo. Such a rational presentation of the human body, while to an extent encourages its idealization, also called for nudes. In Mughal India, though nude European pictures were introduced, the anatomical study of the human body does not seem to have aroused the interest of the artists or their patrons. Actually, in India there never emerged any real effort on the part of the artists to study anatomy.[81] It is only rarely that we have instances of the depiction of the human body with muscular articulation seen in the works of Basawan and others; and these merely suggest adaptation from European examples.

In ancient Indian art (leaving aside the Hellenistic Gandhara art),[82] it is only surface anatomy which seems to attract the artist, or a sculptor. Here, too, set or ideal proportions of the human body tended to be followed. Slender or heavy forms were presented without any indication of muscular movement. Human figures are often shown so laden with ornaments that the decorative aspect prevails over the physical. Finally, symbolic poses, in accordance with iconographic traditions, introduced a seeming affectedness that obscured any sense of reality. Such stylized forms were certainly the opposite of the natural forms that Renaissance art strove for.

In the medieval pre-Mughal Indian art, human figures appear even more stylized, with certain symbolic features used to define status.

The Mughal school is thus fundamentally different from its precursors in that here an artist's goal appears to be the portrayal of the objective reality and the presentation of nature with minute and almost photographic fidelity—the very tenets of Renaissance art. Basawan among Akbar's painters, perhaps succeeded most in the sphere and well deserves Abu'l Fazl's praise of him as a master painter with excellence in various branches of painting, including 'the drawing of features' (portraits).[83] His masterpieces include 'Flute-player' (*c.* 1590):[84] 'Dervish' (*c.* 1590)[85] and 'Jain ascetic' (*c.* 1590-5).[86] The flute-player, shown against a flat ground, is dramatically posed as if dancing in response to the tune being played by him. The heavily folded, long flowing sheet of cloth thrown across the shoulders provide a rhythmic pattern. This portrait is superb in the rendering of the mood of the musician, in the realism of the physical features drawn, the stress on modelling and the presentation of mass and volume. The influence of European engravings and paintings is also manifest in some studies of his such as 'Allegorical Figures', 'Praying Lady', 'Young Woman with an Old Man', and 'Woman on a Monster's Head' (all lodged in the Musee Guimet, Paris).[87]

The presentation of a real character is also revealed in Basawan's portrait representing a wandering *dervish*. In it, the lively facial features, eyes with an intense gaze, body slightly bent, and lean and thin, imbued with gentle movement, is supremely naturalistic. The Mughal painter's realistic approach to his subject as found here shows a marked departure from the mannered style of portraits of the Persian school. The portrait of a Jain ascetic is unusual in being imbued with psychological insight. The holy man clad in a white flowing costume (*dhoti*) and a long transparent sheet of white cloth thrown across the shoulders is depicted as wandering around, with holy books under his arm. His facial features present him engrossed in thought. A gentle movement of his clothes suggest the morning breeze. The ascetic's figure shown amidst unending space, reminds one of the Renaissance fashion of landscape background and emphasis on aerial perspective in portrait painting.

Basawan's contemporary Mansur, infused in portrait painting his own touch of originality. The portrait of a '*Vina*-player' (*c.* 1600) is a psychological one where he has successfully captured the musician's feelings—the musician's reclining head over the *vina* imparts a lyrical quality to the portrait.[88] The flower plants arcading the human figure hint at a vertical movement in the landscape. No definite horizon-line is shown, but the rows of birds on high margin are suggestive of an aerial perspective. In another portrait, 'Huntsman Holding a Falcon' (*c.* 1600-5), a fight of birds shown on the high margin denotes the aerial perspective.[89] These examples suggest an introduction of landscape elements in the handling of space in Mughal portraiture. This technique of Renaissance art found more fuller expression during the seventeenth century, especially in the works of Bichitr and Govardhan.

The naturalism in portraiture may be judged by the extent to which ordinary men are portrayed, since here other aspects, heroic, majestic, decorative, etc., necessarily fall away. Here, an unascribed portrait of a learned man (*c.* 1595-1600) deserves mention.[90] His face is shown in full profile and the body in a three-quarter view: he is depicted engrossed in reading a book resting on his bulging stomach and its folios turned by hand. It reveals the most frank and intimate expression of deep thoughtful mood. The scholar leans comfortably against a pillow. The loosely slipped scarf, the cuddled figure of the dozing dog, and lastly the solitary background add to the serenity of the view. Here the details rendered with deep shading and the naturalism achieved in the depiction of forms are in full consonance with Renaissance art. This quality of portraiture vividly speaks of the artist's originality, while combining the techniques of Indian painting with the spirit of Renaissance realism.

The portrait of a seated man, most likely a musician (judged by the *rubab*, a musical instrument shown lying on his right side), is a good-humoured portrait with a definite understanding of the subject's mood at the time.[91] In it, the cloth with deep folds, the wrinkles and details of the physical features, all speak of a pronounced impact of Renaissance art, especially in shading and modelling.

La'l is another prolific painter of Akbar's court who successfully, captured human moods and feelings. His painting 'An Old Man Writing in a Book, Seated in a Landscape' (*c.* 1590-1600) clearly shows a sense of strain reflected in the face of the old man.[92] Presentation of such psychological portraits, flourished at Akbar's atelier, and later became the mainstay of Mughal art.

It is noteworthy that the portraits of ordinary people in the Mughal school, in general, are spontaneous pictures, altogether different from the stately ones of the royalty or nobles, which often appear mannered and idealized. In the latter the figures appear stereotyped and typified both in positioning and posture. The formalized expression, however, does not effect the sensitive rendering of the characteristic features or the subject. The spontaneous portraits are studies focused mainly on the presentation of a particular mood and action, and thus belong to the category of intimate psychological portraits. In the portrayal of a common man, an artist seems to possess close familiarity with the subject and knowledge pertaining to his inner character. This relationship of the artist with the subject relieves him from observing the prescribed conventions of drawing and composition and the spontaneity in the artist's expression is manifest. Indeed, the portraits of ordinary men in Mughal art are often filled with a feeling of warmth. The Mughal artist's achievement in portraiture reaches a high point in a miniature such as '*Rubab* Player, His Companion, and a Peasant' (*c.* 1615-20), ascribed to Bichitr. Havell notes

> a one eyed [?] musician is singing with great gusto a song which excites the hilarity of his listener, the bowman holding an arrow in his left hand and apparently beating time with his right foot. The facial expression of both is admirably rendered, and the imperturbable countenance of the servant [peasant] squatting in the foreground with his bundle, between the legs, is equally true to life.[93]

As in Renaissance art, a kind of idealization in human portraiture also took place in Mughal school. This included the mode of presenting the figure in isolation amidst a vast landscape; or perceptibly larger in its surroundings and thus dominating the whole landscape; or against the background of a vast open sky filled with billowing clouds.

In the allegorical picture 'Jahangir Embracing Shah Abbas', Abu'l Hasan presents a symbolic depiction of the Mughal Emperor's power and superiority over the Shah of Iran, who is represented as the lesser partner with the figure of Jahangir shown majestically towering over him.[94] The magnification of the favoured subject to emphasize his special secular status, or to attach divinity, has long been a tradition in Indian sculpture and painting. In the Mathura school, precedence is given to Buddha, whose size is enlarged in accordance with the tradition that he had a superhuman stature, or sometimes to express his supernatural grandeur.[95] Further in the Ajanta painting the images of Buddha and Bodhisattva and of the rulers have been shown distinctly large in size in assemblies or groups of men and women.[96] The Mughal painter might not have been aware of it, but he continues to use this device of classical Indian iconography with European symbols, viz., cherubs, putti, cupids, etc., to symbolize power and glory of the Mughal emperors and high-ranking nobles.

In an allegorical portrait of Asaf Khan (*c.* 1625-30), executed by Bichitr, the figure of the main character dominates the whole composition and it looms large over a vast city containing clusters of buildings, high minarets and the bands of cavalry—all shown on a drastically diminished scale, suggestive of aerial perspective.[97] The presentation of an elephant with its rider holding the Mughal flag, and captives with their hands and feet chained on either side of the protagonist, is a symbolic depiction of the power of this noble, shown in a posture of thanks-giving, witnessed by cherubs emerging from the floating clouds holding an inscribed scroll. Similarly, in Bichitr's portrait of I'tibar Khan (*c.* 1620-5), the main figure is composed almost on the same lines. In it, the background comprising the army, river with boats and a walled city with clusters of trees inside presented on a drastically miniaturized scale, reminds one of the vanishing-point perspective.[98]

Bichitr's famous portrait of Shah Jahan (*c.* 1635) in the Chester Beatty Library, Dublin, excels both in its idealization and in the use of symbols.[99] In it, the figure of Shah Jahan is prominently depicted with a large radiating halo, standing on a terrestrial globe with the conventional symbol of the lion and the sheep and two angels descending amidst billowing clouds and holding the royal insignia (a European crown). In addition, on either side of the subject there are two groups of holy men emerging from the clouds with their hands lifted in prayer, diminutive, with details deliberately blurred. Here, while most symbolism comes right out of the conventions of European painting practically unaltered, the introduction of the holy men in groups—the Muslim theologians amidst clouds—is an innovation of Bichitr. It certainly enriches the visual vocabulary of symbols in Mughal iconography. Lastly, the presentation of a noble, shown perceptibly small in size, with a sword hung around his neck—a symbolic representation of an individual's surrender in the east—at the bottom towards the right corner, again testifies to Bichitr's ingenuity in the application of symbols.

In another portrait of Shah Jahan (*c.* 1635-7), also at the Chester Beatty Library, ascribed to Payag, he is drawn, standing on a terrestrial globe holding a matchlock.[100] The background comprises horsemen storming a fort and a group of men presenting themselves before the

Emperor, all depicted on a drastically reduced scale and blurred in effect. The artist's understanding of the aerial perspective is here in full accordance of Renaissance art. By now, the mode of drawing the main character much larger than other objects seems to have become the mainstay of the Mughal artists in the presentation of royal or aristocratic portraits.

Mughal portraits are distinct since these are not in full harmony with either the defined principles of Islamic aesthetics or ancient and medieval Indian art. Undoubtedly, Mughal artists achieved great success in executing truly life-like images of their subjects by completely absorbing elements of Renaissance humanism in their art. Indeed a few masters of the Mughal school, viz., Basawan, Bichitr, Daulat, Govardhan, Mirar (or Murar), and Payag could even reach the acumen of the great Renaissance artists.

Incidentally, the trend to show a circular nimbus or flame-shaped nimbus known in various arts since the twelfth century added a symbolic sanctity to the human figure. The device had earlier existed in ancient Indian art, but seems to have been re-introduced into Mughal painting under the influence of European art.

Till Akbar's time, it is true, no symbols were attached to the portrait of an individual. In the presentation of other subjects too, this abstention prevailed, with the exception of an aureole—the symbol of divine light—and the birds of paradise, derived from the paintings of Islamic lands. In case of European symbols, their application remained strictly confined to the adapted or imitated pictures inspired by European examples. However, later in the seventeenth century, under Jahangir and Shah Jahan, European symbols began to be freely employed in portraitures to provide a vision emphasizing divinity in the likenesses of the Emperor and others. In the context of the rendering of symbolic images, Basawan, a prolific painter in Akbar's court, was the foremost. He shows a fascination for European emblematic pictures/figures, and exhibited considerable ingenuity in their adaptation by introducing some alterations suitable to the taste of the Mughal court. The application of European symbols, viz., halo, angels, cherubs and God the Father, in Mughal portraits added an air of spirituality to the picture, while to a modern viewer it imparts to it a curiously Christian context. In Renaissance art, there was a fashion to represent historic heroes of secular life with the images of saints and other figures revered by the Church in the panels embellishing the buildings of churches, both sets of people thus were immortalized. The Mughal portraits, too, convey the same message. However, the concept of immortality promised to a man through his portrait was not new to Akbar. Abu'l Fazl writes:

> His Majesty himself sat for his likeness, and also ordered to have the likenesses taken of all the grandees of the realm. An immense album was thus formed: those that have passed away have received a new life, and those who are still alive have immortality promised them.[101]

The motifs of cherubs emerging from clouds, holding a European crown, playing musical instruments and the large golden halo are all European symbols. The cherubs holding the crown seem to have been derived from the European pictures on 'Coronation of the Virgin'.

Similarly, the depiction of celestial beings, the angels holding the inscribed scroll and holy book, emerging from the clouds juxtaposed to the rainbow on the top margin of Emperor Babur's posthumous portrait, executed during Shah Jahan's time (*c.* 1640), are in association with the symbols noticed above but with some alterations.[102] These signs and symbols while express the sanctity attached to the man, also hint at the exaltation of the dead.

In the Mughal school, next to portraiture, the most famous genre was the picturization of birds, animals and plants with blossoms, for which Jahangir's reign is celebrated. The pictures on natural history, too, reveal many elements of humanism. In them, an emphasis on 'naturalism' was naturally great. The figures of birds and animals invariably appear life like and these are no more prototype of the ancient past. The spirited drawings of the animals, shown with the maximum possible details, display a scientific precision in the presentation of form and colour. These pictures are fine examples of a vivid and minutely detailed brush. Here nothing eludes the artist's eye, whether it is the texture of the hair or fur, or peculiarities of the horns and the ears, the mane, the tail or the plumage. The large number of the pictures of birds and animals, mostly ascribed to Abu'l Hasan, Govardhan, Inayat, Mansur, Mirar and Pidarath distinctly suggest that there was an emphasis on the delineation of their likenesses from life. In general, an intimate, careful observation of the object was the basis of their life-like pictures. The painters accompanied the royal entourage and were engaged in portraying rarities of nature from actual observation. Mention may be made of the picture of a falcon executed by Ustad Mansur, at the command of Jahangir in 1619:

What can I write of the beauty and colour of this falcon? There were many beautiful black markings on each wing, and back, and sides. As it was something out of common, I ordered Ustad Mansur who has the title of *Nadir ul Asr* (Unique of the Age) to paint and preserve its likeness.[103]

In another instance, in the following year—1620—Mansur executed the likeness of a bird, called *saj* (dipper), caught at Sukh Nag in Kashmir.[104] This study is a fine example of the Renaissance mode of aerial perspective and landscape background.[105] In the present picture, this is achieved by the juxtapositioning of another bird smaller in size and apparently viewed from a distance, and the receding contours or the hills painted in blurred colour, thus suggesting scale perspective besides giving relief to the central figure.

In line with the emphasis on human portraiture associated with Renaissance, Mughal studies of birds and animals, aimed at the subject standing out amidst its surroundings either by composing it in isolation, or by enlarging its figure and diminishing the size of other objects depicted in its surroundings. Mansur's pictures 'Himalayan Cheer Pheasant' (*c.* 1612),[106] 'Himalayan Blue-throated Barbet' *(c.* 1615-20)[107] and 'Chameleon on a Branch' (*c.* 1610-20)[108] are some of the examples exhibiting this particular device. In all these examples, Mansur's compositional technique can be seen in the way he subordinates the background to the principal object, and thereby enhances the effect of the main figure. It was the ingenuity of the Mughal artists that the elements of humanism as gleaned in the human portraits of the Renaissance were extended to the picturization of birds and animals as well. In the works of the Mughal artists, the rendering of the form and colour and the graphic description of details is perfectly balanced with the naturalistic approach to the subject. Of a drawing 'Siberian Crane' (*c.* 1610-20), Havell says that as an ornithological study it rivals the work of the best Japanese masters. He adds, 'the delicate feathers of the white plumage and microscopic details of the bird's anatomy are drawn with infinite patience and scientific exactitude'.[109] Some Mughal artists went further and sought to depict the feelings or mood of the animal. Kuhnel and Goetz hold that the miniature 'Two Magpies' (*c.* 1610-20) reminds one of 'the Dutch specialist painters of the 17th century, who portrayed subjects from the animal kingdom with equal knowledge, but their paintings are seldom so full of feelings as this one from India'.[110]

Realism is seen in Mughal painters work right from the beginning. For instance, the depiction of animals in the illustrations of *Anwar-i Suhaili* (School of Oriental and African Studies, London). *Circa* 1570, appear more natural and more self-possessed than their Iranian or Indian predecessors.[111] The Mughal painter already aimed at the portrayal of the physical reality, and this aspect of the Mughal painter's aesthetics lends his creations a quality of exceptional charm. Grousset has rightly remarked that the Mughal studies of wild life are frank material, intended to give earthly pleasure.[112] The lively naturalism achieved by Jahangir's painters got accentuated under the influence of Renaissance art that was so distinctly felt in the treatment of space, landscape background and modelling.

The oil medium was the favourite of the Renaissance artists and it replaced the tempera technique of earlier European art, since in the latter, different tones of a pigment can not be smoothly blended and the continuous progression of values necessary for a three-dimensional effects is difficult to achieve. As against this, oil being a slow-drying medium could produce a variety of effects from thin, translucent films (called 'glazes') to the thickest impasto; the tones could also yield a continuous scale of hues including rich velvety dark shades previously unknown. Undoubtedly, without 'oil' the Flemish masters' conquest of visible reality would have been much more limited. The Mughal patron, though he had access to European oil paintings, never obtained a liking for this medium; and his artists invariably worked in tempera technique. Their success nevertheless in achieving a three-dimensional effect and a variety of hues of a pigment can well be appreciated by looking at the almost identical copies of the European works executed by them. In 1616, Roe notices Jahangir to have ordered his painters for copies of a European picture:

> I was sent for to the *durbar*. The business was about a picture I had lately given the King, and was confident that noe man in India could equall yt. . . . At night he sent for mee, beeing hastie to triumph in his woorkman, and showed me six pictures, five made by his man, all pasted on one table, so like that I was by candle light troubled to discerne which was which; I confess beyond all expectation; yet I showed myne owne and the differences, which were in arte apparent, but not to be judged by a common eye.[113]

Mention may be made of Kesavdas—a painter in Akbar's court, best known for his copies of European works. His painting 'St. Matthew and the Angel', executed in 1587-8, was based on a print of an engraving by Philip Galle after Martin van Heemskrek's 'St. Matthew the Evangelist', and is almost European in character.[114] In his copy, the Mughal painter has successfully delineated the folds in the robe of the saint and the facial expression in his figure. Kesavdas's other painting 'Joseph Telling his Dream to his Father' (*c.* 1600), based on an engraving by George Pencz, dated 1544, is another outstanding Mughal copy of a European work revealing the artist's full control on European technique and style.[115] In his painting of St. Jerome adapted from Mario Cartaro's print of an engraving of Michelangelo's Noah from Sistine Chapel, Kesavdas's understanding of the subject is explicit in the rendering of the muscular modelling close to the style of Michelangelo.[116] Bailey observes that Kesavdas has excelled here.[117] In fact, the pulsating flesh of his image is more Michelangelesque than the Italian engraving he copied. We know that almost identical Mughal versions of European engravings or pictures were not uncommon in Mughal India. Abu'l Hasan with equal mastery adapted his technique to the trends and modes of Renaissance art. His painting 'St. John' executed in monochrome at the age of thirteen, in 1601, after an engraving by Durer, clearly speaks of this deep understanding of three-dimensional representation.[118] Another painting by him 'Roman Sea-god Neptune Riding on a Water Horse', the European source of which is not clear, is fully expressive of the tenets of Renaissance art.[119] The number of Mughal paintings showing a straightforward imitation of European themes and adaptation of their techniques and methods, is quite large. In general, these exhibit great understanding of the *chiaroscuro* technique—effect of light and shade, modelling of physical features and visual effects in the treatment of space. The deep shading, controlled light effect and heavy modelling were employed in the Mughal style to project volume as well. The Mughal painters understood the principles of light and shade so much as to use spotlight-effect and cast-shadows in their work. Otherwise the oriental method was to depict objects fully bathed in light and to treat day and night scenes in the same fashion with the difference of the introduction of a candle in the foreground, or a starlit sky with moon to convey the impression that the event was taking place in darkness. On the other hand, some of the seventeenth-century miniatures on subjects like 'Ascetics Seated Round a Fire', or 'A Prince Visiting an Ascetic During the Night', or 'An Assembly of Learned Men During the Night' show glowing faces of individuals, and rest of the scene finished in dark pigments: no symbols are needed to tell us that we have a night scene here.

European perspective, as we have seen, largely effected the Mughal visual perception and the methods of handling space in painting. However, the Mughal painter never fully understood it, and therefore, the convergence of angels and diagonal views of buildings do not appear with the same facility as in European art. A gradual receding effect in landscape is not always well achieved in their work. Mughal artists failed to grasp the mathematical and scientifically accurate methods of creating illusions of reality on a two-dimensional plane. One must here realize that the adoption of Renaissance humanism in Mughal art was not the result of an intellectual or scientific movement; and this certainly handicapped it in appreciating the full force of Europe's achievement in art.

Mughal painters could not, after all, liberate themselves from the canons of the conventional arts of Persia and India, though their conscious effort to switch over to the methods and techniques of Renaissance art showed, as we have seen, both skill and ingenuity. Welch's comments on an unascribed miniature 'A Group of Ascetics' (*c.* 1625) may here be recalled: 'As an artist, he invites comparison to Basawan and Daulat, who shared his spirituality uplifting Rembrandtesque world of softly rounded, almost liquid forms and soulfully picturesque portraiture. . . .'[120] Here an artist's knowledge of modelling and shading to suggest volume and his deep insights into character make the work extraordinary. Similarly, the Mughal paintings: 'Holy Men' (*c.* 1650), 'A Gathering of Mystics' (*c.* 1650-5). 'Prince and Courtiers at Camp' (*c.* 1650), 'A Qazi Caught by Surprise with a Young Man' (*c.* 1640), and 'Officers and Wise Men' (*c.* 1655) though relatively conventional Mughal portraits, are noteworthy for their visual realism, carefully delineated effect of light and shade, and the naturalistic modelling clearly derived from the European *chiaroscuro* technique akin to the High Renaissance style.[121]

The modes and trends of the Renaissance art of Europe, with their humanist messages, gained popularity at the Mughal school, but faded away afterwards since other contemporary or near-contemporary schools of Indian art hardly got effected by them. However, during the late nineteenth century, with the awakening among the Indian intelligentsia, especially in Bengal, there emerged a change in the ideas about art and aesthetics. With the rise of nationalism there emerged a renewed interest and pride in the cultural heritage. Raja Ravi Varma's (b.1848) paintings, representative of Western academic manner and imbibing tenets of Renaissance art of Europe turned out to be a strong channel of transference of Western realism into Indian art. In response to the emerging nationalism Varma turned to the themes from Indian mythology and history but adhered to Western technique and style of painting. His narratives and portraits are best known for the *chiaroscuro* effect of light and shade, heavy modelling and deep shading—all complementary to naturalism in art. His human figures are idealized to show the physical charm of the human body. Indian art witnessed another change at the end of the nineteenth century: and with the rise of the new 'Indian style', heralded by Abanindranath Tagore and followed by Nandlal Bose, A.R. Chugtai and others, it led to the development of the Bengal school of painting (also called the Nationalist school) which totally discarded Western Academic art. This phenomenon is to be probed since an element of revival of the classical art and heritage was common to both the Renaissance of Italy and the Bengal school; even so the latter sought to uproot all traces of the former. The basic contradiction was in their approach to art. In the European, its basis was purely scientific and mathematical concepts, encompassing 'modernization', while in the latter the main thrust was to glorify the past and to insist on a total denial of Western art concepts. Thus, the chapter of 'humanism' in art that entered Indian art with the Mughal school, faded away completely with the rise of the Nationalist school.

NOTES

1. *Baburnama*, tr. A.S. Beveridge, New Delhi, rpt., 1979, p. 291.
2. Ibid., pp. 14-15.
3. *Tuzuk-i Jahangiri*, tr. A. Rogers, ed. H. Beveridge, New Delhi, rpt. 1994, vol. 1, pp. 33-4.
4. *Ain-i Akbari*, tr. H. Blochmann, 3rd edn., New Delhi, 1977, vol. 1, p. 113.
5. Ibid., p. 115.
6. Ibid.
7. For reproduction, see Som Prakash Verma, *Mughal Painters and Their Work: A Bibliographical Survey and Comprehensive Catalogue*, New Delhi, Oxford University Press, 1994, p. 128, pl. XXXIII.

8. Jeremiah P. Losty, *The Art of the Book in India*, London, British Library, 1982, p. 101, pl. on p. 100. See also Verma, op. cit., pl. XLIX.
9. *Zakhiratu'l Khawanin of Shaikh Farid Bhakkari*, ed. Sayed Moinul Haq, vol. 1, Karachi, 1961, pp. 47-8. A similar account is given in the *Ma'asiru'l Umara of Shah Nawaz Khan*, tr. H. Beveridge, vol. 1, Calcutta, 1911, p. 99.
10. *Tuzuk-i Jahangiri*, vol. II, pp. 116-17.
11. 'Khan 'Alam with Shah 'Abbas' published by A.K. Coomaraswamy, *Catalogue of the Indian Collections in the Museum of Fine Arts, Boston, Pt. VI (Mughal Painting)*, Boston, 1930, pp. 46-8, pl. 35; 'Shah 'Abbas', published by A.A. Ivanova et al., *Albom Indivskikh-i-Persidskikh Miniatyer xx-viii*, Moscow, 1962, pl. 15; 'Shah Abbas', 'Timurides de l'Inde', *Athar-e-Iran*, vol. II, Haarlem, 1937, 1994-6, fig. 68. See also A.K. Das, 'Bishandas', *Chhavi*, *Golden Jubilee Volume*, ed. Anand Krishna, Bararas, Bharat Kala Bhavan, 1971, pp. 188-90.
12. *Tuzuk-i Jahangiri*, vol. II, p. 117.
13. *Khatirat-i Mutribi Samaraqandi*, ed. Abdul Ghani Mirzoyef, Karachi, 1977, p. 31. Mutribi's account has been overlooked by historians of Mughal art presumably because it had not been published, let alone translated. We are indebted to Professor Riazul Islam of the University of Karachi (Pakistan) for making this text available to us.
14. Ibid., pp. 61-2.
15. V. Smith, *A History of Fine Art in India and Ceylon*, Oxford, 1911, pp. 478-80.
16. T. Falk and M. Archer, *Indian Miniatures in the India Office Library*, London, 1981, p. 66.
17. See 'Portrait of Mulla Sa'id Ulla' (B.M. Add. 18801, no. 32); 'Jaswant Singh' (Prince of Wales Museum of Western India, Mumbai, no. 15, 278); Aziz Khan Chaghata (Johnson Album, v. 23 (9), India Office Library, London.
18. See 'Baqir Khan' (Johnson Album, v. 25 (9) India Office Library; 'Jan Nisar Khan' (Kevorkian Album, Metropolitan Museum of Art, New York); 'Itmadudaula' (Kevorkian Album, Freer Gallery of Art, Washington, D.C.).
19. See 'Shah Jahan' (Chester Beatty Library, Dublin, Album (A), no. 16); 'Shah Jahan with a Courtier', published by I. Stchoukine, *La Peinture Indienne a l'epoge des Grands Moghols du Louvre*, Paris, 1929, pl. 39; 'Muhammad Jam Qudsi', published by E.B. Havell, *Indian Sculpture and Painting*, Murray, London, 1908, pls. 58-9.
20. See 'Dara Shukoh', published by M.C. Beach, *The Grand Mogul: Imperial Painting in India (1600-1660)*, Sterling and Francine Clark Art Institute, Williamstown, Mass, 1978, plate on p. 112; 'Shah Jahan and Dara Shukoh', published by Godard, op. cit., fig. 74.

21. See 'Abyssinian minister', published by Beach, op. cit., plate on p. 126; 'Shah Jahan', ibid., plate on p. 127.
22. 'Prince and a musician' (John Album, v. 4 (5), Indian Office Library.
23. 'Azam Khan', published by Godard, op. cit., fig. 103; 'Shayista Khan', ibid., fig. 104.
24. 'Izzat Khan' (BM, Add. 18801, no. 44).
25. 'Holymen', published by Ivanova et al., op. cit., pl. 13; 'Wanderer', ibid., p. 12.
26. N. Ray, *Mughal Court Painting*, Indian Museum, Calcutta, 1975, p. 97.
27. R.H. Pinder-Wilson, *Paintings from the Muslim Courts of India*, World of Islam Festival Co., London, 1976, p. 21. See also T.W. Arnold and L. Binyon, *The Court Painters of the Grand Moghuls*, Oxford, 1921, p. 52: 'Under Shah Jahan painting continued to have the same character as under Jahangir. Many artists worked during both reigns and so to distinguish between these periods is probably not feasible'. See also, ibid., p. 56.
28. Charles Trinkaus and Naomi Miller, 'Humanism', *Encyclopaedia of World Art*, London, Mc-Graw Hill Company Inc., 1963, p. 723.
29. Edward Mcnall Burns et al., *World Civilization, Their History and Their Culture*, vol. B, Special Indian Edition, Delhi, 1991, p. 606.
30. Abu'l Fazl, *Ain-i Akbari*, tr. H. Blochmann, vol. 1, New Delhi, rpt. from 3rd edn., 1977, p. 114.
31. Milo C. Beach, 'A European Source for Early Mughal Painting', *Oriental Art*, vol. XXII, no. 2, London, 1976, p. 182, fig. 2.
32. *Akbarnama*, tr. H. Beveridge, vol. III, Delhi, Second Indian rpt., 1977, p. 37.
33. Ibid., pp. 349-50.
34. *Muntakhab-ut Tawarikh*, tr. W.H. Lowe, vol. II, Delhi, rpt. p. 215.
35. S.J. Monserrate, *The Commentary of Father Monserrate, S.J. on his Journey to the Court of Akbar*, tr. J.S. Hoyland, annotated by S.N. Banerjee, London, 1922, p. 2 & n.1.
36. Ibid., p. 29.
37. Gauvin Alexander Bailey, 'The Jesuits and the Grand Mogul: Renaissance Art at the Imperial Court of India, 1580-1630', *Occasional Papers*, Smithsonian Institution, Washington, D.C., vol. 2, 1998, p. 16.
38. Edmund W. Smith, *Mogul Architecture of Fathpur Sikri*, pt. 1, Allahabad, 1984, pl. CIX.
39. E. Maclagan, *The Jesuits and the Great Mogul*, London, Burn Oates and Washbourne Ltd., 1932, p. 191 (The book is in eight volume, but for some reason only seven are mentioned as having been presented to Akbar).
40. Ibid.

41. Ernst Kuhnel and Hermann Goetz, *Indian Book Painting*, London, Kegan Paul, Trench Trubner Co. Ltd., 1926, pp. 2-4, 47, 58; Richard Ettinghausaen, 'New Pictorial Evidence of Catholic Missionary Activity in Mughal India (early XVII century)', *Perennitas*, Munster, 1963, p. 391 & n. 33, figs. 4-5.
42. C.H. Payne, *Akbar and the Jesuits*, London, Routledge, 1926, p. 67.
43. Bailey, op. cit., p. 27, figs. 19-20, 21-2.
44. William Foster, ed., *The Embassy of Sir Thomas Roe to India, 1615-19*, Oxford University Press, 1926, p. 187.
45. Ibid., p. 447.
46. Ibid., p. 427.
47. Toby Falk and Mildred Archer, op. cit., p. 78, pls. on p. 392; Verma, op. cit., pp. 150-1, pl. XI.
48. J.M. Rogers, *Mughal Miniatures*, London, British Museum, 1993, p. 105, fig. 73.
49. Ibid., p. 103, fig. 71.
50. Payne, *Jahangir and the Jesuits*, London, Routledge, 1930, p. 65; Maclagan, op. cit., p. 239.
51. Monserrate, op. cit., pp. 48-9, 58-9.
52. Francis Goldie, *First Christian Missions to the Great Mogul*, London, 1897, pp. 168-70.
53. Payne, *Akbar and the Jesuits*, op. cit., pp. 162-3.
54. Maclagan, p. 234 & n. 49.
55. Payne, *Akbar and the Jesuits*, pp. 19-20; Maclagan, p. 226.
56. Payne, *Akbar and the Jesuits*, p. 154.
57. Payne, *Jahangir and the Jesuits*, op. cit., pp. 49-50.
58. Maclagan, p. 248, n. 115.
59. Ibid., pp. 238-9. See also, Payne, *Jahangir and the Jesuits*, pp. 63-5.
60. William Foster, ed., *Early Travels in India, 1583-1619*, rpt., Delhi, 1968, pp. 162-3.
61. S.M. Sen, tr. and ed., *The Indian Travels of Thevenot and Careri*, New Delhi, 1949, p. 85.
62. Foster, *The Embassy of Sir Thomas &c.*, op. cit., p. 211.
63. Ibid., p. 77.
64. Ibid., p. 459.
65. *The Voyage of Nicholas Downton to the East Indies, 1614-15*, London, Hakluyt Society, 1939, p. 187.
66. Foster, *The Embassy of Sir Thomas Roe &c.*, p. 99.
67. *The Voyage of Nicholas Downton &c.*, op. cit., p. xii; Ahsan Jan Qaisar. *The Indian Response to European Technology and Culture (AD 1498-1707)*, New Delhi, Oxford University Press, 1982, p. 87.
68. Foster, *The Embassy of Sir Thomas Roe &c.*, pp. 125-6.
69. Ibid., p. 357.
70. Ibid., pp. 226-7.

71. Foster, *The English Factories in India 1608-1621*, Oxford, 1906, pp. 38, 54; Qaisar, op. cit., p. 89.
72. Foster, *The Embassy of Sir Thomas Roe & c.*, p. 167.
73. Ibid., p. 215.
74. Ibid., pp. 143, 415. See also Foster, *Letters Received by the East India Company from its Servants in the East*, vol. III, London, 1899, p. 64.
75. Payne, *Akbar and the Jesuits*, p. 170.
76. Foster, *Letters Received by the East India Company & c.*, op. cit., p. 64.
77. Ibid., vol. IV, p. 82.
78. W.H. Moreland and P. Geyl, *Jahangir's India* (tr. of Francisco Pelsaert's Remonstrantie), rpt., Delhi, 1972, p. 26.
79. *Ain-i Akbari*, op. cit., pp. 113-14.
80. For their reproductions, see Verma, op. cit., pls. XXVI, XXXIII, XLIX.
81. Verma, *Art and Material Culture in the Paintings of Akbar's Court*, New Delhi, Vikas Publishing House, 1978, p. 28.
82. Madeleine Hallade, *The Gandhara Style and the Evolution of Buddhist Art*, London, Thames and Hudson, 1968, p. 41.
83. *Ain-i Akbari*, p. 114.
84. Amina Okada, *Imperial Mughal Painters, Indian Miniatures from the Sixteenth and Seventeenth Centuries*, tr. Deke Dusinberre, Flammarion, no date, p. 91, fig. 91.
85. Ibid., p. 92, fig. 95.
86. Ibid., pp. 92-3, fig. 1.
87. Ibid., pp. 88-9, figs. 85, 87, 89-90.
88. Reproduced and described: Verma, *Mughal Painter of Flora and Fauna, Ustad Mansur*, New Delhi, Abhinav Publications, 1999, pp. 110-11, pl. III.
89. For reproduction, see S.C. Welch, *Art of Mughal India: Painting and Precious Objects*, New York, 1963, p. 31, pl. 19.
90. Michael Brand and Glenn D. Lowry, *Akbar's India, Art from the Mughal City of Victory*, Asia Society Galleries, New York, 1985, pp. 146-7, no. 41, pl. on p. 79.
91. Reproduced: Okada, op. cit., p. 91, fig. 93.
92. Verma, 'Lal: The Forgotten Master', in Asok K. Das, ed., *Mughal Masters, Further Studies*, Mumbai, 1998, p. 80, fig. 12.
93. E.B. Havell, *The Art Heritage of India*, Bombay, Taraporevala & Sons Co., 1964, p. 91, pl. 61 (A); Verma, *Mughal Painters and Their Work & c.*, op. cit., p. 106, pl. xiv.
94. M.C. Beach, *The Imperial Image: Paintings for the Mughal Court*, Freer Gallery of Art, Washington, D.C., 1981, pp. 169-70, pl. on p. 74; Verma, 'Symbols and Motifs in the Mughal School of Art', in Qaisar and Verma, eds., *Art and Culture: Painting and Perspective*, vol. II, New Delhi, Abhinav Publications, 2002, pp. 50-1, pl. 38.

95. Hallade, op. cit., p. 109.
96. For their reproductions, see A. Ghosh, ed., *Ajanta Murals*, New Delhi, 1967, pl. LXXVI, figs. 7-9.
97. See Verma, 'Symbols and Motifs & c.', op. cit., p. 51, pl. 43; Okada, p. 166, fig. 196.
98. Okada, p. 166, fig. 197.
99. Verma, 'Symbols and Motifs & c.', p. 51, pl. 44.
100. Reproduced: Okada, p. 208, fig. 247.
101. *Ain-i Akbari*, p. 115.
102. F.R. Martin, *The Miniature Painting and Painters of Persia, India and Turkey*, rpt., Delhi, Low Price Publication, 1993, pl. 212.
103. *Tuzuk-i Jahangiri*, tr. A. Rogers, ed. H. Beveridge, vol. II, Delhi, 2nd rpt., 1994, pp. 107-8. For a picture of this bird, see Verma, *Mughal Painter of Flora and Fauna & c.*, op. cit., p. 114, pl. VIII.
104. *Tuzuk-i Jahangiri*, op. cit., p. 157.
105. Verma, *Mughal Painter of Flora and Fauna & c.*, pp. 118-19, pl. XIII.
106. Ibid., pp. 112-13, pl. VI.
107. Ibid., pp. 113-14, pl. VII.
108. Ibid., pp. 115-16, pl. X.
109. E.B. Havell, *Indian Sculpture and Painting*, London, Murray, 1908, p. 214, pl. 61.
110. Kuhnel and Goetz, op. cit., pp. 6, 56, pl. 10.
111. D. Barrett and B. Gray, *Painting of India*, Lausanne, World Publication, 1963, p. 81, pl. on p. 80.
112. R. Grousset, *Civilization of the East*, vol. 2, New York, 1931, p. 374.
113. Foster, *Embassy of Sir Thomas Roe & c.*, p. 199.
114. Beach, 'The Mughal Painter Kesu Das', *Archives of Asian Art*, vol. XXX, London, 1976-77, pp. 35-6, figs. 1-2.
115. Ibid., p. 42, figs. 9 and 11.
116. Bailey, p. 20, fig. 9.
117. Ibid., p. 20, fig. 10.
118. J.M. Rogers, op. cit., 1993, p. 78, fig. 49.
119. Reproduced and described: Chandramani Singh, 'European Themes in Early Mughal Miniatures', in Anand Krishna, ed., *Chhavi*, Banaras, 1971, pp. 405-7, pl. 35.
120. S.C. Welch, *Imperial Mughal Painting*, New York, George Braziller, 1978, p. 87, pl. 24.
121. For their reproductions, see Joseph M. Dye, 'Payag', in Pratapaditya Pal, ed., *Master Artists of the Imperial Mughal Court*, Bombay, Marg Publications, 1991, pp. 129-34, figs. 12-15; Okada, p. 211, figs. 251-2; Beach, *The Grand Mogul & c.*, op. cit., p. 151, no. 52, pl. on p. 152.

CHAPTER 9

Shajra-i-Suhraward: A Sixteenth-Century *Tazkira* of the Suhrawardi Sufi Saints

IQTIDAR HUSAIN SIDDIQUI

This *tazkira* (biographical dictionary) was compiled by Ahmad Khan Akbar Shahi in AD 1596, during the reign of Emperor Akbar.[1] The compiler was the grandson of Shaikh Samauddin Kambo, the leading Suhrawardi Sufi who was the patron saint of the Lodi Sultans. This is the second *tazkira* compiled by a Suhrawardi Sufi after Jamali Kambo's *Siyar ul-Arifin*. Unlike the *Siyar ul-Arifin*, the *Shajra-i-Suhraward* is exclusively related to the Suhrawardi Sufis who flourished in India since the thirteenth century AD. A comparative study of the *Siyar ul-Arifin* and the *Shajra-i-Suhraward* shows that the latter contains additional information about the fifteenth- and sixteenth-century Suhrawardi Sufis. Moreover, we find bits of information about certain early Sufis that help us in correcting historiographic errors, committed by modern scholars on account of their reliance on the legends incorporated by Jamali Kambo in his *Siyar ul-Arifin*. Being a heir to the living tradition of the Suhrawardi *silsilah*, Ahmad Khan Akbar Shahi was in a position to collect information from senior relatives and Sufi literature, including his family records. It is also noteworthy that like other Sufi *tazkira* writers, Ahmad Khan Akbar Shahi has also included popular legends about the miraculous powers possessed by the early Sufis. However, the importance of the work lies in the fact that it contains useful information also and can be used with caution. In the following lines its contents have been analysed.

Let us begin with what helps us point out the pitfalls that some senior scholars have failed to escape because they accepted Jamali's account uncritically. For example, Jamali writes about Shaikh

Jalaluddin Tabrizi, the leading Suhrawardi Sufi who migrated from Baghdad to India and settled in Delhi during the reign of Sultan Shamsuddin Iltutmish (AD 1211-36). Being of charismatic personality, he gained popularity within a short time. Shaikh Najmuddin Sughra, the Shaikh ul-Islam[2] of Delhi became jealous of him and then plotted to defame him. He hired Gauher, a dancing girl, to allege that the Shaikh had illicit relations with her. The Sultan was informed and a *mahzar* (special tribunal) was ordered by the latter to inquire into the allegation. Shaikh Bahauddin Zakariya was invited from Multan to act as the *hakam* (chairman or arbiter) to conduct the proceedings of the *mahzar*. On Shaikh Zakariya's arrival in Delhi, the day was fixed for the settlement of the case. When the *mahzar* was held, the Sultan also came to the Jama Mosque to attend it. Gauhar who was presented as the main witness got nervous and then confessed that she was bribed to malign Shaikh Jalaluddin Tabrizi. Thereupon, the Sultan dismissed Najmuddin Sughra and the Shaikh was honourably exonerated.[3] K.A. Nizami accepted this story uncritically, although it seems to have been structured by the later Suhrawardis to glorify their Shaikh and tarnish the image of the Shaikh ul-Islam of Delhi. Probably, the statement by Shaikh Nizamuddin (Auliya) about the banishment of Shaikh Jalaluddin Tabrizi from Delhi has escaped his notice.[4]

The reference made by Shaikh Nizamuddin (Auliya) to this episode tends to reveal that Shaikh Najmuddin Sughra retained his post of Shaikh ul-Islam as well as the confidence of Sultan Iltutmish till his end. The Sultan did not interfere with the Shaikh ul-Islam and Shaikh Jalaluddin Tabrizi was banished by the latter. According to Shaikh Nizamuddin (Auliya), Shaikh Jalaluddin Tabrizi stayed in Badaon for some time after he had left Delhi. One day, when he was taking a walk along with his companions, he stoped and said to them: 'Let us prepare to offer funeral prayer for Najmuddin Sughra for he has passed away.' Having offered the prayer in absentia, the Shaikh remarked: 'He (Najmuddin Sughra) banished me from Delhi, God has removed him from the world.'[5]

As for the actual cause of Shaikh Jalaluddin Tabrizi's banishment from Delhi; our early sources do not mention it. The statement by Shaikh Nizamuddin (Auliya), quoted above indicates that the Shaikh ul-Islam of Delhi had exiled the Shaikh from the city. In addition to the story narrated by Jamali,[6] the compiler of the *Shajra-i-Suhraward* mentions another story that seems to have angered the Shaikh ul-

Islam. According to it, Shaikh Jalaluddin Tabrizi bought a slave boy for 1,500 *tankas* out of compassion and decided to bring him up. But the Shaikh ul-Islam became suspicious of his conduct.[7] It is also worth mentioning that the picture of Shaikh Jalaluddin Tabrizi that emerges on going through the *malfuzat* of the early great Chishti and Suhrawardi Sufis is that of a great spiritualist, distinguished for his selfless love of man and God. The references found contained in the *Fawaid-ul-Fuad* and *Jami'ul-'ulum* to him is that he was held by scholars and commoners in esteem and remembered by the great Shaikh after his death. He was regarded as an exemplar in renunciation and detachment from worldly affairs. He did not stay in any town for long and moved from one place to another after a short stay.[8] Shaikh Fariduddin Ganj-i-Shakar, the thirteenth century leading Chishti saint cherished his memory, he met him and received his blessing when he was a child.[9] Shaikh Nizamuddin (Auliya) and Shaikh Nasiruddin Chiragh-i-Dilli are also reported to have praised him frequently for his spiritual excellence and charismatic qualities.[10]

Some words are in order about the structured stories found contained in the *Shajra-i-Suhraward*. Like the *Siyar ul-Arifin*, the *Shajra-i-Suhraward* also contains the popular but structured stories interspersed in the biographical details of the thirteenth- and fourteenth-century Suhrawardi Sufis. For instance, Jamali Kambo narrates the following story in order to glorify Shaikh Sadruddin 'Arif, the son and spiritual successor of Shaikh Bahauddin Zakariya of Multan:

> Prince Muhammad Khan (eldest son of Sultan Ghiyasuddin Balban and the governor of Multan) divorced his wife in a fit of anger. Later, he came to his senses, he felt sorry and wanted to keep her as his wife. But the *Sharia* (canon law) did not permit remarriage unless she was married to some other person who spent a night with her and then divorced her. As Shaikh Sadruddin 'Arif was pious man, he was approached by the Prince to do the needful. The Shaikh married the princess. Next day, the Shaikh said that he would not divorce the lady because she was not willing to seek divorce from him. Thereupon the prince got annoyed with the Shaikh and decided to harm him. But, before he could lay his hand, he was informed of the Mongol invasion and had to move immediately with his army to meet the invaders. In a fiercely fought battle the Prince was killed and thus the Shaikh was saved from his wrath.[11]

This story is also contained in the *Shajra-i-Suhraward* with minor additions. The princess is mentioned as the daughter of Sultan Ruknuddin Firuzshah, the son and immediate successor of Sultan Iltutmish. She is also said to have been a beautiful lady of charming features. And, that the prince (Muhammad) divorced her under the influence of alcohol. Since he could not part company with her, Qazi Asiruddin Khwarazmi, advised him to approach Shaikh Sadruddin 'Arif and seek his help. The other details are the same. This story does not stand the test of historical scrutiny because the Shaikh passed away in AD 1285, while Prince, Muhammad Khan was killed by the Mongol invaders in 1287. Moreover, the elegies composed by Amir Khusrau and Amir Hasan Sijzi in verse and prose respectively, portray the prince as a man of noble character free from vices, he neither drank nor indulged in the pleasure of the flesh.[12] Ziauddin Barani also praises the prince for his being fond of the company of the men of piety and learning. Shaikh Sadruddin 'Arif is also reported to have joined the 'gathering of *ulama* and poets at his court'.[13] Had the dispute between these two great men of history taken place, it would not have escaped the notice of Isami and Ziauddin Barani. Particularly, Isami was inclined to incorporate in his *Futuh-us-Salatin* all interesting tales and anecdotes, in order to adorn it. Isami would rather have us believe that Sultan Balban had the innocent son of an old woman killed along with other persons involved in a case of forgery. The woman prayed to God seeking redress. The prince met his death on the battlefield in consequence.[14] It may be surmised that the story was not invented till Isami's day, i.e. the fourteenth century. It was either invented by Jamali Kambo or by some other Suhrawardi protagonist earlier in the fifteenth century. This story has been accepted uncritically by the modern scholars.[15]

As regards the biographical details furnished by the compiler about Shaikh Jalaluddin Bukhari Jahanian-i-Jahangasht, they supplement the information available in other sources. We are informed that he was given the title of Jahanian-i-Jahangasht by his *pir* (preceptor) as *Iddi* (i.e. the Idd festival gift).[16] The information about the establishment of the trust by Sultan Firozshah for the maintenance of the institutions of public utility, attached to the mausoleum of his son, Prince Fath Khan, is also worth citing. Sultan Firoz Shah is said to have had a beautiful mosque, a grand *madrasa* (college) and a large *hauz* (cistern) constructed around the mausoleum. The Sultan endowed the income accruing from fifty-two villages and several royal gardens for running the *madrasa* and *langar* (free public kitchen).

The students and poor people were fed daily. The *waqfnama* (document) relating to the endowment is said to have been executed in the presence of the leading *ulama*, *mashaikh* (Sufi saints) and the *qazis* of the capital in AD 1367 Shaikh Jahanian-i-Jahangasht was present in Delhi at that time and could also put his signature on it as a witness. The compiler says that he himself read the *waqfnama* in the possession of the descendants of Maulana Hafiz Shahin, who was appointed by the Sultan as the *Mutwali* (custodian) of the *waqf*.[17]

The most interesting part of the work begins with the account of the fifteenth- and sixteenth-century Suhrawardi Sufis. It furnishes information about the Suhrawardi Sufis who migrated from Multan and Uchh during the Lodi period. The Lodi Sultans went out of their way to foster close relations with them. We are informed that Sultan Bahlul Lodi (1451-88) gave his daughter in marriage to Shah Abdullah Qureshi, the descendant of Shaikh Bahauddin Zakariya. The Sultan assigned, in addition to rich dowry, the *iqta* of Phulet (in Muzaffarnagar district of U.P.).[18] The other important Sufi was Shaikh Samauddin Kambo who also hailed from Multan during the same time. As he was the grandfather of the compiler, he receives a more detailed treatment in the *Shajra-i-Suhraward*. He became the patron saint of the ruling dynasty. Both Sultan Bahlul Lodi and his son Sultan Sikandar (Lodi) paid visits to his *khanqah*. Being a scholar of Islamic jurisprudence, the Shaikh performed the combined role of a *fiqih* (doctor of *Sharia* law) and a Sufi Shaikh. Shaikh Samauddin was also an exponent of Ibn al-Arabi's philosophy and wrote treatises relating to it. His commentary (*Sharh*) on Ibn al-Arabi's doctrine of al-Wafud gained popularity as it was characterized by his insightful knowledge of different scholars of Sufism.[19] It may also be recalled that his close association with the Lodi Sultans also contributed to his popularity. Shaikh Rizq Ullah Mushtaqi writes that when Sultan Bahlul died near Jalali town, the nobles invited the prince (later Sultan Sikandar) there for his enthronement. Before his departure from Delhi, he paid a visit to Shaikh Samauddin. The Shaikh recited a Quranic verse and then explained its meaning: 'May God render you fortunate in both the worlds'.[20]

The *Shajra-i-Suhraward* also provides us with insights into the cultural efflorescence that resulted from the enlightened state policies followed by the Lodi Sultans. The Lodi Sultans, Bahlul and Sikandar were great patrons of learning, with the result that people took interest in the education of their children. Education was necessary not only for men to become religious scholars but was also a mark of social status.[21] The sons and grandsons of Shaikh Samauddin emerged as leading scholars and served as *danishmands* (scholars of law) or Sufi Shaikhs. Shaikh Abdullah, son of Shaikh Samauddin was a devout Sufi who practised extreme type of austerity, resided in the forest of Malwa in isolation for quite some time and earned the epithet of 'Bayabani'. As for the remaining two sons, Shaikh Jamaluddin Dehlavi and Shaikh Qadan, they specialized in Islamic jurisprudence and were included among the leading *fuqha* (experts of canon law). Shaikh Ladan was selected by Sultan Sikandar Lodi as his adviser on religious issues.[22] Shaikh Jamal was appointed by Islam Shah (1545-53) as the Chief Qazi of the Sur empire. He died in 1575 during the reign of Emperor Akbar. On his death, Makhdum ul-Mulk, the Shaikh ul-Islam of Akbar, paid him a compliment in these words: 'Today, the Imam-i-Azam (the title of Imam Abu Hanifa) has passed away.'[23]

Other eminent Suhrawardi Sufis of the sixteenth century are also mentioned in the work. For example, Jamali Kambo, the son-in-law and the Khalifa of Shaikh Samauddin, is referred to in connection with the popularity of *natiya kalam* (poems composed in praise of the Prophet). Mullah Abdul Qadir Badaoni corroborates the compiler of the *Shajra-i-Suhraward* when he states that Jamali's one *na'ṭ* became so popular that it was translated by Jamali himself in *Hindvi* (local dialect spoken in Delhi and the area around) for the *qawwals* who sang it both in original and *Hindvi* translation.[24] Our author states that one night Shaikh Abdul Wahab Bukhari, the descendant of Shaikh Jahanian-i-Jahangasht and the Khalifa of Shaikh Abdullah Qureshi saw the Prophet in a dream asking him to felicitate Jamali on his behalf for composing the beautiful *n'at*.[25] Shaikh Abdul Wahab Bukhari is also praised for his learning and devotion to religion.

Lastly, mention may be made of the controversy regarding the origin of Kambos of the subcontinent. The Kambos originally belonged to the low caste of Hindus. They lived in the Punjab, worked as peasants in the countryside and as daily wage-earners in the urban centres. Like other low caste citizens, they embraced Islam. In Multan they appear to have benefited from their association with the Suhrawardi Sufis and began to move socially upward. Since our author was himself a Kambo, he would have us believe that his ancestors were ethnically different from the Kambos of the Punjab. He claims that his ancestors came from Arabia and had nothing to do with the Kambos of the Punjab. They were devoted to religion, spent their time in prayer and other religious activities, observed silence most of the time and talked little. Impressed by them, people called them *kumgo* (who talk little). Their descendants followed them and maintained their tradition. But the epithet *kumgo* used for them was corrupted by the uneducated people as Kambo.[26] This statement suggests that on account of the high social status enjoyed by the Kambos from Multan in Delhi and Agra since the Lodi period, they kept themselves aloof from the rustic Kambos of the Punjab. Kambos had emerged as a new social formation during the fourteenth century. Education helped them in their upward social mobility.[27] In short, the *Shajra-i-Suhraward* is not devoid of historical information. Every scholar interested in the study of history and culture would find it a useful source of information.

NOTES

1. The rare manuscript copy of the *Shajra-i-Suhraward* is available in the Rampur Raza Library, Rampur, U.P. It was brought to completion in 1596 when the Suhrawardi *silsilah* was in the decline.
2. The function of the Shaikh ul-Islam was to look after the management of the institution, called *khanqah* in India and *ribat* in Middle East. It was a spacious building constructed outside the city for providing security and financial help to the travellers.
3. Shaikh Jamali (Kombo) Dehlavi, *Siyar ul-Arifin*, Delhi, AH 1311, pp. 165, 167-8.
4. Khaliq Ahmad Nizami, *Some Aspects of Religion and Politics in India during the Thirteenth Century*, Aligarh, Department of History, 1961, pp. 163-4.
5. Cf. Hasan Sijzi, *Fawaid-ul-Fuad*, Lucknow, AH 1885, p. 144.
6. *Shajra-i-Suhraward*, ff. 47b., 48a.
7. Ibid., ff. 46a-47a.
8. *Fawaid-ul-Fuad*, pp.165-6; Hamid Qalandar, *Khairul-Majalis*, ed. K.A. Nizami (Aligarh, 1959), pp. 79-80; Ali bin As'ad, *Jamiʿul-ʿulum* (Malfuzat of Shaikh Jalaluddin Bukhari, known as Makhdum Jahanian-i-Jahangasht), ed. Qazi Sajjad Husain, New Delhi, 1987, p. 258.
9. *Khair ul-Majalis*, p. 220.
10. *Fawaid ul-Fuad*, pp. 132-3; *Khair ul-Majalis*, p. 220.
11. Cf. *Siyar ul-ʿArifin*, p. 135.
12. Besides the Diwan of Amir Khusrau, *The Muntakhab-u't-Tawarikh of Abdul Qadir Badaoni*, vol. 1, also contains these elegies.
13. Ziauddin Barani, *Tarikh-i-Firozshahi*, Calcutta, 1862, pp. 77-80, 127-8, 131.
14. Isami, *Futuh us-Salatin*, ed. S.A. Usha, Madras, 1948, pp. 182-3.

15. Cf. K.A. Nizami, *Some Aspects of Religion and Politics* . . . , p. 226; S. Athar Abbas Rizvi, *A History of Sufism*, vol. 1, New Delhi, 1997, pp. 203-83.
16. *Shajra-i-Suhraward*, ff. 36b-37a.
17. Ibid., f. 38a.
18. *Shajra-i-Suhraward*, 58b.
19. Ibid., 13b-14a.
20. *Waqi'at-i-Mushtaqi*, Eng. tr. Iqtidar Husain Siddiqui, New Delhi, 1993, p. 31.
21. Ibid., p. 17.
22. Ibid., p. 67.
23. *Shajra-i-Suhraward*, ff. 14a-15b.
24. *Muntakhab u't-Tawarikh*, vol. 1.
25. *Shajra-i-Suhraward*, f. 111a.
26. Ibid., f. 9a.
27. Ain-ul-Mulk Mahru, *Insha-i-Mahru*, ed. Sh. Abdur Rashid, Lahore, 1965, document no. 29, pp. 65-7; also Iqtidar Husain Siddiqui, *Mughal Relations with the Indian Ruling Elite*, New Delhi, 1983, pp. 92-4.

CHAPTER 10

Shaikh Ahmad Sirhindi and the Organization of the Naqshbandi *Silsilah* in India

IQBAL SABIR

The Naqshbandi *silsilah* was introduced in India by Khwaja Baqi Billah. He earned great fame and popularity in Delhi where he had settled down in AD 1599. A large multitude of people joined his mystic circle. However, on account of his poor health and busy schedule of prayers and meditation, he could not pay attention to the organization of the *silsilah* and its spread in India. Moreover, after his arrival in Delhi he survived for four years only. He was, however, fortunate enough to have received Shaikh Ahmad of Sirhind, among his *murids*, who emerged as a great spiritual leader, popularly known as *Mujaddid-i Alf-i Thani* (the Reformer of the Second Millennium of Islam). Having assumed the leadership of the *silsilah* on the death of Baqi Billah in AH 1012/AD 1603 as his chief *khalifa* (spiritual successor), he undertook this great mission. He organized the Naqshbandi *silsilah* in India in a very systematic manner by deputing his followers (*khalifas*) to the important cities and towns. These representatives of the Shaikh worked enthusiastically for the progress of the Naqshbandi order and attracted people in large number to their master's fold. If, on one hand, they fulfilled the spiritual expectations and religious urges of the masses, on the other, they also came to wield a considerable and generally sobering influence on the ruling elite which helped them in their organizing activities. As they enjoyed respect and reverence among all sections of the Muslim society, thousands of people joined the Naqshbandi *silsilah* and came into contact with Shaikh Ahmad Sirhindi through his representatives. The present study is an attempt to analyse Shaikh Ahmad Sirhindi's endeavours for the organization of the Naqshbandi *silsilah* in the Indian subcontinent during the first quarter of the seventeenth century.

BURHANPUR

The Shaikh, first of all, turned his attention to Burhanpur[1] which was an important centre of the Sufis and Sufism in central India in those days. A number of Sufis of different *silsilahs* had flourished there since its foundation and attracted thousands of people to their mystic folds.[2] Sirhindi, therefore, deputed his senior most *khalifa*, Mir Muhammad Nu'man, to this famous city, as his spiritual representative. Born in AH 977/AD 1569 in Samarqand,[3] Mir Muhammad Nu'man took keen interest in *tasawwuf* (Islamic mysticism) since his very boyhood. He kept the company of saintly people and spent his time in meditation and offering prayers. In AH 1008/AD 1600 he came to Delhi and joined the mystic discipline of Khwaja Baqi Billah. The mentor's love and affection so deeply influenced Muhammad Nu'man that he decided to permanently stay with him and determined to lead a life of renunciation. On Baqi Billah's death in AH 1012/AD 1603, Muhammad Nu'man came under the direct spiritual guidance of Shaikh Ahmad Sirhindi who took him to Sirhind, looked after him and his family for about six years.[4]

Subsequently, Shaikh Ahmad Sirhindi conferred the Khilafat upon Muhammad Nu'man. In AH 1018/AD 1609, he deputed the Mir to Burhanpur in order to propagate the Naqshbandi *silsilah* and ideology. Nu'man faced many difficulties at the beginning of his stay in the city. It appears that the presence of Shaikh Isa Jundullah[5] and Shaikh Muhammad bin Fazlullah,[6] who had enjoyed great fame and popularity in Burhanpur and the surrounding areas for several years, caused great difficulties and proved a hindrance in the way of Muhammad Nu'man. They seem to have jointly opposed his arrival and missionary activities in the town, and held him as their spiritual rival. Though the evidence in this connection is lacking, it is probable that they were opposed to the Naqshbandi *silsilah* on account of Ahmad Sirhindi's rejection of *Wahdat-ul-wujud*, the spiritual ideology of Shaikh Muhiyuddin Ibn Arabi. After all, Muhammad Nu'man was so much disgusted with local environment that he had to return to Sirhind twice in order to apprise his *pir* of the situation in Burhanpur. The Mir even requested Ahmad Sirhindi for not sending him there again. Nevertheless, Shaikh Ahmad, on both the occasions, emphasizing the importance of Burhanpur, strongly asked Muhammad Nu'man to go back and revive his work of preaching the Naqshbandi *silsilah*. He also exhorted Mir to work with patience and courage in a calm and quiet manner. The Shaikh extended his blessings and wished great success in near future.[7]

Accordingly, Muhammad Nu'man again reached Burhanpur, established his *khanqah* and devoted himself to the spread of the *silsilah* in the region. He frequently communicated his problems to Shaikh Ahmad Sirhindi and sought his advice in every important matter. The Shaikh too, paid great attention to Muhammad Nu'man's work. They both continued correspondence with each other. There are several letters to this effect in the *Maktubat-i Imam-i Rabbani*. In fact, these letters provided moral support as well as spiritual inspiration to Mir Muhammad Nu'man and even created self-confidence in him. Once he informed Shaikh Ahmad that some of his opponents were causing him trouble. Sirhindi did not react upon this. Rather he asked him to continue his work and not to retaliate against them.[8] Complying with the mentor's instructions, Mir Muhammad Nu'man, despite the lack of local support, carried on his mission and gradually gained success. People began to contact with him and ultimately his fame spread far and wide. The author of *Mirat-i Jahan Numa* informs that a large multitude of people benefited from his spiritual radiance. It is reported that no sooner they saw Muhammad Nu'man, than they tore off their garments in a state of spiritual ecstasy.[9] His compassion-radiating personality became the symbol of attraction for the other saints. Many of them are said to have joined his mystic fold. According to the *Zubdat-ul Maqamat* and the *Hazarat-ul Quds*, Nu'man started the process of social association and assimilation.[10] Shaikh Ahmad Sirhindi seemed highly glad to learn his senior follower's success and popularity in Burhanpur. He expected his *khalifa* to cover and spiritually illumine the whole region of the Deccan.[11]

Shaikh Ahmad Sirhindi attached great importance to Burhanpur and wanted to make it an important centre of the Naqshbandi *silsilah*. When, on one occasion, Mir Muhammad Nu'man wrote to him that some of his new *murids* were seeking spiritual training on the pattern of the Qadiriyya *silsilah*, the Shaikh strongly disagreed with them. Rather he insisted on imparting the Naqshbandi teachings only.[12]

Moreover, when he (Shaikh Ahmad) invited Muhammad Nu'man to visit Sirhind, he advised him to come alone.[13] The Shaikh was so confident of the Mir that he could not tolerate him to be disgraced and insulted. Once he was wrongly reported by some persons from Burhanpur that the Mir was not paying any attention to his disciples but taking interest in the construction of his house and spending *futuh* (gift) for his own purpose. But the Shaikh, rejecting this false news, vehemently criticized those who levelled the charges and made complaint against him. He also warned them for their disobedience and disrespectful attitude to their spiritual master. Sirhindi praised Muhammad Nu'man for his bright character and unbound success in Burhanpur and highlighted his spiritual excellences.

Sirhindi's letters to Mir Muhammad Nu'man provide interesting information of Islamic theology and mysticism. In one of his *muktubat* he says. 'The way which leads to the excellences (*kamalat*) of the Prophecy (*nabuwwat*), is associated with the Naqshbandi *silsilah*. That is why the deeds of the Naqshbandi saints are in line with the companions of the Holy Prophet.'[14] Sirhindi attached little importance to the miracles (*karamat*). Once he wrote to Mir Muhammad Nu'man that he should not concentrate in performing miracles as it was not the condition for spiritual development and all the great Sufis, except a few, laid no stress on this aspect.[15] He always enjoined Mir to strictly follow and preach the *Shariah*, the laws of Islam, specially among the ruling class. Once the Shaikh wrote to him, 'The duty of a Muslim Emperor is to enforce *Shariah* in his dominion. The carelessness of a single moment in this great task causes harm to both Islam and the Muslims.'[16]

Mir Muhammad Nu'man was also on friendly terms with Abdur Rahim Khan-i Khanan. According to *Zubdat-ul Maqamat*, Khan-i Khanan visited him in Burhanpur during his viceroyalty of the Deccan. It is related when Jahangir dismissed him from the governship of the Deccan and became hostile towards him, Khan-i Khanan sought Muhammad Nu'man's spiritual blessings.[17] It appears from the *Maktubat-i Imam-i Rabbani* that he helped the Mir and took interest in his religious activities. In a letter to Abdur Rahim, Shaikh Ahmad Sirhindi writes,

> The presence of Mir Muhammad Nu'man in that region is most important. I regard his blessings and spiritual attention towards you as invaluable. These are the source of your stability and promotion. More than a year ago he

wrote to me of your virtues and your attention to the Naqshbandi saints. He also sought my help to block your transfer from the Deccan. I directed my spiritual attention towards you and found that you were destined to make progress.[18]

The fame and popularity of Mir Muhammad Nu'man could not be tolerated by his opponents. They poisoned the ears of the Mughal Emperor against him. They told Jahangir that his activities in Burhanpur could lead to political disturbances in the Empire as more than one lakh Uzbeks had been enlisted in his mystic discipline.[19] According to *Hazarat-ul Quds*, the Emperor called him to the Royal Court at Agra to give explanations of the charges against him. Jahangir is said to have asked Mahabat Khan to inquire into the matter. But the latter's satisfactory remarks notwithstanding, the Emperor set him free on the condition that he would not return to Burhanpur. In compliance with Jahangir's order Muhammad Nu'man had to permanently reside at Agra where he died on 18th Safar AH 1058/ 5 March 1648 AD.[20]

The other saint who maintained the traditions laid down by Mir Muhammad Nu'man and made determined efforts for the development of the Naqshbandi *silsilah* in Burhanpur during the closing years of the life and even after the death of the *Mujaddid-i Alf-i Thani*, in AH 1034 /AD 1624, was Khwaja Muhammad Hashim Kishmi. Though his ancestors owed spiritual allegiance to the Kubrawi *silsilah* and in his boyhood he, too, had come into contact with Kubrawi saints but later he felt attracted towards the Naqshbandi *silsilah*.[21]

It was in his youth that Hashim left for India and spent a period of one year in journeying through various places. Finally he came to Burhanpur in AH 1029/AD 1619. and met Mir Muhammad Nu'man who accorded a warm welcome to him.[22] Hashim joined Muhammad Nu'man's mystic discipline and also got married to his daughter.[23] Later, Muhammad Nu'man introduced Hashim Kishmi, through correspondence, to Shaikh Ahmad Sirhindi. It is reported that the Mir's introductory remarks so deeply impressed Ahmad Sirhindi that he invited Hashim Kishmi to Sirhind.[24]

On reaching Sirhind, where he stayed for about two years, Hashim Kishmi received spiritual training directly from Shaikh Ahmad. There he generally spent his time mostly in serving and attending the spiritual discourses of Shaikh Ahmad Sirhindi. Very often he worked as the latter's secretary as well by assisting him in his academic matters. He also accompanied the Shaikh to different places during his journeys with the royal army.[25] When Sirhindi was in Ajmer, Hashim Kishmi was present there.[26]

Having bestowed the Khilafat upon Khwaja Hashim, Shaikh Ahmad Sirhindi, seven months before his death, sent Muhammad Hashim back to Burhanpur for looking after his family and propagating the Naqshbandi *silsilah* there.[27] As a Naqshbandi Sufi, he too acquired great fame and popularity in that town. His achievements earned him respect and admiration. People joined him in large number and, according to *Hazarat-ul Quds* many high officials and nobles also attended his spiritual assemblies.[28] He also made correspondence with Shaikh Ahmad and received instructions from him for his preaching activities.[29] The *Maktubat-i Imam-i Rabbani* contains many letters to Khwaja Hashim which throw light on the relationship between him and the Shaikh.[30] Hashim visited Sirhind second time on his *pir's* demise in AH 1034/AD 1624 and remained there for some time in the company of Shaikh Ahmad's sons and other *khalifas*.[31] Afterwards he returned to Burhanpur where he lived for the rest of his life. Kishmi died in AH 1054/AD 1644. and was buried on the bank of river Tapti.[32]

Apart from his organizational efforts in Burhanpur, Hashim Kishmi's contribution to the development of the Naqshbandi *silsilah* not only in Burhanpur but in the whole subcontinent, also lies in his producing the famous works entitled: *Zubdat-ul Maqamat*[33] and *Nasmat-ul Quds*.[34] The former occupies a significant place in the Sufi literature produced in medieval India. It is considered a *magnum opus* of the Naqshbandi Mujaddidi saints. The later work contains biographical accounts of the Naqshbandi saints of Central Asia. These works reflect Hashim Kishmi's scholarship and his knowledge of the religious literature. He also compiled the third volume of the *Maktubat-i Imam-i Rabbani*.[35]

Though some other *khalifas* of Shaikh Ahmad Sirhindi are also reported to have visited Burhanpur but no Naqshbandi *tazkira* writer and chronicler has recorded their role and contribution to the expansion of the Naqshbandi *silsilah* there. It appears that they could not stay there permanently.[36]

AGRA

The next important place which attracted Shaikh Ahmad Sirhindi's attention for the organizational work was Agra, the then capital of the Mughal empire. Many important personalities of different persuasions resided there. The Shaikh himself had been there for several years in his youth. His year-long stay there and association with the *ulama*, nobles and Sufis in the capital had made him fully acquainted with the social, political and religious condition of the city.[37] Though, after the accession of Jahangir, the atmosphere, to some extent, had changed, yet Shaikh Ahmad still preferred the capital of the empire for Islamic missionary activities. In comparison with the civilian people, Sirhindi selected the Mughal army for his religious and mystic propagation. It was Shaikh Badiuddin of Saharanpur whom Sirhindi deputed to this task. He belonged to a respectable family of Saharanpur, now in western Uttar Pradesh, and had been a student of Ahmad Sirhindi.[38] Later he joined the mystic fold of the Shaikh and devoted himself to meditation and prayers. After some time Shaikh Ahmad conferred his Khilafat on him and asked him to go to Saharanpur in order to propagate the Naqshbandi *silsilah* and initiate his own disciples. But soon Shaikh Ahmad deputed Badiuddin to Agra to spread his teachings in the Mughal army.[39] Sirhindi strictly asked Shaikh Badiuddin to be determined and not to leave the Mughal capital without his prior permission. The author of the *Zubdat-ul Maqamat* says that Badiuddin attracted a large number of people and earned great fame. He got tremendous success in inculcating a deep sense of peity among both the influential and fellow mystics alike.[40] But contrary to the will of Shaikh Ahmad, Badiuddin left Agra for Saharanpur due to some personal matter. Though he went to Sirhind to apprise Shaikh Ahmad of his departure from Agra but the Shaikh expressed annoyance at his disciple's violation of his orders.[41] On Sirhindi's displeasure Badiuddin promised to return to Agra and perform his duties. But this time Shaikh Ahmad asked him to go to Agra on his own risk. However, Badiuddin reached Agra.[42] Khwaja Muhammad Hashim Kishmi says that in Agra many soldiers of the Mughal army visited Badiuddin and the latter exhorted them to strictly follow the *Shariah* and told them to perform spiritual exercises and meditation.[43] It appears that Badiuddin discussed many controversial topics of *tasawwuf* with them. He got success in the beginning of his mission and many persons approached him to receive the teachings of the Naqshbandi *silsilah*.[44] But at the same time it also appears that some mischievous persons became his enemy on account of his growing popularity. In one of his letters to Shaikh Ahmad Sirhindi, Badiuddin says that such people often cause trouble to him and abuse his spiritual ancestors particularly Khwaja Bahauddin

Naqshbandi and Khwaja Baqi Billah.[45] They also made propaganda against his spiritual mentor, Shaikh Ahmad Sirhindi. Despite these circumstances Shaikh Badiuddin carried on his work and attracted people towards him. He discussed controversial problems of Sufism with the persons who had no faith in mystic revelation and inspiration. It provided an opportunity to make propaganda against him and his spiritual mentor, Shaikh Ahmad Sirhindi. Consequently Jahangir summoned Shaikh Ahmad to Agra and, ordered his imprisonment in the Gwalior Fort.[46] Shaikh Badiuddin afterwards shifted to his hometown Saharanpur and lived there for the rest of his life.[47]

JAUNPUR

Jaunpur was an important city of medieval India. In the Sultanate period it had been a centre of great political and cultural importance under the Sharqi rulers. Even after its annexation to the Mughal empire, it maintained its dignity as a great seat of learning. Shaikh Ahmad Sirhindi realized the importance of this city and decided to introduce his mystic and religious ideology there. He appointed his *khalifa*, Shaikh Tahir Badakhshi in this city.

According to *Zubdat-ul Maqamat*, Shaikh Tahir, a native of Badkhshan in Afghanistan, had been a soldier in his youth. But later he gave up the military service and led a sufi life on the instruction of the Holy Prophet whom he saw along with the first Pious Caliph Abu Bakr Siddiq and other companions in a dream.[48] For some time he wandered about various places and called on many saints to benefit from them. It is reported that he distributed all his clothes among the poor and needy persons, and wore garments of a *dervish*.[49]

Having visited many cities and villages Shaikh Tahir Badakhshi ultimately reached Delhi and came into contact with Khwaja Baqi Billah who imparted spiritual education to him. When the Khwaja passed away, Tahir Badakhshi joined the circle of Shaikh Ahmad and performed spiritual exercises under him at Sirhind. The contemporary *tazkiras* say that Shaikh Ahmad highly regarded the mystical achievement of Muhammad Tahir and even sometimes informed his other disciple of his rapid success.[50]

In AH 1017/AD 1608 Sirhindi conferred the Khilafat on him and sent him to Jaunpur in order to get the Naqshbandi *silsilah* introduced and popularized there.[51] It appears that in the beginning Shaikh Tahir also had to face some difficulty. People avoided his company under the impression that he was a *malamati* Sufi (those Sufis who lived in isolation). Once he himself wrote to his spiritual mentor about the circumstances in Jaunpur[52] but Sirhindi, however, asked him to be determined and devoted to his mystical task.[53] Afterwards, people felt attracted towards and evinced enthusiasm in accepting and joining the Naqshbandi order.[54]

ALLAHABAD

Sirhindi did not neglect the importance of Allahabad as well. He himself seems to have visited this city on one occasion.[55] He sent Saiyid Mohibullah, who belonged to Manikpur, near Allahabad, as his deputy in this city. Previously Mohibullah was a disciple of Shaikh Muhammad bin Fazlullah of Burhanpur. He resided there for a long time and often visited Mir Muhammad Nu'man to receive the teachings of the Naqshbandi *silsilah*. Through these frequent visits to the Mir's *khanqah*, where the letters of Shaikh Ahmad Sirhindi were read out and his teachings imparted to the audience, Saiyid Mohibullah came to know about Sirhindi. The latter dispatched an epistle to him even before he reached Sirhind.[56] The Saiyid was so highly impressed by the personality of Shaikh Ahmad that he joined his mystic discipline and started spiritual exercises under him. Having conferred the Khilafat upon him, the Shaikh asked Mohibullah to stay at Allahabad and make the Naqshbandi *silsilah* popular in that region.[57]

DEOBAND

Deoband was another town to which Ahmad Sirhindi turned his attention. He deputed Shaikh Ahmad Deobani (Deobandi), one of his close *khalifas*, to this town for the propagation of the *silsilah*. Shaikh Ahmad of Deoband had spent a long time of his life in travelling to various places before he came into contact with and studied theology and *tasawwuf* under Shaikh Ahmad Sirhindi.[58] He visited Burhanpur and received Khilafat from Shaikh Fazlullah but soon he again turned to Ahmad Sirhindi. Having performed spiritual exercises under the latter's guidance for several years, Ahmad Deobandi received the *Khilafatnama*.[59] Initially he worked for some time in his native town and attracted many people towards him. But later he shifted to Agra where some Qasim Khan, a royal official of Bengal, came into his contact. Though a Shia, Qasim Khan was so deeply impressed by spiritual excellence possessed by Ahmad Deobandi that he became a Sunni. Deobandi also visited Bengal on the request of Qasim Khan. The *Hazarat-ul Quds* says that Ahmad Deobandi earned great fame and popularity there. Finally he returned to Agra and died there at the age of seventy.[60]

BENGAL AND BIHAR

Shaikh Ahmad also paid attention to the provinces of Bengal and Bihar. He deputed Shaikh Hamid Bengali to Malda as his chief disciple in Bengal. Hamid first of all met Shaikh Ahmad in Agra.[61] It is reported that Hamid Bengali in those days did not believe in Sufism and even did not like Sirhindi on account of his mystical thought. In the meantime Shaikh Ahmad visited Agra and stayed with his old friend Mufti Khwaja Abdur Rahman. Shaikh Hamid had already reached there from Lahore and was staying at the house of the same Mufti. But on being informed of Shaikh Ahmad Sirhindi's arrival, he shifted to another place with a view to avoid his company. But after two days, due to some important matter, he had to come to the Mufti's house where he found Shaikh Ahmad Sirhindi. The latter so deeply influenced Shaikh Hamid by attracting him towards his spiritual excellence, that he not only developed friendly relations with Sirhindi but also decided to accompany him to Sirhind.[62] Subsequently, he joined his mystic discipline. After performing spiritual exercises for several years Shaikh Hamid received Khilafat and was asked by his *pir* to go to his home-town Malda in Bengal in order to popularize the Naqshbandi *silsilah* there.[63]

On reaching Bengal, Shaikh Hamid started his activities there. Both *Hazarat-ul Quds* and *Zubdat-ul Maqamat* state that he also earned great fame and attracted many people to his *khanqah* at Malda. They obtained his spiritual blessings and performed Naqshbandi practices.[64]

As far as Bihar was concerned, Shaikh Ahmad Sirhindi selected Patna as the centre of his mission in that province. It was Shaikh Nur Muhammad whom Shaikh Ahmad sent to Patna to undertake his spiritual mission. Nur Muhammad was a native of Patna. He first came into contact with Khwaja Baqi Billah who assigned him to the care of Shaikh Ahmad Sirhindi. Having received spiritual training for some years, he received the Khilafat from Shaikh Ahmad Sirhindi in AH 1015/AD 1606.[65] The latter asked him to stay at Patna for propagating the Naqshbandi teaching in Bihar. In compliance with his *pir's* instructions, Nur Muhammad reached there and constructed a small house (hut) near the banks of the river Ganga.[66] Thousands of people came to his *khanqah* to obtain his spiritual blessings. Shaikh Nur Muhammad imparted religious and mystical education to his visitors and described the teachings of the Naqshbandi *silsilah* to them.[67]

Later on Shaikh Abdul Haiy, another *khalifa* of Shaikh Ahmad Sirhindi, was also deputed by the latter as his representative to Patna. Abdul Haiy originally belonged to Hisar Shadman, a town in Asfaniyan in Central Asia (now in Tajikistan). He migrated to India and settled down in Patna where he came to know about Shaikh Ahmad's spiritual greatness. Subsequently he reached Sirhind and joined the mystic fold of the Shaikh. At Sirhind, Abdul Haiy also compiled, on the instructions of Sirhindi's son, Khwaja Muhammad Ma'sum, the second volume of the *Maktubat-i Imam-i Rabbani*.[68] After imparting spiritual education and giving mystical training to Shaikh Abdul Haiy, Ahmad Sirhindi conferred his Khilafat upon him. He was also asked to go to Patna to popularize the Naqshbandi teachings and thought.[69]

Contrary to Shaikh Nur Muhammad, who lived a secluded life near the river Ganga, Abdul Haiy took his abode in the heart of the city and devoted himself to his master's mission.[70] Shaikh Ahmad Sirhindi was extremely impressed by the mystical performance of Shaikh Abdul Haiy that he wrote about him in a very high esteem in one of his letters to Shaikh Nur Muhammad.[71] The author of *Hazarat-ul Quds* says that in a short span of time Shaikh Abdul Haiy became the centre of attraction of thousands of people. Even *ulama*, Sufis, and government officials came to him and obtained his spiritual blessings. Very soon he earned fame and popularity. A large number of people from all sections of the society became his *murid* and many of them received Khilafat.[72] Shaikh Ahmad Sirhindi regarded the presence of his *khalifas* in Patna as a great achievement. Once he wrote to some of his sincere friends that the existence of both Shaikh Nur Muhammad and Shaikh Abdul Haiy in Patna at the same time is the conjunction of two auspicious stars.[73]

KASHMIR

Though the *Hazarat-ul Quds* and the *Zubdat-ul Maqamat* are silent about Shaikh Ahmad Sirhindi's mission in Kashmir but the *Maktubat-i*

Imam-i Rabbani reveal that the *khalifas* of the saint were also deputed to this mountainous state.[74] As for Sirhindi's relations with the Kashmiri *ulama* and Sufis, he had been in close contact with some of them during his studies at Siyalkot. Both Maulana Muhammad Kamal and Shaikh Ya'qub Sarafi Kubrawi, under whom Sirhindi completed his higher education, belonged to Kashmir. Shaikh Ahmad's good friend Maulana Hasan Kashmiri, who first introduced him to Khwaja Baqi Billah, also came from Kashmir.[75] Moreover, the Shaikh is also reported to have visited Kashmir on Emperor Jahangir's invitation.[76] He, therefore, must have sent his representative to this state.

PUNJAB

Punjab was the native state of Shaikh Ahmad. It, therefore, drew more and more attention of the saint for the propagation of his mystic and religious mission. He himself resided at Sirhind which was an important town of Punjab at that time. Many of his disciples and *khalifas* had gathered there after coming from far and near. The Shaikh, despite his busy schedule of prayers and meditation, attended his followers, taught them Islamic theology, imparted spiritual education to them and guided their mystical performance. Moreover, the local population and the inhabitants of the adjoining areas also thronged to Shaikh Ahmad for spiritual solace. Many of them approached him for being aware of the different aspects of the religious laws, i.e. the *Shariah*, many visited him to quench their spiritual thirst, many of them desired to listen to his discourses and a large number of people went to the Shaikh's *khanqah* only in order to obtain his spiritual blessings for the fulfilment of their worldly needs. The saint got them convinced and satisfied. All of them gained their goals. Moreover, the *khalifas* of the Shaikh also worked to develop his master's mission in his home-town. Similarly Shaikh Ahmad Sirhindi's sons too assisted him with full enthusiasm in his mystic and religious activities. His eldest son Khwaja Muhammad Sadiq helped his father in imparting spiritual training to the disciples. He also supervised other important matters of the *khanqah* both in the presence and absence of Shaikh Ahmad Sirhindi. After the sad demise of Khwaja Muhammad Sadiq in AH 1025/AD 1616, the whole responsibility of the *khanqah* fell upon the shoulder of his younger brothers Khwaja Muhammad Sa'id and Khwaja Muhammad Ma'sum. Both these brothers played an important part in the development of their father's religious task. All the visitors of the *khanqah* were highly impressed by their scholarly approach and spiritual attainments. These brothers maintained their father's traditions even during his imprisonment and his journeys to various places along with the royal army.[77]

Moreover, Shaikh Badruddin, another *khalifa* of Sirhindi, also actively participated in the popularization of the Naqshbandi *silsilah* in Sirhind and the surrounding areas. He had been a student of Shaikh Ahmad and received spiritual education under him. It is stated that Sirhindi trained Badruddin step by step in his mystical discipline with paternal affection and treated him like his own son. Shaikh Badruddin joined Shaikh Ahmad's mystic discipline at the age of fifteen and lived with his spiritual mentor for a considerable time.[78] He is also reported to have compiled and translated some of the Sufi works but these could not survive. He produced the famous work *Hazarat-ul Quds* in two volumes which contains biographical and other details of the Naqshbandi saints of Central Asia and India.[79] Badruddin initiated many persons into his own mystic discipline. Even his uncle and some ladies of his family joined his spiritual circle. The Naqshbandi Mujaddidi *tazkiras* reveal him as a popular Sufi among the inhabitants of Sirhind town.[80]

Next to Sirhind, Shaikh Ahmad turned to Lahore which was the most important city of Punjab in those days. Having received the Khilafat from Khwaja Baqi Billah, he himself visited Lahore where a large number of *ulama*, *mashaikh*, eminent Muslims and even common people showed great enthusiasm and respect for him and his religious mission. He now decided to make this city a permanent centre of his spiritual activities. He appointed his *khalifa*, Khwaja Muhammad Sadiq, to this task. Originally, the latter belonged to Kishm in Badakhshan. But later on, having migrated to India, he joined the royal service under Abdur Rahim Khan-i Khanan. Subsequently he was introduced by Khan-i Khanan to Khwaja Baqi Billah. Sadiq kept the company of the saint and performed spiritual exercises. After the Khwaja's death, he joined Shaikh Ahmad Sirhindi who, after bestowing the Khilafat upon him, sent him to Lahore (as his deputy) for the propagation of the Naqshbandi *silsilah*.[81] After some time Sirhindi, deputed his another *khalifa*, Shaikh Tahir to Lahore. Tahir was so deeply devoted to his *pir*, Ahmad Sirhindi, that the latter used to say that he was greatly indebted to Shaikh Tahir Lahori. His simplicity and modesty was famous among the other followers of his master. Shaikh Ahmad loved Shaikh Tahir so much that he sometimes asked him to lead the congregational prayer and himself offered *namaz* behind him. Shaikh Tahir was also the tutor of Sirhindi's sons.[82]

Shaikh Ahmad had authorized Shaikh Tahir to initiate disciples into both the Naqshbandi and the Qadri *silsilahs.* In Lahore, Shaikh Tahir completely dedicated himself to the development of his master's mission. He imparted the teachings of his mentor to all his visitors and disciples.[83] According to *Zubdat-ul Maqamat*, he did not have any contact or association with the worldly minded people and never accepted any thing given to him by them. He earned his livelihood through legal means by transcribing the copies of manuscripts.[84] He used to visit Sirhind every year[85] till his death on 20 Muharram AH 1040/29 August AD 1630.[86]

Moreover, during the closing years of Sirhindi's life, two more *khalifas* of the saint, namely, Maulana Abdul Wahid and Maulana Amanullah, were also assigned the duties of preaching the Naqshbandi order in Lahore. They both enthusiastically worked for Shaikh Ahmad Sirhindi's mission after his passing away.[87]

Ahmad Sirhindi's other eminent *khalifa* who played a significant role in the spiritual history of Punjab was Shaikh Adam Banuri, who throughout his life fought against the religious innovations as well as the non-Islamic trends among the Muslims. After instructing him on the mystic path and imparting spiritual education to him, Shaikh Ahmad Sirhindi authorized Adam Banuri as his *khalifa.* The author of *Hazarat-ul Quds* says that *Amr bil Ma'ruf* (the Command to do what is lawful), and *Nehi un il-Munkar* (the Prohibition of unlawful), was the main object of Shaikh Adam's life.[88]

The Shaikh resided at Banur, his native village in Punjab. A large number of people, especially the military men, felt attracted towards him to become his *murids.* Whosoever desired to join his mystic circle (*halqa-i iradat*), Shaikh Adam first asked him to perform *tauba* (repentence), and then to be strict on the path of the *Shariah.* It is stated that many sufis of different *silsilahs* also became the followers of Shaikh Adam Banuri.[89] In AH 1053/AD 1643 Shaikh Adam went to Mecca for Hajj pilgrimage and then visited the tomb of the Holy Prophet at Medina where he died after staying for some years and was buried in the famous graveyard known as the Jannat-ul Baqi' near the grave of the third Pious Caliph, Usman bin Affan.[90]

Moreover, we are also informed of Sirhindi's *khalifas* who made endeavours to preach and popularize the Naqshbandi *silsilah* in different regions in Afghanistan and Central Asia. Maulana Ahmad Baraki and Maulana Hasan Baraki are the best examples in this regard. Sheikh Ahmad deputed them as his representative for this purpose in those lands.[91]

Thus we see that Shaikh Ahmad Sirhindi propagated the Naqshbandi *silsilah* in India in a very organized way by appointing his followers throughout the subcontinent. To almost all the important cities and towns of the country, especially of the Mughal empire, he deputed his *khalifas* and followers for this great religious task. Hardly there was any famous city which did not have any Naqshbandi Sufi authorized by Shaikh Ahmad Sirhindi. That is why Emperor Jahangir too had to accept that Shaikh Ahmad Sirhindi's disciples are found in every city of the Mughal empire.[92]

NOTES

1. A famous city in the present Madhya Pradesh Province of India, Burhanpur was built by Nasir Khan Faruqi, the ruler of Khandesh in AD 1400 in the memory of Shaikh Burhanuddin Gharib, a *khalifa* of Shaikh Nizamuddin Auliya of Delhi. It is related that Nasir Khan Faruqi and his father Malik Raja Faruqi were the disciples of Shaikh Zainuddin, the spiritual successor of Shaikh Burhanuddin Gharib. See Muhammad Qasim Hindu Shah Farishta, *Gulshan-i Ibrahimi* (*Tarikh-i Farishta*), Lucknow, Newal Kishore, AH 1322, p. 279; Munshi Thakur Lal, *Dastur-ul Amal-i Shahanshahi* (Ms. in British Museum/Rotograph in the Research Library, Department of History, AMU, Aligarh), ff. 43-4; Ghulam Ali Azad Bilgirami, *Rauzat-ul Auliya,* Hyderabad, Safdari Press, AH 1310 (AD 1892-93), p. 33.
2. It is said that Shaikh Burhanuddin's spiritual descendants played an important part in making Burhanpur a prominent Chishti centre. They worked zealously to extend their influence in the town and attracted thousands of people to their mystical fold. Even the rulers of Khandesh felt deeply attracted towards them. A large number of Chishti *khanqahs* existed there.

   Shaikh Azizullah Mutawakkil (ob. 912/1506-7), is reported to be the first eminent saint of the Chishti order in Burhanpur. He was the spiritual descendant of Shaikh Fariduddin Ganj-i Shakar. Shaikh Azizullah left a deep impact upon the inhabitants of the town and enlisted a large number of people into his mystic circle. See Shaikh Abdul Haq Muhaddith, *Akhbar-ul Akhyar*, Delhi, Matba'-i Mujtabai, AD 1332, pp. 278-9; K.A. Nizami, *Tarikh-i Mashaikh-i Chisht,* I, Delhi, 1979, pp. 222-66 and also his article

'Sufi Movement in the Deccan', published in the *History of Medieval Deccan*, II, ed. H.K. Sherwani, Hyderabad, Govt. of Andhra Pradesh, 1974, pp. 176-99.

For the details of the Sufis of different *silsilahs* in Burhanpur, see Nizami's article 'Sufi-Movement in the Deccan', in Sherwani, op. cit., pp. 176-99.

3. Muhammad Nu'man originally belonged to Kishm, a town in Afghanistan. His father Mir Shamsuddin Yahya, popularly known as Mir Buzurg (ob. AH 944/AD 1586, came from a distinguished Saiyid family of saintly scholars, and himself was a famous *alim* and sufi of his time. Mirza Muhammad Hakim, the ruler of Kabul, is reported to have held Mir Yahya in high esteem and entertained him at his court. It is said that when Mirza Hakim died in AH 993/AD 1585 and Emperor Akbar appointed Raja Man Singh as the new governor of Kabul, Mir Buzurg could not tolerate a non-Muslim ruler in his country and prayed for his own death. Accordingly he died in AH 994/AD 1586 and was buried in Kabul. See Badruddin Sirhindi, *Hazarat-ul Quds,* II, Lahore, Punjab Waqf Board, p. 299.

   But the author of *Zubdat-ul Maqamat*, Khwaja Muhammad Hashim Kishmi, reports that Mir Buzurg was buried in Kishm which seems correct as he himself belonged to the same town. See *Zubdat-ul Maqamat*, Kanpur, Newal Kishore Press, 1890, p. 327.
4. Hashim Kishmi, *Zubdat-ul Maqamat*, Kanpur, Newal Kishore Press, 1890, pp. 328-31; Badruddin Sirhindi, op. cit., pp. 300-2.
5. He was the disciple and Khalifa of Shaikh Arif, a follower of Saiyid Muhammad Ghauth of Gwalior. It is related that he had a thorough command over the works of Muhiyyuddin Ibn Arabi and wrote a number of treatises explaining the theory of 'Wahdat-ul Wajud. He died in AH 1031/AD 1621-2. He is also reported to have written a commentary on the Quran. See Nizami, 'Sufi Movement in the Deccan', in Sherwani, op. cit., pp. 176-99.
6. A famous saint and scholar of Burhanpur who held an important position among the people. Born in AH 992/AD 1545-6 in Gujarat, he studied under eminent *ulama* and scholars of his time, in India and in Mecca and Madina. It is said that Miran Muhammad II, the ruler of Khandesh, paid great respect to and invited him to stay at Burhanpur. Shaikh Muhammad was a strict adherent of the *Shariah*. He produced a number of treatises which cover a vide range of Islamic theology and Sufism. The Shaikh died on 2nd Ramazan 1029/1 August 1620. For his detailed study see Saiyid Imamuddin, *Barkat-ul Auliya* (Urdu), Delhi, Afzal-ul Matabi', AD 1322, pp. 95-7.
7. *Zubdat-ul Maqamat*, p. 331.
8. *Maktubat-i Imam-i Rabbani* (Turkish edn.), Istanbul, Isik Kitabvi, 1977, vol. I, letter no. 119.

9. Muhammad Baqa, *Mirat-i-Jahan Numa* (Ms. in British Museum Rotograph in the Research Library, Department of History, AMU), f. 112a.
10. *Zubdat-ul Maqamat*, p. 332; *Hazarat-ul Quds*, II, p. 303.
11. *Maktubat*, vol. I, letter no. 246.
12. Ibid., letter nos. 119, 238.
13. Ibid., letter no. 257.
14. Ibid., letter no. 313.
15. *Zubdat-ul Maqamat*, p. 277.
16. Ibid.
17. Ibid.
18. *Maktubat*, vol. II, letter no. 62.
19. In this connection the statement of Saiyid Athar Abbas Rizvi is misleading. He says, 'Although Akbar and Jahangir would never have been so rash as to dispatch such a large military force composed of a single racial group to one outpost, it is probable that some newly arrived Uzbeks soldiers did become disciples of Mir Muhammad Nu'man (see, *A History of Sufism in India*, vol. II, Delhi, Munshiram Manoharlal, 1983, p. 224). It may be noted here that Mir Muhammad Nu'man or his supporters never claimed such a large number of military or civilian Uzbeks to have been initiated into his mystic fold. The *Hazarat-ul Quds* (vol. II) clearly reveals that the rivals of the Mir fabricated this false accusation and incited the Mughal Emperor Jahangir (see p. 272).
20. *Hazarat-ul Quds*, II, p. 272.
21. *Zubdat-ul Maqamat*, p. 1.
22. Ibid., p. 326.
23. Zawwar Husain, *Hazrat-i Mujaddid-i Alf-i Thani*, Karachi, Idarah-i Mujaddidiyah, 1975, p. 789.
24. *Maktubat*, vol. II, letter no. 1.
25. *Zubdat-ul Maqamat*, p. 3; *Hazarat-ul Quds*, II, p. 369.
26. *Zubtal-ul Maqamat*, p. 282; *Maktubat*, vol. III, letter no. 106.
27. *Hazarat-ul Quds*, p. 370; *Maktubat*, vol. III, letter no. 106.
28. *Hazarat-ul Quds*, II, p. 370.
29. *Maktubat*, vol. III, letter no. 42.
30. See *Maktubat-i Imam-i Rabbani,* vol. I, letter nos. 310, 313; vol. II, letter nos. 65, 74, 93, 97; vol. III, letter nos. 42, 53, 69, 75, 90, 92, 96.
31. *Zubdat-ul Maqamat*, p. 285.
32. *Hazarat-ul Quds*, II, p. 383; Zawwar Husain, op. cit., p. 793; Abdul Haiy, *Nuzhat-ul Khawatir*, vol. 5, Hyderabad, Idarah-i Dairat-ul Ma'arif, 1976, p. 406.

    It may be mentioned here that Muhammad Aslam, basing on the information contained in the tablet (*katbah*) fixed on Kiṣhmi's grave, gives the latter's year of demise as AH 1045/AD 1635 (see, *Tarikh-i-Maqalat*, Delhi, Nadwat-ul Musannifin, 1970, p. 163) which is not correct. In this connection Zawwar Husain also criticizes Aslam's view (see *Hazrat-i-Mujaddid-i Alf-i Thani*, p. 793).

33. The *Zubdat-ul Maqamat* was first published in 1885 by Matba'-i Mahmud, Lucknow. The Newal Kishore Press of Kanpur also published it in 1890. The present writer has used the Newal Kishore (Kanpur) edition of the *Zubdat-ul Maqamat* in the preparation of this article.
34. The manuscript of this work belongs to the Leningrad University Library, Russia, see, C.A. Storey, *Persian Literature*, vol. I, pt. 2, London, Luzac & Company, 1972.
35. *Hazarat-ul Quds*, II, p. 370.

    In this connection also see the Preface of the third volume of the *Maktubat*. It may be mentioned here that Khwaja Hashim was a poet as well. Almost all the contemporary and later Naqshbandi sources refer to his poetic compositions (see *Hazarat-ul Quds*, p. 377; *Nuzhat-ul Khawatir*, vol. 5, p. 406; Thomas William Beale, *An Oriental Biographical Dictionary* (rpt.), New Delhi, Manohar, 1971, p. 158). Moreover, Hashim himself has given two of his poems at the end of the *Zubdat-ul Maqamat* (see p. 399).

    The collection of his poetic verses known as *Diwan-i Hashim* seems to have been completed in his lifetime (see William Beale, op. cit., p. 158; C.A. Storey, p. 988; also see *Nuzhat-ul Khawatir*, vol. 5, p. 406).

    For his details see: Iqbal Sabir, 'Khwaja Muhammad Hashim Kishmi: A Famous Seventeenth Century Naqshbandi Sufi of Burhanpur', in *Sufis, Sultans and Feudal Orders: Professor Nurul Hasan Commemoration Volume*, ed. Mansura Haidar, New Delhi, Manohar and Centre of Advanced Study, Department of History, AMU, Aligarh, 2004, pp. 63-70.
36. *Hazarat-ul Quds*, II, pp. 333, 349. Mention may be made here of another outstanding Sufi who played an important part in disseminating the Naqshbandi teaching in Burhanpur during the second half of the seventeenth century whose name was Shaikh Abul Muzaffar Sufi Burhanpuri. But he was a *khalifa* of Khwaja Muhammad Ma'sum, the son and successor of Shaikh Ahmad Sirhindi. Abul Muzaffar belonged to a noble family of the Deccan but later he turned to Sufi life and worked zealously to popularize the *silsilah* and its practices as well as thought. His piety and scholarship had a tremendous impact upon the inhabitants of the town. Thousands of people are said to have joined the circle of his *murids*. He died in 1108/1696 in Burhanpur. For his details, see *Barkat-ul Auliya*, p. 138; *Nuzhat-ul Khawatir*, vol. 6, Hyderabad, Idarah-i Dairat-ul Ma'arif, 1978, p. 18; Muhammad Abdul Jabbar Khan, *Tarikh-i Auliya-i Deccan*, vol. I, Hyderabad, Matba-i-Hasan, AD 1328, p. 149.

37. See Iqbal Sabir, 'Hazrat Mujaddid-i Alf-i Thani Ahd-i Akbari Mein', *Ziya-i Wajih*, vol. 9, no. 6, June 1998, ed. Wajahatullah Khan, Rampur, Jamia Furqania, pp. 19-24.
38. *Zubdat-ul Maqamat*, p. 346.
39. Ibid., p. 347.
40. Ibid., p. 348.
41. Ibid.
42. Ibid.
43. Ibid.
44. Ibid., p. 350.
45. Ibid.
46. Ibid., p. 348.
47. Ibid., p. 349.
48. Ibid., p. 364.
49. Ibid.
50. Ibid., p. 365.
51. *Hazrat-ul Quds*, II, 342.
52. *Zubdat-ul Maqamat*, p. 366.
53. *Maktubat*, vol. I, letter no. 217.
54. *Zubdat-ul Maqamat*, p. 366.
55. *Maktubat*, vol. I, letter no. 313.
56. *Zubdat-ul Maqamat*, p. 382; *Maktubat*, vol. I, letter no. 272 (It appears from this letter that Saiyid Mohibullah was very fond of *sama*, i.e. mystical songs, in his early days but due to Shaikh Ahmad's influence he gradually gave up this habit, see, letter no. 285.)
57. *Zubdat-ul Maqamat*, pp. 382-3.
58. *Hazarat-ul Quds*, II p. 349.
59. Ibid.
60. Ibid., pp. 50-1.
61. *Zubdat-ul Maqamat*, p. 354.
62. Ibid., p. 355.
63. Ibid., p. 135.
64. *Hazarat-ul Quds*, II, p. 317.
65. *Zubdat-ul Maqamat*, p. 351.
66. Ibid.
67. Ibid., p. 353.
68. Ibid., p. 376.
69. Ibid.
70. Ibid.
71. *Maktubat*, vol. II, letter no. 85.
72. *Hazarat-ul Quds*, II, p. 366
73. Ibid.; *Zubdat-ul Maqamat*, p. 376.
74. Two letters are incorporated in the first volume of the *Maktubat-i Imam-i Rabbani* (letter nos. 295 and 303) which are addressed to some Haji

Yusuf Kashmiri. It appears from the contents of the letters that he was Shaikh Ahmad Sirhindi's *khalifa* in Kashmiri.

75. For details, see *Zubdat-ul Maqamat*, pp. 32-8.
    The first volume of the *Muktubat* contains four letters addressed to him also (letter nos. 99, 100, 101 and 279).
76. *Zubdat-ul Maqamat*, p. 159; also Ali Akbar Husaini, *Majma'-ul Auliya* (MS.), IOL, no. 145, f. 442.
77. For details, see *Zubdat-ul Maqamat*, pp. 300-25 and *Hazarat-ul Quds*, pp. 220-95.
78. *Hazarat-ul Quds*, II, p. 386.
79. The first volume of the *Hazarat-ul Quds*, begins with the details of the Holy Prophet, the First Pious Caliph Abu Bakr Siddiq, Salman Farsi and Imam Jafar Sadiq, and Supplying the accounts of almost all the Naqshbandi saints of Central Asia, it concludes with the details of Khwaja Baqi Billah, his sons and *khalifas* whereas the second volume is devoted to Shaikh Ahmad Sirhindi, his sons and *khalifas.*
80. *Hazarat-ul Quds*, II, pp. 387-413.
81. Ibid., pp. 345-7.
82. *Zubdat-ul Maqamat*, pp. 340-1.
83. Ibid., pp. 342-6.
84. Ibid., p. 346.
85. Ibid.
86. *Hazarat-ul Quds*, II, p. 327.
87. *Zubdat-ul Maqamat*, pp. 388-9.
88. Ibid., p. 383.
89. *Hazarat-ul Quds*, II, p. 384.
90. The author of the *Hazarat-ul Quds* says that Shaikh Adam Banuri had been banished to Mecca by the order of Emperor Shah Jahan because, on account of a considerable large number of his Afghan followers, the Shaikh had become suspect in the eyes of the Mughals. See p. 388.
91. *Zubdat-ul Maqamat*, pp. 368-70.
92. *Tuzuk-i Jahangiri*, ed. Sir Syed Ahmad Khan, Aligarh, Private Press, 1864, p. 272.

CHAPTER 11

The Position of Hindus in the Mughal *Suba* of Malwa

SYED BASHIR HASAN

The condition of various religious communities in medieval times has become the subject of practically a national debate in recent years for well-known reasons. Historians have, of course, been long concerned with it. One way of looking at the fortunes of individual communities is to isolate localities or regions, and treat their history comprehensively by making use of literary, epigraphic, archival and archaeological material. What follows is a preliminary study of the fortunes of the Hindus in the *suba* of Malwa during the Mughal period (sixteenth to seventeenth centuries). It is hoped that this preliminary study can be supplemented by scholars more conversant with Hindu religious texts and secular literature.

Malwa was a preponderantly Hindu province under the Mughals. The region came under Muslim domination in 1305 when the independent existence of the kingdom of the Parmaras came to an end.[1] An independent Muslim kingdom was established in Malwa by Dilawar Khan Ghuri in 1401-2 who was sent by the Sultan of Delhi as governor in 1390-1.[2] Under the Sultans, the Hindus had an important role to play and were associated in the administration. During the reign of Nasir Shah (1501-10), Basant Rai appearing to be a Rajput, held the highest post of a *wazir*. He was reappointed to the same post by Sultan Mahmud Khalji II, the third son of Nasir Shah. However, Basant Rai was murdered by a section of Muslim nobles as a result of party politics among the nobles in order to secure more power.[3] Mahmud Khalji II also had to flee from Mandu, his capital, to save himself from Muhafiz Khan, the *wazir* who succeeded Basant Rai and had become too powerful. It was at this critical moment that Rai Chand Purbiya of Chanderi and his Rajputs came to the assistance of the Sultan. He was appointed chief adviser of the Sultan and was given the title of Medini Rai. Being restored on the throne of Malwa and in recognition of the services of Medini Rai, Mahmud Khalji II honoured him with the post of *wazir*.

During the next few years, Medini Rai due to his bravery and loyalty, grew very powerful. He succeeded in removing the Muslim *amirs* from all posts of influence and became practically an arbiter of the state. The rivalry between the two ultimately resulted in the flight of Mahmud Khalji II to Gujarat. Muzaffar Shah II, the Sultan of Gujarat restored Mahmud Khalji II to the throne of Malwa in AD 1518 and Medini Rai sought help from Rana Sanga of Chittor. Later Medini Rai occupied Chanderi.[4] Thus the Hindus formed a considerable section in the nobility of the Sultans of Malwa and held both lower and higher posts in the administration. They also got themselves involved in the factional politics of the nobility, particularly during the reign of Mahmud Khalji II for gaining greater influence over the Sultan or for achieving higher positions for themselves and for their supporters.

For the Hindus' position in Malwa under the Mughals, one naturally turns to the chapter on Malwa in Abul Fazl's *Ain-i-Akbari*. In the detailed statistical tables of the *mahals* (*parganas*) appended to this chapter, the Mughal historian records the clan or caste of *zamindars* against each *mahal*. This gives sufficient information regarding the concentration and political domination of a particular caste of Hindus in different regions or Mughal administrative subdivisions of *sarkars* in *suba* Malwa.

The *sarkar* of Garha in the *suba* of Malwa occupied the largest area in this province. Lying in eastern part of the *suba*, the bulk of the *sarkar* consisted of the region known as Gondwana.[5] The *Ain* in its *mahal* list of the *sarkar* shows that it was totally under Gond *zamindars* except that of *pargana* Jetha where Gonds and Brahmans are specified as *zamindars*.[6] The principal chieftaincy of Gondwana was that of Garha or Garha-Katanga.[7] Abul Fazl writes:

> In the spacious territories of Hindustan there is a country called Gondwana, viz. the country inhabited by the Gond tribe. . . . This country is called Garha-Katanga. It is an extensive country full of forts, prosperous towns and cities, as that the persons balanced in mind, have stated that Garha-Katanga contained 70 thousand villages. Out of them Garha is a large city, and Katanga was the name of a village. And therefore, the country has become known

by this double name. The capital of the country is the fort of Churagarh (Chauragarh). . . .[8]

Since the *Ain* assigns *haveli* to Garha, we may assume that both Garha and Chauragarh were recognized as headquarters of the *sarkar*. Besides Garha, there were a number of chiefs (*rajas*) in Godwana. They are referred to as the *rajas* of Karaula, Haria, Silwani, Dangi, Kathola, Magadh, Mandla, Deohar and Lanji.[9] Besides these rulers, we find references to the *raja* of Bairagarh[10] and a chieftain named Krishna Rai holding Amoda (Amodgarh of the *Ain*)[11] which was a *pargana* of *sarkar* Garha. Since the *Ain* mentions all *parganas* (except Jetha) as the territories of the *zamindars* of Gond tribe, it may be assumed that the above-mentioned *rajas* belonged to the same tribe as this region was completely dominated by the chiefs of Gond tribe giving its name as Gondwana to this region.

In 1564-5, Asaf Khan, the Mughal *jagirdar* of Kara, attacked the country of Garha-Katanga and defeated the forces of Rani Durgawati and the Rani died by committing suicide in the battlefield.[12] After her death, Raja Bir Narayan, the son of the Rani also died fighting and the fort of Chauragarh was captured.[13] Thus the political status of the Gond *rajas*, after Bir Narayan, was reduced to that of the subordinates of the Mughal empire.

While the eastern part of *suba* Malwa was exclusively dominated by the Gonds, western Malwa was largely dominated by Rajputs. Other castes are also recorded but very occasionally. Among the Rajputs,[14] we find a variety of clans. The *sarkars* of Ujjain and Raisen are shown as completely in possession of the Rajput *zamindars*.[15]

The Rathors are entered in three *parganas* only; Ujjain in *sarkar* Ujjain[16] and Paplun and Muhammadpur in *sarkar* Sarangpur.[17] As against the Rathors, the Chauhan *zamindars* were more numerous. They are recorded against the *parganas* of Jhajhon and Deohari Khurd in *sarkar* Chanderi;[18] Ashta, Agra, Talain, Sarangpur, Sandarsi, Shujapur, Naugam in *sarkar* Sarangpur[19] and Baraudah in *sarkar* Mandsaur.[20]

The Khichis are a well-known offshoot of the Chauhans. Abul Fazl has entered them as the caste of the *zamindars* against Dub Jakar in *sarkar* Chanderi and Bazilpur and Zirapur in *sarkar* Sarangpur.[21] We find a reference of one Gharib Das, a Khichi chief, who was granted Sironj (the famous textile town of Malwa) in *jagir* by Akbar.[22] After the fall and dispersal of the Parmaras in Malwa, the

Khichis supplanted the Dods, a far-flung branch of the Parmaras and spread themselves eastward. In the thirteenth century, their dominion is said to have shrunk to the region which now bears the name of Khichiwara. These Khichis were a constant source of trouble to Muslim potentates till the reign of Akbar. The Mughal emperors as a matter of policy gave *jagirs* to Rathors in Malwa in order to keep down the older element of the Rajput population in the *suba*. These in turn relegated the Khichis to an inferior political and social position.[23]

Interestingly, the *zamindars* of the famous Sisodia clan were recorded only in the *sarkar* of Mandsaur. Abul Fazl, in his *mahal* list, assigns *parganas* of Ringnod, Basaherah (Jarret-Basad) and Jamiawara to Sisodia chiefs.[24] There is only one place where the Solankis are mentioned in the *mahal* list of *sarkar* Raisen.[25]

Similarly the Rajput clans like Dhakrah (Dhakar),[26] Bais and Jadon are recorded in the *sarkar* of Ujjain only. The Dhakrah is entered against *pargana* Unhel, and Jadon (Yadu) and Bais against *pargana* Nolai.[27]

Another clan of the Rajputs, the Bundelas are of somewhat inferior position among the Rajputs. Abul Fazl has recorded them at one place only in *pargana* Bara in *sarkar* Chanderi.[28] Similar to Bundelas were the Dhandels, mentioned in the *Ain* against *pargana* Sahar Baba Haji in *sarkar* Sarangpur,[29] a branch of Hara Rajputs giving their name to a territory called Dhandhelkhand in Bundelkhand. The Dhandels are regarded a shade higher than the Bundelas.[30]

Among the other castes, the Khatris have been recorded as zamindars in *sarkar* Chanderi against the *parganas* of Mianah and Mahadpur.[31] In the same *sarkar* of Chanderi, the Bagris (Baugrees), are mentioned in its *mahal* list against the *parganas* of Udaipur and Bandarjhilla (Jhilla).[32] The two modern scholars, who have worked on tribes and castes of India, have surprisingly omitted the Bagri caste in their monumental works. However, Malcolm records the Bagris, as the lowest caste of the Hindus who were professed robbers and thieves. He traces their origin in Malwa from the western parts of India, chiefly from the neighbourhood of Chittor.[33]

A very interesting clan is that of the Ujjainias, who shared the *zamindaris* of *parganas* Ujjain, Unhel and Dipalpur in *sarkar* Ujjain. Their name is clearly derived from the ancient town of Ujjain, and they are said to have belonged to the clan of Panwars.[34]

Apart from the above clans and castes, Abul Fazl has recorded

Mehtar, Soriah, Magwar, Dodia or Deora, etc., in the *sarkars* of Ujjain, Sarangpur, Mandsaur and Kotri Pirawa. In several other cases, the Mughal chronicle simply enters 'Rajput' as the caste of the *zamindars* in various *sarkars* of Malwa.

The Brahmans (*zunnar-dar*) had also their share in the *zamindari* of Malwa. The *Ain* records Brahmans as a caste of the *zamindars* against the *parganas* Bhorasa (Bhonrasa), Bandarjhilla, Bajhar (Pachar), Beli, Tumun and Korai (Korwai) in *sarkar* Chanderi and against Bamangaon and Barodara in *sarkar* Bijagarh.[35] In the modern district of Indore, the 'Shrigaur or Shrigauda' and Dasora sub-divisions of the Brahmans trace their settlement in the district since ancient times and due to long historical connection with Malwa, the 'Shrigaur or Shrigauda' Brahmans are called 'Malvi Brahmans'.[36]

The caste of Ahir is recorded against the *parganas* of Itawa, Badarwas and Ahak, Beli and Chanderi in *sarkar* Chanderi and against Ujenwas, Tharod (Tirod), Baraltah and Ghiyaspur in *sarkar* Mandsaur. The Gujars had their share in the *zamindari* in *pargana* Kalakot only in *sarkar* Chanderi. The Jats are entered against *pargana* Bandarjhilla in *sarkar* Chanderi, along with Brahman and Bagri.

The Bania caste (Baqqal) is recorded as *zamindar* in three *parganas* of *sarkar* of Chanderi namely Udaipur, Ranod and Larwala (Karwala). Tavernier, a French traveller, who visited Malwa in the seventeenth century informs us that the town of Sironj (*sarkar* Chanderi) was largely inhabited by 'Banian' (Bania) merchants and artisans.[37] Malcolm in his Memoir of Central India, found in early 1820s that the 'Soucars and Shroffs' (bankers and money-brokers) and 'Bunnias' (Banias) in Malwa were both Jains and Vaishnavites; but the greater number was that of the Jains. A considerable number of Banias in Malwa are either from Gujarat or Marwar. The Banias of Gujarat originally settled in Ujjain some time in the sixteenth century. Some Bania families of Indore came to be settled there during the prosperous period of the Sultans of Malwa.[38] The Banias were mostly involved in the trade and commerce of Malwa.

The caste of writers and village accountant, the Kayastha (Kayath in the *Ain*), is entered as the caste of *zamindars* in the *parganas* of Mungaoli in *sarkar* Chanderi, Beawar in *sarkar* Sarangpur and Kotri Pirawa in *sarkar* Kotri Pirawa.

Such a bigger hold of the Hindus as zamindars, their inclusion in the provincial administration and above all the cordial attitude of the Mughal emperors and the provincial bureaucracy towards the Hindus in Malwa not only enabled them to continue with the construction of new temples and repair and maintain older ones but also to enjoy freedom in religious activities throughout the province. The epigraphic records left by the builders of these temples and afterwards by the pilgrims refer to the construction of new temples practically in every emperor's time right from Akbar down to Aurangzeb (see Table, nos. 64, 98, 99, 143, 186, 191). There are three temples which explicitly record their construction during Akbar's reign. The Shaiva temple in the town of Maheshwar in *sarkar* Mandu (district Indore) dedicated to Kaleshwar Mahadeva bears an inscription recording its construction in VS 1627 (AD 1570)[39] (see Table, no. 98). Similarly another Shaiva temple known as Matangeshwar also bears an inscription dated VS 1627 (AD 1570)[40] (see Table, no. 99). Another Shaiva temple dedicated to Tilabhandeshwar Mahadeva was built at Ujjain in AD 1600[41] (see Table, no. 186).

The construction of new temples also continued during the reign of Akbar's son and successor Jahangir. A Shaiva temple dedicated to a goddess in the town of Bhonrasa in *sarkar* Chanderi (district Vidisha) bears an inscription recording its construction in VS 1681 (AD 1624) (see Table, no. 191). It also mentions the name of the builder, which is illegible.[42]

However, there is no temple in Malwa bearing an explicit date of construction during the reign of Shah Jahan. But there are two temples built in the districts of Guna and Mandsaur during the reign of Aurangzeb. A temple at Dhakoni (district Guna) was constructed in VS 1737 (AD 1680) by one *raja* of Chanderi according to an inscription at its entrance[43] (see Table, no. 64). Another table at village Satkheda dedicated to Kala-Bhairava was also built in AD 1680[44] (see Table, no. 143).

Besides these, there are a number of temples built during the reign of Mughal emperors as the archeologists have given their date of construction in the sixteenth-seventeenth centuries. In this category are the two Shaiva temples built at Hinglajgarh[45] and one Vaishnava temple at Athana[46] in the district of Mandsaur (see Table, nos. 105, 123 and 124). A temple dedicated to Nau Durga Mata[47] at Antri Buzurg in the same district was constructed either during the period of Malwa Sultans or in the time of Mughals (see Table, no. 104). Similarly, a group of four Shaiva temples in the town of Dharmapuri situated on the north bank of river Narmada in the district of Dhar is assigned the date of sixteenth-seventeenth century[48] (see Table, no. 34). The Shaiva temple of Pataleshwar Mahadeva at Nagda in the district of Dewas was constructed in the sixteenth-seventeenth century[49] (see Table, no. 8). A Shaiva temple called Jaleshwar Mahadeva[50] at Maheshwar in the district of Indore was constructed in the seventeenth-eighteenth century (see Table, no. 97). Since we find no temple with clear date of Shah Jahan's period, we may assume that a few of them might have been constructed in his time.

The survival of a large number of ancient and medieval temples including those built during the period of independent Muslim Kingdom of Malwa bear testimony to the fact that they were well-attended and worshipped unhindered during the Mughal period. A large number of them were repaired from time to time and many of them are being worshipped by the Hindus to the present day.

Besides the religious importance of the temples, there were a large number of towns, villages and rivers in Malwa which were greatly esteemed by the Hindus and served as the centres of Hindu pilgrimages. Ujjain, situated on the banks of river Sipra, held great sanctity among the Hindus. Abul Fazl also refers to Ujjain as a place of great sanctity.[51] Jahangir who visited Malwa in 1617 and stayed there for about seven months also went to Ujjain.[52] He narrates Ujjain as one of the old cities and one of the seven established places of worship of the Hindus. He also refers to a superstition of the Hindus that once in some year at an uncertain time the water of river Sipra turns into milk. Even the Muslim inhabitants of Ujjain also shared this belief. However, Jahangir rejected this belief of the people of Ujjain.[53] The town had a large number of Hindu temples and among them a temple at Unk-Pat was held in great veneration as being a place where Krishna and his brother Balbhadder or Baldeo received their elementary education.[54] Similarly, the temple of Ganesha called Chintaman was visited by numerous processions at certain stated periods.[55] During his stay at Mandu, the former capital of Malwa Sultans, Jahangir refers the bank of river Narmada as a sacred place of pilgrimage of the Hindus.[56] The town named Bagli in the district of Dewas appears to have been a place of pilgrimage as there is a local legend that Lord Rama sent Sita in exile to this place and her sons Lava and Kusa were born here.[57] A small village named Bandarabhan situated at the confluence of the rivers Tawa and Narmada in Hoshangabad district also earned sanctity and became a place of pilgrimage.[58] Similarly, another village called Pamli in the same district situated at the confluence of the rivers Palakmati and

Narmada was held sacred. Nearby this place is a sacred grove called Pandodwip and the Hindus believed that the Pandavas made a horse sacrifice there.[59] A tank in Alot town in district Ratlam was held sacred by the Hindus where pilgrims took holy bath on occasions of Hindu festivals.[60]

There existed a bitter rivalry in Malwa between the Hindus and Jains on one hand and between the Shaivites and the Vaishnavites on the other. This acrimony resulted in capturing each other's temples. The Hindus captured two Jain temples, the one at Sandalpur (district Dewas) and the other at Kothdi in the district of Mandsaur (see Table, nos. 10 and 135). Similarly, the Jains occupied two Hindu temples at Gyaraspur in the Vidisha district (see Table, nos. 195 and 196). The rivalry of the Shaivites and the Vaishnavites led to the capture of two Vaishnavite temples by the Shaivites at Dhamnar and Dhundheri (see Table, nos. 109 and 114) in the district of Mandsaur while the Vaishnavites occupied three Shaivite temples standing at Kohala in the same district (see Table, nos. 132, 133 and 134). These acts of sacrilege resulting out of sectarian conflict might have also resulted in the destruction of temples of these communities as is the case of the Vrindavan temples.[61]

As regards the position of Hindus in the provincial bureaucracy of *suba* Malwa under the Mughals, the information is, however, scanty but sufficient to throw light on their participation in the administration. When Prince Murad was governor of Malwa (1590-1), Akbar directed him to consult Ismail Quli Khan and Raja Jagannath on vital matters of statecraft since both had distinguished themselves by loyalty to the prince. The latter was one of the several important officers who accompanied Prince Murad to the government of *suba* Malwa.[62] The emperor seems to have transferred his *jagir* from Punjab to Malwa on his posting with the prince there.[63]

Khwaja Sabir Nasiri Khan who held Malwa twice as governor (1631-2 to 1634-5 and 1634-5 to 1637-8) had a trusted Hindu officer named Govind Das. When the governor initiated action against Marvi Gond who had deprived Bhupat, son of Sangram, the Mughal-friendly *zamindar* of Kunar to succeed, the rebel Gond had tried to open negotiations through Mirza Wali and Govind Das, the two trusted officers of Khan-i-Dauran, Nasiri Khan.[64]

We find Hindu nobles appointed as *subadars* in Mughal provinces but none of them got an opportunity in Malwa. However, we find appointments of Hindus as deputy *subadars* in Malwa. When Prince

Azam was appointed *subadar* of Malwa in 1685-6, Muluk Chand was his deputy *subadar*. His brave and loyal services in the *suba* earned for him the title of *Rai-i-Rayan* with promotion from the emperor.[65]

As regards the posting of *diwans* in *suba* Malwa, the information is scanty. However, we find one Hindu *diwan* appointed in Malwa by Jahangir in 1618. Rai Kahnur or Rai Kunwar who had formerly served as *diwan* in *suba* Gujarat was appointed as the *diwan* of Malwa.[66]

In the lower category of officials, we find reference of Chaudharis (Hindu) holding office in *pargana* Dhar of *sarkar* Mandu in a hereditary manner.[67] We may assume that such a hereditary continuation of offices particularly in the revenue sphere was there in *suba* Malwa. We find an interesting piece of information of gallantry of one Gopal posted as the Chaudhari of Sironj (*sarkar* Chanderi) in 1704 who saved the imperial treasures from Maratha attack by helping Mughal officer Firuz Jang and the emperor rewarded the Chaudhari for his bravery.[68] Another reference of lower category Hindu official in *suba* Malwa comes from Ujjain. Here one Manorath Ram was posted as the Kotwal of *sarkar* Ujjain during the reign of Aurangzeb.[69]

In fact, the subordinate ranks were monopolized by the Hindus in the revenue and accounts department. In most of the cases even personal assistants of most of the executive heads were also Hindus.[70]

Our evidence thus shows that the Hindus in Malwa in Mughal times had a fairly prosperous existence in the *suba*, preserving their temples, pilgrimage centres and festivals and occupying a largely comfortable position in the economy and society of the sixteenth- and seventeenth-century Malwa. They had a fairly large share in the administration. In its own way, this evidence constitutes one building block for a large view of the religious situation in the Mughal empire.

TABLE: REMAINS OF HINDU TEMPLES AND RELIGIOUS BUILDINGS IN MODERN DISTRICT WITHIN MUGHAL *SUBA* OF MALWA[71]

S. No.	Place	Description	Period/Date	Source
		District Dewas		
1.	Bagli	Shaiva Temple called Jatashankar temple located in this town is believed to be very old. Throughout the year water trickles on the idol of Shiva from the Go-mukh.	–	*MPDG*, Dewas (1993), p. 327.
2.	-do-	A temple called Sitamandir in the adjoining villages of Nimanpur and Pipri is also very old. It was renovated after 1956.	–	Ibid.
3.	Bijwad (Bijwar)	Shaiva temple known as Bijeshwar Mahadeva on the bank of the stream Dhatuni, flowing to the west of Bijwad. Some fine carved stones taken from the ruins of the Jain temples located nearby are used in this temple.	Eleventh-twelfth century AD	Ibid.; *AMM*, S.No. 282.
4.	Bhaurasa	A town situated 16 km east of Dewas town. A Shaiva temple Known as Bhaoreshwar Mahadeva stands here from which the town got its name. Constructed by the use of much stone material taken from an older Jain temple.	–	*MPDG*, Dewas (1993), p. 328.
5.	Dewas	Headquarters of the district. An old temple of Seelnoth Mahadeva stands towards the east of the town.	–	Ibid.
6.	Gandharvapuri or Gandhawal	Temple called Gandharvasen, according to local legend was constructed by Vikramaditya's father Gandharvasen who gave the village its present name.	–	Ibid., p. 330.
7.	Karnawad	An old village having temple of Karaneshwar bearing two inscriptions dated VS 1215 (AD 1158) and VS 1925 (AD 1868).	–	Ibid., p. 331.

8.	Ṅagda	A Shaiva temple of Pataleshvar Mahadeva. An underground shrine with a *linga* inside.	Sixteenth-seventeenth century AD	*AMM*, S.No. 1148.
9.	Nemawar	A Shaiva temple of Siddheshvar Mahadeva situated on the north bank of river Narmada. Built on a raised stone-plinth, it has a sabhamandapa or a pillared hall in front, approached by three projecting porches and surmounted by a tall *shikhara* or spire. Later repairs and additions are visible. It is one of the most beautiful temples in north India. Built under the Parmaras of Malwa.	Eleventh-twelfth century AD	*MPDG*, Dewas (1993), pp.332-34; *AMM*, S.No. 1234.
10.	Sandalpur	A temple of Mahadeva originally built by the Jains for their pilgrimage. The local Hindus converted it into a Saivic one. This act enraged the Jain community of this village and they left the place enmasse and migrated to Khategon, 5 km. away from Sandalpur.	–	*MPDG*, Dewas, (1993), p. 334.
11.	Sonkatch	An important town of Dewas district. Several old temples stand here including the two famed locally as Pipaleshvar and Nagchandkeshwar temples.	–	Ibid., p. 336.
		District Dhar		
12.	Achana	A Shaiva Temple.	–	*AMM*, S.No. 1; *MPDG*, Dhar (1984), p. 291.
13.	Amjhera	A village about 40 km north-west of Dhar. A Shaiva temple called Rajeshwar Mahadeva.	–	*AMM*, S.No. 43.
14.	-do-	A Shaiva temple of Shiva.	–	Ibid., S.No. 44.
15.	-do-	A Shaiva temple of Chamunda.	–	Ibid., S.No. 45.

(*Contd.*)

S. No.	Place	Description	Period/Date	Source
16.	-do-	A Shaiva temple of Ambika.	–	Ibid., S.No. 46.
17.	-do-	A Shaiva temple of Ratneshwar.	–	Ibid., S.No. 47.
18.	-do-	A Vaishnava temple of Chaturbhujanath	–	Ibid., S.No. 48.
19.	-do-	A Vaishnava temple of Laxmi Narayan.	–	Ibid., S.No. 49.
20.	Ansukhedi	A small village 32 km west of Dhar. Here stands a Shaiva temple.	–	*MPDG*, Dhar (1984) p. 291 *AMM*, S.No. 72
21.	Badnawar	A Shaiva temple of Shiva with signs of later repairs.	Eleventh-twelfth century AD	*AMM*, S.No. 90.
22.	Bagh	A Shaiva temple of Mahakal.	Tenth-eleventh century AD	Ibid., S.No. 103.
23.	-do-	A Shaiva temple of goddess Bageshwari.	–	Ibid., S.No. 106.
24.	Chikalda	A Shaiva temple stands here.	–	Ibid., S.No. 408.
25.	-do-	A temple dedicated to snake god Takshakeshwar.	–	Ibid., S.No. 409.
26.	-do-	A temple dedicated to snake god Bhilatdeva.	–	Ibid., S.No. 410.
27.	Chhayan	A temple locally called Deva Dharmaraja.	–	Ibid., S.No. 401.
28.	Dasai	A Shaiva temple stands here.	–	Ibid., S.No. 433.
29.	-do-	A Shaiva temple called Mukteshwar Mahadeva.	–	Ibid. S.No. 434.
30.	-do-	A Vaishnava temple of Rama.	–	Ibid., S.No. 435.
31.	Dehri	A Shaiva temple of Mahadeva	–	Ibid., S.No. 436.
32.	Deola	A Vaishnava temple of Narasimha.	–	Ibid., S.No. 450.
33.	Dharmapuri	Situated on the north bank of river Narmada, about 72 km south-east of Dhar. Four Shaiva temples in a group are located here.	Twelfth-thirteenth century AD	*MPDG*, Dhar (1984), p. 301; *AMM*, S.No. 479.

34.	-do-	A group of four other Shaiva temples are located about a km to the east of Dharmapuri, called Nageshwar.	Sixteenth-seventeenth century AD	*MPDG*, Dhar (1984), p. 301; *AMM*, S.No. 480.
35.	Dholya	A temple called Jal Mandir.	–	*AMM*, S.No. 488.
36.	-do-	A Shaiva temple of Shiva.	–	Ibid., S.No. 489.
37.	Dightan	A Shaiva temple known as Kukteshwar Mahadeva.	–	Ibid., S.No. 498.
38.	Ekalbara	A Shaiva temple of Baijnath Mahadeva.	–	Ibid., S.No. 516.
39.	Gangali	The small village possesses an old Shaiva temple of Nandikeshwar.	–	*MPDG*, Dhar (1984), p. 302, *AMM*, S.No. 537.
40.	Jamli	A small village north-west of Manawar has a magnificent Shaiva temple of Mahadeva. Consists of shrine with *shikhara* and a porch in front.	Tenth-eleventh century AD	*MPDG*, Dhar (1984), p. 302, *AMM*, S.No. 716.
41.	Kanwan	Village situated about 17 km south of Badnawar town, contains old temples dedicated to Kalika and Koteshwar Mahadeva. There is an inscription on a pillar.	–	*MPDG*, Dhar (1984), p. 302.
42.	Kothda	Village on north bank of river Narmada about 16 km south-east of Kukshi town, contains an old Shaiva temple of Koteshwar Mahadeva bearing a nagari inscription.	–	Ibid., p. 303.
43.	Manawar	A town 72 km to the south-east of Dhar has an old Shaiva temple.	–	Ibid., p. 310.
44.	Perkheda	Shaiva temple of Bhogishwar Mahadeva.	–	*AMM*, S.No. 1326.
45.	-do-	Shaiva temple dedicated to Nilkantheswar Mahadeva.	–	Ibid., S.No. 1327.
46.	Sadalpur	Contains old Vaishnava temples.	–	*MPDG*, Dhar (1984), p. 312.
47.	Saon	A temple known as of Devadharmaraja.	–	*AMM*, S.No. 1469.
48.	Singhana	Shaiva temple of Harasiddhi.	–	Ibid., S.No. 1554.

(*Contd.*)

S. No.	Place	Description	Period/Date	Source
49.	Sultanpur	Shaiva temple dedicated to Shiva.	–	Ibid., S.No. 1594.
50.	-do-	Shaiva temple dedicatd to Ganga Mahadeva.	–	Ibid., S.No. 1595.
		District Guna		
51.	Anghora	A Shaiva temple stands here originally dedicated to goddess Mahishamardini, with the sanctum and a porch probably constructed later. It contains a pilgrims record on floor slab recording the date VS 1157 (AD 1000).	Ninth-tenth century AD	Ibid., S.No. 61.
52.	-do-	A Shaiva temple stands in a jungle two miles north-west of the village.	–	Ibid., S.No. 62.
53.	Bajranggarh	A Shaiva temple with a cell and a porch in front in ruined condition. The image of Mahishamardini placed in the modern Visabhuja temple here is believed to belong to this temple.	Tenth-twelfth century AD	Ibid., S.No. 118.
54.	-do-	A Vaishnava temple of Sitarama.	–	Ibid., S.No. 122.
55.	-do-	A Vaishnava temple of Hanuman.	–	Ibid., S.No. 23.
56.	Chanchoda	A Shaiva temple of Bagjeshwar Mahadeva with collection of old sculptures.	–	Ibid., S.No. 322.
57.	Chanderi	A Shaiva temple of goddess called Jogeshwari.	–	Ibid., S.No. 392.
58.	-do-	A Shaiva temple of Mansimheshwar Mahadeva. Contains an inscription recording its construction by Man Singh, a Bundela chief of Chanderi in VS 1784 (AD 1727).	AD 1727	Ibid., S.No. 393.
59.	-do-	A Shaiva temple called Panchamadhi.	–	Ibid., S.No. 394.
60.	-do-	A Shaiva temple known as Kalyan Rai's temple.	–	Ibid., S.No. 395.

61.	Deokani	Shaiva temples, small shrines in a group dedicated to Shiva, Devi, etc.	Twelfth-thirteenth century AD	Ibid., S.No. 442.
62.	-do-	A temple stands a quarter mile east of a *garhi*. Consists of a shrine and sabhamandapa. Its *shikhara* is lost.	"	Ibid., S.No. 445.
63.	-do-	A Shaiva temple of Ganesha. Consists of a small shrine with the figure of Ganesha in the centre of the dedicatory block of the lintel of the door-frame.	"	Ibid., S.No. 445.
64.	Dhakoni	A temple built in the reign of one Raja of Chanderi in VS 1737 (AD 1680) as recorded in an inscription at its entrance.	AD 1680	Ibid., S.No. 457.
65.	Indore	A Shaiva temple dedicated to Garagaj Mahadeva. Shrine is star-shaped in plan.	Eighth-ninth century AD	Ibid., S.No. 700.
66.	-do-	A Vaishnava temple consists of a shrine with the *shikhara* lost. Its exterior is also damaged. Stands half a mile west of the village.	Ninth-tenth AD	Ibid., S.No. 701.
67.	Kadwaha	A Shaiva temple bearing a Sanskrit inscription recording the names of two kings, Jayantavarman and Gopala.	Tenth century AD	Ibid., S.No. 748.
68.	-do-	A Shaiva temple known as Chandal Madhi stands a mile north of the village.	Tenth-eleventh century AD	Ibid., S.No. 749.
69.	-do-	Shaiva temples in a group locally called Murayatas. Located on the river bank.	"	Ibid., S.No. 750.
70.	-do-	Standing east of the village refer Shaiva temples are set in a group.	"	Ibid., S.No. 751.
71.	-do-	Shaiva temples in a group located north of the village.	"	Ibid., S.No. 752.
72.	-do-	Shaiva temples in a group located west of the village.	"	Ibid., S.No. 753.

(Contd.)

S. No.	Place	Description	Period/Date	Source
73.	Lakhari	Shaiva temples, both standing in a row on a common plinth. Each consists of a shrine and a porch erected on pillars in front having sculptures of Brahma, Shiva, Vishnu and Navagrahas. Pilgrims record dated VS 1000 (AD 943) is there. Door-frame of one is intact, the other ones fallen down.	Ninth-tenth century AD	Ibid., S.No. 906.
74.	-do-	Another temple located east of the village locally called Madh. Consists of a shrine with a *sabhamandapa* in front. Signs of later repairs are noticeable.	Eleventh-twelfth century AD	Ibid., S.No. 908.
75.	Madankhedi	A Vaishnava temple dedicated to Vishnu.	"	Ibid., S.No. 919.
76.	Mahuvan	A Shaiva temple stands two furlong south-west of the village and consists of a shrine with a Nandi pavilion in front.	Tenth-twelfth century AD	Ibid., S.No. 947.
77.	-do-	A Shaiva temple dedicated to Shiva. Contains a *linga* and sculptures of Mahishamardini in shrine.	"	Ibid., S.No. 948.
78.	-do-	A Shaiva temples, three in a group on a mound on river bank.	"	Ibid., S.No. 949.
79.	Mamon	A Shaiva temple dedicated to Shiva, located south-east of village. Consists of a shrine with sculpture of Shiva-Parvati in ruins.	Tenth century AD	Ibid., S.No. 971.
80.	Mohanpur	A Vaishnava temple dedicated to Nrisimha. Largely renovated in a later period.	Tenth-twelfth century AD	Ibid., S.No. 1127.

81.	Ranod	Shaiva monastery locally known as Khokhai Matha. Constructed with large blocks of stones. Also large stone slabs used in its roofing. The two-storeyed building consists of a court, corridors at sides and a series of rooms. Contains undated inscription recording its re-construction by an ascetic of the Mattamayura sect named Vyomakesha. This inscription may be assigned to tenth-eleveth centuries AD. It also refers to the line of ascetics of the sect and mentions king Avantivarman.	Tenth-eleventh century AD	Ibid. S.No. 1394.
82.	Sakarra	A Shiva temple, Consists of a shrine and a pillared hall in front. The *shikhara* is lost. Contains an image of Ganesha at centre of the door-frame, lintel and figures of Brahma, Surya and Ganesha in niches of the exterior.	Eleventh century AD	Ibid., S.No. 1441.
83.	-do-	A temple stands near the above mentioned temple. Consists of a shrine and a porch in front. Images of Surya, Ganesha and Vishnu sculptured in niches of the exterior.	"	Ibid., 1441.
84.	-do-	Another temple stands on the northern bank of a tank. Consists of a shrine and and a porch in front. Images of Varahi, Vaishnavi and Parvati in the niches of the exterior.	"	Ibid., S.No. 1442.
85.	-do-	A temple stands near the above-mentioned temple. Consists of a shrine and a porch in front. The *shikhara* is lost. Images of Parvati, Ardhanarishvara and Brahma in the niches of the exterior.	"	Ibid. S.No. 1443.

(*Contd.*)

S. No.	Place	Description	Period/Date	Source
		District Hoshangabad		
86.	Bandarbhan	Small village situated at the confluence of the Tawa and the Narmada rivers, 5 miles east of Hoshangabad. An old temple stands here.	–	*CPDG*, Hoshangabad district (1908), p. 289.
87.	Handia	An old town on the bank of the river Narmada, 13 miles north of Harda. Here stands a Shaiva temple called Siddhnath temple containing an old image of Shiva. An imposing structure, built of carved stone in a conical shape.	–	Ibid., p. 299.
88.	Pamli	Small village, 7 miles north-west of Sohagpur at the confluence of the Palakmati River and the Narmada. Here stands an old Shiva temple and an image of Mahadeva.	–	Ibid., p. 299.
89.	Tigharia	Small village, 12 miles south-west of Hoshangabad. An old Shaiva temple dedicated to Mahadeva stands here.	–	Ibid., p. 363.
		District Indore		
90.	Choli	A Shaiva temple stands here.	–	*AMM*, S.No.414.
91.	-do-	A Shaiva temple dedicated to Somnath.	–	Ibid., S.No. 415.
92.	-do-	A Shaiva temple dedicated to Ganesha.	–	Ibid., S.No. 416.
93.	Depalpur	In a village Kiraki or Karki, about 10 km from Depalpur stands a Shaiva temple dedicated to Mangaleshwar Mahadeva. Its shrine has been rebuilt but the ***mandapa*** is old.	Thirteenth century AD	Ibid., S.No. 451; *MPDG*, Indore (1971), pp. 709-10.

94.	Devguradya	A Shaiva temple dedicated to Gupteshwar Mahadeva. An earlier structure later rebuilt by Ahilyabai Holkar in the eighteenth century.	–	*AMM*, S.No. 456.
95.	Indore	A Vaishnava temple of Khedapati, built in AD 1741.	AD 1741	Ibid., S.No. 706.
96.	Kalmer	A village, north-west of Indore has a temple of Hanuman. There is an old figure of Rama carved on stone.	–	*MPDG*, Indore, (1971), p. 722.
97.	Maheshwar	A Shaiva temple dedicated to Jaleshwar Mahadeva.	Seventeenth-eighteenth century AD	*AMM*, S.No. 934.
98.	-do-	A Shaiva temple of Kaleshwar Mahadvea bearing an inscription dated VS 1627 (AD 1570).	Sixteenth century AD	Ibid., S.No. 935.
99.	-do-	A Shaiva temple dedicated to Matangeshwar Mahadeva with inscription dated VS 1627 (AD 1570).	"	Ibid., S.No. 936.
		District Mandsaur		
100.	Achera	Vaishnava temple locally known as Das Hanuman. The shrine is empty.	–	*AMM*, S.No. 4.
101.	Afzalpur	A Shaiva temple stands here.	–	Ibid., S.No. 7.
102.	-do-	Vaishnava temple of Laxmi Narayan.	–	Ibid., S.No. 11.
103.	-do-	Vaishnava temple of Rama.	–	Ibid., S.No. 12.
104.	Antri Buzurg	Village situated on the northern bank of Retam River, 15 km south-west of Manasa. There are several old temples, one of which dedicated to Nau Durga Mata was built during the Muslim period.	–	*MPDG*, Mandsaur (1993), p. 282.
105.	Athana	A Vishnava temple of Laxmi Narayan.	Seventeenth century AD	*AMM*, S.No. 80.
106.	Bichor	A temple with only the platform now existing.	Fourteenth-fifteenth century AD	Ibid., S.No. 215.

(*Contd.*)

S. No.	Place	Description	Period/Date	Source
107.	Bunjar	A Shaiva temple of goddess Umari Mata.	–	Ibid., S.No. 306.
108.	Chimrolia	A Shaiva temple dedicated to Jayanath Mahadeva.	–	Ibid., S.No. 411.
109.	Dhamnar	Rock-cut Shaiva temple. Dhamnar caves probably named after the temple of Dharmarajeshwar, carved in one of these caves. Originally the temple was a Vaishnava one, though presently known as Shaiva temple enshrining a Shiva lingam called Dharmanath. Consists of a shrine with a *shikhara*, a *sabhamandapa* and a porch, all hewn out of rock. An image of Chaturbhuja Vishnu is also there.	Seventh-eighth AD	*MPDG*, Mandsaur (1993), p. 285; *AMM*, S.No. 464.
110.	Dhanakhedi	Rock-cut cells. Two in a hill south-east of village.	–	*AMM*, S.No. 467.
111.	-do-	Rock-cut cells. Two in hill known as Ganesh Pahadi with a rock-cut image of Ganesha.	–	Ibid., S.No. 468.
112.	-do-	A Rock-cut temple. A miniature shrine, hewn in hill, west of the village.	–	Ibid., S.No. 469.
113.	Dhundheri	Vaishnava temple enshrining an image of Chaturbhuj or Vishnu carrying *varadaksha*, *gada*, *chakra* and *sankha*. It stands now renovated but the original temple is assignable to circa eleventh century.	Eleventh century AD	*IAR* (1985-86), p. 133.
114.	-do-	The other temple that stands here in a dilapidated condition is dedicated to Shiva. A Sivalinga is presently kept in the *sabhamandapa* but originally this temple is a Vaishnava one.	"	Ibid., p. 133.
115.	Dudakhedi	A temple dedicated to a goddess.	–	AMM, S.No. 509.
116.	Garoth	An old temple called Porwalka Mandir later rebuilt.	–	Ibid., S.No. 540.
117.	Ghusai	A Shaiva temple dedicated to Bhairvaji.	–	Ibid., S.No. 556.
118.	-do-	A Shaiva temple dedicated to Mahadeva.	–	Ibid., S.No. 557.
119.	-do-	A Shaiva temple dedicated to Amareshwar Mahadeva.	–	Ibid., S.No. 558.

120.	-do-	A Vaishnava temple dedicated to Vishnu.	–	Ibid., S.No. 559.
121.	-do-	A temple called Yajnakund.	–	Ibid., S.No. 560.
122.	-do-	Temples in a group stand on the bank of an old tank.	–	Ibid., S.No. 561.
123.	Hinglajgarh	A Shaiva temple dedicated to Hinglajmata.	Sixteenth-seventeenth century AD	Ibid., S.No. 682.
124.	-do-	A Shaiva temple of Chaturmukha Mahadeva.	”	Ibid., S.No. 683.
125.	Kadvada	A Vaishnava temple of Chaturbhuja with signs of later repairs.	–	Ibid., S.No. 742.
126.	Kanjarda	A Vaishnava temple dedicated to Vishnu.	–	Ibid., S.No. 784.
127.	-do-	A Shaiva temple of Shiva called Godya Mahadeva.	–	Ibid., S.No. 785.
128.	Karadia	A Shaiva temple dedicated to Mahadeva.	–	Ibid., S.No. 787.
129.	Kethuli	A Vaishnava temple of Sheshashayi Vishnu.	Thirteenth-fourteenth century AD	Ibid., S.No. 817.
130.	Khundoro	A Shaiva temple dedicated to Shiva.	–	Ibid., S.No. 854.
131.	-do-	Three temples stand here.	–	Ibid., S.No. 855.
132.	Kohala	A Vaishnava temple of Varaha. Consists of a sanctum, an *antarala*, an open *sabhamandapa*. Stands on a spacious platform. A fine example of Parmara temple architecture. Originally dedicated to Shiva.	Eleventh century AD	*IAR* (1985-86), p. 133.
133.	-do-	A Vaishnava temple of Laxmi Narayan stands on a high and spacious platform. Renovated and white-washed in modern times. It was originally dedicated to Shiva.	”	Ibid., p. 134.
134.	-do-	A Vaishnava temple of Chaturbhuja. Close resemblance in plan to that of the Laxmi-Narayan temple. Its inscription records its date of construction as VS 1166 (AD 1109). It was originally dedicated to Shiva.	AD 1109	Ibid., p. 134.

(*Contd.*)

S. No.	Place	Description	Period/Date	Source
135.	Kothdi	A large village about 13 km from Bhanpura. There are several old temples, one of which is called Jain Bhajan Jabareshwar Rama (Mighty Rama, the destroyer of Jains). Originally a Jain temple but Hindus occupied it and installed the images of Rama, Laxman and Sita in the shrine towards the end of the fourteenth century.	–	*MPDG*, Mandsaur (1993), pp. 292-3.
136.	Modi	A Shaiva temple dedicated to Lakulisha Shiva with inscription dated VS 1317 (AD 1251).	Thirteenth century AD	*AMM*, S.No. 1123.
137.	Morwan	A Shaiva temple of Shitala Mata.	Eleventh-twelfth century AD	Ibid., S.No. 1131.
138.	Navli	A Shaiva temple of Nandikeshwar Mahadeva.	Twelfth-thirteenth century AD	Ibid., S.No. 1226.
139.	-do-	A temple dedicated to a Devi.	"	Ibid., S.No. 1229.
140.	Nimthur	A Shaiva temple dedicated to Panch-Mukhi Mahadeva with inscription recording its construction in the tenth century AD.	Tenth century AD	Ibid., S.No. 1241.
141.	Runja	A Shaiva monastery of a Gosain.	–	Ibid., S.No. 1427.
142.	Sandhara	A Vaishnava temple of Chaturbhuja Vishnu.	Eleventh-twelfth century AD	Ibid., S.No. 1460.
143.	Satkheda	A village about 17 km south-west of Garoth. Famous for its temple of Kala-Bhairava built in AD 1680.	AD 1680	*MPDG*, Mandsaur (1993), p. 304.
		District Nimar		
144.	Balakwada	A temple dedicated to goddess Bhavani.	–	AMM, S.No. 124.
145.	Gwalanghat	A temple of Bijasani.	–	Ibid., S.No. 609.

146.	Kasrawad	A Shaiva temple dedicated to Gangleshwar Mahadeva.	–	Ibid., S.No. 810.
147.	Khargone	A temple of Navagrahas or nine planets.	–	Ibid., S.No. 832.
148.	Sendhwa	A temple.	Eleventh-twelfth century AD	Ibid., S.No. 1503.
149.	Un	A Shaiva temple known as Mahakaleshwar Mandir stands in the village. Consists of a shrine with a *shikhara* and a porch in front. Built under the Parmaras of Malwa.	Eleventh century AD	Ibid., S.No. 1755.
150.	-do-	A Shaiva temple called Gupteshwar Mahadeva. A Parmara construction consists of a shrine and a porch in front. The *shikhara* is lost.	"	Ibid., S.No. 1756.
151.	-do-	A Shaiva temple dedicated to Balleshwar Mahadeva. Stands west of village. Consists of a shrine and a porch in front of *shikhara* with later repairs.	"	Ibid., S.No. 1757.
152.	-do-	A Shiva temple dedicated to Nilakantheshwar Mahadeva. Consists of shrine with a *shikhara* and a porch in front. Constructed under the Parmaras of Malwa.	"	Ibid., S.No. 1758.
153.	-do-	Shaiva temple known as Mahakaleshwar stands on the bank of a stream to the east of the village. Consists of a shrine with a *shikhara* and a porch in front. Constructed during the reign of the Parmaras of Malwa.	"	Ibid., S.No. 1759.
		District Raisen		
154.	Bhojpur	Small village situated 29 km south-east of Bhopal. Here stands a great Shaiva temple of simple structure, square in plan. This temple remained incomplete in construction.	Eleventh or thirteenth century AD	*MPDG*, Raisen (1979), p. 341.

(*Contd.*)

S. No.	Place	Description	Period/Date	Source
		District Ratlam		
155.	Bilpank	Shaiva temple dedicated to Mahadeva. Consists of a sanctum, an *antarala*, a *sabhamandapa* and an *ardha-mandapa*. Grandest temple of western Malwa. An inscription mentions that the temple was renovated by Siddharaja Jai Singh. Present temple is a specimen of Parmara-Chalukya architecture.	Eleventh century AD	*MPDG* (1994), pp. 362-3; *IAR* (1985-6), pp. 139-40.
156.	Birmawal	Temple known as Devi temple contains an image of Mahishamardini Durga, locally called Kamleshwari. Original temple assignable to *c.* tenth century AD. Renovated during modern times.	Tenth century AD	*IAR (1985-6)*, p. 139.
157.	Dharad	Shaiva temple known as Mahakaleshwar temple. Recently renovated. The sanctum and the *antarala* are original.	"	Ibid.
158.	Ringnod	Shaiva temple called Mahadeva temple stands 11 km from Ringnod on the bank of river Sipra. Built during the reign of Parmaras of Malwa.	Twelfth century AD	*MPDG*, Ratlam (1994), p. 368.
159.	Sailana	Town situated about 22 km to the south-west of Ratlam. An old temple stands at a place called Jesnagar, 3 km from Sailana known as Kalyan Kedareshwar. Ratan Singh's grandson, founder of Sailana state, is said to have visited this temple in 1730s.	–	Ibid., pp. 368-9.
160.	-do-	Shaiva temple called Bara Kedareshwar stands within 3 km of the town.	–	Ibid., p. 369.
161.	Sipawara	Village situated on the confluence of the rivers Chambal and Sipra. Near the village stands an old Shaiva temple dedicated to Kamleshwar Mahadeva.	–	Ibid., p. 370.

162.	Uchangarh	A village about 40 km to the west of Ratlam. Here stands an old temple dedicated to Rajapuramataji or Khakai Mata on the bank of Mahi River.	–	Ibid., pp. 370-1.
		District Ujjain		
163.	Agar	A vaishnava temple of Varaha. Constructued out of old temple materials and enshrines an old image of Varaha datable to tenth and eleventh centuries AD.	–	*AMM*, S.No. 16.
164.	Badi-Delchi	Here stands a Shaiva temple of goddess Hinglajmata.	–	Ibid., S.No. 88.
165.	Bherongarh	A Shaiva temple dedicated to Kala-Bhairava.	–	Ibid., S.No. 207.
166.	-do-	A Shaiva temple called Ukreshwar Mahadeva.	–	Ibid., S.No. 208.
167.	-do-	A Shaiva temple dedicated to Tarakeshwar Mahadeva.	–	Ibid., S.No. 209.
168.	-do-	A Shaiva temple dedicated to Siddhavata.	–	Ibid., S.No. 210.
169.	Bhonrasa	A Shaiva temple of Bhairavanath.	–	Ibid., S.No. 261.
170.	Bichrod	Two Shaiva temples in a group.	–	Ibid., S.No. 267.
171.	-do-	A Shaiva temple dedicated to goddess Shitala Mata.	–	Ibid., S.No. 268.
172.	Dangarwa	A Shaiva temple dedicated to Mahadeva.	–	Ibid., S.No. 432.
173.	Dhanvantari	A Shaiva temple dedicated to Shiva.	–	Ibid., S.No. 470.
174.	Gandhawal	A temple of Gadharvasena. Consists of a shrine and shikhara with signs of later repairs.	Eleventh-twelfth century AD	Ibid., S.No. 531.
175.	Jalwa	A Shaiva temple dedicated to Shiva.	–	Ibid., S.No. 713.
176.	Karedi	A Shaiva temple dedicated to a goddess called Mahakali.	–	Ibid., S.No. 790.
177.	Karnavad	A Shaiva temple known as Karneshwar Mahadeva with inscription dated VS 1275 (AD 1218).	AD 1218	Ibid., S.No. 803.
178.	Karohan	A Shaiva temple dedicated to Shiva.	–	Ibid., S.No. 805.
179.	Khacharod	A Vaishnava temple of Narsimha.	–	Ibid., S.No. 820.
180.	-do-	A temple known as Jankidas.	–	Ibid., S.No. 821.
181.	Mahu	A Shaiva temple stands here.	–	Ibid., S.No. 941.

(*Contd.*)

S. No.	Place	Description	Period/Date	Source
182.	-do-	A Shaiva temple dedicated to goddess Kali.	–	Ibid., S.No. 942.
183.	Makla	A Shaiva temple dedicated to Mahakaleshwar.	Eleventh-twelfth century AD	Ibid., S.No. 958; *IAR* (1985-6), pp. 137-8.
184.	Mehidpur	A Vaishnava temple dedicated to Chaturbhuja Vishnu with inscription dated VS 1344 (AD 1287).	AD 1287	*AMM*, S.No. 107.
185.	Sundarsi	A Shaiva temple dedicated to Mahakaleshwar bearing inscription dated VS 1224 (AD 1167).	Twelfth century AD	Ibid., S.No. 1603.
186.	Ujjain	A Shaiva temple known as Tilabhandeshwar Mahadeva.	AD 1600	Ibid, S.No. 1741.
187.	-do-	A temple of Ganesha surnamed Chintamun.	–	*AR*, p. 42.
		District Vidisha		
188.	Badoh	A Shaiva temple locally known as Gadarmal Mandir. Repairs to its *shikhara* were done in late historical times.	Ninth century AD	*AMM*, S.No. 93; *MPDG*, Vidisha (1979), pp. 311-12.
189.	-do-	Temples grouped together called Sat-Madh (i.e. seven shrines). Now stand only six shrines.	Tenth-twelfth century AD	*AMM*, S.No. 94; *MPDG*, Vidisha (1979), p. 313.
190.	Bagrod	A Shiva temple dedicated to Shiva.	–	*AMM*, S.No.112.
191.	Bhonrasa	A Shaiva temple dedicated to a goddess bearing an inscription dated VS 1681 (AD 1624) recording its construction by (name illegible).	AD 1624	*AMM*, S.No. 251.
192.	Gyaraspur	A temple locally called Athkhamba. Now stands with only eight pillars of its *sabhamandapa* and door-frame of the shrine. One of its pillars bears a pilgrim's record dated VS 1039 (AD 982).	Ninth century AD	Ibid., S.No. 657; *MPDG*. Vidisha (1979), p. 323.

193.	-do-	A Vaishnava temple to south-west of village locally called Bajra Math. Three shrines, originally dedicated to Shiva, Surya and Vishnu but now Jain images are enshrined.	"	*AMM*, S.No. 658; *MPDG*, Vidisha (1979), p. 323.
194.	-do-	A mile south-west of village a temple stands locally called as Mahadevi Mandir. Originally dedicated to a goddess but now images of Jain Tirthankaras are enshrined.	"	*AMM*, S.No. 659; *MPDG*, Vidisha (1979), p. 324.
195.	-do-	Temple stands in the eastern part of the village. Only its platform, sculptures and pillars with bracket, etc., and a very richly carved torana gateway now exists. Its gateway is known as Hindola ***torana***.	"	*AMM*, S.No.660; *MPDG*, Vidisha (1979), p. 324.
196.	Lateri	A large village about 29 km south-west of Sironj. Here stands an old Shaiva temple known as Nilkantheswar temple.	Tenth century AD	*MPDG*, Vidisha (1979), p. 326.
197.	Pathari	A Shaiva temple called Kukdeshwar Mahadeva. Çonsists of a shrine with shikhara and a porch in front.	Tenth-eleventh century AD	Ibid., p. 327; *AMM*, S.No. 1313.
198.	Sironj	The Girdhari temple situated in the town assigned to eleventh century AD.	Eleventh century AD	*MPDG*, Vidisha (1979), p. 329.
199.	-do-	An old Shaiva temple known as Jatashankar.	–	Ibid.
200.	-do-	An old temple known as Mahamaya.	–	Ibid.
201.	Udaypur	A Shaiva temple of Nilkantheswar Mahadeva. A beautiful temple with inscriptions, one of which records its construction by Parmara King Udayaditya in VS 1116 (AD 1059).	AD 1059	*AMM*, S.No. 1691; *MPDG*, Vidisha (1979), p. 334.
202.	-do-	A temple known as Pisnarika Mandir. Consists of a shrine with a ***shikhara*** and a porch in front.	Eleventh-twelfth century AD	*AMM*, S.No. 1693; *MPDG*, Vidisha (1979), p. 336.

NOTES

1. Kailash Chand Jain, *Malwa Through the Ages (from the Earliest Time to 1305* AD), Delhi, Motilal Banarsidass, 1972, p. 376.
2. U.N. Day, *Medieval Malwa*, Delhi, Munshiram Manoharlal, 1965, pp. 12-21.
3. Ibid., pp. 268-9.
4. *A Comprehensive History of India*, ed. Mohammad Habib and K.A. Nizami, vol. V, New Delhi, People's Publishing House, rpt. 1982, pp. 928-33.
5. Abul Fazl, *Akbarnama*, *Bib. Ind.* (ed. Abdur Rahim), 3 vols., Calcutta, 1873-81. See vol. II, p. 208.
6. Abul Fazl, *Ain-i Akbari*, 3 vols., Lucknow, Newal Kishore, 1903. See vol. II, pp. 96-7.
7. *Akbarnama*, II, p. 208.
8. Ibid.
9. Ibid., p. 209. Most of the chieftaincies of Gondwana region lying in *sarkar* Garha of *suba* Malwa have been identified and located on the map. See Irfan Habib, *An Atlas of the Mughal Empire*, New Delhi, Oxford Unviersity Press, 1982, Sheet 9A.
10. *Akbarnama*, II, p. 215.
11. D.S. Chauhan, 'A Study of the Later History of the Rajgond Kingdom of Garha-Mandla 1564-1678', *PIHC* (Mysore Session), Aligarh, 1966, p. 156.
12. For details of the events, see *Akbarnama*, II, pp. 212-16; The whole episode of the heroic death of the Rani still forms part of beautiful folklores in the region. See Suresh Mishra, *Garh ke Gond Rajya ka Utthan aur Patan*, Jabalpur, Rani Durgawati Vishwavidyalaya, 1986, p. 61.
13. *Tabaqat-i Akbari*, Lucknow: Newal Kishore, 1875, p. 26.
14. Abul Fazl has omitted the clans at many places. See *Ain-i Akbari*, II, pp. 94-102.
15. Ibid., II, pp. 95-6.
16. Ibid., p. 95.
17. Ibid., pp. 98-9.
18. Ibid., p. 97.
19. Ibid., p. 98-9.
20. Ibid., p. 102.
21. Ibid., p. 98-9.
22. John Malcolm, *A Memoir of Central India including Malwa*, 2 vols., London, Parbury, Allen & Co., 1832. See vol. 1, pp. 45-6, 464.
23. K.R. Qanungo, *Sher Shah and his Times*, Calcutta, Orient Longmans, 1965, pp. 325-6.
24. *Ain-i Akbari*, II, pp. 101-2.

25. Ibid., p. 96.
26. It is doubtful if they are proper Rajputs. R.V. Russell and Hira Lal, *The Tribes and Castes of the Central Provinces of India*, 4 vols., Delhi, Rajdhani Book Centre, rpt. 1975. See vol. IV, p. 446.
27. *Ain-i Akbari*, II, pp. 95-6.
28. Ibid., p. 97.
29. Ibid., pp. 98-9.
30. H.M. Elliot, *Memoirs on the . . . Races of the North-Western Provinces of India, being an Amplified Edition of the Original Supplemental Glossary*, revised by John Beames, vol. 1, London, Trubner & Co., 1869, p. 79.
31. *Ain-i Akbari*, II, p. 98. Akbar's famous minister, Raja Todarmal, was a Khatri.
32. Ibid., p. 98.
33. R.V. Russel, *The Tribes and Castes of the Central Provinces of India*, vol. II, rpt. 1975, Delhi; William Crooke, *The Tribes and Castes of the North Western India*, 4 vols., Delhi, Cosmo Publications, rpt. 1974. See vol. I. Perhaps both of them failed to trace the caste of Bagri referred to by Abul Fazl in the *Ain*, John Malcom, vol. II, p. 182.
34. William Crooke, op. cit., vol. IV, rpt. Delhi, 1974, p. 421.
35. *Ain-i Akbari*, II, pp. 97-9.
36. *Madhya Pradesh District Gazetteers* (hereafter *MPDG*), Indore (Bhopal, 1971), p. 141.
37. Jean Baptiste Tavernier, *Travels in India*, vol. 1, New Delhi, Oriental Books Reprint Corporation, 1977, p. 46.
38. John Malcolm, II, pp. 159-60.
39. *The Descriptive and Classified List of Archaeological Monuments in Madhya Bharat* (cited hereafter *AMM*), ed. D.R. Patil, *Gwalior*, n.d.., S.No. 935.
40. Ibid., S.No. 936.
41. Ibid., S.No. 1741.
42. Ibid., S.No. 251
43. Ibid., S.No. 457.
44. *MPDG*, Mandsaur (1993), p. 304.
45. *AMM*. S.Nos. 682, 683.
46. Ibid., S.No. 80.
47. *MPDG*, Mandsaur (1993), p. 282.
48. *MPDG*, Dhar (1984), p. 301; *AMM*, S.No. 480.
49. *AMM*, S.No. 1148.
50. Ibid., S.No. 934.
51. *Ain-i Akbari*, II, p. 93.
52. *Tuzuk-i Jahangiri*, ed. Sayed Ahmad, Aligarh, Private Press of Sayed Ahmad, pp. 172-94.
53. Ibid., p. 175.

54. William Hunter, 'Narative of a Journey from Agra to Qujein', *Asiatick Researches: or Transactions of the Society, Institued in Bengal*, vol. VI, Calcutta: East India Company's Press, 1795, p. 40.
55. Ibid., p. 42.
56. *Tuzuk-i Jahangiri*, p. 180.
57. *MPDG*, Dewas (1993), p. 327.
58. *Central Provinces District Gazetters*, Hoshangabad District, vol. A Descriptive (ed. G.L. Corbett and R.V. Russell), Calcutta, 1908, rpt. Bhopal, 1997, p. 289.
59. Ibid., p. 344.
60. *MPDG*, Ratlam (1994), p. 361.
61. Suresh Pandey, 'Who Destroyed Vrindavan Temples', in *Reason and Archaeology*, ed. K.M. Shrimali, Delhi, Association for the Study of History and Archaeology (ASHA), 1998, pp. 169-71.
62. *Akbarnama*, III, p. 538.
63. Kunwar Refaqat Ali Khan, *The Kachhwahas under Akbar and Jahangir,* New Delhi, Kitab Publishing House, 1976, p. 146.
64. Abdul Hamid Lahori, *Badshahnama*, ed. Maulvis Kabiruddin Ahmad and Abdur Rahim, 2 vols. *Bib. Ind.*, Calcutta, 1867. See vol. II, pp. 370-2.
65. Saqi Mustaid Khan, *Maasir-i Alamgiri*, ed. Agha Ahmad Ali, *Bib. Ind.* Calcutta, 1871, pp. 266-7.
66. *Tuzuk-i Jahangiri*, p. 233.
67. Syed Bashir Hasan, 'Administration of Jagirs in Malwa in Mid-seventeenth Century Malwa: The Dhar Documents', *Medieval India 2*, ed. Shahabuddin Iraqi, New Delhi, Manohar, 2008, pp. 217-30.
68. Raghubir Singh, *Malwa in Transition or A Century of Anarchy 1698-1765,* Bombay, D.B. Taraporevala, Sons & Co., 1936, rpt., Delhi, Asian Educational Services, 1993, pp. 60-2.
69. M.P. Singh, *Town, Market, Mint and Port in the Mughal Empire 1556-1707*, New Delhi, Adam Publishers and Distributors, 1985, p. 43.
70. This was the general feature practically in the administration of all provinces where the population of the Hindus was considerably large.

CHAPTER 12

Iranis and Commerce: A Case Study of Shaista Khan in Gujarat and Bengal

MOHAMMAD AFZAL KHAN

It is widely recognized that members of the Mughal nobility were not averse to pursuing commercial and economic activities. There are cases of members of every section of the ruling class, from princes to petty officers, participating in this activity.[1] The Mughal nobles, whether *jagirdars* or *naqdis* (receiving pay from treasury), derived their income mainly in cash, and they are said to have accumulated enormous assets by way of cash and jewels. Nobles who had large amounts of cash in hand, often invested it in trade, either by engaging in trade directly or by making advances to merchants.[2] They also invested some amount in sea-borne trade. Tavernier says, 'on arrival for embarkation at Surat, you find plenty of money. For it is the principal trade of the nobles of India to place their money on speculation for Harmuz, Bassora and Mocha and even for Bantam, Achin and Philippenes.'[3]

Apart from the capital advances, the Mughal nobles and sometimes members of the royal family were also engaged in business investment.[4] In 1640-1, for instance, Shah Jahan and Asaf Khan invested Rs.100,000 in cloth at Ahmedabad for Mokha and ordered weavers and dyers not to work for anyone else until this order had been supplied.[5]

Sometimes they had their own ships which sailed to different ports laden with either their own goods or, in some cases, with the cargo of other merchants.[6] It is well known, that

> Private trade or *Sauda-i-Khas* of the Governor was a characteristic feature of India's economic life in the 17th and 18th centuries. Many influential personages such as Mirza Ishaq Beg (Governor of Surat), Mir Jumla, Shuja, Shaista Khan and Azim-ush Shan (in Bengal) were involved in this device.[7]

Shaista Khan happens to be one of the nobles, about whose commercial activities we have considerable information.

He sought to obtain gains from trade during his viceroyalty of Gujarat (1646-7 and 1651-3) and Bengal (1664-77 and 1679-89). He appears to have tried to monopolize and control trade of many important articles. While governor of Gujarat, in 1647, he forced the *banjaras* to sell him sugar and thus made a profit gain of Rs. 1,000. His rigorous attempt to monopolize the commodity caused a great scarcity of the commodity. 'Sugar is scarce and dear, the governor's tyranny having deterred the merchants from bringing any down.'[8] He also wanted to engross all the indigo collected in the city of Ahmedabad and its environs. He summoned the English indigo brokers which caused much resentment among the factors.[9] In June 1647 the factors at Ahmedabad reported about the arbitrary behaviour of the governor towards the indigo dealers. Again on 10 July 1647 they reported that trade in Gujarat was at a standstill, owing to the governor's tyrannical behaviour and the troubles with the carters who brought down the goods from Agra.[10]

In August 1647 saltpetre of the English was seized. George Tash negotiated with Shaista Khan who, after much trouble, allowed the factors to weigh only that much quantity of saltpetre for which they had paid. They were thus allowed to take saltpetre worth only Rs. 1,500, which they had disbursed for saltpetre in Malpur.[11] The Dutch were faced with somewhat similar conditions. Their saltpetre was taken by the governor who just paid them what they had disbursed thereon.[12]

Shaista Khan also tried to engross the cloth trade of Gujarat. Many obstacles were put in the procurement of 'chints and tappichindaes by the English and Dutch merchants for their Bantam investment'.[13]

In 1653, claiming to have received orders from the king, he stopped saltpetre export of the English merchants. They were refused permission to put it aboard the ships at Diu or to embark the goods at any other port than Surat.[14] The English and Dutch factors alleged that Shaista Khan wholly ruined the trade of Ahmedabad directly by seizing upon their goods, or indirectly by sharing in their profit of whatever was bought or sold.[15] Aurangzeb's prohibitory orders to the officers in Gujarat asking them not to buy grain cheap and sell it dear, suggests that such interference with the market had been common[16] and that Shaista Khan was not an exception.

In Bengal too, Shaista Khan appears to have tried to profit by interfering with commerce. The English records are full of references to his extortions and covetousness.[17] Despite imperial *farmans* and official permits he is alleged to have stopped trade in saltpetre and the merchandise of the English merchants at every post and ferry and charged them customs-duty over and over again. Thomas Bowrey says, 'Dacca could take a large quantity of Europe goods if it were under another Nabob, the present being most covetous'.[18] He realized the cesses (*abwabs*) abolished by imperial charters and monopolized the internal trade of Bengal in commodities of daily use such as salt, *supari* (betel-nuts) and even the fodder of animals.[19] Shaista Khan's private enterprise provided great obstacles to free trade in Bengal.

Shaista Khan used to have salt, *supari* and other articles brought down by boats, and sold them in Bengal on profitable rates. He also sold these articles to the merchants and traders at Dacca and thus prevented them from making purchases and sales on their own account. This act of Shaista Khan's injustice was reported to Aurangzeb, and Shaista Khan was, therefore, recalled to the court in 1677.[20] Perhaps salt was the most profitable commodity in Bengal during those days, owing to the meagreness of local supply. One may easily presume the volume of his trade in this single commodity by the fact that he had large emporiums of salt at several places on the bank of the Bangsha River. In 1677 (when he was recalled to the court) these emporiums held salt worth Rs. 1,52,000 which he left in the custody of one of his subordinate officers as he could not transport it before his departure from Bengal.[21] These salt depots occupied a large area of land and when the new governor Prince Muhammad Azam planned to construct a large market complex for which ample space was required, he demolished the depots and threw the salt into the river.[22]

It was proverbial that Shaista Khan had amassed a large amount of wealth. The property, which after his death, was taken into the imperial exchequer, was held to be beyond computation.[23] Besides his trading activities he is said to have accumulated Rs.17 crore by procuring two or three *tolas* of gold for one gold *muhr*,[24] which is, perhaps, an exaggerated reference to his insistence on higher rates for his *muhrs*. It is said that in thirteen years (1664-77) as governor of Bengal he accumulated Rs.380 million.[25] Shaista Khan's monopoly in bees wax[26] and the extent of his possessions is further corroborated by Shah Nawaz Khan's account who on the testimony of a reliable source says that once when Aurangzeb was hunting, some wax was needed. But the officials deputed to collect the wax could not procure even a grain of it. The *Khan-i-Saman* reported that it was only available in the stores of Shaista Khan at Delhi. An order was issued to borrow some to meet urgent requirements. As the Khan, at that time, was in Bengal it would have taken a long time to have his permission. Shaista Khan's agent in Delhi, therefore offered 200 maunds of wax, and one or two thousand articles of wax, each weighing 2-3 maunds, on his own account, and that too with an excuse of not being able to furnish more in the absence of his master. It is also said that the wax was stored in wells specially dug for the purpose and during summer water was put into them to keep the wax from melting.[27]

The general allegation that Shaista Khan's activities were ruinous for European trade in Bengal seems exaggerated. On several occasions, as is evident from the English Factory Records, he granted the factors privileges such as exemption from customs duty and permission to trade in saltpetre.[28]

True, Shaista Khan sent his *darogha* (agent) to Patna, the principal place of saltpetre manufacture, with a commission to buy 20,000 maunds of saltpetre in May 1664, and with orders to forbid the Dutch and the English from procuring any saltpetre before the imperial requirement was obtained. Job Charnock, the English factor at Patna, misconstrued this order and alleged that Shaista Khan wanted to take the whole trade into his own hands and to sell saltpetre again to the English and the Dutch at profitable rates.[29] Similarly, writing from Hugli to the Surat Factors on 21 June 1664 William Blake warned the factors that Shaista Khan wanted to engross all those goods in which he thought of commercial gains.[30] But Shaista Khan's attempt to procure saltpetre for himself was in compliance with the imperial requisition of a large quantity of saltpetre required for king's wars in the Deccan and Arakan. Whether the imperial requisition was fulfilled is not known. Charnock himself admits that if he was supplied with necessary funds, he would be able to procure 25,000 or 30,000 maunds of saltpetre yearly, 'whereas hitherto 18,000 had been the limit'.[31] In 1665 factors from Bengal wrote that 'if (we) had moneys, 1,000 tonns might easily yearly be procured'.[32]

Stewart also believes that Shaista Khan's administration provided a favourable environment for the English Company's trade to grow.[33] Whereas in 1659 its Bengal investment amounted to only £10,000, it was raised to £85,000 in 1674, to £100,000 in 1677 and to over £1,50,000 in 1681.[34] An analysis of Shaista Khan's *parwanas* which he granted to the English, from time to time, shows that his attitude towards them was not unfriendly. In almost all of his *parwanas* he ordered his underlings that henceforth they were bound not to cheat the English traders and not to create any restraint in the transportation of their goods either on land or on water. He also condemns those officials who committed malpractices. He ordered the officials to provide all kinds of help to the factors in their dealings with their local agents and other traders.[35]

Shihabuddin Talish remarks that the former governors of Bengal used to farm out (*ijara*) trade in most of the articles of food and clothing and all merchandise and then sell them at arbitrarily set rates, which the necessitious people had to agree to. Whenever ships brought elephants and other articles to the ports of Bengal, the *subedar's* men used to confiscate (*qurq*) them and take whatever they selected at prices of their own liking. Shaista Khan, on taking charge of the province, is said to have forbidden these practices and to have moreover decreed that there should be freedom for everyone to buy and sell.[36]

Shaista Khan governed Bengal for about a quarter century and during his government peace and commerce flourished. The commodities of daily use were so cheap that 320 *seers* or 8 maunds of rice was sold to Re. 1.[37] Talish remarks that it was due to Shaista Khan's excellent arrangements that from the beginning till the writing of his book the price of grain in the army had been almost equal to the price in Dacca.[38]

On the whole it appears that Shaista Khan participated actively in trading activities, and enforced monopolies wherever possible. But the English factors' accounts tend to exaggerate his faults. Where his own interests were not involved, he was not unfriendly to the Europeans and during his governorship of Bengal the trade of the English and Dutch Companies flourished.

NOTES

1. Tapan Raychaudhuri and Irfan Habib, eds., *The Cambridge Economic History of India*, vol. I, *c.1200-c.1750*, Delhi, 1982, p. 182 (hereafter *CEHI*). For revenue collectors called *Shiqqdars* being engaged in commercial activities see Fray Sebastian Manrique, *Travels of Fray Sebastian*

Manrique (1628-41), tr. C.E. Luard and H. Hosten, Hakluyt Society, 1927, vol. I, pp. 440-1, who mentions that the *shiqqdar* of Pipli sent a 'big new ship' to Cochin loaded with different kinds of merchandise.

2. M. Athar Ali, *The Mughal Nobility under Aurangzeb*, Bombay, 1966, p. 154.
3. Tavernier, *Travels in India (1640-67)*, tr. V. Ball, ed. William Crooke, London, 1889, vol. I, p. 422.
4. Empress Nur Jahan and her brother Asaf Khan had extensive trade interests in the Persian Gulf and until their ships were laden or goods were sold none else could do so. See B.G. Gokhale, *Surat in the Seventeenth Century*, Bombay, 1979, p. 55.
5. *Daqh Register (1640-41)*, p. 308 as cited by Tapan Ray Chaudhuri in *CEHI*, vol. I, p. 183n.
6. Dara Shukoh had his own junks which sailed to Persia. Shah Jahan's ship *Ganjawar* together with five junks of Surat was forced to anchor at Gombroon by the customs officers who overrated all the goods and levied 20 per cent of customs. See *English Factories in India*, hereafter *EFI (1646-50)*, pp. 318, 324. Cf. Iftikhar Ahmad Khan, 'Indian Merchants in Iran in the 17th Century' (unpublished), in the cyclostyled volume of *Aligarh Papers on Medieval Indian History*, presented at 44th Session of Indian History Congress held at Burdwan in 1983, p. 158.
7. Jagdish Narain Sarkar, 'Private Trade in Seventeenth Century India', in *JBRS*, vol. 49, 1963, p. 200; also see by the same author, *Studies in Economic Life in Mughal India*, Delhi, 1975, pp. 181-2.
8. *EFI (1646-50)*, p. 155.
9. They are found apprehensive of Shaista Khan's ambitions for becoming 'the sole merchant of this place' and declare that if he succeeded in engrossing the indigo 'we may then expect shortly to fetch our butter and rice from him'. See the letter of George Tash, Hugh Fenn and Anthony Smith, factors at Ahmedabad, to the President and Council at Surat, dated 17 May 1647 in *EFI (1646-50)*, p. 130; see also Irfan Habib, *The Agrarian System of Mughal India (1556-1707)*, Bombay, 1963, p. 80n.
10. *EFI (1646-50)*, pp. 133, 136.
11. It was contrary to Shaista Khan's previous promises publicly made allowing the English merchants to procure 5,000 maunds of saltpetre and for that he had also taken a bribe of Rs. 280. See *EFI (1646-50)*, p. 150.
12. Ibid., p. 156.
13. Ibid., pp. 160-1.
14. Ibid. (*1651-54*), p. 215.
15. Ibid. (*1646-50*), p. 187.
16. Ali Mohammad Khan, *Mirat-i-Ahmadi*, ed. Syed Nawab Ali, Baroda, 1927, vol. I, pp. 286-88; Cf. *CEHI*, vol. I, p. 183; also see *Mughal Nobility*, op. cit., p. 159.

17. *EFI*, relevant volumes passim; also Charles Stewart, *The History of Bengal*, 2nd edn., Calcutta, 1910, pp. 338-53; C.R. Wilson, *The Early Annals of the English in Bengal: Being the Bengal Public Consultations for the first half of the Eighteenth Century*, Calcutta, 1895, pp. 48, 79, 90, 98, 111, 118.
18. *A Geographical Account of Countries Round the Bay of Bengal, 1669-79*, ed. R.C. Temple, Cambridge, 1905, p. 146n.
19. Streynsham Master, *The Diaries of Streynsham Master, 1675-80* (hereafter Master), ed. R.C. Temple, London, 1911, vol. II, pp. 80-81; Cf. J.N. Sarkar, *The History of Bengal, Muslim Period (1200-1757)*, Patna, 1973, p. 374.
20. S.K. Bhuyan, *Annals of the Delhi Badshahate*, Gauhati, 1947, pp. 167-8.
21. Ibid., pp. 169-70.
22. Ibid., p. 170.
23. Shahnawaz Khan, *Maasir-ul Umara* (hereafter *MU*), ed. Maulavi Abdur Rahim and Mirza Ashraf Ali, *Bib. Ind.*, Calcutta, 1889, vol. II, p. 705; Cf. Niccolao Manucci, *Storia do Mogor 1653-1708*, tr. William Irvine, London, 1907, vol. II, p. 322.
24. Bhuyan, op. cit., p. 168.
25. Master, op. cit., vol. I, p. 493.
26. *CEHI*, vol. I, p. 183; Cf. Master, vol. I, pp. 15, 53, 321; vol. II, 26, 27, 83.
27. *MU*, vol. II, p. 706.
28. *EFI (1661-64)*, p. 395; *(1665-67)*, pp. 135, 138; *(1668-69)*, p. 316, etc.
29. Ibid. *(1661-64)*, pp. 395-6.
30. Ibid., p. 395.
31. Ibid., p. 396.
32. Ibid. (*1665-67*), p. 139.
33. *History of Bengal*, op. cit., p. 331. This shows unrestrained trading activities of English factors in Bengal.
34. *EFI*, vol. X, p. 275 as cited by M. Mohar Ali, 'Nawab Shaista Khan and the East India Company's Trade in Bengal, 1664-1669, in *J.A.S. Pak*, vol. X, no. 2, December 1965, p. 89. This expansion in the volume of Bengal trade led the Company in 1682 to separate the Bengal factories from the control of the Madras Council and to set them on an independent footing. William Hedges was appointed agent and governor with special powers in the Bay of Bengal with his seat at Hugly, the first military establishment of the Company in Bengal. See Stewart, op. cit., pp. 339-40.
35. See copies of *parwanas* of Shaista Khan in the collection of *Farmans, Nishans and Parwanas*, issued in favour of English East India Company, from 1637 to 1712, British Museum, Add. 24039. These are sufficient

proof against the charges of avarice and oppression on the part of Shaista Khan.

36. Shihabuddin Talish, *Fathiyah-i Ibriyah*, Or. Ms. Bodl. 589, ff. 127 (a)-(b); also see Jadunath Sarkar, 'Shaista Khan in Bengal, 1664-1666', in *JASB* (second series), vol. 2, June 1906, p. 263.
37. Ghulam Husain Salim, *Riyaz-us Salatin*, tr. Abdus Salam, rpt., Delhi, 1975, p. 228.
38. *Fathiyah-i Ibriyah*, op. cit., ff. 160 (a)-(b).

CHAPTER 13

Banjaron ki Baori at Sikar (Rajasthan): A Study of Medieval Hydraulic Technology

M.K. PUNDHIR

India has a long tradition of building various types of hydraulic structures to store, conserve and manage water. One of these structures is step well which is known by a number of names. In Delhi and Agra region[1] step well is known as *baoli* and in Rajasthan it is termed as *baori*. In Gujarat, *vapi, vauvavdi, vai* are the terms used for the step wells.[2] In the Indian classic *Shilpa Shashtra* and in inscriptions, the word *vapi* and *vapika* has been used for step wells.[3] Even travellers in their accounts frequently used the terms *bauri* and *baori* for step wells.[4]

Examples of the earliest structural step well came from the seventh century from the Saurashtra region which was associated with a temple in the Barda hill area.[5] The concept and construction of the step wells were evolved with the passage of time. In Rajasthan, the earliest known example was found at Osian which was built in the eighth century AD, whereas in Karnataka the earliest construction of the step well can be ascribed to the seventh century found in Aihole attached with a temple.[6] During the medieval period a number of step wells were constructed in Delhi and Agra region which are still found intact.[7]

Banjaron ki Baori is located in the centre of city of Sikar, a northern town[8] of Shaikhawati region. The city[9] is situated 27°37′ north of latitude and 75°20′ east of longitude[10] to the north of Jaipur and south of Jhunjhunu.[11] It is surrounded by important towns such as Fathapur, Ramgarh, Lachhmangarh, Pilani, Chirawa, Nawalgarh, Jhunjhunu, Churu, Chomu, Sri Madhopur and Neem ka Khana and is at a distance of 108 km from Jaipur.[12] The city was founded in AD 1687 on the site of the town known of Vir Bhan ko Bas.[13] So far as nomenclature of the town of Sikar is concerned, no recorded evidence regarding the designation is available. As per the tradition, Sikar is a colloquial corruption of the word *shikhar.*[14] During the medieval period, Sikar was one of the major centres on the internal as well as external trade routes, which were crisscrossing the whole of Rajasthan.[15] Internally, trade route from Bikaner to Jaipur used to pass either from Churu and Sikar or from Sodawa and Sikar.[16] Trade route connecting Rajasthan with external region such as Multan also passed through Sikar.[17] Besides, Jaipur rulers also established a mint at Sikar where silver and copper coins were struck.[18]

Banjaron ki Baori is situated in the heart of present city of Sikar. The structure derives its nomenclature from the Banjaron ka Bagh where it is located. The garden where Banjaras[19] enroute used to stay in Sikar during the medieval times. To cater the water neads of caravans of Banjaras, a masonry step well was constructed to manage the water storage and source of water during the later medieval period. On the basis of the shape of arches and building technique, construction of the step well can be assigned to the seventeenth century.

The step well consists of three well-defined structural elements, i.e. the well, the square shaft and the stepped corridor (Fig. 13.1 and Pls 13.1-13.4). The alignment of the structure of the step well runs from north to south. The shaft and stepped corridor are encircled by a high enclosure wall though both are built as a compact structure. The well exists outside the main structure on the northern side (Figs. 13.1 & 13.2 and Pl. 13.4 A & B). The entrance to the stepped corridor has been provided on the southern side. It is a high-rise arched gatehouse, but presently it is mutilated, vandalized and encroached upon. Beyond the arched entrance, there are two rooms flanking the passage of 4 m width in the gatehouse. After the passage, a rectangular platform is provided from where the stepped corridor (Figs. 13.1 & 13.2 and Pl. 13.1 A) descends to the shaft. The corridor consists of parallel steps punctuated by an arched gateway (Figs. 13.1 & 13.2 and Pls. 13.1, 13.2 & 13.3), which divides the corridor into two parts. There are 40 steps in the first part reaching up to the arched gateway and after that the second part starts which comprises 7 steps, providing the approach to the gate of the shaft. The arched gateway is 3.05 m wide having a pointed arch. The width of the passage is 5.5 m and consists of arched niches on both sides of the passage (Pls. 13.1 A and 13.2 A & B).

The shaft (Fig. 13.1) of the step well is almost square, measuring 8 × 10 m. It has an entrance on the southern side. The entrance gateway (Pls. 13.2 A & 13.3 B) of the shaft is smaller in comparison to the arched gateway existing in the middle of the stepped corridor. The gateway is 2.5 m wide with a depressed pointed arch and enshrines six steps of equal tread and riser to enter into the shaft. The shaft comprises staggered lateral staircases (Figs. 13.1 & 13.2) set one after another from south to north, going deep until it touches the eastern wall of the shaft. The lateral staircases are arranged in a way that two staircases, where one descends from east to west and another from west to east from the same platform and reached down on the two separate platforms existing on the same level. Another set of two staircases, one leads down from west to east and another from east to west from two separate platforms of the same level and both descend on the same platform. In such a way, lateral staircases form the shape of English alphabet V and inverted V alternatively. Through the lateral staircases one can go down to the depth from south to north in the shaft. On all sides except the southern wall of the shaft are provided with steps inside after a gap of considerable vertical height which have been constructed to give the walls more strength as it descends to considerable depth. In the eastern wall, a number of rectangular holes (Pls. 13.2 A & 13.3 A) after a gap of certain vertical heights is provided, which connect the shaft with the northern side well. These holes are meant to maintain the level of water equal both in the well and the shaft. As the water table rises or descends in the well, connecting holes facilitate the water level accordingly in the shaft. When water level goes down in the shaft, one has to approach the water descending through the lateral staircases. The technique of lateral staircases is meant to go to maximum depth by occupying minimum space.

Undressed stone also known as rubble has been used as the main building material and lime and *surkhi* as mortar in the construction of the step well (Pls. 13.2 A, 13.3 A & 13.4 B). Owing to the use of undressed stone as building material, the whole structure is plastered with lime mixed *surkhi* whose thickness at some places is approx. 4″. Consequently, we find no decorative feature or pattern on the walls of the step well. For the treads of the step, slabs of stone with one chiselled smoothened surface are used. The riser of the steps is again slabs of stone placed vertically under the edge of the tread stone. Arches of the gateway are devoid (Pl. 13.2 B) of its true elements, i.e. keystone and voussoirs and made of rubble and mortar again of lime and *surkhi* in corbelled process.

The source of water, a vertical well (Figs. 13.1 & 13.2 and Pl. 13.4 A & B), is situated on the north side out of the main structure of the step well though it is an integral part of it. It is masonry well constructed with stone rubble and mortar of lime mixed *surkhi*. It is little merged in the northern wall of shaft and provided with holes to maintain the same level of water both in the shaft and the well. The well has sunk deeper vertically than the shaft and has a natural spring, which serves as the perennial source of water. The well is equipped with the technique of hauling up water through a *pur* or bucket drawn by bulls. Two masonry pillars are constructed diagonally above the ring of the well, which holds the pulley and a masonry slop is also built to accommodate the run of bulls while pulling the bucket filled with water from the well.

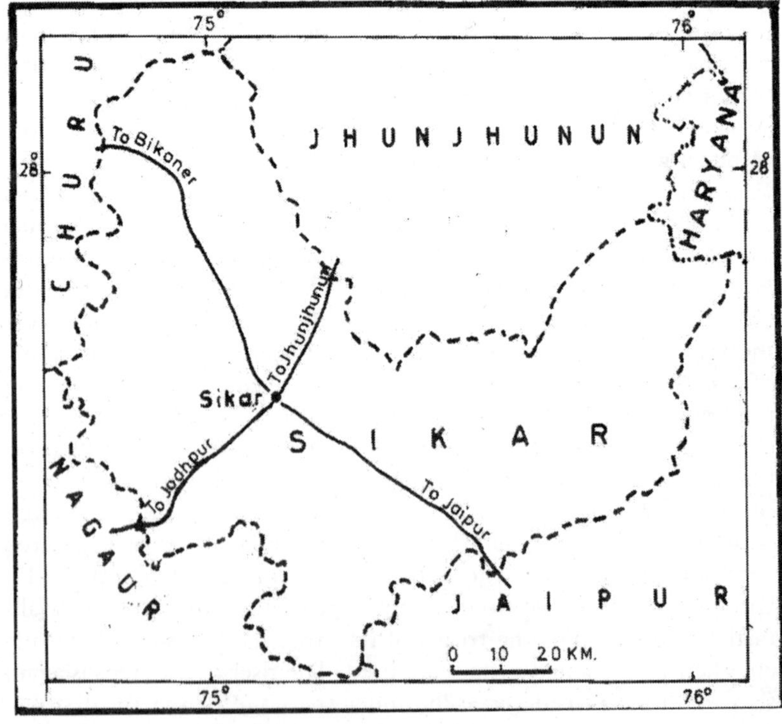

Map Showing Location of Sikar

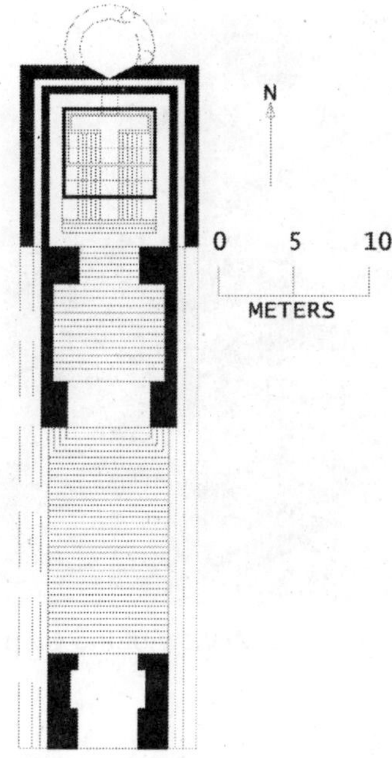

Fig. 13.1: Banjaron ki Baori Sikar (Ground Plan)

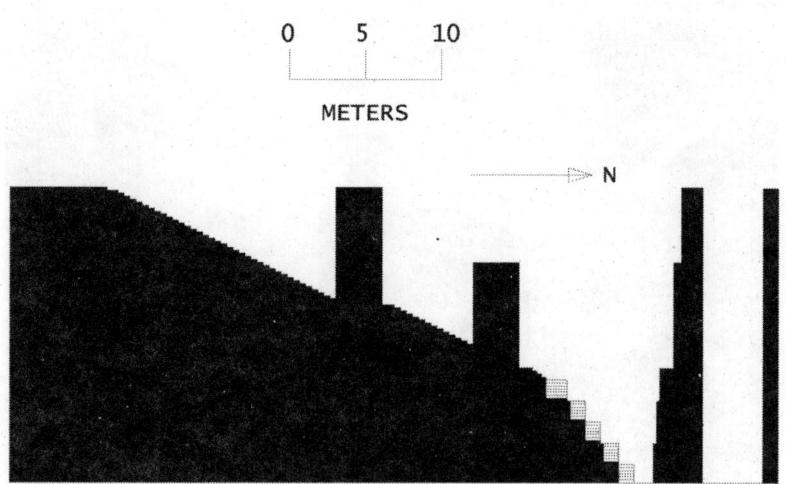

Fig. 13.2: Banjaron ki Baori Sikar (Elevation)

Plate 13.1 (A): A View of the Step Well

Plate 13.2 (B): A Closer View of the Step Well

Plate 13.2 (A): A Closer View of Arched Gateways of the Stepped Corridor

Plate 13.2 (B): A Closer View of Arch of the Gateway

Plate 13.3 (A): A Closer View of the Shaft with Rectangular Holes

Plate 13.3 (B): A Closer View of the Stepped Corridor

Plate 13.4 (A): A View of the Well

Plate 13.4 (B): An Inner View of the Well

NOTES

1. Juta Jain Neubauer, *The Stepwells of Gujarat in Art Historical Perspective*, New Delhi, Abhinav Publications, 1981, p. XIII.
2. Ibid., p. 1.
3. Ibid.
4. James Tod, *Travels in Western India*, Delhi, Orient Publishers, 1971.
5. Juta Jain Neubauer, *The Stepwells of Gujarat*, p. XIV.
6. Ibid.
7. Ibid.
8. See map showing the location of Sikar.
9. Sikar was an important town of Shaikhawati as one half of the land of the Shaikhawati Confederation was held by the chiefs of Sikar and Khetri. As per estimate, revenue from Sikar including Khandela was Rs. 8,00,000 which was approximately 35 per cent of the total revenue of Shaikhawati region at the beginning of the nineteenth century. James Tod, *Annals and Antiquities of Rajasthan*, Delhi, Low Price Publications, 1993, pp. 1426-7.
10. E. Thornton, *A Gazetteer of the Territories under the Government of the East India Company and of the Native States of the Continent of India*, Delhi, Neeraj Publications, 1984, pp. 867-8.
11. *Rajasthan District Gazetteers: Sikar*, by B.D. Agarwal, Jaipur, 1978, p. 430.
12. Ibid.
13. Ibid., p. 432, cf. H.S. Arya, *Shaikhawati Ke Thikanon Ka Itihas Evam Yogdan*, Jaipur, Panchsheel Prakashan, 1987, p. 59.
14. Ibid., p. 432.
15. B.L. Gupta, *Trade and Commerce in Rajasthan during the 18th Century*, Jaipur, Jaipur Publication House, 1987, pp. 130, 133-4.
16. Ibid., p. 130. There are three internal trade routes which connected Bikaner with Jaipur used by Banjaras, out of which two were being passed through Sikar.
17. Ibid., p. 133.
18. Ibid., p. 167. Jaipur, Sawai Madhopur and Sikar were the three places where coins were being minted in Jaipur State.
19. B.L. Gupta, op. cit.

CHAPTER 14

A Walk into Oblivion of Pargana Amarsar: The Environmental Dimension

SUMBUL HALIM KHAN

Pargana Amarsar[1] located in the Mughal period in *sarkar* Nagaur, *suba* Ajmer had a sizeable area coverage in the sixteenth century. However, one finds a consistent shrinking of this extensive area in the seventeenth and eighteenth century till in the modern times it loses its identity to tehsil Bairath in district Jaipur. The intention in this paper is to investigate the *raison d'être* a *pargana*—Amarsar—of substantial *raqba* undergoes such a transmogrification. What is that which makes or mars the identity of a *pargana* or for that matter why a one time important *pargana* cannot survive the exigencies? This problem leads us to focus on the influence exercised by the morphology, the behaviour of water, soil profile, and physiography of a *pargana*.

The measured area of *pargana* Amarsar at the close of the sixteenth century[2] and in 1701-8[3] indicates a larger measured area in the earlier period than in the latter, viz., 12,74,713 and 94,776 *bighas* respectively. Both the measurements being in *bigha-i-daftari*.

Amarsar was one of the coveted areas for Jai Singh Sawai, testimony to which is borne out by his constantly seeking the *pargana* in *ijara*.[4] The reason for doing so could have been guided by the area being extremely fertile, or carrying some strategic importance or a possible missing link for a larger political interest. While there is no allusion to the former, the last reason appears more plausible from the point of view of the expansionist approach of Amber *rajas* in relation to their *watan* area.[5]

The Amber *rajas* having submitted at the imperial court were assigned *mansabs*, the payment of which was made to them from the *jagirs* of their ancestral domain, the remaining area was given from outside their *watan*. At his accession, Jai Singh Sawai's *watan* area consisted of Amber, Dausa, and Baswa. However, the concept of *watan* gradually began encompassing such territories where their *zamindari* rights prevailed. It is worth noting that despite the clear distinction between *mahal-i-watan* and *zamindari*, both were opted in close proximity—therefore becoming complementary to each other. Preference for the *parganas* indexed in the same *dastur* circle was greater. At a time when the request for an assignment of a *jagir* could not materialize, the Raja settled for *ijaras*. Short-term *ijaras* were constantly renewed, later *tankhwah jagirs* in this area were sought and finally claims of *watan* were made.

Pargana Amarsar comprised 181 villages, out of which 141 were original (*asli*) and the rest were attached to other *parganas* (*dakhli*).[6] To gauge the varying size of the settlements one can broadly classify these villages into—large, medium and small. The percentage distribution of the three types of villages was 43.3 per cent as large, 54.6 per cent as medium, and 2.1 per cent as small. The above percentage of villages facilitates discerning that large villages were considerable, which is normally an indication of good cultivated land and assured water supply. Medium villages are the largest in number showing a comparatively less conducive condition. Small villages are exceptionally few in number and these were villages newly populated and therefore having only cultivable area. One can determine that settlement conditions were in general encouraging in the *pargana*.[7]

TABLE 14.1: TOTAL AREA OF THE VILLAGES AND THE PERCENTAGE OF CULTIVABLE AND *PARAT* LAND IN *PARGANA* AMARSAR

Village	Total Area	Cultivable Area	% of Cultivable Area	*Parat*	% of *Parat*
Pachahri Surpuro					
Syayampur	40000	34000	85.00	6000	15.00
Tihervas	40000	32000	80.00	8000	20.00
Dasnali	35000	31200	89.14	3800	10.86
Khejdoli	28000	25000	89.29	3000	10.71
Vathavsi	25000	20000	80.00	5000	20.00
Amarpuro	25000	21000	84.00	4000	16.00
Ronovalvas	25000	21000	84.00	4000	16.00
Syampuro, Kishanpuro					

Kucivach	25000	20000	80.00	5000	20.00
Kararhvas	25000	21000	84.00	4000	16.00
Moridas	22000	18000	81.82	4000	18.18
Mudrohvas Khurampuro	22000	20000	90.91	2000	9.09
Nathusar	22000	18000	81.82	4000	18.18
Harsoli	21400	18200	85.05	3200	14.95
Garh	21000	18700	89.05	2300	10.95
Bhadalavas Hagum Bhojpuro	20000	17500	87.50	2500	12.50
Nalvo	20000	17000	85.00	3000	15.00
Kothrivas	19000	16000	84.21	3000	15.79
Silalo	18700	17500	93.58	1200	6.42
Jotusar	18000	13000	72.22	5000	27.78
Sargadh	18000	15000	83.33	3000	16.67
Khatuvas Kehrpur	18000	14500	80.56	3500	19.44
Madodugra	18000	12000	66.67	6000	33.33
Dhanuto	17000	14800	87.06	2200	12.94
Dhovalovas	17000	15000	88.24	2000	11.76
Lakhriju	17000	17000	100.00	0	0.00
Dholasarhi	16000	14000	87.50	2000	12.50
Doralo	16000	14500	90.63	1500	9.38
Nagal Koju	16000	14500	90.63	1500	9.38
Mehbhorrhakovas	15000	10000	66.67	5000	33.33
Vadhavas	15000	13500	90.00	1500	10.00
Chachvasath	15000	13500	90.00	1500	10.00
Sidhoduvas	15000	13000	86.67	2000	13.33
Laiasarvas	14000	12500	89.29	1500	10.71
Nathanvas Ranipur Jodhpur	14000	12000	85.71	2000	14.29
Tilokpur	13000	11700	90.00	1300	10.00
Karirivas	13000	11300	86.92	1700	13.08
Vijaipur	13000	10000	76.92	3000	23.08
Mehrosi	13000	11000	84.62	2000	15.38
Qasba Amarsar	12000	10000	83.33	2000	16.67
Vavrhi	12000	10000	83.33	2000	16.67
Dhuharhsar	12000	10000	83.33	2000	16.67
Suhlavas	12000	10000	83.33	2000	16.67
Surero	12000	10000	83.33	2000	16.67
Surani	12000	10500	87.50	1500	12.50
Khachravas	12000	10000	83.33	2000	16.67
Lisarho	12000	10600	88.33	1400	11.67
Nagal Kalan	12000	10000	83.33	2000	16.67
Nagala Ramsingh	12000	10800	90.00	1200	10.00
Asti Buzurg	11000	10000	90.91	1000	9.09
Alodo	10000	8500	85.00	1500	15.00

Charanvas	10000	7000	70.00	3000	30.00
Dalapatipuro	10000	8500	85.00	1500	15.00
Samadhri	10000	8800	88.00	1200	12.00
Gojavas	10000	7000	70.00	3000	30.00
Godhavas Kakrovas	10000	8000	80.00	2000	20.00
Lavi	10000	8000	80.00	2000	20.00
Lunavas	10000	7000	70.00	3000	30.00
Mudli	10000	80000	80.00	2000	20.00
Madhbherho	10000	9000	90.00	1000	10.00
Muthavas	1000	7500	75.00	2500	25.00
Nahri Salahdipur	1000	8200	82.00	1800	18.00
Vagarsikavas	9000	8200	91.11	800	8.89
Sihorhi	9000	8000	88.89	1000	11.11
Ajarsar	9000	8000	88.89	1000	11.11
Gehravarho	9000	7000	77.78	2000	22.22
Vanathlo	8000	7500	93.75	500	6.25
Vuharli	8000	6500	81.25	1500	18.75
Vajavas	8000	6500	81.25	1500	18.75
Chachasarhi	8000	6500	81.25	1500	18.75
Chainpuro	8000	7300	91.25	700	8.75
Dhisdevlo	8000	7000	87.50	1000	12.50
Sundarpuro	8000	7000	87.50	1000	12.50
Guvarhi	8000	7500	93.75	500	6.25
Kolvo	8000	7500	93.75	500	6.25
Nagal Ganga	8000	7000	87.50	1000	12.50
Udarhguvari	7300	5500	75.34	1800	24.66
Ahirvas	7000	5200	74.29	1800	25.71
Aspuro	7000	6300	90.00	700	10.00
Vilanderpur	7000	6200	88.57	800	11.43
Pirthipur	7000	5500	78.57	1500	21.43
Parharavas	7000	4500	64.29	2500	35.71
Junso	7000	6000	85.71	1000	14.29
Jasacharan	7000	7000	100.00	0	0.00
Dhighapuro	7000	6500	92.86	500	7.14
Ruhlan	7000	6000	85.71	1000	14.29
Rilavato	7000	6000	85.71	1000	14.29
Raipuro	7000	6000	85.71	1000	14.29
Kilanpur	7000	6000	85.71	1000	14.29
Madni	7000	6000	85.71	1000	14.29
Motilavas	7000	5000	71.43	2000	28.57
Hasairho Khurd	7000	5500	78.57	1500	21.43
Hathohro	7000	6000	85.71	1000	14.29
Haspur	7000	7000	100.00	0	0.00
Vudovasi	6000	5500	91.67	500	8.33

Pithalpur	6000	5000	83.33	1000	16.67
Basrhi Buzurg	6000	5200	86.67	800	13.33
Jalpavali	6000	5200	86.67	800	13.33
Sukho	6000	5400	90.00	600	10.00
Khorho	6000	4200	70.00	1800	30.00
Mirai	6000	5000	83.33	1000	16.67
Nagal Govinda	6000	5000	83.33	1000	16.67
Hingonovas	6000	5500	91.67	500	8.33
Asti Khurd	5000	4500	90.00	500	10.00
Vuvavna	5000	4000	80.00	1000	20.00
Javas	5000	4600	92.00	400	8.00
Savalpuro	5000	4500	90.00	500	10.00
Kalervas	5000	4400	88.00	600	12.00
Kanhipur	5000	4500	90.00	500	10.00
Narsinghpur	5000	3000	60.00	2000	40.00
Nivavas	5000	4300	86.00	700	14.00
Nahro	5000	4600	92.00	400	8.00
Narai	5000	4000	80.00	1000	20.00
Vasrhi Khurd	4000	3600	90.00	400	10.00
Jalalpur	4000	3600	90.00	400	10.00
Kali Kherho	4000	3500	87.50	500	12.50
Guthilo	4000	3700	92.50	300	7.50
Gudri	4000	3700	92.50	300	7.50
Ladpura	4000	3500	87.50	500	12.50
Malikpur Khurd	4000	3500	87.50	500	12.50
Malikpur Kalan	4000	3300	82.50	700	17.50
Mangarh	4000	3500	87.50	500	12.50
Nosal	4000	3500	87.50	500	12.50
Barnas	3500	3200	91.43	300	8.57
Kishanpur	3500	2800	80.00	700	20.00
Turkavas	3000	2800	93.33	200	6.67
Datilo	3000	2700	90.00	300	10.00
Siharh	3000	2600	86.67	400	13.33
Khativas	3000	2200	73.33	800	26.67
Hasterha Buzurg	2500	2000	80.00	500	20.00
Dongavas	2000	2000	100.00	0	0.00
Tatro	2000	1800	90.00	200	10.00
Raichandpur	2000	1900	95.00	100	5.00
Kaho	2000	1500	75.00	500	25.00
Vorkavas	2000	1500	75.00	500	25.00
Merhmajro	2000	1800	90.00	200	10.00
Bhurtharha	1500	1300	86.67	200	13.33
Andesari Majro Kathubhusar	1400	1200	85.71	200	14.29

Ramchand Charan Vas	1000	1000	100.00	0	0.00
Hevokovas	800	800	100.00	0	0.00
Abhai Ramcharan Ka Vas	800	800	100.00	0	0.00
Madho Ka Vas	350	350	100.00	0	0.00

A regular feature of the village landscape was the *parat* or fallow land. Ordinarily understood, fallow land is left in order to help soil retain its strength to take up fresh cultivation. Fallow land can be both current and regular. Current fallow can perhaps be classified as those which form a part of crop rotation and crop pattern. Why are current fallows necessary in crop rotation? The explanation can be supplied by soil conditions and availability of irrigational facilities, and soil moisture required at the time of sowing, which determines the choice of crops taken up in the season. The cropping pattern followed in irrigated areas varies in different agro-climatic zones, e.g. presently there are nine such identified agro-climatic zones in Rajasthan,[8] and our region belongs to IIIa in Table 14.2.

TABLE 14.2: PRESENT AGRO CLIMATIC ZONES AND THEIR CROPPING PATTERN

Ia.	All tehsils of districts Bikaner, Barmer, Jaisalmer, Phalodi, Shergarh, Osian and Jodhpur, Dungargarh, Sujangarh, Ratnagarh, and Sardrshahr district Churu	Bajra – fallow Guar – fallow Kharif pulses – fallow Groundnut – fallow Jowar - fallow
Ib.	All tehsils of district Sriganga-nagar	Cotton – wheat/barley Urad – mustard Bajra – sorghum – gram Sesame – coriander Maize – potato – wheat Sorghum – wheat – green gram
IIa.	All tehsils of district Nagaur, Sikar, and Jhunjhunu: tehsils Taranagar, Churu and Reajgarh of Churu district	Moth – fallow Bajra – fallow sorghum + kharif – pulses – fallow Guar – fallow Sesame + moong – fallow Bajra – wheat Sorghum – barley Bajra – gram Guar – wheat

IIb.	All tehsils of district Jalore and Pali: Reodher, Sirohi and Shivganj tehsils of district Sirohi: Bilara, Bhopalgarh tehsils of district Jodhpur	Moth – fallow Bajra – fallow sorghum + kharif – pulses – fallow Guar – fallow Sesame + moong – fallow Bajra – wheat Sorghum – barley Bajra – gram Guar – wheat
IIIa.	All tehsils of districts Tonk, Jaipur and Ajmer	Bajra – wheat Bajra – gram Bajra – mustard Sorghum – gram Fallow – mustard Sorghum/bajra – barley Cowpea/moong/urad – wheat/barley
IIIb.	All tehsils of districts: Alwar, Bharatpur, Doiur and Sawai Madhopur (except Khandar and Sawai Madhopur tehsils of Sawai Madhopur)	Fallow – mustard Bajra – wheat Bajra – barley Bajra arhar mix Sesame arhar mix Cowpea – mustard Moong – mustard Urad – mustard Fallow – gourd – wheat Fallow – gourd – barley Bajra – gram Fallow – gram
IVa.	All tehsils of district Bhilwara: all tehsils except Dharvavad, Salumber and Sarada of district Udaipur: all tehsils except Choti Sadri, Pratapgarh, Arnode and Badi Sadri of district Chittorgarh: also Abu road and Pindwara tehsils of Sirohi district	Bajra/Jowar – Mustard Moong – maize – wheat Sorghum – chickpea Maize – chickpea Cowpea – safflower Maize/bajra/sorghum – barley Sesame – rabi sorghum Maize + black gram Maize + pigeon pea Maize + castor Sorghum + pigeon pea Cotton + blackgram
IVb.	All tehsils of districts Banswara and Dungarpur: Choti sadri, Badi Sadri, Pratapgarh and Arnod tehsils of district Chittorgarh; tehsil Daryabad, Salumber and Sarada of district Udaipur	Maize/paddy/cotton/jowar/groundnut/sesame – fallow Kharif pulses/arhar – fallow Maize – wheat/gram Urad/moong/groundnut/sesame – wheat Maize – urad

V	All tehsils of districts Bundi, Kota and Jhalawar; tehsils Sawaimadhopur and Khandar of district Sawaimadhopur	Rice – wheat Soyabean – wheat Jowar – gram Maize – wheat Maize – gram maize mustard Sugar cane – ratoon Chari – barseem Kharif pulses – wheat/gram Fallow – gram Fallow – mustard Fallow – wheat Fallow – coriander Fallow - linseed

Likewise, there is a difference between irrigated and unirrigated crop patterns. Illustratively, the following is the present pattern of crop rotation adopted in the unirrigated area and irrigated area of Jaipur district.[9]

UNIRRIGATED CONDITIONS

Bajra	Fallow – Pulses – Fallow
Jowar	Fallow – Fallow – Gram
Bajra	Fallow – Fallow – Gram
Fallow	Mustard – Fallow – Gram
Fallow	Wheat
Groundnut	Wheat
Fallow	Mustard
Bajra	Fallow
Jowar	Fallow
Fallow	Gram

IRRIGATED CONDITIONS

Bajra	Wheat/Barley
Maize	Wheat/Barley
Groundnut	Wheat/Barley
Pulses	Wheat
Maize	Potato – Wheat
Bajra	Wheat – Moong
Fallow	Wheat/Barley
Fallow	Mustard
Jowar	Gram
Cotton	Fallow – Fallow – Wheat

We have testimony to Mughal administration taking cognizance of the irrigational facilities provided (viz., *pival*, *dhenkli*, or *tal*) while determining the land revenue of an area.[10]

Fallow from the above graphic appears to be common in those areas which fall in a particular agro-climatic zone or is suffering from lack of irrigational facilities. Availability of water in the soil profile obtainable to a particular agro-climatic zone as well as for irrigational purpose is an underlined element for regular cultivation and non-appearance of fallows.

To understand the significance of soil one has to admit that soil is one of the most significant ecological factors. It is derived from the transformation of surface rocks. Plants depend on it for their nutrients, water, mineral supply and anchorage. Sand and clay constitute the hard mineral fractions of the soil. Soil water acts as a solvent and as a transporting agent. It also maintains the soil texture and compactness of soil particles which make it the perfect habitat for plants. There are recognized classifications of soil texture namely sandy soil, clay soil, sandy loam soil, clay loam soil and sill loam soil.[11] Our documentary evidence does not assist us to form an idea as to which category soil in our period belonged. Variance in soil profile however did have an impact on *dastur* rates of individual crops, e.g. the rates of *magro* (hilly land) had a lower *dastur* rate as compared to *goriwa* (sandy).[12] One has also to concede that soil texture in the sixteenth-seventeenth century would have been far more better than in the same area presently.[13]

In order to appreciate the climatic and geomorphic characteristics one can notice that the landforms of Rajasthan are dictated by the Aravalli hill system that stretches across the State from the south-west to the north-east. Its climate is mainly described by rainfall and temperature components. The effect of these is modified by the existing landforms and their usage. In Rajasthan, the Aravalli range demarcates the climate pattern of rainfall distribution. The climate west of the Aravalli range is semi-dry and dry. This part receives very little annual rain. High temperature and high velocity winds and dust storms are a regular feature, particularly in summer months. The rainfall distribution pattern on the eastern flank of the mountains is quite variable and receives much rain when compared to the western side. Our region falls in the eastern flank.

It appears that water played a vital role in not only the selection of crops to be sown in an area but also the selection of harvest in which the crop was sown. A perusal of the data available indicates that in this area more *rabi* crops were preferred as compared to *kharif*.[14] This also confirms our suspicion that irrigation was a problem in the area, since most of these crops appear to be rain-fed.

The crops sown in *pargana* Amarsar were *jowar*, *makka*, *varh* (sugar cane), indigo, *sunn* (jute) and *vani* (cotton). The combination appears varied in view of the nature of the soil and water requirement of each crop. Jowar or *sorghum vulgare* is an important crop of Rajasthan. It is a *kharif* crop but it is also grown during summer with the help of irrigation. The utility of the crop is that it can be used both for fodder and grain. *Jowar* is drought resistant to a considerable extent. Therefore it is an ideal crop for areas of low and uncertain rainfall. *Jowar* resists wilting and remains stunted during dry periods and resumes growth after rain. The soil preferable for the crop is clay loam for better yields. *Jowar* tolerates saline soil. The seeds of edible *jowar* are sown far apart while *chari-jowar* used for fodder is grown compactly.[15]

Makka or maize grows best on well-drained fertile loamy soil and requires plenty of moisture during its early phase of growth. It needs heavy manuring and more attention than other *kharif* crops. The fertile moisture-retentive soil is regarded suitable for this crop.

Sugar cane roots are left while reaping the crop for one harvest. At the end of the second harvest, the roots also are removed before fresh seeds are sown. Water should be available in abundance for a good yield.

The seeds of indigo are sown broadcast in the month of June or as soon as rain sets in. When the young plants are above the ground the grass is weeded out by a process of hand hoeing. Reaping commences around the month of October. An important feature of indigo cultivation is the variation of the period of occupation of the soil. In some localities the crop is obtained in three months from the time of sowing, in other localities as much as eighteen months are needed. Earlier the system of taking several cuttings a year and allowing the plant to occupy the soil for two to three years was followed.[16]

Soil where cotton is grown is fertile though light. The plant is grown as a mixed crop usually with *til* (sesame), *arhar* (*Caganus indicus*), *sunn* (*Crotacaria juncea*), etc. The ground is prepared by ploughing and manuring. The cotton seed is broadcast in the month of April-June. The land is lightly ploughed immediately and later on again ploughed. Picking commences in October and is completed by the end of the year. The best soil for growing cotton is rich loam which is usually directly manured. On better grade of soil the crop is gradually grown alone, except where rows of *arhar* are sown at intervals of five to seven yards, but on poor soil it is almost invariably associated with four or five subordinate crops of which *arhar* and *til* are chief. If allowed to remain after January, watered and hoed two to three times, a second gathering in an even better quality can be obtained in May and June.[17]

The crop pattern of our region thus shows remarkable diversity as we find a dry crop like *bajra* on the one hand and wet crops like cotton, sugar cane, maize and indigo being sown in a *pargana*.

A close scrutiny would also reveal that the fallow area mentioned in our ten-yearly account does not represent a single strip of land which we can class as being unirrigated but in actuality it represented various patches of land within a village mentioned together. There is a strong apprehension that the fallow area may not have stayed in the same magnitude in the following year but the mean of fallow land continued in the official records.

In the end one can conclude that the consistent shrinking of *pargana*. Amarsar can possibly be explained by (a) decreasing revenue resources due to significant area being in *parat*, (b) the soil and soil water balance further deteriorated over a period of time, (c) water supply and irrigational facilities were lacking to sustain its identity, therefore, its villages were attached to the *pargana* of Bairath, which was in close proximity to Amarsar. Finally Bairath was elevated from the modest origin of a *pargana* of 34 villages[18] to tehsil Bairath of modern times which came to comprise among other villages, Amarsar in the Jaipur district.[19] In this interesting development, the function of water supply cannot be underestimated since Banganga which was about 164 km, an important river of Jaipur region originates in the hills of Bairath tehsil.[20]

NOTES

1. Amarsar is located at 27^0 -75^0, 6A, Irfan Habib, *An Atlas of the Mughal Empire Political and Economic Maps with Detailed Notes, Bibliography and Index*, New Delhi, Oxford University Press, 1982.
2. Abul Fazl, *Ain-i-Akbari*, ed. Blochmann, vol. 1, pp. 356 & 512, Calcutta, 1872.
3. *Taqsim Dahsala Pargana Amarsar*, VS 1758-65/AD 1701-8.

4. Wakil Report dated 15 September 1712; *Parwana*, dated 1717; *Parwana* 25 March 1718 O.H.R., No. 18, C.U. Wills et al., *Report on Panchpana Singhana, Sikar, Khandela etc.*, 1933.
5. S.P. Gupta, 'Expansion of the Territories of the Kachhwahas in Mughal Times', *Proceedings of Indian History Congress*, 1965.
6. Taqsim Dahsala Pargana Amarsar, vs 1758-67/1701-10; Taqsim vs 1768/1702, vs 1770/1713, etc.
7. For a detailed study of the interplay of environment and settlement see R.C. Sharma, *Settlement Geography of the Indian Desert*, New Delhi, 1990.
8. G.P. Khurana, 'Soil Climate, Land Use Characteristics and Associated Features for Agricultural Production in Rajasthan', pp. 124-36, published in *Rajasthan: A Unique State.*
9. *Rajasthan District Gazetteer*, Jaipur by Savitri Gupta, Directorate Distt. Gazetteer, Govt. of Rajasthan, Jaipur, 1987, p. 126.
10. *Dastur-ul Amal Pargana Amarsar*, vs 1783/1726, cf. S.P. Gupta, *The Agrarian System of Eastern Rajasthan*, New Delhi, Manohar, 1986.
11. B.K. Sharma, *Industrial Chemistry and Environmental Chemistry*, Meerut, Goyal Publishing House, 2006.
12. *Dastur-ul Amal Pargana Phagui*, vs 1691, cf. *Agrarian System*, op. cit.
13. *Industrial Chemistry*, op. cit., p. 178.
14. *Arhsatta Pargana Amarsar*, vs 1770/1713.
15. *Dastur-ul amal Pargana Amarsar*, vs 1783, *Agrarian System*, op. cit.
16. George Watt, *A Dictionary of Economic Products of India*, vol. IV, Calcutta, 1890, pp. 676-7.
17. Ibid., pp. 602-3.
18. *Arhsatta Pargana Bairath*, vs 1780/1723 & vs 1783/1726.
19. C.S. Gupta, *Census of India*, 1961, vol. XIV, Rajasthan, pt. IX A, Census Atlas, Census Operation, Rajasthan, 1967.
20. See, *An Atlas of the Mughal Empire*, op. cit. Also see *Rajasthan District Gazetteer*, op. cit.

CHAPTER 15

Ecology, Social Stratification and Agrarian Production in Medieval Rajasthan*

MAYANK KUMAR

As such, environment and technology or means of production, in themselves, are neutral to the socio-politico-economic set-up and are non-discriminatory. However, the opposite of it is also equally true in stratified societies since the ancient past. The access point of different sections of the society or individual influences the notion or perception of environment and technology. Human negotiations with the environment and/or technology by different sections of society or an individual form a very diverse experience. Thus, human interactions with the environment and technology cannot be treated as homogeneous. It is layered with several mediators, commonly known as 'socio-politico-economic factors'. At the larger social levels, it is not the invention of technology, rather proliferation is more important. Proliferation is governed by several factors, most important being the attitude to adapt to new and better technology closely followed by availability of necessary capital. It is aptly argued by Lynn White Jr. that, 'Iron was long a rare and costly metal, used exclusively for arms and for cutting edges.'[1] Thus, proliferation of iron for mundane agricultural purposes was slow as it was a capital-intensive proposition. On the other hand, use of stirrup for better and more

*An earlier version of the paper was presented at 'The Environment and Indian History', National Conference organised by The C.P. Ramaswami Aiyar Institute of Indological Research, Chennai, January 2008. I am thankful to G.S.L. Devra, Mahesh Rangarajan, Rajat Dutta for their valuable suggestions. I would also like to thank participants of the conference for their comments, especially Arun Bandopadhyay and Ranjan Chakrabarti.

effective cavalry witnessed active political interventions. 'Martel's diversion of a considerable part of the Church's vast riches to military purposes therefore was contemporary with the shift of the focus of the Frankish army from infantry to cavalry.'[2]

Further, it is to be noted that, almost all the human interventions in nature were mediated by the use of knowledge and/or technology. The access to knowledge, which made interaction with the environment easy and fruitful, was usually monopolized by the dominant sections of the society. It was more so because the application of this knowledge and technology required greater investment. Absence of the required capital with the mass was a major deterrent in the expansion and proliferation of the available technologies. A plausible reason for the same can be offered in terms of retaining control over human resources, the most viable source of energy in the pre-Industrial Revolution era.[3]

It appears that negotiations with nature when mediated by technology is a complex process and this paper examines the intricacies of human interventions in the environment with specific reference to agrarian technologies in early modern Rajasthan. It is all the more important because, it has been suggested than man lived in harmony with nature during the pre-colonial period and nature was basically benevolent. Such generalisations are not tenable in the light of empirical evidences from early modern Rajasthan. The role and impact of social stratification *vis-à-vis* nature and technology have been examined and the notions of homogeneity have been questioned.

Any study of the medieval period in India suffers from paucity of historical evidences, especially with reference to the impact on society and social responses to the natural uncertainties.[4] However, there are several categories of official documentation available for this period in the Rajasthan Archives. These sources delineate the official response to the natural distress and at the same time by implication these provide us glimpses of contemporary socio-political responses and concerns. We can further substantiate these with the literary and epigraphic sources available in good measure.

The archival administrative records are often in the nature of official correspondence between the rulers on the one hand, and officials posted in different parts of the concerned state on the other hand. Some of these were part of the royal communication and some of these were official directives. These doduments have been consulted extensively by several historians from different perspectives.[5] An important category of official document available in archival repositories is the *arzdasht* or petition written by the *amils*, *faujdar* or other *pargana* officials to the ruler at Amber. These officials regularly reported to the ruling authorities about various revenue and administrative details of the areas under their control. These documents were written in response to the problems faced by concerned officials and therefore provide useful insights into the various concerns of state and the common man. Simultaneously, they also give us the responses/remedies, evolved to solve the problem. The other important archival source this used in this study is the *Arhsattas* or ledgers of receipts and expenditure maintained at the *pargana* level.

As far as the north-western region, i.e. Marwar, is concerned, we have used a very informative document known as the *Sanad Parwana Bahi*. The term *'sanad'* and *'parwana'* explain the functions that the documents performed. These are primarily imperial directives issued to the *pargana* officials in response to various complaints and representations received by it. The subject matter of these documents range from, routine complaints due of revenue against the state officials, to the mutual disputes over the share of water of a well.[6] The *kagad bahi* of Bikaner is particularly significant for a better comprehensive document of the land revenue system. A good deal of light is thrown on the problems faced by the peasants, the primary producing class, and the methods of redress adopted by the state. Various kinds of concession and help were offered by the state to the peasantry, as monsoon failures were frequent in this region. Along with directives issued to the traders to not to hoard the grain, details of various concessions offered by the state in times of natural exigencies have also been recorded in the *kagad bahi*.

It will be relevant at this point to provide the details of land-man ratio, ratio between land available for agriculture and land being actually under cultivation. Any conjecture about the number of people living in this region during the pre-census period is doubtful. Tod tried to give an estimate about the number of people living in the region in the first half of the nineteenth century. He estimated a population of 5,39,250 for the state of Bikaner and an average density of 10 persons per sq km. For Jaisalmer it was 74,400 with an average density of 1 person per sq km. For Jodhpur State a total of 20,00,000 persons. For Shaikhawati he gives the average density as 30 persons per sq km, leading to a population of 4,24,800. Hence, the total population of the arid region was about 3,038,450 with an average density of 14 persons per sq km. However, the most authentic record for the contemporary period, *Ain-i-Akbari* by Abul Fazl, does not give any idea about the number of people. Moreland remarks, 'Rajputana was in general sparsely inhabited'[7] at the beginning of the seventeenth century.

A brief delineation of the ecological settings of Rajasthan will equip us better to appreciate the necessity and significance of technological inputs for agriculture. As far as general weather is concerned, heat dominates the scene in the whole of Rajasthan except some hilly parts.[8] In the summers, the temperature rises above 40 °C as the maximum occasionally reaching 50 °C at places in the desert area.[9] As such, a large part of India can be termed as semi-arid, but the relative absence of perennial rivers further worsens the conditions in Rajasthan. Rivers like the Looni, Chambal, and Betwa are highly seasonal; there are no snow-fed rivers in Rajasthan unlike in the Punjab, north India, or Assam. Rainfall also varies greatly, depending upon the direction of the monsoons and other related factors. In the western part, i.e. Jaisalmer, Bikaner and greater part of Marwar, the annual rainfall scarcely averages more than 12 cm. Since the clouds have to pass extensive heated tracts of sand before reaching these plains they are emptied of much of their moisture upon reaching the high ranges in the Kathiawar and the nearer slopes of the Aravallis.[10] However, in south-west Rajasthan, which is more directly reached and with less intermediate evaporation, by the periodical rains, rainfall is much more abundant; and at Abu sometimes it even exceeds 250 cm. Except in the south-west highlands of the Aravallis, rain is most abundant in south-east Rajasthan. In this part of the country, if the south-west rains fail to come on time, the southeast rains usually come to the rescue later in the season, so that the region is rarely subjected to the extreme droughts of the northwestern tracts.[11] If the eastern winds are strong, they bring hard rains from the Bay of Bengal; whereas if the south-west monsoon prevails, the rain is comparatively late and light. Sometimes a good bout of rainfall comes from both the seas, but rarely so. Rainfall varies substantially from year to year and even within a year.[12] Similar variations are visible in the natural vegetation as well. North-western Rajasthan is bereft of any forest cover, and grass and bushes dominate the landscape,[13] whereas the south-eastern part has a greater forest cover. To this effect, we have references of several *shikargahs* of the Mughal period.[14] This semi-arid bio-geographic zone was home to four large cats—lions, tigers, cheetahs and leopards. However, lions became extinct by the 1870s and cheetahs by the 1900s.[15]

Traditions have played a very significant role in the functioning of the pre-colonial social formations, especially in India and 'traditions were sufficient as long as the social order was one defined exclusively by birth.'[16] Society was characterized by the hierarchical order based on birth, where duties and privileges provided the functional framework.[17] Although the role of various sections of the society were defined by the larger framework provided by tradition, the vagaries of a monsoon-based agricultural production forced a level of flexibility on the part of different sections of society. Simultaneously, it is necessary to bear in mind another important limitations pointed out by James C. Scott. He argued that

> [T]he key to successful statecraft was typically the ability to attract and hold a substantial productive population within a reasonable radius of the court. Given the relative sparseness of the population and the ease of physical flight, the control of arable land was pointless unless there was a population to work it.[18]

However, such generalizations are problematic as they attribute little significance to the role of local social and environmental conditions in modulating the socio-political apparatus. The might of the political power cannot be measured solely in terms of the geographical expanse. 'A growing, productive population settled in the ambit of a monarch's capital was a more reliable indicator of a kingdom's power than its physical extent',[19] seems to be closer to reality. There seems to be a continuous attempt on the part of the political apparatus to increase the number of settlements in their territory.[20] Any migration during the years of distress was avoided by offering several concessions[21] and at times the already migrated peasantry was retrieved back on the promise of concessions and remittances in revenue demand.[22]

The socio-political stratification was further accentuated due to the difference in the access to the instruments of the productive resources among different sections of the society. Here it is pertinent upon us to point out at that unlike colonial states, pre-colonial political systems were extensions of kin-relations.[23] The polity and kinship systems coexisted and were intermixed, implying empowerment based on family ties. The structure was hierarchical with the ruler as the head of the clan, who had acquired territorial rights and established the principality; then came the *thikanadars* (nobles) who were his *sagas* (blood relatives)—brothers, sons and other close relatives. The dominant sections of the village society comprised various strata of the rural aristocracy (like the *jagirdars*, *bhumias* and *bohras*) who owed their status partly to hereditary superior proprietary rights in land and partly to their position in the apparatus of the revenue administration.[24] Moneylenders known as *mahajan/bohra* were the source of capital for the ordinary peasantry. The rulers offered a certain amount of patronage and protection to the *mahajans*, as the state recognised their importance.[25] The paucity of natural resources necessitated greater ties of interdependence between, and among, the ruling class and the peasantry at large. It was manifested in the flexibility in their relationships with respect to method and quantum of revenue realization.

A brief sketch of agriculture will place us in a better position to appreciate the dependence over irrigation facilities. In India, two crops have been a general norm, but in Rajasthan due to scarcity of water, at times it was difficult to raise even one crop.[26] The long-term and the short-term variations in the rainfall could ruin the crops and dry up pasturage, thereby make sustenance difficult. For instance, in VS 1660, it was reported to the state that in *qasba* Aaveri, rain measuring ten fingers fell on *sawan sudi* 11, so ploughing could be done only for 4-5 days.[27] Similarly, for *pargana* Amber in VS 1648/AD 1591, it was reported by *purohit* Harsram, that from *sawan vadi* 7 to *sawan sudi* 1, there was little rainfall in the *pargana* and because of strong winds, ploughing was not done and production fell sharply[28] which often forced migration of the peasantry.[29]

Choice of crop varied according to the variations in the climatic patterns. The flexibility seems to be inbuilt in agricultural societies—if rains were delayed, peasants shifted to cultivation of *moth* which has the shortest maturity period. Amar Chand and Sahib Ram, *vakil* of the Amber court inform us that due to meagre and delayed rains till the month of *Bhadava*,[30] only *moth* could be sown.[31] *Vakil* Ajitdas and Man Ram informs that due to drought, not even *moth* could be sown.[32] The statement that 'not even *moth* could be grown', testifies to the fact that *moth* was the last crop that could be sown in the case of delayed rains. During delayed or insufficient rainfall, land is ploughed extensively to make it soft and then seeds were sown. Kanwar Pal and Bhopat Ram inform the administration on *Kati Sudi* 9, vs 1641, that in the regions which have received insufficient rains, land is being worked upon to make it soft so as to sow the seeds.[33] Kanwar Pal and Hari Valabh Das supplement the information that wherever soil is hard, it needs one more shower and wherever rains have been insufficient, artificial irrigation through wells was arranged as well.[34] A close look at the revenue collection based on the agricultural production from the various parts of the Kingdom of Marwar clearly establishes the correlation between investment made by the ruling elite towards development of irrigation facilities and the agricultural potential.

The harsh environmental conditions of Rajasthan necessitated capital investment to sustain agricultural production. An analysis of ownership of key agricultural assets like ploughs, bullocks and Persian wheel, by individual cultivators point out economic disparity prevalent in the society. For *pargana* Pinyan, Dilbagh Singh has calculated that, 'there were 423 ploughs and there were a total of 315 *gavetis* and 76 *pahis*. Therefore, on a rough average each cultivator had at his disposal slightly more than one plough, which would have been sufficient only for cultivating a marginal holding, the *gavetis* being in a better position than the *pahis*. The individual breakdown was as follows:

4 ploughs held by 1 cultivator
3 ploughs held by 1 cultivator
2 ploughs held by 25 cultivators
1 plough held by 350 cultivators
0.5 plough held by 33 cultivators

This means that the better-off section, i.e. those with more than two ploughs formed only about 1 per cent of the total number of cultivators, the middle section 6 per cent and the poor section formed about 93 per cent.[35]

For the Harauti region, documents furnish information on the patterns of ploughs owned by *karsas*. In *mauza* Jholpa, 244 ploughs were distributed over 82 *karsas*, giving an average of 3 ploughs per head. However, the image undergoes a change if we consider individual cases. It shows that 13 *karsas* had less than one plough, 13 had up to 2 ploughs, 50 possessed 3 to 5 ploughs each and 5 had more than 5 ploughs whereas 2 Jat *karsas* possessed 33 ploughs each.[36]

The significance of the number of ploughs owned by peasants is self-explanatory, as a greater number would ensure greater capacity to cultivate more land. However, the significance of the number of ploughs in cultivation can be realized from the following popular saying:

Cultivating with one plough unit was a liability while two plough units were gainful employment, three plough units were proper cultivation and four plough units were a source of power. It very aptly relates the numbers of ploughs with economic power.[37]

The ownership of the number of bullocks is also a very important indicator of the economic status and a closer analysis point out the economic disparity. In *pargana* Chatsu 2,448 *asamis* owned 6,200 bullocks at an average of 2.5 bullocks per *asami*. However, the actual distribution of bullocks was quite unequal. 24 per cent *asamis* had one bullocks, 44 per cent *asamis* possessed 2 bullocks, 15 per cent *asamis* owned 3 bullocks, 8 per cent *asamis* were owners of 4 bullocks and remaining 9 per cent *asamis* had more than 4 bullocks.[38]

Similarly, in *pargana* Malrana there were 2,195 *asamis* sharing 5,988 bullocks. The individual ownership of bullocks is as follows: 12 per cent *asamis* had 1 bullock, 45 per cent *asamis* owned 2 bullocks, 23 per cent *asamis* possessed 3 bullocks, 10 per cent *asamis* had 4 bullocks and the remaining 10 per cent *asamis* owned more than 4 bullocks.[39] The economic disparity is visible even in terms of caste of the peasant.

Tables 15.1 and 15.2 show the number of bullocks owned by various castes for *qasba* Chatsu and Mauza Pachal.[40]

TABLE 15.1: CASTE-WISE BREAK-UP OF CATTLE IN *QASBA* CHATSU

Caste of *Asami*	Number of *Asamis*	Cattle
Mali	70	133
Gujar	8	18
Teli	28	51
Brahman	51	115
Lodha	5	17
Kumhar	4	11
Kayastha	5	11
Rajputs	3	12
Deswali	3	10
Meena	2	2
Nagori	14	35

TABLE 15.2: CASTE-WISE BREAK-UP IN MAUZA PACHAL

Caste of *Asami*	Number of *Asamis*	Cattle
Patel	2	12
Jat	12	30
Brahman	5	15
Khati	1	2
Miscellaneous	10	35

To sustain agricultural production in the semi-arid and arid region, means of irrigation were needed. The cost of construction of masonry well was beyond the capacity of a common peasant. The character of the subsoil renders the construction of wells or tanks expensive and labour-intensive. Munhot Nainsi's *Marwar Pargana Ri Vigat* carefully distinguishes between earthen and brick lined wells. In *pargana* Merta, out of 6,947 to 7,782 wells, only 20 wells were brick lined.[41] In Jalore, out of 693, only 147 were *pukka kuwa* (brick lined wells). Thus the *kachcha* wells heavily outnumbered the brick lined ones.[42] The much higher cost of construction of masonry well was perhaps a factor. For example, in AD 1738, in *qasba* Sawai Jaipur, the cost of a masonry well was Rs. 300 while a *kachcha* well was sold for Rs. 84 in a village of *pargana* Phagi in AD 1764. In *pargana* Dausa there were 513 wells distributed over eighteen villages, out of which 478 were *kachcha* and 35 *pukka*, nine of the latter being equipped with a *dhenkali*—a water-lifting device.[43]

In this context, the references to Persian wheels and other water-lifting devices is significant. In Rajasthan, possession of land was not enough, the availability of artificial irrigation was also necessary to stabilise and increase production. The cultivators who owned wells were able to grow superior food crops and cash crops like cotton, as these crops required regular and frequent water supply.

The significance of artificial irrigation device is clearly brought out from the statistical account of the *parganas* of Marwar as provided by Nainsi. He has enumerated not only the villages with mechanisms of irrigation but also the number of such mechanisms.[44] The significance of irrigation devices can be inferred from the evidence that villages given on *patta* were classified according to the availability of irrigation device in the villages.[45] The state was well aware of the potential of irrigation devices in surplus availability from any given region. The ownership of these devices was confined to the upper strata of society. It can be inferred that other cultivators might have rented Persian wheels. This is strengthened by the evidence provided by the *qanungo bahi*, which records that there were more than one pair of bullocks (*bhaoli*) attached to a Persian wheel, and the owners of these were different *asamis*, except for one pair which belonged to the Persian wheel owner. It means that the owners of the bullocks did not own the Persian wheel, and they irrigated their fields with the water-lifting machine belonging to some other *asami*.[46]

As pointed out above, the irrigation mechanism was an economic asset. These could be purchased, sold, or mortgaged by the owner. As ownership was an economic asset, it was also a criterion of social status. Generally, the ownership of these were confined to the upper strata of society who had enough capital to dig the well and construct the relevant mechanism to harness its potential. The importance of irrigation can be gauged by comparing the productivity of irrigated and non-irrigated lands. Madhvi Bajekal has calculated that in AD 1713-14, the differential in the yields of irrigated and non-irrigated rabi food grains was estimated to be 6.75 *maunds* per *bigha* and 3 *maunds* per *bigha* respectively.[47]

Besides wells, tanks/reservoirs played an important role in irrigation. The rulers and nobles had constructed numerous tanks/ reservoirs, both small and large. Sur Sagar, Farasat Sagar, Vasant Sagar in Marwar,[48] Ghadisar,[49] in Jaisalmer, Jai Samand,[50] Raj Samand,[51] Pichhola Jheel[52] in Mewar region, etc., were large reservoirs of water.

The consequences of the availability of artificial irrigation can be seen in the kinds of crops grown by various sections of society and resultant perpetuation of the economic disparity already prevalent in the society. The majority of the upper caste peasants raised cotton and other cash crops. Two Rajput peasants raised cotton on 75 and 60 per cent of land they cultivated respectively.[53] However, it is very significant that the size of land holdings broadly corresponded to the agricultural resources in terms of technological inputs like ploughs, seeds, Persian wheel and cattle. Peasants with adequate technological inputs could only raise crops meant for the markets.

It has been argued that the *zamindars*, revenue grantees, revenue officials and village headmen were endowed with a greater command over resources, which enabled them to produce cash crops for the markets. The possible cause for this might be the availability of capital for investment and the ability to take risks involved in the production of commercial crops. Whereas, ordinary peasants were unable to cultivate cash crops because these generally required a larger investment in terms of technological inputs than an average peasant could afford.[54]

Loans were sought to procure the means of cultivation—seed, manure, plough, bullocks, etc.

In many cases the peasant indebtedness was collective and we find the entire *ryots* of villages borrowing money from the *bohra*—the moneylender, to purchase seeds, manure, ploughs and bullocks so that they could cultivate the fallow lands of the village, construct ponds and dig wells. The *ryots* had to pay the debt at the time of next harvest with interest usually through their traditional representatives, the *zamindars* or the *patels*.[55]

The indigent peasants, usually the *paltis* and a category of *pahis*, were wholly depended on the *mahajan* for the resources needed for cultivation. The *mahajans* provided such loans to the peasants on various conditions, which is quite evident from the following example: the *ryot* of *qasba* Mauzabad borrowed bullocks, ploughs and seeds from the *bohra*. The subsistence loans were also sought by the peasantry and extended by the *bohras*. Similarly, in the village Sitarampur, *pargana* Fagi, we find that *paltis* borrowed money from the *bohra* to procure seeds and subsistence. At times the *mahajans* rented out their ploughs and bullocks and charged interest on lending seed and subsistence.[56] At the same time, the rulers offered a certain amount of patronage and protection to the *mahajans*, as even the state was aware of their importance.

The adverse effects of climatic conditions on the production possibilities could be mitigated with the ingenuity of human interference. If the conditions so provided, the introduction of better techniques could have lead to better results. The geography of the region was conducive for cultivation of cash crops, but required input, either in the form of human labour or technological support (dependable means of irrigation).

The above discussion very clearly points out that harsh environmental conditions of semi-arid and arid parts of Rajasthan necessitated a greater capital investment. The social distribution of various agricultural assets—size of land-holdings, bullocks, irrigational devices, etc., was highly unequal and it was reflected in the social stratification. The ownership of these assets greatly affected the production capabilities of different sections of the society. The capability of various classes to invest capital in agricultural production greatly determined the output and in this respect, economic disparity played a crucial role. Even though the environmental constraints were same for various sections of the society, classes with capability to invest in technological inputs received higher and secure returns. The above discussion clearly points out the need for greater capital investment to sustain and develop agriculture in the region. At the same time, we have already pointed out the economic disparities prevalent in the society forcing lower classes to search for credit to expand or even to continue with cultivation.

The economic disparity was compounded by the recurrent visits of drought in Rajasthan. The droughts undermined the limited capacity of the lower classes to continue agricultural production without borrowing heavily, which perpetuated the social inequality.

In the agrarian economy of this semi-arid and arid region, failure of monsoons very often led to droughts. Due to excessive dependence on the rains and the relative absence of perennial rivers further compounded the problem in Rajasthan. Cultivation of single crop a year in most of the arid part of the region further reduced the possibilities of accumulation of grains and thereby squeezed the capacity to cope with the vagaries of monsoons. Possibility of cultivation of particular crop in a season was determined by the timely onset of the rains. Choice of crop varied according to the variations in the climatic patterns.

Analysis of the land and pattern of social stratification in Rajasthan clearly highlights that land was available in abundance but means of cultivation and means of irrigation played a decisive role. In other words, the lack of capital with the primary producers was a major constraint in the expansion of cultivation. As such, given the level of technology, there were limited possibilities for development and sustenance of agriculture in the arid region, even with the availability of capital. Moreover, the agricultural output varied a lot in the normal years as well. The environmental features constrained agricultural production as Monsoons were erratic in the region. The cost of construction of wells or installation of water-lifting devices thereupon was capital-intensive. At the same time the recurrent drought and accompanying famine often eliminated the meagre resources—bullocks, seeds, etc.—possessed by the peasantry.

NOTES

1. Lynn White Jr., *Medieval Technology and Social Change*, New Delhi, Oxford University Press, 1979, p. 40.
2. Ibid.

3. Slavery, slaves, serfs and caste system were the tools to control and manipulate human resources.
4. At another plane, this concern led with the social responses of the lower rung of society gave rise to 'subaltern studies'. Sumit Sarkar, 'The Decline of the Subaltern Studies', in Sumit Sarkar, *Writing Social History*, New Delhi, Oxford University Press, 1998, pp. 82-108.
5. Satish Chandra, *Medieval India: Society, The Jagirdari Crisis and the Village*, New Delhi: Macmillan, 1982; G.D. Sharma, *Rajput Polity: A Study of Politics and Administration of the State of Marwar, 1638-1749*, New Delhi, Manohar, 1977; G.S.L. Devra, *Rajasthan ki Prashashnik Vyavastha*, Bikaner, Dharti Prakashan, 1981; S.P. Gupta, *The Agrarian of Eastern Rajasthan*, New Delhi, Manohar, 1986; Dilbagh Singh, *The State, Landlords and Peasants*, New Delhi, Manohar, 1990; B.L. Bhadani, *Peasants, Artisans and Entrepreneurs: Economy of Marwar in the Seventeenth Century*, Jaipur, Rawat Publications, 1999.
6. As the environment had imposed limitations on resource generation in the region, there were conflicts over the distribution of resources. These limitations compelled the state to extend several concessions in times of natural calamity. These documents are important as they also highlight the various concessions offered by the state in the times of natural calamity, the incentives to be offered for rehabilitation of a deserted villages, to check migration due to famine or drought, highlighting the concerns of the state in this desert region.
7. W.H. Moreland, *India at the Death of Akbar: An Economic Study*, New Delhi, Macmillan Co. Limited, 1920, p. 22.
8. On his way Babur had realised that north-east Rajasthan is very hot. Zahirud Din Muhammad Babur, *Babur-Nama*, tr. A.S. Beveridge, New Delhi, Oriental Books Reprints, 1970, p. 577; Abul Fazl and Jahangir have placed it in the second of the seven categories in which whole world was traditionally divided. The second category implied equitive heat and winter. Abul Fazl, *Ain-i-Akbari*, vol. II, tr. Col. H.S. Jarrett, New Delhi, Oriental Books Reprint Corporation, 1978, p. 273; Jahangir, *Tuzuk-i-Jahangiri*, ed. and tr. H. Beveridge, Delhi, Munshiram Manoharlal, 1968, pp. 340-1.
9. Abdul Qadir Badauni, *Muntakhab ut Tawarikh*, vol. II, tr. W.H. Lowe, Delhi, Renaissance Publishing House, 1986, p. 239.
10. *The Rajputana Gazetteer*, vol. I, Calcutta, Office of the Superintendent of Government Printing, 1879, p. 20.
11. *The Imperial Gazetteer of India*, vol. XXI, London, Clareandon Press, 1909, p. 92.
12. *Arzdasht*, *Asad Vadi* 1, vs 1638 and *Bhadva Sudi* 6, vs 1638, Historical Section, Jaipur Records, Rajasthan State Archives, Bikaner (henceforth, HS, JR, RSAB).
13. Irfan Habib, *Atlas of the Mughal Empire*, Delhi, 1982, Sheet No. 6 A

& B, New Delhi, Oxford University Press, 1982. 'The Geographical Background', in Irfan Habib and Tapan Raychaudhuri, eds., *The Cambridge Economic History of India*, vol. I, Cambridge, Cambridge University Press, 1982, pp. 1-13.

14. *Arzdasht, Migsar Vadi* 13, vs 1640, HS, JR, RSAB; GSL. Devra, 'Desertification and problem of Delimitation of Rajputana desert during the medieval period' *Human Ecology*, 7, 1999, pp. 97-107.
15. Divyabhanusinh, *The End of a Trail: The Cheetah in India*, New Delhi, Oxford University Press, 1999. Some of the famous protected areas here are Ranthambore, Sariska, Mount Abu and Sitamata. Deep Narayan Pandey, *Beyond Vanishing Woods: Participatory Survival Options for Wildlife, Forests and People*, Udaipur, Himanshu Publications, 1998, p. 36.
16. Nicholas Xenon, *Scarcity and Modernity*, New York, Routledge, 1989, p. 16.
17. Dipankar Gupta, 'Continuous Hierarchies and Discreet Castes', in Dipankar Gupta, ed., *Social Stratification*, New Delhi, Oxford University Press, p. 141.
18. James C. Scott, *Seeing like a State: How Certain Schemes to Improve the Human Conditions Have Failed*, New Haven and London, Yale University Press, 1998, p. 185. However, Sumit Guha has argued that South-East Asia has always seen greater density since ancient times. Sumit Guha, *Health and Population in South Asia from the Earliest Times to the Present*, New Delhi, Permanent Black, 2001.
19. Ibid., p. 185.
20. *Arzdasht, Jeth Sudi* 4, vs 1742, *Falgun Sudi* 2, vs 1743 and *Jeth Sudi* 4, vs 1742, HS, JR, RSAB.
21. The pre-colonial kingdom thus rode a narrow path between a level of taxes and coercive exactions that would precipitate wholesale flight. Scott, op. cit., p. 185.
22. *Arzdasht*, *Magh Vadi* 9, vs 1765, *Asad Sudi* 2, vs 1762, Jeth *Vadi* 7, vs 1752, and *Chait Vadi* 3, vs 1752, HS, JR, RSAB.
23. Sharma, op. cit.
24. Gupta, *Agrarian System*, op. cit., pp. 134-43 and Singh, op. cit., pp. 42-50.
25. Dilbagh Singh, 'The Role of the Mahajanas in the Rural Economy in Eastern Rajasthan during the 18th Century', *Social Scientist*, vol. 2(10), 1974, pp. 22-31.
26. Munhta Nainsi, *Marwar ra Pargana ri Vigat*, vol. II, ed. Narain Singh Bhati, Jodhpur: Rajasthan Oriental Research Institute (hereafter RORI), 1968, pp. 12, 36, 258-9, etc.
27. *Arzdasht*, *Sawan Sudi* 11, vs 1659, HS, JR, RSAB.
28. *Arzdasht*, *Sawan Sudi* 1, vs 1647, HS, JR, RSAB.
29. An *arzdasht* written by Mouji Ram dated *Kati Sudi* 15, vs 1774, HS,

JR, RSAB, informs the state about meagre rainfall leading to drought. This resulted in the migration of the peasantry. In his *arzdasht* dated *Jeth Sudi* 1, vs 1762, HS, JR, RSAB, Lal Chand Dala Ram informs about migration of peasantry due to drought and resultant decline in revenue collection. Similarly another *arzdasht* by Ajit Das, Man Ram dated *Chait Vadi* 3, vs 1752, HS, JR, RSAB, informs that villages were deserted.

30. Traditionally *Bhadva* is the third month of rainy season and usually the last one also.
31. *Arzdasht, Bhadva Vadi* 7, vs 1660 & *Arzdasht Sawan Sudi* 9, vs 1638, HS, JR, RSAB.
32. *Arzdasht, Falgun Sudi* 11, vs 1638, HS, JR, RSAB.
33. *Arzdasht, Kartik Sudi* 9, vs 1641, HS, JR, RSAB.
34. *Arzdasht, Asoj Vadi* 7, vs 1642, HS, JR, RSAB.
35. Singh, op. cit., p. 34.
36. Jhada Pargana Barsana ko Mauza Jholparo, vs 1856, Dusri Manzil, Basta no. 41, Kota Records, R.S.A. Bikaner.
37. J.S. Gehlot, *Rajasthani Krishi Kahavaten*, Jodhpur, Pragati Publishers, 1941, p. 56.
38. *Arshattas, Pargana* Chatsu, vs 1666, HS, JR, RSAB.
39. *Arshattas, Pargana* Malrana, vs 1666, HS, JR, RSAB.
40. Singh, op. cit., p. 34.
41. Nainsi, op. cit., vol. II, pp. 89-213.
42. Bhadani, op. cit., p. 45.
43. Singh, op. cit., p. 52.
44. Nainsi, op. cit., vol. I, 1968, pp. 209, 211, 213, 214, 215 447, 449, 450, 452, 455; vol. II, 1969, pp. 14, 124, 126, 129, 131, 133, 134.
45. *Sanad Parwana Bahi*, no. 2, vs 1822, Jodh. Rec. RSAB.
46. Bhadani, op. cit., pp. 116-17.
47. Madhvi Bajekal, 'Agricultural Production in Six Selected Qasbas of Eastern Rajasthan (*c.* 1700-1780)', thesis submitted to the University of London, 1990, p. 43.
48. Nainsi, op. cit., vol. I, pp. 579-99.
49. Munhta Nainsi, *Khyat*, ed. Badri Prasad Sakariya, vol. I, Jodhpur: RORI, 1960, p. 73.
50. Nainsi, *Khyat*, vol. I, p. 31.
51. Ibid.
52. Ibid.
53. Bhadani, op. cit., p. 116.
54. Irfan Habib, 'Potentialities of Capitalist Development in the Economy of Mughal India', *Enquiry* (New Series), vol. III, no. 3, Delhi, 1971, p. 20.
55. Singh, 'The Role of the Mahajans', op. cit., pp. 22-3.
56. Ibid.

REVIEWS

Hamid Qalandar, *Khair-ul-Majalis**

IQTIDAR HUSAIN SIDDIQUI

The Indo-Persian literature produced during the Delhi Sultanate period is of historical significance in that we find new genres invented that inspired Persian writers in other Persian-speaking countries also. In fact, the early Indo-Persian writers performed an important role in the progress of Persian prose. Besides the translation into Persian of Arabic and Sanskrit classics, no doubt, a pioneering effort, the works of Persian lexicography, historiography, *Sufi Malfuzat*, fiction (i.e. *dastan-writing* in Persian prose) are important. They remain not only unequalled much less excelled by their counterparts in foreign lands but also set trends in Persian language. As for the compilation of *Sufi Malfuzat* (collection of discourses or utterances), it began with the compilation of *Fawaid-ul-Fuad* by Mir Hasan Sijzi, the *murid* (disciple) of Shaikh Nizamuddin Chishti (Auliya). Sijzi noted down whatever he heard his *pir* say to his *murids* in the assembly just after he returned home. His collection served as a model to others later.

Inspired by Hasan Sijzi, Hamid Qalandar put down the utterances of Shaikh Nasiruddin Chiragh-i-Delhi and entitled his collection *Khairul-Majalis* (Auspicious Assemblies). He also wrote on return from the hospice of the Shaikh the discourse or whatever was uttered by the Shaikh in the assembly. The problems discussed provide us with insights into the life and culture of the age and help us in delineating the society. Herein we find interesting evidence that not only corroborates that which is available in histories but also of supplementary nature. For example, the prices of essential commodities had gone up causing misery to the poor during the reign of Sultan Muhammad bin Tughlaq and remained so in the early years of the reign of Firozshah also. Nostalgic of the prosperity and cheapness of Sultan Alauddin's reign, Shaikh Nasiruddin laments comparing the

*Translated into English by Ishrat Husain Ansari and Hamid Afaq Siddiqui, Idara-i-Adabiyat-i-Delhi, 2010.

present with the past (i.e. the reign of Alauddin Khalji, 1296-1316); there was reliance on God during those days. Then he recalled the abundance of money and cheapness of essential commodities. One *maund* wheat could be had for 7½ *jitals*, 1 *maund* sugar for half a dirham and ordinary sugar for 1 *jital* a *maund*. Clothes and other articles too were also cheap. If someone desired to give a feast or hold an assembly, so much food was available in two *tankas* and four *tankas* that it was enough for the entire assemblage. Thereafter he recalled the *langars* (free kitchens) run by the dervishes in the city (Delhi) and its suburbs. Mention is made of the *langars* maintained by Ramzan Qalandar and Malik Yar Paran where people were served food in large number. Similarly, flesh arranged by Shaikh Badruddin Samarqandi on certain occasions for feeding people on large scale are described. He was a friend of Shaikh Nizamuddin Auliya and they paid visits to each other. Samarqandi was fond of *sama* and evinced too much interest in it. When it was *Urs* (death anniversary of a saint), the Shaikh invited all the *langardaran* (fellow Sufis) and they came from the adjoining places. What an auspicious and blessed age was this, people lived in comfort and were happy. Today, neither the *langardaran* (those who ran *langars*), not the *langars* and devotees have remained (pp. 141-2).

All this is corroborated by Ain-ul-Mulk Mahru, the governor of Multan, when he criticized the conduct of the artisans who did not reduce their wages when the prices had come down. He complains that the artisans charged two or three *jitals* for their work for the whole day during the times of Sultan Alauddin Khalji. 'A weaver, he says, used to charge two *jitals* for weaving a *chadar* (sheet), but, today he charges thirty *jitals* for it. The tailor, who charged four *jitals* for stitching single *Yakta* (unique garment without a lining), today (i.e. Firozshah's reign) he is not happy even if he is paid thirty *jitals* for the same work. They justify their action complaining about the rise in the prices of food grains by way of excuse, although compared to the recent past the prices have again become low. They persist in changing what they charged during the time of famine (cf. Ainul Mulk Mahru, *Insha-i-Mahru*, ed. Shaikh Abdur Rashid, Lahore, 1965, letter no. 20, pp. 47-8).

Likewise, we find interesting information about certain political events that is wanting in the contemporary histories. For instance, the following reference to the Mongol invasion under the command of Targhi of India and the siege of Delhi in AD 1303, casts light on the disturbance caused by it around Delhi as well as the mode of warfare in the Sultanate of Delhi. It shows that by the time of Sultan Alauddin Khalji, the Delhi army had full knowledge of the Mongol mode of warfare and adapted it to its need. In the lands under their occupation the Mongols took recourse to the scorched earth policy when they found the invader too powerful for them. The Sultan of Delhi began to use, the same weapon when he was not able to face the Mongols in the open. Furthermore, we also find herein information about the Sultan's concern for the safety of his people. The Shaikh is reported to have told the visitors:

> when I came on this occasion (to Delhi from Awadh) on the sixth or seventh day, Iqbal (the disciple of Shaikh Nizamuddin Auliya) came and said: 'Get ready'. I said, 'what is the matter?' Khwaja Iqbal replied: 'There is great anxiety about the Mongols. Sultan Alauddin (Khalji) at this very moment has sent one of his men to the Shaikh (Nizamuddin Auliya)'. He said: 'The Sultan says that there is a Mongol alarm, and wants you to come inside the city'. The Shaikh will do so not tomorrow, but the day after tomorrow. At the same time he brought news that the soldiers had been detailed to bring people from the surrounding countryside and to destroy all villages and burn the standing crops: My mount was in the village of Maulana Fakhruddin Zarradi (also a disciple of Shaikh Nizamuddin), one of his relatives had a village. The animals in Fakhruddin's village had been sent there. (p. 205)

Also worth quoting is the reference contained in the *Khair-ul-Majalis* to the estrangement of relationship between Shaikh Nizamuddin (Auliya) and Sultan Qutbuddin Mubarakshah Khalji (reigned: 1317-20). Once Shaikh Nasiruddin Chiragh told the visitors that some people said to the Sultan that Shaikh Nizamuddin accepted the gifts presented by the servants of the court but not those from the Sultan. Being displeased, the Sultan issued the order that no state employee should visit the Shaikh and thought that the *langar* of the Shaikh could not be maintained without assistance from the state officers. When the Shaikh knew about the royal order, he asked the *murid-in-charge* of the kitchen to enhance the quantity of food cooked for feeding people. After some time, when the Sultan enquired whether the Shaikh was still able to maintain the *langar*. He was told that the people who got food, their number had increased. More money was being spent. The Sultan realized that he was wrong (pp. 203-4). All this explodes the myth created by the later writers that the Sultan was bent upon doing harm to the Shaikh but was murdered by his own favourite, Khusrau Khan. That the Sultan met the tragic and on account of his hostility towards the Shaikh.

In short, the *Khairul-Majalis* forms an important part of the source of information about the life and culture in the Sultanate of Delhi. This work not only helps us analyse the elements of change and continuity in history but also shifts our focus from preoccupation with battles, factionalism and intrigues at the royal court. It provides us with insights into problems and tensions faced by people in medieval Indian society. Its translation from Persian into English makes it accessible to the scholars who could not utilize it in Persian.

Mulla Qāti'i Harvi, *Tazkira-i-Majma'al-Shu'ra-i Jahangir Shahi**

IQTIDAR HUSAIN SIDDIQUI

The present edition of the *Tazkira-i-Majma'al-Shu'ra-i Jahangir Shahi* is to be warmly welcomed since we have here a biographical dictionary of 153 Persian poets, many of whom served in important positions in Indian and Khurasan regions during the sixteenth century. Mulla Qāti'i, himself a poet and scholar of merit, lived a long life, serving the Mughal emperors from Humayun to Jahangir. His notices of the poet-grandees who migrated from Khurasan and Central Asia as well as those who belonged to India and had won the favour of the Mughal emperors, though brief, are important in as much as they contain bits of rare information not found in other contemporary sources. Further, the compiler's reminiscences of historical events, incorporated in the biographical notices provide us with some new evidence. These additional pieces of information certainly enhance the historical value of this *Tazkira*.

Mulla Qāti'i's family hailed from Herat as his surname Harevi suggests. The family seems to have migrated to Qandahar during the early sixteenth century. On Humayun's return from Iran to Qandahar, which he wrested from Mirza Kamran, Humayun entrusted its charge to Bairam Khan, Mulla Qāti'i joined the latter. It was at this time in Qandhar that he met Hakim 'Ain al-Mulk Shirazi, a leading physician and scholar. According to Qāti'i, the large hearted patronage extended by Bairam Khan to men of learning and talent had turned Qandhar into a rendezvous for scholars and poets. Bairam Khan is also said to have built a rich library near his own residence where Qāti'i spent most of his time in the company of Hakim 'Ain al-Mulk. He says that Bairam Khan also used to join them in the library and talked to them in the most civil manner (p. 54). In 1551-2, when Mirza Hindal was killed by Mirza Kamran's men, and Humayun

*Edited by Muhammad Saleem Akhtar, Karachi, 1977.

assigned the territory of Ghazni to Prince Akbar, Qāti'i was sent along with Khwaja Jahan, Mir Katib and Qasim 'Ali Khan to Ghazni. Having spent some time in Ghazni, he decided to leave for the pilgrimage to Mecca and Madina.

Qāti'i's notices of the expert calligraphist shows that Humayun and Akbar patronized men of talent. Humayun patronized Ashraf, the disciple of Mulla Dost Mohammad, a leading calligraphist (p. 61).

Like his father, Emperor Akbar also evinced interest in calligraphy. On his return from Arabia, Qāti'i joined the group of calligraphists at Akbar's court (p. 12). He seems to have been commissioned along with other expert calligraphists, such as Khwaja Mahmud Ishaq, Mir Kulang, Mir Hafiz Muhammad Amin, the disciple of Mir Saiyid Ahmad, and Khwaja Husain Harevi to prepare the copies of the books for the king's library. The *Qissa-i-Hamza (Dastan-i-Amir Hamza)* is said to have been copied and bound by them for the royal library (p. 12). Among them Khwaja Husain Harevi was an important grandee who enjoyed a *jagir*, yielding seventy to eighty lakh *dams* annually. Mulla Qāti'i being his friend was given a village by him out of his *jagir* (p. 13).

As an illustration of the historical information contained in the notices of the Indian, Central Asian and Irani poets, we may begin with the notice of Mulla Mazhar Kashmiri. The compiler, describing the pleasant climate, scenic beauty and physical charm of the valley and people of Kashmir, says about Mirza Haidar Dughlat that the people of Kashmir, on account of the interest taken and training given by Mirza Haidar, gained skill (in different arts and crafts). Before him, there were no musical instruments (perhaps Central Asian instruments), music, poetry (i.e. Persian) and sciences. The Mirza's effort and training made them skilful in arts and poetry (p. 12). Qāti'i also describes Mulla Mazhar Kashmiri as a special recipient of divine grace, and states that the Kashmiris held him in high respect for his spiritual excellence (p. 13).

We also find interesting information about the early career of Khwaja Kalan, the premier noble of Babur, who wrote poetry under the pen name of Sipahi. Qāti'i writes about him: 'He was the most distinguished and the highest of the nobles of Hazarat Firdaus Makani, Babur Badshah. He arrayed forces and fought battles against 'Ubaid Khan (the successor of Shaibani Khan Uzbek in Central Asia).

[Once] Ubaid Khan commanded fifty-seven thousand men from Ilachoban

(Turks), while Babur had only two or three thousand horse men with him. In the ensuing battle, people were killed in large numbers on both sides. A few great Khwajas (descendants of Khwaja Ahrar Naqshband and the relations of Khwaja Kalan) also obtained martyrdom. Khwaja Kalan accompanied the king (Babur) and fought in every battle. When His Majesty, the King (Babur), found that many Muslims were killed, he left Transoxiana for Badakhshan.

Humayun was posted in Badakhshan, and Babur himself came to Kabul. Khwaja Kalan Beg was entrusted with the charge of Qandahar and allowed to exercise full authority there. In Qandahar, many scholars and poets came from Herat and joined his service. He did all of them great favour, with the result that Qandahar became a 'second Herat' as a centre of learning. After the defeat of Sam Mirza (the Safavid Prince who attacked Qandahar), Shah Tahmasp came in person to invest Qandahar (AD 1526). Khwaja Kalan determined to defend the fort, but his people persuaded him to come to terms, saying: 'He is not Sam Mirza but Shah Tahmasp, who has taken a decision to massacre all people (in Qandahar) after victory'. Some of them also suggested that he should vacate Qandahar. Khwaja Kalan then left Qandahar for the Panjab. His lieutenant, Khwaja Muhammad had the keys of Qandahar made of gold and then proceeded to see Shah Tahmasp. Being an eloquent man, he pleased Shah Tahmasp who asked him to ask for the grant of the country for himself. The Khwaja said: 'I request your Majesty to spare the people of Qandahar'. The Shah said: 'I have forgiven the people of Qandahar'. Thereupon, having surrendered the keys of Qandahar to the Shah, the Khwaja came to Bhakkar (pp. 29-30). These details are not furnished anywhere else to us.

Equally important are the details about the scholars who were attracted by Akbar's patronage and came from different countries to join his court. They got suitable positions in accordance with their qualifications. For instance, Mulla Chalebi, who originally hailed from Iraq and got educated in the Ottoman empire, came to India during Akbar's reign. Akbar found him a gifted man and appointed him as qazi to administer justice. Though he is said to have performed his judicial functions competently, at times he suffered from mental disbalance. He was addicted to opium, and ultimately resigned his office and led a retired life (p. 35).

In the notice of Shaikh Abu Nasr Farahi, the compiler takes the opportunity to praise the climate and fruits of Farah (a town in western Afghanistan). 'Particularly, the pomegranates there are of large size, delicious and very juicy. Every grain (of pomegranate) is of beautiful red colour, like a ruby'. He himself had stayed there for four months and benefited from his association with local scholars such as Qazi Abu'l Baraka (p. 36).

Mir Jan Siyaqi was a man of the pen and served Bairam Khan as his *Bakhshi*. He enjoyed full authority as *Bakhshi* in Qandahar. On Humayun's return to India (1555), he came with Bairam Khan and remained the most trusted man of his master. On the murder of Bairam Khan, 'the pious Nawab', he took his dead body to Mashad, and distributed money among the Saiyids there (p. 38).

We also find additional information of certain intellectuals of Iran who were compelled to migrate to India. In the notice of Mirza Sharaf, the Sunni qazi and courtier of Shah Tahmasp, we are informed of the eminence of Mulla Abud'l Razzaq as an intellectual, statesman and administrator of Gilan. With his cooperation and help, the ruler of Gilan, Khan Ahmad (1536-76) defended his territory against Shah Tahmasp for about twenty years. When Gilan was at last conquered, Khan Ahmad was imprisoned in the fort of Qanqaha and 'Abdu'l Razzaq was killed (p. 48). The latter's sons, Hakim Abu'l Fath, Hakim Humam and Hakim Nuru'ddin were reduced to poverty. They, therefore, turned to India and joined Akbar's service in 1575, winning Akbar's favour and becoming his trusted courtiers (*vakils*). Hakim Abu'l Fath Gilani, we are told by Qāti'i, had no equal in diagnosing diseases by reading the pulse of the patient. His brother, Hakim Humam, was more learned in sciences than him (p. 48).

In the notice of a *Waqi'a navis* (news reporter), Mulla Shah, with the pen-name Ansi, we are given information about the festivities held in the capital at the time of the coronation of a Mughal king. In 1530 when Humayun ascended the throne, the nobles brilliantly illuminated their boats and vessels on either side of the river Yamuna. There were dazzling lights all around from torches and lamps. He also states about his close association with Mulla Shah. When Qāti'i decided to set-off for pilgrimage to Mecca, some time after the expulsion of Humayun from India in 1540, Mulla Shah too joined the pilgrimage. On the way his party encountered Afghan robbers. Mulla Shah had many *ashrafis* (gold coins) concealed inside the lining of his cloak. He put an expensive gown over it and then rode a fast horse with all the courage he had. When he came face to face with the Afghan highwaymen, he galloped away and was soon beyond their reach. He covered 10 *kurohs* (about 20 miles) without halt and was thus safe. Qāti'i travelled through a safer route with his other companions, and joined Mulla Shah in Sibi (Balochistan). Mirza Askari, whom Humayun had exiled to Arabia, was also with them. Mulla Shah, his sons and his grandsons, Mir Husain and Mir Muhammad Qasim, served under Qulij Khan, one of the high nobles of Akbar. They are portrayed as highly cultured men (pp. 51-2 and editor's note, pp. 221-2).

Ashraf Khan, a Saiyid from Herat, was not only an expert calligrapher and a talented poet but also an erudite scholar. In calligraphy he was the chief disciple of Mulla Dost Salman. Ashraf Khan could write in all the seven hands (*Khats*), and was unrivalled as a *Mir Munshi* (prose-writer). He came to India and joined Akbar's service. 'Most of the royal *farmans*, issued in Hindustan, were drafted by him. One of these *farmans*, addressed to Mulla Niyazi (an Iranian scholar), inviting him to the royal court, was (also) penned by him'. 'It is in my possession', says our author. 'It is characterized by beautiful words and phrases'. He possessed wealth beyond any limit. In every province in Hindustan, he had beautiful houses constructed; later they passed on to his sons and grandsons (p. 53).

Another Saiyid from Herat was Mir Kulang. He was educated in Bukhara, where his family was shifted by the order of 'Ubaidullah Khan in 1539. From Bukhara, a great seat of Muslim learning, he migrated to India in the company of Mir Duri and Khwaja Muhammad Ishaq during the reign of Akbar. He was appointed as a calligraphist in the royal library and commissioned to make the copy of the *Qissa-i-Amir Hamza*. The other scholars associated with this project were Mir Duri and Muhammad Amin, the disciple of celebrated Saiyid Ahmad in calligraphy. The author also worked with them and was especially concerned with the binding of its parts. Mir Kulang and Khwaja Husain Marvi inscribed different portions of the work. Later on, they went to Arabia together for *hajj* (p. 54).

Mention should also be made of the account of Khwaja 'Abdullah Marvaridi, who had Bayani as his pen-name, since it contains interesting information about Shaibani Khan Uzbek. Being a scholar poet, Khwaja 'Abdullah Marvaridi was associated with the court of the Timurid prince, Husain Baiqra in Herat. He held the post of *Sadr us-sudur.* In addition to his *diwan* (collection of poems), he had to his credit a number of treatises on different sciences. On the death of Mirza Husain Baiqra, 'Shaibak Khan (i.e. Shaibani Khan) came to Herat, occupied it and ascended the throne there. The distinguished scholars, who survived the Mirza, and were stipend-holders or served the court in different capacities, attended the darbar of Shaibani Khan. They presented gifts along with their writings. Uzbek nobles were also present in the darbar. First the Master Bihzad (the famous painter) was conducted with his painting to the royal presence. The Khan asked for his pen-case which was brought there immediately. The Khan, having picked up the pen, asked Bihzad to come nearer. Thereupon, he made comments on every part of the painting such as that the nose should have been drawn in that way and that the face was not shown properly. After him Mulla Sultan 'Ali came forward and presented a distich. Again, the Khan picked up his pen and made alterations in the poem, saying that the vowel mark should have been placed on that letter or the dot should have been put in that place, etc. The Mulla and Khwaja 'Abdullah were disappointed, and they lost hope of retaining their positions at the new court. Soon, however, the Khwaja was able to win over the confidence of Shaibani Khan and became his associate. One day, he submitted to the Khan that men of learning and talent, such as Mulla Sultan 'Ali and Bihzad, who were unrivalled in learning and art, deserved royal patronage. 'It looks strange that the Khan has not done favour to them.' The Khan said: 'You are right, I also have the same feeling. But they came on the day when I held the court and all the Uzbek nobles were present. I have impressed upon these Turks that no king anywhere had the mastery over sciences and art like me'. Then he summoned all of them, and had a grand feast arranged in their honour, and their lands and stipends were restored to them (p. 56).

It is worth recalling that Mulla Pir Muhammad Sherwani (later Nasir al-Mulk) has been described by contemporary historians as a man whom power and high position had turned into a tyrant, yet the details provided by Qāti'i about him in the notice of Hakim 'Ain al-Mulk (d. 1594) serve as a corrective. He writes that when he was in the service of Bairam Khan in Qandahar, Pir Muhammad Khan Sherwani and Hadi Sistani, who held the office of *Vakil* with full authority, happened to be the most refined and cultured persons among a galaxy of learned and talented men. And Pir Muhammad was a notable scholar of religious sciences. 'When the king (Humayun) reconquered India (1555), he (Pir Muhammad) exerted himself and displayed courage. Bairam Khan gained power and influence under Akbar; with him Pir Muhammad Khan also rose into prominence and treated people with benevolence and consideration'. As regards his good qualities, Qāti'i remembers one instance: The drum of Pir Muhammad Khan was being beaten at the *darwaza-i la'l* (red gate) where the *sawars* were galloping around. The Khan asked: 'Friends, do you know whose is the drum they are beating?' People wondered as to why he asked the question. Then he told them that the drum belonged to one who was a pauper in Mashad during his student days (i.e. himself) (pp. 59-60).

Hakim 'Ain al-Mulk Shamsu'ddin 'Ali Shirazi was a physician, famed for his expertise in surgery and ophthalmology. In India, Qāti'i says, he was appointed the *hākim* (governor) of Delhi (pp. 58-9).

Some of the foreign dignitaries who had settled down in Sind after the expulsion of Humayun from India in 1540 performed important roles in Thatta and Bandar Lahri. For instance, Mulla Jani who hailed from Merv, now sought refuge in Thatta. Shah Husain, the ruler of Sind, impressed by his verses and eloquence, entrusted him with the charge of Bandar Lahri. He managed the affairs of the port well and collected valuable goods in plenty. Two beautiful gardens were laid out by him in the fashion of Herat. Qāti'i was impressed by his hospitality when he reached Lahri in response to his invitation (p. 114).

Like Mulla Jani, Mir 'Aziz of Kashan was not only a talented poet but also a man of administrative capability. He came from an illustrious family of Ustrabad and served as the *diwan* (finance minister) of 'Isa Khan Tarkhan of Thatta. In Thatta he had a magnificent *hamam* built inside the walls of his mansion. He also had a beautiful garden laid outside the *hamam* with a tank and fountains (p. 61).

We also find interesting information about an Indian scholar and poet of Jewish origin, Mulla Tarzi, of Bani Isra'il whose family seems to have become Muslim a few generations earlier. Qāti'i says about the members of Bani Israil fraternity that in India they were very good Muslims, possessed of saintly virtues. Khwaja Uwais Gwaliari is also praised for his authoritative knowledge of astrology, astronomy, geomancy, and astrolabes, in addition to Islamic sciences and Arabic. He obtained the patronage of both Humayun and Akbar.

Another important Indian Muslim personage whom Qāti'i mentions is Shaikh Gada'i, the first Sadru's-Sudur of Akbar's reign. Afraid of Sher Shah Suri's wrath against the collaborators of the Mughals, Shaikh Gada'i fled to Gujarat after Humayun's expulsion. When Bairam Khan also made good his escape and reached Gujarat, Shaikh Gada'i went out of his way to help him. In this notice of the

Shaikh, we find interesting information about Bairam Khan, not available anywhere else. We learn that Bairam acquired proficiency in Hindvi and composed verses in a mixture of Hindui and Persian. The following couplet, called *rekhta* (a popular form of Hindvi poetry at that time) is said to have been composed by him in Gujarat: *Sad bar guftam ki Takrani jiyo, yakbar na gufti ki piya pani piyo* 'Hundred times I begged: O gracious lady, you did not say even once: Love, have water to drink (pp. 63-4).

We are also informed that after the return of Bairam Khan to India, Shaikh Gada'i joined him, and shared power with him as his most trusted friend. Bairam Khan addressed him out of respect as *Bha'i* (brother) Gada'i (pp. 70-2).

The account furnished of Mulla Khwaja Husain Mervi, another scholar, in the service of Humayun and Akbar is also of some interest. His family is said to have moved to Bukhara during the time of 'Ubaidu'llah Khan Uzbek. Having completed his education in Bukhara, he joined Humayun's service in Kabul. Impressed by his knowledge of different sciences, Humayun called him the most outstanding of the scholars in his service. He arrived in India from Arabia after performing *hajj* there, and joined Akbar's service. For his association with his father and high accomplishments in learning, Akbar is reported to have assigned him a big *jagir*, yielding seventy to eighty lakh *dams* annually. Qāti'i states that the Khwaja, being a generous man, gave his friends lands and villages for their maintenance out of his own grant. One village was given by him to Qāti'i also. The Khwaja had a beautiful building constructed on the bank of the Yamuna in Agra where he hosted banquets for scholars and poets. Another house constructed by him also on the bank of the Yamuna was given away to Qati'i. The Khwaja was himself a good calligraphist, trained in this art by the famous Mir Ali. He could write beautifully in different hands (*khats*) (pp. 119-20).

Mention should also be made of Mulla Sha'uri, who had been the teacher of Mughal princes and nobles in Kabul and got two thousand *bighas* of *madad-i ma'ash* grant (maintenance land) near Chapparghatta, during Akbar's reign. He is said to have come to India after performing *hajj*, and Akbar gave him the land-grant on Shihabu'ddin Ahmad Khan's recommendation. He settled down near Chapparghatta and started farming. He had a palatial building constructed for his residence. A *serai* for the comfort of travellers to and from Bengal was also built by him. Soon the *serai* became famous by the name

Serai Mughal. Everyone who passed through the road, the Mulla received him in all courtesy. He used to walk on foot to receive a guest; only in case the distance was long did he go riding. He also had a *diwan* (collection of poems) to his credit (pp. 83-4).

Qāti'i adds a few words about the importance of certain cities and towns if they had been the abode of great religious divines, scholars or rulers. In this respect, he generally incorporates the popular legends and traditions current during his own days and does not question their authenticity. For example, in the notice of Mir Saiyid Hasan Ghaznavi (the poet), he states that he belonged to Ghazni where four hundred sufi saints lie buried. Then he would have us believe that Salar Mas'ud (who lies buried in Bahraich) was Sultan Mahmud's (d.1030) sister's son and was deputed with an army by his royal uncle to punish a local ruler for maltreating a Muslim; and it goes on to narrate a long, legendary and baseless account of Mahmud's raids up to Jagannath in Orissa (p. 19).

The present critically edited text of the *Tazira-i-Majma'al-Shu'ra-i-Jahangir Shahi* is based on the rare manuscript available in the Bodleian Library, Oxford. The editor has taken pains to correct transcriptional errors, on the basis of a wide reading of the contemporary historical literature, and later *tazkiras* of poets, anthologies, and Persian lexicons of the Mughal period. The copious notes added by him are most helpful in identifying historical figures. Saleem Akhtar has certainly earned the gratitude of all students of the history and culture in India under the Mughals.

Razi uddin Aquil, *Sufism: Culture and Politics, Afghan and Islam in Medieval North India**

IQBAL SABIR

This work will attract every scholar of medieval Indian history because it has been published by the Oxford University Press, which is known for publishing books of academic excellence. The reader is, however, doomed to disappointment. The young author seems to be in a hurry to gain recognition by making unwarranted comments on the scholarly works of the senior scholars, although many works criticized by him have no relevance to the theme of his work. Let us review it chapter-wise.

The work is divided into three parts, containing six chapters, besides the Introduction, Conclusion and Bibliography at the end. Strangely, the introduction begins with the criticism of modern works on economic history of India during the eighteenth century, although, according to the Preface, the theme is sovereignty and governance under the Lodi Sultans and Sher Shah Suri. Having mentioned the modern works on eighteenth-century India, the author complains that the important role played by the Sufis, *ulama* and other scholars in socio-economic life has not been paid attention at all (p. 2). The works published by Muzaffar Alam and Sanjay Subramaniam are praised while Irfan Habib's work on the agrarian system of the Mughals is mentioned as limited to containing only the revenue figures collected from the peasantry (p. 3). According to the author, Marxist historians failed to see that the Sufi literature has great value as a source of information for the scholars of economic history. He is particularly critical of Irfan Habib, calling his article, 'Slavery in the Delhi Sultanate: Thirteenth and Fourteenth Centuries; Evidence from Sufic literature (published in *Indian Historical Review*, vol. 15,

*Oxford University Press, New Delhi, 2007, 268p., Price Rs. 595.

nos. 1-2, 1988-9, pp. 248-56). He states that the author's concern in the article is more to show the prevalence of slavery as a recognized institution than to understand how the Sufis themselves viewed it and worked for its abolition, at least in a limited manner (p. 8). No example is, however, cited to substantiate the statement about the Sufis' opposition to slavery, although a lot of information in this regard is available in original Sufi works produced in Medieval India. This is indicative of the fact that he has not studied Sufi literature and has no working knowledge of Persian language (for an example of Sufis' opposition to slavery, see I.H. Siddiqui's article, 'Advent of Sufism in Medieval Punjab', in *Sufism in Punjab: Mystics, Literature and Shrines*, ed. Surinder Singh and Ishwar Dayal Gaur, Delhi, Aakar Books, 2009, p. 57).

Also unjustified is the criticism of the scholars who have seriously studied the historical role performed by Sufis of Medieval period. Professor Mohammad Habib, K.A. Nizami, A.A. Rizvi, Carl W. Ernst, Bruce Lawrence and I.H. Siddiqui are clubbed together as if they had a similar approach to delineating the missionary activities of the Sufis, even although they greatly differ from each other in this regard. Mohammad Habib emphatically denied the Sufis' role in converting Hindus to Islam. He writes: 'The wholesale conversions attributed to the Muslim mystics of this period are found in later day fabrications only and these works must be totally discarded. The Muslim mystics did not bother about conversions; it was no part of their duty. Muslim mysticism in those days was a postgraduate discipline—a discipline exclusively for Mussalmans who had completed their study of the theological and other sciences' (*cf. Collected Works of Mohammad Habib: Politics and Society*, ed. K.A. Nizami, Aligarh, 1974, vol. 1, p. 76).

The author is critical of Andre Wink for not acknowledging his indebtedness to the modern writers on the history of the Delhi Sultanate, although he himself has plagiarized much from the modern works. He claims to be the first writer to question the traditional approach to the history of Afghan kings, and no mention is made of I.H. Siddiqui's works. It is Siddiqui who pointed out that neither Bahlul was a tribal Afghan nor the Sultanate of Delhi was ever a confederation of tribes. According to him, the modern scholars uncritically followed Rushbrook William, the author of *An Empire Builder of the Sixteenth Century* in this regard. All the details of the circumstances in which Bahlul Lodi occupied the throne of Delhi have been lifted from Siddiqui's work *Some Aspects of Afghan Despotism in India* (Aligarh, 1969) without any acknowledgement.

In discussing Bahlul's invitation to the Afghans of Roh to come to India, help him in his war against the Sharqi Sultan and occupy important positions in his Sultanate, he makes the misleading statement that the early Turkish Sultans of Delhi had laid this tradition of seeking help from the Afghan tribes in their homeland (Roh) (p. 17). No Sultan of Delhi is ever reported to have invited the Afghans from Roh, at least the contemporary sources contain no such information. Also, the author's statement (p. 19) that the Lodi Sultans had their treasures accumulated in the fort of Chunar is incorrect. Lad Malika, the widow, inherited a large treasure from her late husband Taj Khan Karrani and gave it to Sher Khan after her marriage with him. On page 25, Sher Shah is said to have sent his envoy to Iran on the basis of *Tawarikh-i-Dawlat-i-Sher Shahi*, which is a later day fabrication, presented as a work from the pen of the fictitious Hasan Khan, Sher Shah's old companion. Strangely enough, Siddiqui's work *Mughal Relation with the Indian Elite*, which contains a lengthy chapter concerning the nature of this spurious work, is listed in the bibliography of the book under review, but totally ignores the story of Sher Shah's envoy in Iran. In examining the contents of the *Tawarikh-i-Daulat-i Sher Shahi* (of Hasan Ali Khan), Siddiqui discards it as a myth because Humayun stayed in Sind till July 1544, and struggled to find a foothold but in vain. Having failed to seize Sind, he left for Kabul where Kamran Mirza did not welcome him. Ultimately he decided to leave for Iran and seek military help against Kamran. Before Kamran's refusal to welcome him in Kabul, even Humayun had no plan to go to Iran and seek help from its Shah. Discarding the story contained in the *Tawarikh-i-Daulat-i-Sher Shahi* as the stuff of fiction, Siddiqui says on the basis of Badauni's *Muntakhab-ut-Tawarikh* that Sher Shah decided to send Mir Rafiuddin Shirazi to the Ottoman Sultan of Turkey for negotiating a military alliance against Iran after the conquest of Kalinjar fort but his accidental death upset his plan (cf. *Mughal Relations with the Indian Ruling Elite*, pp. 186-7).

Such factual errors are found throughout the lengthy introduction. On page 27, for instance, the author says that the rulers kept the saints in good humour because they could remove them from the throne and bestow it upon someone else who appeared more deserving. This is absolutely incorrect and indicates how immature the author is. No Sufi in Medieval Indian history appears to have become so powerful as to change the king on the throne

Abul Fazl's statement about Sher Shah being a dacoit in his early career is not only discarded, but his *Akbarnama* is also called a source of dubious nature. Sher Shah's own confession in this regard as mentioned by Mushtaqi is called a lie. Qanungo and Siddiqui are also criticized for accepting the evidence of *Akbarnama* and *Waqi'at-i-Musltaqi*. The time suggested by Siddiqui for Sher Shah taking to plundering was just after his dismissal by his father as manager of his *iqta* of Sahasram and appointment of his stepbrother instead. In such circumstances, the sons in polygamous families could turn rebels against their fathers. Abul Fazl could glorify the Mughals but did not concoct stories against historical personages. As regards Mushtaqi, he wrote with a pro-Afghan bias. In short, the lengthy introduction is full of factual errors, historical over-simplification and unjust criticism of the senior writers on the history of the Afghan kings of north India.

The first chapter also contains unjustifiable criticism of modern scholars that due attention has not been paid to the involvement of religion in politics. It is also worth noting that the Sufi *tazkiras* are found replete with fanciful stories, generally the inventions of the writers or the Servitors of the *dargahs* (Sufi shrines). They cannot be taken into consideration without caution. For instance, all the Sultans who rose from below are said to have been blessed by the Sufis with crown in their early career. The author accepts these stories uncritically.

Of the modern writers, I.H. Siddiqui's works are taken as marked with freshness yet he is criticized. As a matter of fact, the author of this book does it, in order to take credit for adding to existing knowledge what Siddiqui has done. He states 'Iqtidar Husain Siddiqui's researches have provided considerable sophistication to our understanding of Afghan history. Siddiqui has pointed out errors in the existing historiography by a more careful reading of the sources. We have referred above his *'Afghan Despotism'* in which he has cogently argued against the characterization of Afghan polity as tribal' (pp. 40-1). Having said all this, he blames Siddiqui for ignoring the crucial linkage between religion and politics. It is not correct because Siddiqui has discussed the problem at length in a separate chapter on *Wajh-i-ma'ash* grants made by the Lodi Sultans, Sher Shah

Sur and his successors and the author has utilized it without acknowledgement (cf. Siddiqui, *Sher Shah Sur and His Dynasty*, pp. 173-99).

Another allegation is that Siddiqui discards a whole corpus of sources in favour of solitary evidence, which provides a different picture (p. 41). As a matter of fact, the so-called corpus is muddled and the solitary evidence used by Siddiqui stands the test of historical scrutiny. Siddiqui's approach is critical and no mature scholar ever disagreed with him over his assessment of the sources.

Aquil is also wrong when he says that Siddiqui's political narrative abruptly comes to a close with the battle of Chausa. No doubt, the decisive battles fought between Humayun and Sher Shah mentioned in brief in Siddiqui's work, yet it contains fresh evidence, not accessible to Ishwari Prasad and Qanungo (cf. *Sher Shah and His Dynasty*, pp. 87-9, 95-6). As usual, Siddiqui does not reproduce what has been written by the earlier writers, he rather acknowledges them. Unlike Siddiqui, Aquil lifts details about disunity among the leading Afghan nobles during their struggle against the foreign Mughals without referring to Siddiqui's work *Mughal Relation with the Indian Ruling Elite* (published by Munshiram Manoharlal, New Delhi, 1983), although it is listed in his bibliography. It is Siddiqui who discussed the national character of struggle against the foreign rulers, Babur and Humayun.

Aquils' work also contains glaring factual errors because of his inability to follow the sources correctly. For instance, he would have us believe that Jamal Khan Sarang Khani was assigned by Sultan Sikandar Lodi the charge of the territorial unit of Jaunpur with the order to maintain two thousand *sawars* (p. 44). How could the vast territorial unit that had a large number of recalcitrant Rajput Zamindars be controlled by such a small contingent? According to Abbas Sarwani, the Sultan ordered Jamal Khan Sarang Khani to maintain twelve thousand *sawars*. Mushtaqi says that Jamal Khan's son and successor Khan Azam Ahmad Khan was allowed to increase the number of *sawars* to twenty thousand (cf. English tr. *Waqi'at-i-mughtaqi*, p. 93). Influenced by Bihari chauvinism, the author seems to be inclined to believe that Sher Shah was born in Sahasram (p. 45).

As regards the details about Sher Shah's education, they have been lifted straight from Siddiqui's work without any acknowledgement (cf. *Medieval India: Essays in Intellectual Thought and Culture*, Manohar, New Delhi, 2002). This work has been mentioned in Aquil's bibliography but not referred to here.

In his narrative of the events that took place in rapid succession and helped Sher Shah gain prominence, the author is confused in fixing their dates. Discarding Mushtaqi, he relies on Abbas Sarwani who was not able to know this sequence. A newcomer from Roh, Abbas Sarwani, compiled the biography of Sher Shah at Emperor Akbar's instance. He gathered information from the old Afghans and incorporated it in his work without trying to know their actual sequence. Unlike Abbas, Mushtaqi was a contemporary Indian, associated with the Afghan nobles having sympathy with their cause. In describing the events that took place since AD 1533 Mushtaqi is, as a writer, more reliable than Abbas. Certainly, any serious scholar interested in Medieval Indian history having gone through modern writings on Sher Shah would agree either with Qanungo or Siddiqui and discard Aquil's work as substandard. It may also be pointed out that Aquil does not mention Pakistani scholar Husain Khan's monograph on Sher Shah but seems to have utilized it. Husain Khan glorifies Sher Shah as a guide of Emperor Akbar and his successors and utilized the fictitious *Tawarikh-i-Daulat-Sher Shahi* in its preparation. Siddiqui examined *Tawarikh-i-Daulat-i-Sher Shahi's* contents and proved that it is not a contemporary source but compiled towards the close of the seventeenth century. Husain Khan purposely does not mention Siddiqui's work in the bibliography. Aquil mentions Siddiqui's work, *Mughal Relations with the Indian Ruling Elite*, in his bibliography, but neither agrees nor disagrees with Siddiqui's analysis. He rather uses it on the basis of Husain Khan's monograph without acknowledgement.

In describing the occupation of Chunar Fort by Sher Shah, the author makes the misleading statement that the Lodi Sultans had accumulated the treasures in it and that Sher Khan got them after his marriage with Lad Malika, the widow of Taj Khan Sarang Khani. There is no evidence to support this statement. Abbas Sarwani states that Lad Malika, the young and beautiful wife of Taj Khan had control over her husband. On the latter's murder by his son born of the senior wife, she not only inherited the wealth but also got control of the fort of Chunar with the support of men in her husband's service. On her supporter's advice she agreed to marry Sher Khan Sur. Thus the treasure accumulated by Taj Khan Sarang Khani was gained by Sher Khan. Having discussed the Chunar affair, the author makes digression and abruptly turns back to discuss the events that took place a few years earlier. For example, the battle of Khanwa fought between Rana Sanga and Babur in 1527 is described. After it the flight of Rana Sanga's allies with Prince Mahmud Lodi, the son of Sultān Sikandar Lodi to Bihar is described in detail. That they seized Bihar from Jalal Khan Nuhani who fled to Bengal. Sher Khan was still looked down by the senior Sarwani, Lodi and Farmuli nobles as a mere upstart. He had to please them by joining them. It is wrong to say that Sher Khan had got into prominence by that time (pp. 68-9). In fact, Sher Khan became the undisputed ruler of Bihar after the flight of the senior Afghan nobles from Bihar to Gujarat in 1533.

Aquil also contradicts Siddiqui regarding the assumption by Sher Khan of the sovereign title of Shah in AD 1535 (p. 72). He states that the discovery of one single coin does not suffice it to say that he had declared himself an independent king. It is really academic dishonesty not to mention the second silver coin mentioned by Siddiqui both in his *Mughal Relations with the Indian Ruling Elite* and the revised edition, *Sher Shah Sur and His Dynasty*. Also no mention is made by him of the copper coins issued by Sher Shah in 1537 that have been mentioned by Qanungo. It may also be added that Aquil betrays his ignorance of political culture of pre-Akbar period. The fact that a noble who revolted against the centre used to assume the sovereign title and called himself Sultan during the Sultanate period should not be lost sight of. Ibn Battuta mentions the rebels with their royal titles in his account of the reign of Sultan Muhammad bin Tughlaq. In *M'abar*, Saiyid Jalal Uddin assumed the title of Sultan Ahsan Shah, in Awadh Ainul-Mulk Mahru assumed the title of Sultan Alauddin Shah, while *Makh* Afghan was declare by his followers as Sultan Nasir Uddin Shah (cf. *Ajaib-ul-Asfar*, Urdu tr. Mohammad Husain, vol. 2, pp. 169, 182, 198). Ibn Battuta is corroborated by Isami in this regard (cf. *Futuh us-Salatin*, Madras, 1948, pp. 292-3, 519, 521).

Like the Introduction and the first chapter, the second chapter is also marred by confusion, repetition of events and factual errors. The author accepts uncritically what he finds in the muddled sources. For instance, Sarwani invents the story that Sher Khan attended the banquet hosted by Babur in Chanderi where Babur found him a man of extraordinary brilliance and also became doubtful of his loyalty to him. That Sher Khan also felt insecure and fled. This is a concoction. Neither Babur nor any other writer refers to Sher Khan's visit to Babur's camp. All the Afghan or non-Afghan Indian nobles whoever paid a visit to Babur are mentioned in the *Baburnama*.

Chapter III, entitled 'Norms of Governance and Aspects of Administration' begins with irrelevant details of the adoption by Muslim of diverse cultural traditions in the conquered non-Arab lands since the early period of Islamic history. Then begins abruptly the discussion of Sultan Balban's relations with Shaikh Fariduddin Ganj-i-Shakar on the basis of K.A. Nizami's work on the life and times of the Sufi saint, without any acknowledgement. In an effort to make his narrative a bit different, popular myths, discarded even by Nizami, are incorporated. For instance, the author would have the reader believe that Sultan Balban gave his daughter to the Shaikh in marriage and six sons and two daughters were born of her (p. 122). This is ridiculous. Neither Shaikh Nizamuddin Auliya nor any other fourteenth century writer mentions the establishment of matrimonial relation between the Shaikh and the Sultan. Even the sixteenth- and seventeenth-century *tazkiras*, *Akhbar ul-Akhiyar* and *Gulzar-i-Abrar* avoid mentioning such fantastic myths. It is true that Balban paid a visit to the Shaikh on his way to Multan during the reign of Sultan Nasiruddin Mahmud and offered money to the Shaikh as *futuh* (unasked for gift). The shaikh was too old to marry or beget children at that time (cf. K.A. Nizami, *The Life and Times of Shaikh Fariduddin Ganj-i-Shakar*, Aligarh, 1955).

Also the details of Bahlul Lodi's relations with Shaikh Samauddin Suhrawardi and other Suhrawardi Sufis have been plagiarized from Siddiqui's works, *Some Aspects of Afghan Despotism* and *Shershah Sur and His Dynasty*, as usual without acknowledgement. Mushtaqi's statement regarding Bahlul's visit to a *majzub* (an ecstatic saint) and his blessing of the throne of Delhi in return of money offered by the former, has been accepted as a fact, although this myth has been refuted even by medieval writers, Nizamuddin Ahmad and Firishta. Mushtaqi being a Sufi, glorifies Sufis by attributing miraculous powers to them. The stories of Sufis bestowing thrones to people are fictitious. Bahlul never dealt in the trade of horses. He belonged to a family of the nobles of the Sultanates, the fact that has been emphasized by Nizamuddin and Firishta.

As regards the portion concerning the administrative system under the Lodis, it is sketchy and replete with confusion. Details copied from Siddiqui's work on Sher Shah have been mixed with what did not exist, much of it is the figment of the author's imagination. For instance, the whole of the empire, according to the author, was divided into nine *vilayats* that came to be known as *subas* under Akbar. The term *vilayat* was never adopted officially and a larger territorial unit was either called officially a *khitta* or an *arsa*. The ideal term for an extensive territorial unit under Sher Shah was *sarkar*, while Malwa and Bengal were known as *khittas*. The trans-Sutlej Punjab, Malwa and Bengal were divided into *sarkars* and supreme officers were posted to supervise the activities of the *faujdars* and other officers posted in each *sarkar*. The region to the south of Multan was not annexed by Sher Shah. It is wrongly included by Aquil in Sher Shah's empire.

Chapter IV begins with the criticism of the modern scholars, which is unjustified, because Hindu-Muslim relations have been paid adequate attention by the modern scholars. All this is now common knowledge. In discussing Sher Shah's policy towards the Rajput land chiefs, the author digresses to discuss the reforms introduced by Sultan Sikandar Lodi. He states that ban was imposed by the Sultan on *taziya* procession (p. 148), although *taziyas* were not known to the Indian Muslims till the end of the first half of the eighteenth century. (The procession of *taziya* was an innovation begun by Najaf Khan in Delhi during the reign of Shah Alam II, cf. S.A.A. Rizvi, *Shah Wali-Allah and His Times*, Camberra, Ma'rifat Publishing House, 1980, p. 340). As a matter of fact, Sikandar Lodi is reported to have banned the procession of Salar Masud's flag (*nezah*) in the Sultanate. Because this occasion provided men and women to mix together. Such errors mar each chapter and make the reading of the work cumbersome.

As for the statement that Sher Shah married Rajput women forcibly in order to strengthen his ties with Rajput chiefs is not supported by any standard medieval source. It is only the fabricated work *Tawarikh i-Daulat Sher Shahi* that contains a fictitious story about the romance between Sher Shah and the daughter of a Rajput soldier. Siddiqui discards it as a story fabricated much later after the fall of the Sur empire, in his *Mughal Relations with the Indian Ruling Elite*. Siddiqui's work has not been taken note of in this regard although it is included in the bibliography.

Sher Shah is reported by Abbas Sarwani to have married Hargusain, the rich widow of Nasir Khan Nuhani. Sarwani does not say anything about her parentage but the author calls her a Brahman woman. She seems to have been the daughter of a Rajput convert to Islam. The Rajputs who converted to Islam did not give up their social customs and practices as the foreigners like Ibn Battuta and Babur marked it (cf. Ibn Battuta, *The Travels*, Eng. tr. Gibb, vol. 3, p. 597). We may cite here the example of Jamal Khan Mewati whose ancestor had converted to Islam in the fourteenth century, gave his daughters the Hindu names of Raj Gusain and Takht Gusain. They were married to Humayun and Bairam Khan-i Khanan respectively. Abdur Rahim Khan-i Khanan was born of the Mewati lady (cf. Sukumar Roy, *Bairam Khan*, Karachi, 1992, pp. 152, 154).

Chapter V, 'The Political and the Sufic Wilayat' also contains factual errors regarding the nature of the relationship between the Sufi saints and the kings. The author would have us believe that Sultan Ibrahim Lodi invited the Sufis and sought their blessing before he had left for Panipat to face the invader, Babur. That the sufis were displeased because they were forced to accompany the Sultan. This is incorrect (p. 176), because no contemporary or later writer have written about it. On page 177, the author falls into error by calling Shaikh Bahauddin Zakariya a fourteenth-century saint, although he flourished during the thirteenth century and died in 1262. Shaikh Bahauddin Zakariya's son, Sheikh Sadruddin Arif is called the preceptor (*pir*) of Shaikh Abdul Wahab Bukhari instead of Shaikh Abdullah Qureshi, a sixteenth-century Sufi and the son-in-law of Sultan Bahlul Lodi. It is extremely unfortunate that the author is ignorant of even elementary facts about the Sufis of the period. In fact, the writers on Sufism believed in the mystical powers of the Sufis, and wrote about them. Many of these writers invented stories to promote the *dargah* cult. We have to use this literature with caution. For example, the anecdotes about conversion by the Sufis of non-Muslim to Islam are a later day concoction. The Sufis did not preach their religion among non-Muslims; they spent their time inside their hospices imparting instructions to their disciples in spiritual exercises and prayers. No contemporary source contains any eye-witness account of a non-Muslim visitor converting to Islam. Only the works written long after the death of an eminent Sufi credit him for having won converts to Islam.

To conclude, it may be said that the young research scholar needs to improve his understanding of the literature culture, apart from the state apparatus under the Lodis and the Surs. The comments made by him on the writings of senior scholars should be based on sound footing. To analyse complex social phenomena, a scholar is required to acquire good working knowledge of Persian language and literature of medieval period. It is all the more surprising that such a work has been published by the Oxford University Press (Delhi), a well established institution known for its high standard of publications the world over.

Iqtidar Husain Siddiqui, *Delhi Sultanate: Urbanization and Social Change**

PARWEZ NAZIR

In contrast to the history of the Mughal period, many aspects of life and culture in India during the Delhi Sultanate period remain unexplored. The reason being the paucity of source material contained in the histories compiled during the pre-Mughal period. With the exception of Zia Uddin Barani's works, *Tarikh-i-Firozshahi* and *Fatawa-i-Jahandari*, the conventional sources of information generally do not deal with matters other than political. To depend upon these chronicles is to limit the scope of history. At the most the narrative of the ruling dynasties that ruled over the Sultanate of Delhi can be prepared on their basis. The important role played by the cultural institutions, bazaars, trade and commerce, merchants engaged in trade who integrated India with international trade and above all, the patterns of political behaviour displayed by the Sultans of strong personality in meeting the requirements of time would not be known unless the relevant evidence is searched in the non-conventional sources. In the preparation of the work under review, an impressive array of new sources have been used offering a paradigm shift. We may now briefly comment on each chapter.

The book is composed of eleven chapters of varying lengths, besides an introduction in the beginning, two appendices and bibliography at the end. In the introduction attention has been focused on the changes—social, political and economic that took place in Makran, Sind and Multan territory (southern Punjab) in the wake of the Arab Conquest in AD 712-13. The Arab settlements in the conquered region exposed this western region to foreign influence that marked the beginning of Medieval Age. Not only the bureaucratic

*Viva Books, New Delhi, 2009, Price Rs. 795, 241p.

system was introduced by the foreign conquerors, the region was also turned into a high road for international trade between the Islamic World and the foreign countries, both south-eastern and middle eastern countries, on account of the involvement of the Arab merchants. Also interesting is its last portion relating to the changes after the annexation of the region to the Ghaznavid empire in the beginning of the eleventh century.

The first chapter entitled, 'The Delhi Sultanate: Political Economy and Public Welfare', discusses first the concepts as worked out by the political thinkers associated with court and their impact on the state and society. Opposed to the idea of free operation of market economy at all times, they advised the Sultan to control the prices if the situation demanded. New sources of information utilized by the author in the preparation of this chapter shed interesting light on the fact that the thinkers and their followers among the rulers were ahead of their counterparts in Europe as far as the concept of political economy is concerned as the sources hitherto unknown reveal. Amir Khusrau's *Aijaz-i-Khusravi* contains reference to *'Ilm-i-ma'ishat* (Economic science) which is of significance. Besides Amir Khusrau's works, such terms used by the medieval writers have been carefully analysed in the book under review. Due emphasis has been placed on Ziauddin Barani's argument that people who supported *laissez-faire* in trade and commerce were of the view that cheapness was brought about by plenty. Incisive comments have been made on modern writings on Sultan Alauddin Khalji's market control system, Moreland's and Irfan Habib's assessments have been commended. Perhaps the discussion of the mechanism worked out by the Sultan to make the system work successfully has been regarded by the author superfluous as found in detail everywhere. But, in view of author's access to miscellaneous sources, one would have liked to have known more about the matter, even the inclusion of a bit of fresh evidence would be of importance.

Chapter two deals with the process of urbanization, introduction of the arcuate system of architecture, the important role played by the *bazaars*, foreign trade, cash nexus, etc. The growth of old towns and the foundation of new urban centres accelerated the process of acculturation. The arrival of the immigrants who represented urban ethos was doubtless a catalyst for social change. The immigrants who included among them men of learning, merchants engaged in foreign trade, warriors and Sufis played an important role in enriching India's culture. Along with the impact of interaction between the old residents and new settlers on the life and culture, the second chapter presents an indepth analysis of the different factors that helped the process of urbanization. Also worth mentioning is the correction of historiographic errors committed by the scholars in identifying the nature and function of buildings and institutions of public utility.

The third chapter titled, 'Economy and Trade' is illuminating in so far as the fresh insights into the multidimensional role performed by the merchant's importance of foreign trade in the Sultanate economy, the importance of *bazaars*, prevalence of cash nexus in place of barter system, the rise of seaports into the emporium of international trade, improvement in the conditions of urban proletariat and diasporas of Indian merchants as well as also the mention of a number of export items that were in great demand in the foreign countries, left unmentioned in modern writings, is concerned. This chapter considerably adds to our knowledge of India's trade relations with foreign countries.

The fourth chapter, 'Food and its Social Significance' is interesting in that we find insights into the introduction of foreign cuisine, addition of caterers' shops in the *bazaars* giving rise to catering profession, the importance of the royal kitchen which generated trade, banquet culture and the boost it gave to the cottage industry of manufacturing vases, goblets, platters of gold, silver and precious stones, besides trade in chinaware. Indeed, this is a pioneering effort in the study of Indian cuisine and the caterer's profession during the Delhi Sultanate period.

Likewise, the fifth chapter discusses the introduction of the new profession of *atishbazan* (experts in pyrotechnique) and corrects the historiographic errors regarding the beginning of the use of gunpowder and firearms in the country. Also interesting is the description of illuminating mosques on the occasion of *Shab-i-barat* (night of offering supererogatory prayers) like the Dipawali, the Hindu festival of light.

As for the next chapter, 'Social Mobility and the Emergence of New Social Groups', it is the revised version of the essay, published in the journal *Medieval India* (Oxford University Press, New Delhi, 1992). It was very well received as a pioneering attempt in the cultural history of the Sultanate of Delhi. Now it contains additional information about the emergence of new social formations. Similarly, the seventh chapter, 'Scientific Development in the Sultanate of Delhi' provides the first valuable information about the scientific instruments and ideas that found their way into India along with elite emigrants from the countries of higher culture as well as the patronage extended by the rulers to the scientists, men of talent and learning. We find herein a detailed description of intellectual life and the progress of creative astronomy, astronomical instruments and time-keeping devices, and the scientific temper.

Chapters eight to ten, which deal with the education system, the literary tradition and the syncretic tradition respectively, are really invaluable. It discusses not only the role played by the *madrasas* in the progress of education, but also that book trade and literary culture which went a long way in financially helping a large number of people engaged in manufacturing paper, ink, book-binding, besides scribes.

The tenth chapter discussing the significance of the translation of Arabic and Sanskrit classics into Persian tells about how the representatives of two different cosmocentric and anthropocentric traditions came closer to each other and that their interaction resulted into the development of the culture of shared values, called today India's composite culture.

The last (eleventh) chapter begins with a reference to the dissolution of the Sultanate towards the close of the fourteenth century and the emergence of regional kingdoms and principalities carved out by the erstwhile governors of the Sultan of Delhi. The ruler of each kingdom and principality assumed the title of Sultan and tried to build his capital into a centre of learning and culture and associate scholars, poets and men of talent with his court. Of these regional kingdoms and principalities, that of Kalpi has been selected for a case study. Malik Mahmud Turk, the *Muqta* of Mahoba seized the village of Kalpi, from its zamindar and had a city built near it which was given the name of Muhammadabad *urf* (alias) Kalpi. After Timur's invasion, the area included in the principality of Kalpi became the core area of the Delhi culture due to the arrival of refugees. The scholars as well as other resourceful persons had fled from Delhi in fear of Timur's invasion and sought refuge in the far-off regional headquarters. With the emergence of Kalpi as the capital of a principality, urban culture permeated in the area around. The *bazaars* established in Kalpi replaced barter system by cash nexus, with the result that trade and commerce received boost and socio-economic growth began. This is suggestive for the scholars to probe into socio-economic change in other principalities in north India during the fifteenth and sixteenth centuries. As a matter of fact, the building material for the rise and splendour of the Mughal empire was prepared in these regional kingdoms and principalities.

The appendices added at the end not only provide additional information about the trade in war horses and the Delhi Sultanate currency respectively but also point out the pitfalls that the modern scholars have failed to escape in their research.

To conclude, I may quote Peter Hardy's remark about Siddiqui's work on the Lodi Sultans and Sher Shah Suri that applies to this work also 'the work of Iqtidar Husain Siddiqui on the Afghans in the fifteenth and sixteenth centuries and on Shershah, has, properly, made the establishment of Mughal rule less remarkable but more intelligible' (Peter Hardy, 'The Authority of Muslim Kings in Medieval South Asia', *Prusartha*, Paris, 1986, p. 37).

Contributors

ALI ATHAR: Associate Professor, Department of History, Aligarh Muslim University, Aligarh.

S. BASHIR HASAN: Senior Research Assistant, Department of History, Aligarh Muslim University, Aligarh.

SHAHABUDDIN IRAQI: Professor, Department of History, Aligarh Muslim University, Aligarh.

MOHAMMAD AFZAL KHAN: Associate Professor, Department of History, Aligarh Muslim University, Aligarh.

SUMBUL HALIM KHAN: Associate Professor, Department of History, Aligarh Muslim University, Aligarh.

MAYANK KUMAR: Fellow, Nehru Memorial Museum & Library, New Delhi.

RAVINDRA KUMAR: Professor of History, IGNOU, New Delhi.

PARWEZ NAZIR: Assistant Professor, Department of History, Aligarh Muslim University, Aligarh.

M.K. PUNDHIR: Assistant Professor, Department of History, Aligarh Muslim University, Aligarh.

(LATE) A.J. QAISAR: Professor (Retired), Department of History, Aligarh Muslim University, Aligarh.

ANEESA IQBAL SABIR: Senior Research Assistant, Department of History, Aligarh Muslim University, Aligarh.

(LATE) IQBAL SABIR: Assistant Professor, Department of History, Aligarh Muslim University, Aligarh.

IQTIDAR HUSAIN SIDDIQUI: Professor (Retired), Department of History, Aligarh Muslim University, Aligarh.

MOHAMMAD UMAR: Professor (Retired), Department of History, Aligarh Muslim University, Aligarh.

RASHMI UPADHYAYA: Assistant Professor, Department of History, Aligarh Muslim University, Aligarh.

S.P. VERMA: Professor (Retired), Department of History, Aligarh Muslim University, Aligarh.